WILLIAM SHAKESPEARE
A Documentary Life

Frontispiece:

THE FLOWER PORTRAIT OF SHAKESPEARE. *This painting, executed on an ancient elm panel now worm-eaten and the worse for surface damage, hangs in the Royal Shakespeare Portrait Gallery in Stratford-upon-Avon. It was acquired around 1840 by one H. C. Clements of Peckham Rye, who claimed that it had been publicly exhibited in London seventy years previous, and that 'many thousands' had flocked to view it. Such exhibition, however, is not otherwise recorded. After Clements's death in 1895 the portrait came into the possession of Mrs. Charles Flower of the celebrated Stratford brewing family. She donated it to the Gallery. Sometimes called the 'Droeshout Original' in earlier days, the painting is clearly related to the engraving that adorns the title-page of the Shakespeare First Folio (see item 212), but more likely as descendant than progenitor — despite the inscription in the upper left-hand corner: 'William Shakespeare 1609'. In the reproduction this inscription is only barely visible. The painting improves upon Droeshout, while simplifying the subject's costume. Examination in 1895–6 indicated that the portrait had undergone repair and restoration. More recently, X-ray photography conducted at the Courtauld Institute revealed, under the present surface, a painting by a mid-fifteenth century Italian artist of the Madonna and Child, with St. John; the outline of the Virgin's shoulder is still discernible under Shakespeare's white wired band. Despite its derivative status, the portrait still commands interest as the earliest painting unquestionably of Shakespeare. (The more celebrated — and superior — Chandos Portrait in the National Portrait Gallery in London is not demonstrably a likeness of the poet, although it has had distinguished advocates.) On the Shakespeare iconography, see M. H. Spielmann, 'Shakespeare's Portraiture', in* Studies in the First Folio *written for the Shakespeare Association (1924), pp. 1–52; also* SL, *passim.*

WILLIAM SHAKESPEARE

A Documentary Life

S. SCHOENBAUM

NEW YORK
OXFORD UNIVERSITY PRESS
in association with
The Scolar Press
1975

Library of Congress Catalog Card Number: 74-77424

Printed in Great Britain by
The Scolar Press, Ilkley, Yorks.

To James G. McManaway

Contents

Preface

My aim in these pages has been to present a straightforward account of Shakespeare's life — in adequate detail, and not shirking vexatious issues like the significance of the marriage records and the second-best bed — and to combine that account with facsimiles, faithfully reproduced, of the documents and records which comprise the biographer's materials. Although many illustrated books have appeared, none to my knowledge has fulfilled a similar service. I am conscious that to some my undertaking may seem improbable. What documents? Which records? 'Everything we know about Shakespear can be put into a half-hour sketch'; so Shaw remarked, echoing what others have been saying since the eighteenth century. In the event he needed one paragraph, not a half-hour, for his sketch. I have required almost three hundred pages (admittedly inclusive of the facsimiles), but then Shaw wrote very concisely.

He also exaggerated, but it would be idle to deny some legitimate basis to scepticism regarding the whole enterprise of Shakespearian biography. There was a time for such a thing in the aftermath of the poet's death, and before all his friends, professional associates, and relations had passed from the scene. Gradually they dropped off: his cherished fellows Condell and Heminges in 1627 and 1630, his elder daughter Susanna in 1649. His sister Joan Hart survived him by forty years, and his second daughter Judith lived into the Restoration; but nobody sought them out for intimate sidelights on 'the famous William Shakespeare', as he was already being called. The reason is not far to seek. Literary biography, as we know it, did not yet exist in those pre-Boswellian days. The way to biographical preferment lay in distinguished service to church or state, not to the ungrateful muse. Donne's life is, to be sure, amply chronicled, but he had the foresight to become Dean of St. Paul's.

Nevertheless we do well to resist luxuriating in a sense of deprivation. Time scattered the Shakespeare papers like leaves before the wind, destroying a number (how many we cannot say), but tucking some safely away in odd corners, and preserving others under the kindly dust of the muniments room. Then, at first tentatively but soon gaining momentum, the movement to recover these relics got under way. Over a period of centuries enthusiasts retrieved them, sometimes by chance but more often by toilsome inquiry. This story I have told in *Shakespeare's Lives*. What they found is insufficient for a portrait in depth of Shakespeare the man, and attempts to render one have always foundered: the three dimensions contract into two, substance becomes shadow, despite the embroidering of fact with fancy or speculation. Yet the records themselves are more numerous than is popularly supposed. They consist of the remarks, sometimes ambiguous and almost always laconic, of contemporaries, and of the public traces people in all periods leave behind: parish register entries, records of investment, litigation, and professional activity; a last will and testament. In the absence of diaries and correspondence, Shakespeare's buried life resists the biographer's inquisitive probings, but those records we have, supplemented by the fruits of the historian's researches, enable us to enter into the quotidian life of a vanished age.

They show how children were educated, families worshipped, and officials busied themselves with the task of local government. The Stratford corporation minutes and accounts chronicle the rise to civic eminence of Shakespeare's father, and his subsequent melancholy eclipse. We see his poet son marrying under awkward circumstances, turning to the courts for the recovery of petty debts, and acquiring social respectability. The tax collector called and found him not at home. In his Cripplegate lodgings he found himself involved in the domestic affairs of his landlord's family. We also see Shakespeare in the context of the London theatrical and publishing industries, and, at last, on his deathbed arranging a disposition of his estate that biology would thwart. 'Look here upon this picture and on this', Hamlet beseeches his mother in the Closet

Scene. We too may choose between pictures. Beside the remotely inscrutable Shakespeare of the bardolaters — smiling and still, out-topping knowledge — we may set another Shakespeare who was in many ways like other, more ordinary, men. This Shakespeare did not disdain to partake of the bread and cheese of life. The existence of such a dimension, apparent from the records, is hostile to the romantic celebration of genius, but to my mind brings us a little closer to the creator of Romeo and Lear and Timon, who after all address us not in the accents of an impersonal deity, but of essential humanity. The mundane concerns of documentary biography bring their own rewards.

The legends provide more colourful fare. They show the Bard suffering ignominious defeat in a toping competition. He poaches and gets caught. Later he becomes the darling of the Queen and (afterwards) the King, as well as a boon tavern companion of the wits. A more self-abnegating biographer might have passed over in silence this accretion of dubious lore. But the *mythos* — as, following Chambers, I term it — has its own wayward interest, and even austere biographers have reckoned with the possibility of a germ of truth here and there. My own treatment of this apocryphal matter is, I trust, not uncritical.

Were I to claim any novelty for my narrative, that claim would have to rest on its lack of novelty. Although I can offer a recently discovered titbit or two (for example, the little book — conceivably once in Shakespeare's library — with an inscription naming his daughter Susanna), I have not turned up the poet's laundry list, a prize coveted by Mr. Anthony Burgess. Nor have I extricated any previously unidentified Dark Lady from the unlaundered bed-linen. I have no new theories respecting the genesis or first performance of any of the plays. In fact, I have no interesting theories at all to offer. These I leave to more adventurous spirits. Of speculation, sometimes masquerading as evident truth, there has, I feel, been sufficient, though it is mostly harmless enough. The present moment is perhaps as reasonable as any for a summing up of knowledge. So I have examined all the documents again, at first hand, and set forth (I hope without special pleading) what they tell us.

I have said *all*, but in fact there is a class of document, more precious than the rest, that I touch upon only in the most external fashion. These are the plays, with their myriad *personae*, and the *Sonnets*, in which the mask does not at all times appear to be fixed firmly in place. 'To live over people's lives is nothing', Henry James once remarked, 'unless we live over their perceptions, live over the growth, the change, the varying intensity of the same — since it was *by* these things they themselves lived.' If the minutiae of Shakespeare's life, the accidents of his existence, elude our ken, the perceptions of which James speaks are available to us in the book of the poet's works. Tolstoy perhaps went too far when he said that there was no point in visiting a great writer, as he was present in his writings; but it is a position with which many — not least, authors — will sympathize. Criticism has lately asked large questions about the relations between the life and the *oeuvre*. Although they interest me very much, these questions (which, as regards Shakespeare, arise in a special way) concern the critical rather than the documentary biographer, and so I have not gone into them here. I may return to them another day.

Surely the principal appeal of this book will reside not in my prose but in the facsimiles, of which I have brought together over two hundred. I must confess that, even after long familiarity with old books and papers, I have not outgrown my naïve sense of wonder in the presence of these remembrances of times past, and I hope that the reader too will share in their capacity for evocation. The facsimiles are not limited to manuscripts. I have included extracts from printed books to convey some of the flavour of my sources, although I have not attempted to present every passage in this fashion. I have also found space for early maps, plans, and prospects, sketches of houses and theatres, and the like. If these items are not, strictly speaking, biographical, they certainly hold interest for the biographer, and they will vary the facsimile diet. Photographs, the staple of pictorial biography, I have tried as much as possible to avoid.

A rather surprisingly large number of my sources, even the manuscript ones, have not previously been reproduced in this way. I have not spared myself pains to present them faithfully. A principal defect of comparable volumes lay, as I saw it, in their unevenness of quality: tone and clarity tended to vary from facsimile to facsimile. Such fluctuation is not always readily avoided. Some archives will allow only their own photographers on the premises, and in certain cases (as when the documents are fragile or damaged) they are reluctant to undertake photography under any circumstances. Wherever possible, however, we secured fresh photographs rather than trust to stock negatives. Next we had the printers make proof copies. I then returned to the archive and checked proof against original. A disadvantage of this scheme, to which I permitted no exceptions, is that the records are widely dispersed. Thus I had to find my way in frozen mid-winter to Hamilton College in upstate New York to examine a single item, the purported Anne Hathaway sketch in a copy of the Shakespeare Third Folio. I was glad I did, though, as my proof copy was, as it turned out, unsatisfactorily faint. Twice I visited California, and also New Jersey, to inspect materials which, in the upshot, I decided against including as not strictly essential. On two occasions I visited Utrecht for unique items in the University Library there. One library I journeyed to had misplaced the book, so I was obliged to come again. I can fairly describe my itinerary as strenuous, as well as costly, but I could not see my way clear to delegating any of the task. To achieve some approximation of uniform quality, it was necessary for the same pair of eyes to function throughout. Now that the whole operation is behind me, I have no regrets about the procedure. For the fact is that proofs were often too light or dark (usually the latter), and not all the photographs met our standard for sharpness of focus. The need to go through the whole process more than once made special demands on staff, who responded with unfailing courtesy. I must also here mention the graciousness of Mr. and Mrs. Paul Mellon, who allowed us to transport the Hollar drawing of Southwark by security van from London to Yorkshire, where it was re-photographed under ideal studio conditions.

Why bother? For one thing, it seemed likely that the project, once done, would not soon be re-done. I wanted to be as scrupulous as possible, so that students, and indeed ordinary readers, might consult the facsimiles with confidence. I also saw my work, whether justly or not, as an act of homage to the many investigators — some famous, others obscure — whose tireless quest rescued the Shakespeare records from the ruins of time. Careless homage is a doubtful compliment. Moreover, I have thought that my book might in its own small way contribute to historical preservation. Documents suffer from handling, and from the effects of moisture and light, especially when on continuous display. Examples are not far to seek. In the nineteenth century, tracing paper was pasted over two of the three pages of 'Sir Thomas More' thought to be in Shakespeare's hand, in a misguided attempt to protect them. These pages now present so dismal a blur that, after much deliberation, I decided no useful purpose would be served in reproducing them here. The marriage licence bond is properly looked after these days, but past abuse has taken its toll, and my facsimile is unavoidably indistinct. During my peregrinations I learned that two familiar documents had been locked up for safe-keeping in a basement during World War II, only to have the writing almost obliterated by water seepage. I was unable to track down any photographs. Fortunately the great majority of the items included in this book are in satisfactory, often excellent, condition. Like all old papers, however, they remain vulnerable. Perhaps with them conveniently available in facsimile form, the need for display and handling, with the attendant risks, will be reduced, and a unique heritage safeguarded. The narrative design, as well as limitations of space, ruled out admitting a number of facsimiles that might otherwise have found a place in my pages: a complete run of Stationers' Register entries, for example, or specimens of the forgeries of William Henry Ireland and J. Payne Collier. These I hope to provide in a supplementary volume in which I shall also include such curiosities as the purported Shakespeare signature in William Lambarde's *Archaionomia*.

Although the rather elaborate format of this book — with text, facsimiles, captions (sometimes lengthy), and notes all co-existing on the page — is calculated to inhibit footnoting by the yard, I have tried to record particular, and sometimes general, debts. I am, however, only too conscious of the inadequacy of conventional acknowledgement in a work that draws so extensively on the entire tradition of Shakespearian biographical scholarship. That tradition is symbolized by Edmond Malone in the eighteenth century and J. O. Halliwell-Phillipps in the nineteenth; Sidney Lee offers a bridge between the Victorian and modern eras, and the present century has produced, as its most notable monument, Sir Edmund Chambers's brilliantly organized synthesis, as well as more specialized contributions by Edgar I. Fripp, Mark Eccles, and others. If B. Roland Lewis includes much that is extraneous, his *Shakespeare Documents* brings together a wealth of useful information. One consults it with caution, but one consults it. G. E. Bentley's biographical handbook is modest in scale but distinguished by the same rigorous scholarship as characterizes his great work on the Jacobean and Caroline stage. The popular biographies of Joseph Q. Adams and A. L. Rowse have limitations which I have commented upon elsewhere, but more than once I have had occasion to give thanks for their existence. These authorities and others have made my own labours possible. I suppose I have turned most often to Chambers and Eccles. Inevitably I have repeated some material from my *Shakespeare's Lives*, but I trust I have profited from the opportunity to reconsider what I have said previously. In my sections on education, religion, London, and the theatres I have been especially cognizant of the importance of sound guides, for on these topics I can claim no special expertise. Like so many other students, I have profitably turned to the *Dictionary of National Biography* for particulars about minor figures (e.g. Peter Bales and Sir William Dethick). Perhaps my multifold obligations are best summed up in my dedication, for I offer this book to a scholar whose humane learning exemplifies what is best in the tradition.

I am grateful to Penguin Books Ltd. for permission to quote from the Introduction to William Shakespeare, *A Midsummer Night's Dream*, edited by Stanley Wells (New Penguin Shakespeare; 1967), and to Jonathan Cape Ltd. and Alfred A. Knopf, Inc., for the use of Anthony Burgess, *Shakespeare* (© Anthony Burgess, 1970).

Some debts are personal. These it is the welcome traditional prerogative of the Preface to enumerate. I fear I cannot bring myself to apologize for the length of the catalogue, but I do regret any inadvertent omissions. My first opportunity to sort out my ideas for a documentary life of Shakespeare came in 1971, during four weeks spent in the tranquil splendour of the Villa Serbelloni through the generosity of the Rockefeller Foundation. Later the same year, on a Bank Holiday weekend in Yorkshire, I was able to formulate my plans more precisely after my host, Dr. R. C. Alston, took me round The Scolar Press and introduced me to the technology of facsimile publishing. Subsequently his dynamic optimism prevented me from entertaining second thoughts about the feasibility of my programme. Dr. Gordon N. Ray, most benevolent of Foundation directors and also an authority on illustrated books, gave advice and encouragement that helped to sustain me.

During the early stages Mr. John R. Turner, then with The Scolar Press, was an effective liaison man in dealings with librarians, archivists, photographers, and printers. Certain institutions — the Bodleian Library, the British Library, the Folger Shakespeare Library, the Public Record Office, and the Shakespeare Birthplace Trust Records Office — were called upon to handle particularly extensive orders which sometimes presented special problems. I should like especially to thank Mr. N. E. Evans at the Public Record Office, and Mr. Robert Bearman and Miss Gwyniver Jones at the Shakespeare Birthplace Trust Records Office, for looking after our requests so efficiently. At my suggestion Mr. W. H. Kelliher, of the Department of Manuscripts of the British Library, examined the two Shakespeare entries in John Manningham's *Diary* with the aid of ultra-violet light, and also under a high-magnification microscope. His findings provided confirmation — if any were needed — that these entries are genuine.

Professor James G. McManaway, Professor Kenneth Muir, and Dr. Stanley Wells found time, despite their strenuous schedules, to read an early draft of my typescript. Dr. Levi Fox perused the Stratford chapters, and Dr. Valerie Pearl a section on Elizabethan London. Without the benefit of their expertise this book would be more imperfect than it is.

A Senior Fellowship from the National Endowment for the Humanities enabled me to have an extended stay in England in 1973–4, and thus to be in close proximity to primary sources vital to my work. Northwestern University, always generously supportive of my research, defrayed secretarial and other expenses connected with the project. Mrs. Linda Yates typed the final draft with intelligence and precision. When the book was in galleys, Mr. Douglas Chambers checked quotations from printed sources, and saved me from more than one egregious lapse. My Clarendon copy-editor, Mr. Bernard Dod, was properly fierce about infelicities. Having already read my typescript, Dr. Wells exceeded the obligations of friendship by volunteering to read a set of page proofs. Mr. J. C. Maxwell, for whose impersonal rigour I have unstinting admiration, did likewise. They have saved me from late error.

All through the production phase I have worked closely with Mr. Sean Magee of The Scolar Press. He is, quite simply, the ablest and most dedicated of editors. Miss Yvonne Skargon designed the book, and although almost every page presented a particular challenge, owing to the outrageous variations in the size of the facsimiles, she met them all without ever betraying the appearance of crisis. My relations with my publishers have long since ripened into friendship. I must particularly mention Dan Davin and Jon Stallworthy at the Clarendon Press, John Commander with The Scolar Press, and James Raimes of Oxford University Press, New York.

My wife good-humouredly looked after the xeroxing, and provided the office-management skills that helped me to cope with an intimidating mass of notes, correspondence, drafts, and proofs. Well-wishers who conferred special favours were Mrs. Donald F. Hyde, Mrs. Elsie Robinson, Miss Shirley Watkins, Professor G. E. Bentley, Mr. Patrick Finn, Dr. O. B. Hardison, Mr. Richard Proudfoot, Dr. Thomas Treadwell, and Mr. Ian Willison. Finally, the special brand of (dare I say it?) feline scepticism of Mr. Oscar Commander helped me to keep my sense of perspective.

London   S.S.
June 1974

A Note on Procedures

In a book such as this, in which facsimile reproductions are married to the text, I have thought it advisable to preserve the idiosyncrasies of old spelling in quotations from manuscript and early printed sources. I have, however, normalized long *s* and final *j*, and the *i-j* and *u-v* equations (e.g. I give *upon* for *vpon*, *have* for *haue*, and *joyed* for *ioyed*). I have also extended abbreviations, except for certain common and untroublesome forms (e.g. *y^e*, *&*, *W^m*, *M^r*). Expansions are introduced silently; to have drawn attention to them by brackets or italic type would have been to disfigure the text and to invite error by complicating the printers' already difficult task. I have been less inclined to tamper with monumental inscriptions; there is something immutable about stone. With punctuation, or its absence, in records I have meddled as sparingly as possible. These procedures reflect a compromise between the requirements of scholars and the convenience of non-specialist readers, and as such they will not, I realize, be a taste for every tooth. But I can say that I have thought hard and long about the several options, and there is precedent for what I have done; purists may console themselves with the facsimiles.

I have sought to make the facsimiles the same size as their originals, although this was not always possible. Some documents remained unco-operatively awkward in their dimensions, and there was no choice but to reduce them, usually only slightly. Where such reduction has taken place, I have noted it.

Ideally I should have liked to include full transcripts of all the documents, but the scale and format of this book — not to mention potential costs — ruled out so ambitious a programme. I have, however, throughout tried to indicate the significance of the records reproduced, and I transcribe crucial passages. In any event the Shakespeare documents are familiar enough, and transcripts are easy to come by. In my captions I have referred readers to the relevant pages of E. K. Chambers, *William Shakespeare: A Study of Facts and Problems* (1930), and B. Roland Lewis, *The Shakespeare Documents* (1940). Transcripts in the latter are occasionally fuller. In certain cases I have cited other authorities — Savage and Fripp, for example, for John Shakespeare in the minutes and accounts of the Stratford corporation. For readers more comfortable with modernized texts I have included references to C. F. Tucker Brooke, *Shakespeare of Stratford* (1926) in the Yale Shakespeare. Fallibility being universal, the ablest scholars sometimes err: I have found that even the great Chambers is, reassuringly, by no means absolutely trustworthy, although the deficiencies usually involve accidentals which leave sense unaffected. Even when due care has been exercised, there is bound at times to be disagreement about particular readings. The vagaries of Elizabethan handwriting, not to mention the condition of some records, make that inevitable. The letter *w* (to mention but one instance) can be troublesome: one man's *William* is another's *william*. Although in some circumstances even a faithful reproduction is no substitute for consultation of the original, the facsimiles will furnish a yardstick for measuring the palaeographer's performance.

That performance achieves a high standard in the Appendix of 'Records, Documents, and Allusions' included by G. Blakemore Evans in the *Riverside Shakespeare*, of which he is the General Editor. This volume, which promises to be widely available, appeared when my own was already entering proof; else I should have included references to Appendix B in my captions.

I like to think of the captions as comprising a species of *catalogue raisonné*. Shelfmarks are supplied for all the manuscript entries, and for all books up to 1640: the period covered by Pollard and Redgrave's *Short-Title Catalogue*. I also give *STC* numbers, and in addition, for plays, the entry numbers in W. W. Greg, *A Bibliography of the English Printed Drama to the Restoration* (1939–59). I have provided essential details about the discovery and first publication of the documents and other records, and where the subsequent history of the item holds special interest (as with the marriage licence bond and the will) I have found space for brief resumés. This information sometimes corrects or supplements that found in my *Shakespeare's Lives* (1970), which gives an account of the gradual recovery of biographical knowledge of the poet. For cross-references in my captions I use the term *item*, followed by the number of the facsimile. In 1973 the book, manuscript, and map departments of the British Museum became divisions of the British Library. With some sentimental reluctance I revised my citations to conform with the new designation.

In captions and footnotes the place of publication, unless otherwise indicated, is London. For quotations from Shakespeare I have used the Peter Alexander edition of *The Complete Works* (1951).

A word about dates. In this period the year (which in England was still reckoned according to the Julian calendar) began officially on Lady Day, 25 March, although popular — as distinguished from legal and governmental — practice varied. Not until the Calendar Act of 1752 was Gregorian reform instituted: eleven days were dropped from that year to correct the discrepancy that had developed between the two calendars, and 1 January became the official first day of the year. In citing dates I have followed the standard practice of revising the year (where appropriate), but not tampering with day or month. Thus in the facsimile of John Manningham's diary entry for a performance of *Twelfth Night* in the Middle Temple, the date appears as 2 February 1601, but in my narrative I give it as 2 February 1602. The whole question is expertly discussed by W. W. Greg, 'Old Style – New Style', in *Collected Papers*, ed. J. C. Maxwell (Oxford, 1966), pp. 366-73.

I have used the following abbreviations:

TB   C. F. Tucker Brooke, *Shakespeare of Stratford: A Handbook for Students* (The Yale Shakespeare; New Haven, 1926).

EKC   E. K. Chambers, *William Shakespeare: A Study of Facts and Problems* (Oxford, 1930), 2 vols.

ME   Mark Eccles, *Shakespeare in Warwickshire* (Madison, Wisc., 1961).

Greg   W. W. Greg, *A Bibliography of the English Printed Drama to the Restoration* (1939–59), 4 vols.

H-P   James Orchard Halliwell-Phillipps.

H-P, *Life*   J. O. Halliwell[-Phillipps], *A Life of William Shakespeare* (1848).

H-P, *Outlines* J. O. Halliwell-Phillipps, *Outlines of the Life of Shakespeare* (7th ed., 1887).

BRL   B. Roland Lewis, *The Shakespeare Documents* (Stanford University, 1940), 2 vols.

MA   *Minutes and Accounts of the Corporation of Stratford-upon-Avon*, ed. Richard Savage and Edgar I. Fripp; Publications of the Dugdale Society, vols. i, iii, v, x (Stratford-upon-Avon, 1921–30).

SL   S. Schoenbaum, *Shakespeare's Lives* (Oxford, 1970).

STC   *A Short-Title Catalogue of Books Printed in England, Scotland, & Ireland And of English Books Printed Abroad 1475–1640*, comp. A. W. Pollard and G. R. Redgrave (1926).

TLS   *The Times Literary Supplement.*

Arber   *A Transcript of the Registers of the Company of Stationers of London; 1554–1640 A.D.*, ed. Edward Arber (1875–94), 5 vols.

B

A Note on Handwriting

The Elizabethans cared about their handwriting. The master calligrapher Peter Bales achieved fame by the improbable feat of transcribing the Bible within the compass of a walnut; Queen Elizabeth wore a specimen of his art mounted in a ring. In 1596 Bales triumphed over Daniel Johnson, a rival master, in a public exhibition, and was rewarded with a golden pen.[1] Hamlet's command of a fair hand comes to his aid when, *en route* to England, he unseals the 'grand commission' in Rosencrantz and Guildenstern's packet:

> Being thus benetted round with villainies —
> Ere I could make a prologue to my brains,
> They had begun the play — I sat me down;
> Devis'd a new commission; wrote it fair.
> I once did hold it, as our statists do,
> A baseness to write fair, and labour'd much
> How to forget that learning; but, sir, now
> It did me yeoman's service.

'To be briefe', declared Martin Billingsley in 1618 in *The Pens Excellencie, or The Secretaries Delight*, 'the Art of *Writing* is so excellent, and of such necessary use, that none ought to be without some knowledge therein, since the excellency of no art without it can bee made knowne or manifest.'

In the grammar schools, masters taught their charges how to hold the pen, and how not to; and how to write fair:

> Leave betwene eche woorde smale a letters space,
> That faire and seemelye your hand maye be redd.
> Keepe even your letters at foote, and at heade:
> Wyth distaunce a lyke betweene letter and letter:
> One out of others showes muche the better.[2]

The most favoured hand was secretary, 'so tearmed . . . partly because it is the Secretaries common hand; and partly also, because it is the onely usuall hand of *England*, for the dispatching of all manner of businesses for the most part whatsoever'.[3] This is the hand that the schoolchildren of Shakespeare's Stratford would have learnt. Richard Quiney, a good penman, used it for the letter he addressed to his 'Loveinge good ffrend & contreymann m^r w^m Shackespere'. In this hand the poet signed his name, and composed (if it is his autograph) an addition to 'Sir Thomas More'. A new hand, however, the fruit of humanistic reform in Italy, was making gradual headway, and would ultimately displace the native English cursive script. But in the sixteenth century instruction in the Italian hand — simpler and more elegant than English secretary — was pretty much limited to the children of the upper classes.

Other hands flourished in the law courts and government departments, where scriveners developed specialized scripts, or set (as distinguished from free) hands, such as the Chancery, Common Pleas, and Pipe Office hands. That special gentle, Jonson's fatuous clerk Dapper in *The Alchemist*, writes '*good* court-hand'; in fact, 'six faire hands'. These scripts had much in common with one another, the letters being formed in a regular and upright manner, and as a rule not joined together.

For a reliable and lucid introduction to the whole subject, the reader may be referred to the manual by Giles E. Dawson and Laetitia Kennedy-Skipton, *Elizabethan Handwriting 1500–1650* (New York, 1966).

---

1   'Peter Bales', *Dictionary of National Biography*, iii. 43–4.
2   John de Beau Chesne and John Baildon, *A Booke Containing Divers Sortes of Hands* [1571], sig. A1.
3   Martin Billingsley, *The Pens Exellencie, or The Secretaries Delight* (1618), sig. C3^v.

I THE SECRETARY ALPHABET. *From John de Beau Chesne and John Baildon,* A Booke Containing Divers Sortes of Hands *[1571], sig. A3. Copy in the British Library; shelfmark: C.44.a.2. STC 6446. John de Beau Chesne was a French writing-master whose* Thresor d'escripture *had been printed in Paris in 1550; for the English edition he enlisted the assistance of John Baildon. The woodcut engravings of the various styles of handwriting in this book were a novel feature at the time.*

2 THE CHANCERY HAND. *From John de Beau Chesne and John Baildon,* A Booke Containing Divers Sortes of Hands *[1571], sig. C4. Copy in the British Library; shelfmark: C. 44.a.2. STC 6446.*

WILLIAM SHAKESPEARE
A Documentary Life

Gent. Mag. Dec.r 92. Pl. II. p.1077.

South East Prospect of Stratford upon Avon.1746.

R. Greene del.

3 SOUTH-EAST PROSPECT OF STRATFORD-UPON-AVON, 1746. *Engraved from a copy by a Mr. Stringer of a drawing by Richard Greene, and reproduced in* The Gentleman's Magazine, *lxii (December 1792), facing p. 1077. 'From its being the birth-place of Shakspeare', Greene addressed Sylvanus Urban, as the editor styled himself, 'I hope you will think it worthy a place in your Magazine, and make no doubt but your engraver will do it justice. It shews the South east prospect of the church, in which are enshrined the bones of our immortal Bard; the tower of a chapel, built of fine squared stone, in a principal part of the tower [sic], by Sir Hugh Clapton. . . . It shews likewise the foot-bridge of timber; the corn and oil-mills; the top of the old town-hall (now elegantly rebuilt). . . .' A surgeon and apothecary of Lichfield, Richard Greene (1716–93) was brother to the Revd. Joseph Greene, the antiquarian headmaster of Stratford grammar school. For other specimens of Richard Greene's work, see items 8 and 12.*

1

Stratford Town and Stratford Church

The story of William Shakespeare's life is a tale of two towns. Stratford bred him; London gave him, literally and figuratively, a stage for his fortune. In an unpretentious market-town he was born and reared in a house which has miraculously survived erosions by time and tourism. Before achieving his majority he took for his bride a local girl past the bloom of youth; she bore him three children, one of whom, the only son, died young. In London, Shakespeare became a common player in plays, then a popular writer of plays — the most popular in his age, although the *literati* did not universally concur in the valuation; eventually he held shares in his theatrical company, which was the foremost in the land. With the pecuniary rewards for the triumphs of his art he invested prudently in dwellings, lands, and tithes. That was in his native Stratford, although he had lodgings in the capital. His last years he passed in a fine house, called New Place, he had purchased in his home town. There, shortly before his death, he drew up a will in which he remembered — in addition to kin — ordinary folk, Stratford neighbours, as well as the colleagues, his 'fellows', he esteemed most in the King's troupe. He neglected to mention noble lords, although to one he had in early days dedicated two poems. In Stratford, Shakespeare died and was buried. Seven years later his collected plays were printed in a handsome folio volume. That event took place in London, which then, as now, was the centre of the publishing trade in England.

A simple life-story, and one often — perhaps more than often enough — retold. Here we shall recount it again, with all the significant records to hand for the first time. Our point of departure is Stratford town and Stratford church.

Taking its source from a spring called Avon Well in the village of Naseby in Northampton-shire, the River Avon flows westward into Warwickshire, past churches, villages, and hamlets — past Guy's Cliff, associated with the legendary earl; past Warwick, fortress of the Kingmaker, with its proud castle tower and turreted walls; past Fulbrook Park (here the waters run deep) and Charlecote, seat of the Lucys and setting for the myth of Shakespeare the Deerslayer — until, broadening, the stream reaches Stratford-upon-Avon.[1] Here the great road, or *stræt*, leading north from London to Henley-in-Arden provided a passage, or *ford*, over the *afon*, which in Welsh signifies *river*. At this point the banks of the Avon gently ascend to a flat ground of light gravel, where early settlers built timber-frame cottages with stone foundations and thatched roofs. Southward lay the region known as Feldon, its fields ripe for pasturage, and (so the topographer John Speed remarked) 'tractable to be stirred for corn'. Beyond this stretch of flat open country, across the Vale of the Red Horse, rose the gently rolling Cotswold Hills. To the north the Forest of Arden, thick with undergrowth, sheltered abundant deer and other small game. The river, dividing champaign from woodland, supplied fresh water and a means of communication.

The settlement has a venerable history. Shortly after Christianity penetrated to the Kingdom of Mercia, we hear of a monastery established at *Stretforde*; much later, in Tudor times, local tradition held that this cloister was built where now stands the collegiate church of the Holy Trinity. In the Domesday Book, Stratford figures as a small manor belonging to the pious Wulfstan, Bishop of Worcester, and extending over fourteen and a half hides — under two thousand acres — with a church and mill. For several centuries the Bishop's successors remained lords of the manor.

---

1   On Stratford history I have profited mainly from Levi Fox, *The Borough Town of Stratford-upon-Avon* (Stratford-upon-Avon, 1953), and, to a lesser extent, from Sidney Lee, *Stratford-on-Avon from the Earliest Times to the Death of Shakespeare* (new ed., 1904); also R. B. Wheler, *History and Antiquities of Stratford-upon-Avon* (Stratford-upon-Avon, [1806]), and Philip Styles, 'Borough of Stratford-upon-Avon', in *The Victoria History of the County of Warwick* (1904–69), iii. A. L. Rowse, *William Shakespeare* (1963), is evocative on the Warwickshire context.

Sam. Ireland. del.

4 AVON HEAD, NASEBY, NORTHAMPTONSHIRE. *From Samuel Ireland,* Picturesque Views on the Upper, or Warwickshire Avon, from its Source at Naseby to its Junction with the Severn at Tewkesbury *(1795), facing p. 1. An engraver by profession, and by avocation a Shakespeare enthusiast, Ireland visited Stratford and its environs in the summer of 1794. The engravings in the* Picturesque Views *derive from sketches he made then. In his peregrinations Ireland was accompanied by his son William Henry, shortly to gain notoriety for his Shakespeare forgeries.*

5 THE OLD MARKET HOUSE. *Shakespeare Birthplace Trust Records Office; shelfmark: ER 1/109, item 72c. This ink-and-water-colour sketch by Captain James Saunders, c. 1821, forms part of the extensive topographical collections of Saunders now in the Birthplace Records Office.*

A captain in the Warwickshire militia, Saunders was mayor of Stratford in 1822, and a friend of Robert Bell Wheler (see below, item 7), whose antiquarian enthusiasm he shared. Most of Saunders's drawings are thought to belong to the first two decades of the last century. He sketched the Market House, to preserve a record of its appearance, just before it was demolished. Item 63, below, is also by Saunders.

Later, when the agricultural labourers became free tenants paying fixed money rents for their holdings under a system known as burgage tenure, individual and communal enterprise was stimulated, and Stratford developed into a thriving agricultural market-place.

'There are (as I take it)', remarked the Elizabethan topographer William Harrison in his *Description of England*, 'few great townes in England, that have not their weekelie markets, one or more granted from the prince, in which all maner of provision for houshold is to be bought and sold, for ease and benefit of the countrie round about.'[1] Richard I was the prince who, in the twelfth century, allowed Stratford a weekly market to be kept on Thursdays. It may well have been first held at Rother Market (*rother*, from the Anglo-Saxon, means *cattle*; the thoroughfare still bears that name), and perhaps afterwards at the place where Bridge Street, Henley Street, and High Street converge. By Shakespeare's day the ancient stone high cross at this intersection had yielded to a covered wooden Market House, open below, with four pillars supporting an upper storey, and a cupola with clock on top. In 1730 the clock was replaced; the town fathers had the whole house taken down in 1821. Today the spot where it stood is a green patch on a traffic roundabout which the visitor may glimpse, through the swirl of modern motor traffic, from the Stratford Information Office on the site where the poet's daughter Judith once lived.[2] The stone foundation of the original market-cross is preserved, unmarked, in the centre of the gravel path that divides the tranquil Birthplace garden. Tradesmen still display all manner of wares every Friday in the market held at Rother Market, but the cattle market is now held on Tuesdays near the railway station.

In the thirteenth century the bishops of Worcester procured royal charters for a series of fairs. The first ran for the three days of the eve, feast, and morrow of the Holy Trinity, the festival of the parish church's dedication, a holiday which attracted many folk from neighbouring villages. A second fair (beginning on the eve of the Exaltation of the Cross) followed, and a third at Ascensiontide. The fourth, proclaimed in 1309, lasted a full sixteen days. These events wonderfully encouraged medieval commerce. Farmers marketed their produce and livestock, while artisans — weavers, dyers, carpenters, shoemakers, and the like, of whom the town now had a full complement — displayed their wares. Not only for the benefit of locals. Travellers on their way to the cloth-making town of Coventry, famous for its cap industry, or the port of Bristol, second only to London, or industrial Birmingham might stop for refreshment at the Bear or Swan, and buy and sell merchandise at Stratford fairs.

So the town flourished. By the King's letters patent in the seventh year of Edward VI's reign, it became an independent township; a corporation possessed of a common seal and consisting of a bailiff and a council of fourteen burgesses and fourteen aldermen. Young men from the nearby villages, not content with their hereditary station as husbandmen, migrated there to learn a trade and improve their lot. The poet's father was one of these. In the sixteenth century, after the establishment of a great theatrical industry in London, the leading acting companies included Stratford in their provincial tours. The Queen's men and the Earl of Leicester's men were the first to come; they played in the Guild Hall in the summer of 1569, when John Shakespeare presided as bailiff. It is true that Stratford remained outside the mainstream of national politics, and to this day it still lies off the beaten track; but in Tudor times the town was not, as some historians have suggested, a torpid backwater. It was a pretty place, leafy with elms — almost a thousand of them on corporation property alone, according to a 1582 survey.

In the reign of Henry VIII, John Leland, Keeper of the King's libraries, made an antiquarian perambulation of England, to seek out the literary remains of ancient writers in monasteries and colleges. Around 1530 Leland set foot in Stratford. 'It hathe 2. or 3. very lardge stretes, besyde bake [i.e. back] lanes', he noted. 'One of the principall stretes ledithe from est to west, anothar from southe to northe. . . . The towne is reasonably well buyldyd of tymbar.'[3] Leland remarks on the 'great fayre' kept once each year on Holyrood Day, 14 September. In the 'right goodly chappell'

---

1 William Harrison, *The Description of England*, in Raphael Holinshed, *The First and Second Volumes of Chronicles* [1587], i. 202.
2 The site of The Cage (see below, p. 240) until recently housed a Wimpy restaurant.
3 John Leland, *Itinerary*, ed. Lucy Toulmin Smith (1907–10), ii. 48.

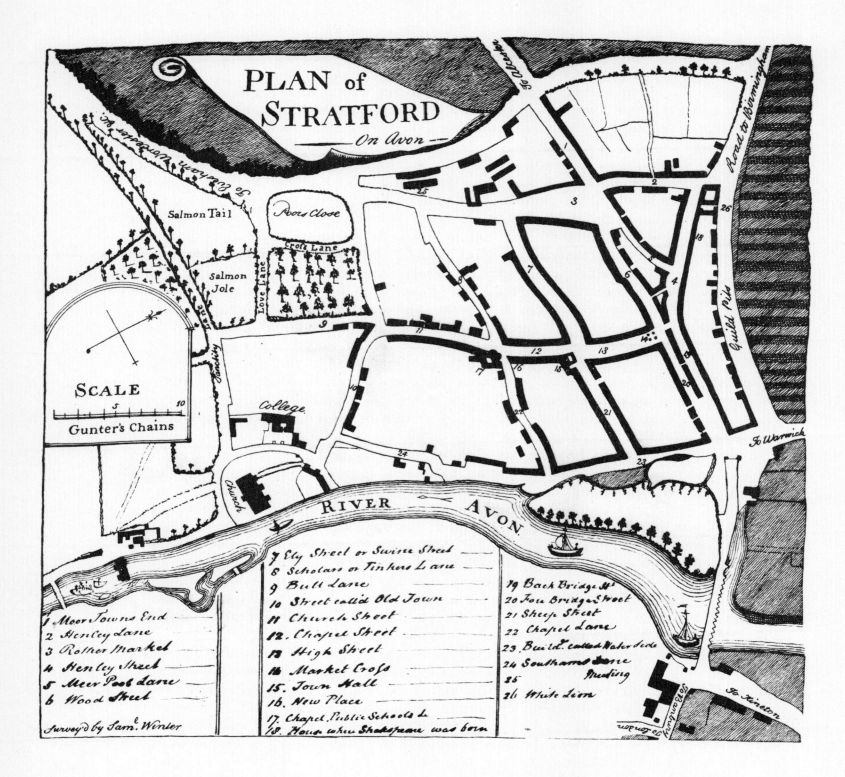

6 WINTER'S PLAN OF STRATFORD, c. 1768. *Shakespeare Birthplace Trust Records Office, ER 1/48.* The earliest known maps of Stratford-upon-Avon were made by Samuel Winter, a schoolmaster under Joseph Greene at the local grammar school; 'Sam Winter our Writing-Master', Greene refers to him. (If Winter was, as H-P reports, a maltster, he shared that sideline with many townsmen.) Winter was buried in Stratford on 1 May 1771.

His town was not all that different from the one Shakespeare knew. The basic street arrangement, laid out in the Middle Ages, consists of three principal thoroughfares running parallel with the river, and three others at right angles. It has served without essential alteration for over seven hundred years. In 1590 the manor possessed 212 houses; in 1759 (according to Winter), 552. In Winter's day these properties remained concentrated in the same few streets, and the borough boundaries had not changed (they were first enlarged in 1879). The population grew from around 1,500 in 1590 to 2,287 in 1765, when the first census was taken. For these and other facts about early Stratford, see Levi Fox, The Borough Town of Stratford-upon-Avon (Stratford-upon-Avon, 1953). Shakespeare's birthplace is identified for the first time in Winter's plans. He drew two. The first, a water-colour made in 1759, is preserved in one of the H-P scrapbooks in the Folger Shakespeare Library (shelfmark: Art Vol. d 74, no. 1a), and included by Fox in his edition of The Correspondence of the Reverend Joseph Greene (1965), facing p. 157. Winter's improved second draft, c. 1768, here reproduced, includes more houses. This version was found and printed by H-P in An Historical Account of the New Place, Stratford-upon-Avon, the Last Residence of Shakespeare (1864), p. 220. The references to the numbers in the plan, which is preserved in a volume entitled Shaksperian Scraps, are in Winter's hand.

in Church Street he paused to admire the Dance of Death 'curiously paynted' on the walls — Reformation not having yet defaced such superstitious images.

This chapel belonged to the religious and fraternal Guild of the Holy Cross. The society's rapid growth after being formed in the thirteenth century testifies to the material prosperity of Stratford. Enriched by donations from its brethren and sisters, the Guild employed four priests to perform masses in the chapel; it relieved the wants of indigent members, and supported the aged in neighbouring alms-houses. In 1427 a flurry of Guild construction produced, among other projects, a schoolhouse near the chapel. Thus was initiated the system of free grammar-school tuition in Stratford, from which in the next century the young Shakespeare would receive the sum of his formal education. By then administration of the school had passed into the hands of the corporation, for the Guild suffered the common fate of Catholic foundations after the Acts of Suppression: lands were seized, revenues confiscated, the Guild itself dissolved.

The Guild Chapel that so impressed Leland had been improved and beautified in the reign of Henry VII by one of Stratford's most successful sons, Sir Hugh Clopton. Actually he was not born there but a mile away, at Clopton manor-house; still he always regarded Stratford as his native town. A younger brother, Clopton went off to London to seek his fortune. There, as a mercer, he amassed great wealth, and was elected alderman, sheriff, and finally in 1492 (the year he was knighted) Lord Mayor. Eventually Clopton took possession of the ancestral mansion and also of his elder brother's inheritance. 'Having never wife nor childern', this self-made man determined to become a great benefactor of Stratford. In addition to rebuilding the chapel, he replaced the inadequate wooden bridge, perilous at times of flood, with another, 'great and sumptuose' (in Leland's phrase). Walled on both sides, with a long stone causeway at the west end, it consists of fourteen massive free-stone arches. On one of the piers was appropriately placed a stone pillar emblazoned with the arms of the city of London and the Clopton family, and beneath it this inscription: 'Sr. Hugh Clopton, Knight, Lord Mayor of London, built this bridge, at his own proper

7 CLOPTON BRIDGE. *From R. B. Wheler,* History and Antiquities of Stratford-upon-Avon *(Stratford-upon-Avon, [1806]), facing p. 110. This engraving is one of eight made by F. Eginton of Birmingham from amateur sketches by the Stratford antiquary, Robert Bell Wheler (1785–1857), and included in the* History and Antiquities. *For an account of Wheler, see* SL, *262–6.*

expence, in the reign of King Henry ye. Seventh.' During the Civil War, parliamentary forces tore down one of the arches, but, restored, the bridge stands to this day, a masterpiece of Tudor engineering. The London traveller bound for Stratford by way of High Wycombe and Oxford must still cross Clopton Bridge to enter the town; so Shakespeare did almost four hundred years ago.

Sir Hugh also built for himself another fine structure, 'a praty howse of brike and tymbar' by the north side of the Guild Chapel. According to Leland, who so describes it,[1] Clopton in his latter days lived in this house and died there; but the King's antiquary is wrong. Clopton granted a life-interest in the dwelling to one Roger Pagett, and in his will, drawn up the day before his death in London, he bequeathed the 'grete house' to his great-nephew William Clopton. By the end of the sixteenth century, when it came into the possession of another son of Stratford who had triumphed in the capital, the house was known as New Place.

A few years after Shakespeare's birth, William Camden, later to become the celebrated head-master of Westminster School, toured England in Leland's footsteps, gathering material for his great topographical and antiquarian survey, *Britannia*, which he composed in choice Elizabethan Latin. Following the Avon's course, Camden arrived in Stratford, by way of Warwick and Charlecote. It made a favourable impression on him, this 'handsome small market town, which owes all of its consequence to two natives of it'. One of these great benefactors was the builder of Clopton Bridge; the other, John de Stratford. The latter figures briefly in Marlowe's *Edward II* as the implacable Bishop of Winchester who demands — and obtains — Edward's crown, and delivers it to the adulterous Queen Isabella and her paramour Young Mortimer. In the next reign John was elevated to the see of Canterbury; ultimately, in 1338, he became Lord Chancellor. When he was not preoccupied with strife of state, John de Stratford's mellower thoughts would turn to the town of his birth, and to the parish church which, as a young man, he had served as rector. This he rebuilt for the greater glory of God, and, in so doing, gave it much of the aspect it holds for the modern pilgrim. Fittingly his remains lie in an alabaster tomb near the high altar.

Holy Trinity Church, built over a period of centuries, stands hard by the Avon's banks at the southern edge of Stratford, in the neighbourhood known as Old Town.[2] A long avenue of lime trees leads to the north entrance of the church. They have stood there for centuries, their boughs 'so intermingled as to produce a solemn, yet grateful shade'; so, in 1814, wrote the author of *The Beauties of England and Wales*. The splendid edifice — almost 200 feet long by 70 wide — finds its reflection in the river's placid waters. The beauty of Holy Trinity, as well as its romantic situation, has driven beholders to strange fits of doggerel:

> Church of the Holy Cross, to God and Glory,
> Mellowed by age and just a trifle hoary;
> Christians and Clergy, blessed with light Divine,
> Still love to linger at this Sacred Shrine.[3]

In design the church is cruciform: chancel and nave, running east and west, are crossed by the north and south transepts. The square tower at their point of intersection is surmounted by a lofty octagonal stone steeple — a late improvement, for the spire that Shakespeare knew was a smaller timber one. In the eighteenth century the parishioners decided that this steeple was too mean and diminutive, and anyway it was always wanting repair; so they hired an architect to replace it with another of Warwick hewn stone.

On either side of the avenue of lime trees, Stratford folk lie buried. Here the poet's father and mother were laid to rest, as was his daughter Judith. Within the church itself are interred the more illustrious dead of Stratford, and some have imposing monuments. One of these belongs to Sir Hugh Clopton, despite the fact that he lies in London, in the parish church of St. Margaret,

---

1 The quoted phrase is the first reference to brick in Stratford; brick did not become popular, except for chimneys, until after the Restoration (*Victoria History*, iii. 223).

2 A detailed account (which I have found most valuable) of Holy Trinity is J. Harvey Bloom, *Shakespeare's Church, otherwise the Collegiate Church of the Holy Trinity of Stratford-upon-Avon* (1902).

3 *A Short History of Stratford-on-Avon, Written in Ballad Form by an Old Warwickshire Boy*, Privately Printed (1926), verse 12.

A South West View *of the* Col:st *Church* Stratford upon Avon. R:Greene Del 1762.

8 SOUTH-WEST VIEW OF HOLY TRINITY CHURCH, 1762. *Ink-and-water-colour, by Richard Greene, in the Folger Shakespeare Library; shelfmark: Art Vol. d 70, no. 2a. Formerly in the collection of H-P, it is described by him as 'One of the earliest drawings of the Church known to exist' (Calendar of the Shakespearean Rarities (1891), p. 117). The sketch shows the old wooden steeple, replaced the following year with the present stone one.*

Lothbury. Although Jonson eulogized Shakespeare as a monument without a tomb, he was not for that reason denied his memorial, complete with effigy, in the north wall of the chancel. It is today the principal attraction for visitors. In medieval times the church's chief glory was the great rood loft, carved with images, and painted red and gold. It has long since disappeared — part of the toll Reformation took of the church — along with a local master's ceiling paintings that depicted Saint George and the Dragon, the Last Judgement, and the history of the Holy Cross.

The church's harmonious interior proportions have, however, survived vicissitudes (the chancel fell into decay and was boarded up; two years after Shakespeare's burial there, it was declared 'ruinous'). Much of the effect we owe to John de Stratford. Parts of the ancient fabric — tower, transepts, portions of the nave — date back to the early thirteenth century, but he altered and added a good deal. The north aisle he widened, and installed in it a chapel in honour of the Holy Virgin, which after his time was wholly usurped by tombs and monuments of the Cloptons; so it is

Sam. Ireland. delt

9 STRATFORD CHURCH. *From Samuel Ireland*, Picturesque Views on the Upper, or Warwickshire Avon, from its Source at Naseby, to its Junction with the Severn at Tewkesbury (*1795*), *facing p. 210.*

called Clopton Chapel. John also rebuilt the south aisle, and placed there a chapel to Saint Thomas à Becket. In 1332 he founded a chantry of this chapel, and endowed in perpetuity five priests to chant masses at the altar for himself, his family, the Kings of England, and the Bishops of Worcester. John's nephew, Ralph de Stratford, in 1351 built for the habitation of these priests a house adjoining the western side of the churchyard. This structure came to be styled the College of Stratford, after the chapter, or college, of priests who dwelt there under a warden and served the church. That is why Holy Trinity is described as a collegiate church.

In the fifteenth century the Dean of Lichfield provided endowment for four singing boys, who were accommodated in a steep-gabled two-storey house approached by steps from the chancel, through a doorway just below the Shakespeare monument. Gradually this dwelling fell into decay, and in time it became a charnel-house. An immense quantity of bones accumulated there, we learn from a late seventeenth-century report; enough to load a great number of wagons.[1] It was already a charnel-house in Shakespeare's day. Perhaps he had it in mind when Juliet protests to Friar Lawrence,

> chain me with roaring bears,
> Or hide me nightly in a charnel house,
> O'er-cover'd quite with dead men's rattling bones,
> With reeky shanks and yellow chapless skulls.

The bone-house was demolished in 1801, but the doorway to it, now walled up, still stands.

Others who followed John de Stratford further beautified the church. Most important of these is Dr. Thomas Balsall, warden of the College in Edward IV's reign. He reconstructed the chancel from the ground up, installing the five bays on either side with their large uniform windows with

---

1 See William Hall's letter (1694) to Edward Thwaites, reproduced below, item 205, p. 251.

cusped and crenellated transoms; also the dividing buttresses floridly ornamented in late Gothic style with angels, dragons, and grotesques. To one of Balsall's master masons we probably also owe the baptismal font. Only the shattered bowl today survives, on its new pedestal near to Shakespeare's grave, for it was in time superseded by a new font of late Renaissance design.[1] The original

10 PARISH REGISTERS, STRATFORD-UPON-AVON. Shakespeare Birthplace Trust Records Office, ER 1/III, f. 100. This sketch of the first, and oldest, volume of the Stratford registers was made around the middle of the nineteenth century by F. W. Fairholt, the engraver and antiquary who illustrated H-P, Life (1848). Richard Savage used the drawing for the frontispiece to his edition of The Registers of Stratford-on-Avon, in the County of Warwick *(1897–1905), vol. i, for the Parish Register Society. It is here reproduced from the original in a Fairholt scrapbook. The title, as recorded in the sketch, is not precisely accurate.*

All but one of the entries in the Stratford registers concerning Shakespeare, his relations and descendants, appear in the first volume. It is a large folio, measuring 17½in. × 7½in. × 3in., bound in brown leather, with brass corner pieces ornamented with the Tudor rose, and the remains of the brass clasps depicted by Fairholt. The front cover bears the inscription 'Stratforde/upon Aven/400 Leaves/1600:/R/Elizabeth. 42/42'. Actually the volume contains 335 numbered leaves. It records baptisms (1558–1653, 1687–1776), marriages (1558–1651, 1687–1754), and burials (1558–1653, 1687–1776). This register was kept in Holy Trinity Church until 28 September 1966, when the vicar, the Revd. T. Bland, entrusted it for safe-keeping to the Chairman of the Birthplace Trust.

The entry for the burial of Judith Shakespeare (see below, item 217) occurs in the second volume, which covers the period from 1653 to 1686. This register was deposited with the Shakespeare Birthplace Trust in 1971.

1   The relic was formerly kept at the back of the nave.

was discarded, and turned up long afterwards in the garden of a parish clerk, one Thomas Paine, who died in 1747. He was using it as a water-cistern. This is the font in which William Shakespeare and his brothers and sisters were christened.

A record of the baptisms was entered in the parish register, which also recorded burials and weddings. Such registers had been first instituted in 1538, when the Vicar General, Thomas Cromwell, put forth an edict for the keeping of these essential data in each parish of England. They were not, however, always regularly maintained. The order was renewed in 1547, when Edward VI was king, and some years later Queen Elizabeth enjoined every parish priest to subscribe to this oath: 'I shall keepe the register booke according to the Queenes Majesties injunction.' The Stratford registers commence in March 1558, the first year of her reign. A single hand is responsible for all entries — whether of christenings, weddings, or deaths — up to mid-September 1600. Evidently these belong to a copyist, probably Richard Byfield, who became vicar of Stratford in 1597, just after the promulgation of a new provincial constitution. The Archbishop and Clergy of Canterbury now required each parish to procure parchment register books at its own expense, and to transfer into them (from the paper books formerly in use) the names of those baptized, married, or buried during the reign of Elizabeth; moreover, the vicar and church-wardens were to examine and certify each page of these records. This explains why the extant registers for Stratford begin in 1558, and why the year 1600 is inscribed on the cover of the first volume. The entry for William Shakespeare's baptism is, then, not the original but an early transcript.[1]

These registers chronicle the most crucial events — birth, marriage, death — in the family of John Shakespeare. Normally one might expect such records, limited to the bare citation of names and dates, to be straightforward enough, but a special problem bedevilled the earliest authorities who consulted the parish books. For a second John Shakespeare, contemporary with ours, has left his trail in the registers, as well as in other Stratford records. This Shakespeare was a corvisor, or shoemaker, from nearby Warwick who succeeded to the family business when his brother drowned in the Avon. The shoemaker apparently married three times, and his offspring — Ursula, Humphrey, and Philip — duly enter the baptismal register. Having filled some minor corporation posts and become Master of his guild, he seems to have left Stratford for good by the mid-nineties. A John Shakespeare was buried in St. Mary's in Warwick on 7 February 1624. Actually the coincidence, while curious, need not startle us, for Shakespeares, their names spelt with exotic variety, were thick on the ground in Warwickshire and the adjoining counties. (As early as 1248 a William Sakspere of Clopton in Gloucestershire was hanged for robbery.) The confusions caused by the two John Shakespeares were successfully sorted out by the close of the eighteenth century through the industry of Edmond Malone, greatest of Shakespeare scholars.

The career of John Shakespeare is amply and reliably documented. To him and to his antecedents we now turn.

---

1 *The Registers of Stratford-on-Avon, in the County of Warwick*, ed. Richard Savage (Parish Register Society; 1897–1905), i, pref., pp. vi–vii.

2

The Shakespeares:

from Snitterfield to Stratford

Three and a half miles north-east of Stratford, and just north of the old turnpike road leading from the market-town to Warwick, sits, perched on a hill, the quiet little village of Snitterfield. Here Shakespeare's grandfather Richard settled some time before 1529. In those days, as now, a single structure dominated the village: the handsome, large parish church of St. James the Great with its long nave and imposing west tower. The clerestory then was new, as was the slate roof fetched (some say) from Fulbrook Castle. Within are Renaissance stalls elaborately carved with vines, and an octagonal baptismal font, still in use, dating from the fourteenth century; in all likelihood the poet's father was christened there — we do not have registers for christenings as early as that. At Hill Field the old mill by the stream has long since disappeared, and few evidences remain of the timber-frame cottages with timber-frame barns and timbered pigeon-houses. Snitterfield is situated in pleasantly undulating countryside, with scattered woodland, thickets of small trees and shrubs, heath, and yellow-blossoming gorse. Here, in several manors, Richard Shakespeare rented land, tilled the soil, and pastured his livestock.[1]

The court and manorial records of the area chronicle the everyday vexations and (less frequently) rewards of a farmer's life. Presumably Richard mended his hedges when ordered in 1538 to do so. A jury charged him with overburdening the common with his cattle. He paid fines for neglecting to yoke or ring his swine, and for letting his livestock run loose on the meadows — that was in 1560, when every tenant was ordered to 'make his hedges & ditches betwixt the end of the lane of Richard Shakespere & the hedge called dawkins hedge'. When he could not get by with an acceptable excuse, he paid his twopence fine rather than attend the manor court held twice yearly at Warwick, a six miles' journey from Snitterfield. A prosperous alderman of Stratford, the vintner and clothier Thomas Atwood *alias* Taylor, bequeathed Richard the four oxen already in his keeping. He helped to appraise the goods of a deceased vicar, as well as of other neighbours. (This was the office of friends and good neighbours, 'persons two at the least, to whom the person dying was indebted'; so the statutes of the realm decreed, to which Henry Swinburne, the supreme Elizabethan authority on testaments, adds, 'it is not sufficient to make an inventarie, conteining all and singular the goods of the deceased, unless the same be particularly valued and praised [i.e. appraised] by some honest and skilfull persons, to be the just value thereof in their judgements and consciences . . . .'[2]) When Richard died, before 10 February 1561, his own goods were valued at £38.17s. — almost £5 more than the vicar's. Richard Shakespeare's house abutted on the High Street, probably the high road to Warwick, and had land that stretched down to the brook which flows through Snitterfield and on down to the Avon. This property he rented from Robert Arden of Wilmcote. Arden had a daughter, Mary, who would marry John Shakespeare.

Richard had at least two sons. A Thomas Shakespeare who paid the largest rent, £4, of all the tenants who farmed in the Hales manor may have been his issue, but proof is wanting. Henry Shakespeare, however, was certainly Richard's son. Like Thomas, he held land in the Hales manor, but he also farmed at Ingon in the nearby parish of Hampton Lucy, which lies on the

---

1   On Richard Shakespeare and his sons, ME (7–12) concisely sums up knowledge.
2   Henry Swinburne, *A Briefe Treatise of Testaments and Last Willes* (1590), f. 220; cited by H-P, *Outlines*, ii. 245.

C

left bank of the Avon and extends to the ridge dividing the fertile valley from the Forest of Arden; his brother John would also hold land in Ingon Meadow. Henry was something of a ne'er-do-well. He got into a fray with one Edward Cornwall, drew blood, and was fined, but did not show up in court to answer the charge. He was imprisoned for trespass; he incurred debts and failed to honour them. On one occasion Henry refused to pay his tithe (there was a quarrel between claimants) and for a time suffered excommunication. The authorities fined him for wearing a hat instead of a cap to church — maybe a principle was involved, for many, especially Puritans, resented the Statute of Caps, promulgated to encourage the depressed craft of cappers. He was also fined for not labouring with teams to mend the Queen's highway, and 'for having a diche betweene redd hill and Burman in decaye for want of repayringe'. (These fields, still called Burman and Red Hill, may to this day be identified a short distance east of Snitterfield church, on the right-hand side of the road leading to Luscombe.) Once when he was in jail in the High Street for debt, his surety William Rounde marched over to Henry's house and appropriated two oxen which the latter had bought but characteristically not paid for. Yet when he died in his own house there was, a witness declared, plenty of money in his coffers, corn and hay 'of a great value' in the barn, and a mare in the stable. This was the poet's Uncle Harry. In the parish church of Hampton Lucy (re-built in the early nineteenth century) he had two children baptized: Lettice in 1582 and James in 1585. Shakespeare as a boy likely enough crossed the fields to Ingon to visit his uncle and aunt and cousins. Little James died in 1589. Henry was buried in Snitterfield on 29 December 1596, and two months later 'Margaret Sakspere, being tymes the wyff of Henry Shakspere' followed him to the grave.

Richard Shakespeare's other son John was another sort. Not content with raising crops and pasturing herds with his father in Snitterfield and his brother in Ingon, he migrated in mid-century to Stratford. There he undertook an apprenticeship of at least seven years to become a glover and whittawer, or dresser of white leather. In this craft he 'tawed' the hides of deer and horses, and also of goats and sheep and hounds (but not cattle or pigs); he made and sold not only gloves but all manner of soft leather goods: belts, purses, aprons, and the like. (The dramatist recalls the glover in his shop in *The Merry Wives of Windsor*, when Mistress Quickly tries to place Master Slender — 'Does he not wear a great round beard', she asks, 'like a glover's paring-knife?') It was a good trade to be in, protected against foreign competition by Act of Parliament. On market and fair days, the glovers commanded the most strategically located standing-place in the market square, at the Market Cross under the clock. The seventeenth-century gossip John Aubrey, celebrated for his *Brief Lives*, reports that John Shakespeare was a butcher, but this is unlikely; stringent regulations governing the wholesomeness of meat kept the two occupations separate.[1] Anyway Ralph Cawdrey was the local butcher licensed by the council. John's entrance into the trade of glove-making may have been facilitated by his father's connections. As we have seen, Richard knew Alderman Atwood. Maybe he was also acquainted with John Townsend of the Wold in Snitterfield. Townsend had a daughter, Joan, who married a prominent Stratford citizen, Thomas Dickson *alias* Waterman, also an alderman, and landlord of the Swan Inn in Bridge Street. By trade this Dickson was a glover, and possibly the master under whom John Shakespeare served out his apprenticeship.

He enters the historical record ingloriously on 29 April 1552, when he paid a shilling fine for having amassed an unauthorized refuse heap (*sterquinarium*) in Henley Street. On that occasion John was not the only offender penalized for failure to use the 'comyn mukhyll' standing at the country end of the street, before the house of William Chambers the wheelwright; Humphrey Reynolds and Adrian Quiney were similarly fined that day. John Shakespeare's muck-hill (in the view of our foremost authority on the plague in Elizabethan England) has come to symbolize Tudor methods of sanitation.[2] Such filth spawned pestilence; at the same time, the stiff penalties imposed — equal to two days' pay for an artisan — show that the community worried about the wholesomeness of its lanes and gutters. The record has an additional interest, for it reveals that by the spring of 1552 John Shakespeare was residing as a tenant or householder in Henley Street.

1   See Charles Isaac Elton, *William Shakespeare: His Family and Friends* (1904), pp. 349–50; also below, item 57, p. 58.
2   F.P. Wilson, *The Plague in Shakespeare's London* (Oxford, 1927), p. 26.

11 JOHN SHAKESPEARE'S MIDDEN HEAP, 29 APRIL 1552. *Public Record Office, Special Collections, Court Rolls, S.C. 2/207, no. 82. Transcript: BRL, i. 52. This citation, from a View of Frankpledge taken by the court leet for the King's manor of Stratford, was discovered in the Carlton Ride Record Office by the antiquary Joseph Hunter, an assistant keeper of the public records, and published by him in* New Illustrations of the Life, Studies, and Writings of Shakespeare *(1845), i. 18. H-P, Life, p. 23, gave a fuller extract. The document was later removed to the Public Record Office in London.*

That must have been in the western part of the big double house; the wing which, in afterdays known as the Birthplace, has made of Stratford a secular shrine.

Soon John was acquiring more property. In 1556 he purchased from one George Turnor a freehold estate with garden and croft (*unum tenementum cum Gardino & Crofto*) in Greenhill Street, the road that would afterwards be called More Towns End. The same year he bought another house with adjacent garden in Henley Street from Edward West. This was to be the eastern wing, known to posterity as the Woolshop. At some time — just when is not recorded — workmen joined together the two houses to form the present impressive structure, which gives the appearance of being a single half-timbered house of three gables. It was put up in the late fifteenth or early sixteenth century. Because of its associations, the house has not wanted fanciful appreciation. 'Shadows and weird noises are in the rafters, the wind is in the chimneys, crickets are on the hearth, fairies glisten in the light of the dying fire, through leaded windows shines the moon, without is the *to-whit, to-whoo* of the loved brown owl.'[1]

However this may be, the dwelling consists of a stone groundsill, or low foundation wall, upon which rests a sturdy oak superstructure. Wattle and daub fill in the spaces of the rectangles formed by the beams. In the centre a massive chimney stack consolidated the structure, which was covered by a timber roof — in time to come this would be replaced with tile. Late in the sixteenth century a rear wing of timber and plaster, similar to the rest, was added; it projects into the pleasant garden. John Shakespeare was still living in Henley Street in 1597, when for fifty shillings he sold a narrow strip of land — only a half-yard wide by twenty-eight yards in length — to a draper, George Badger, who (it seems likely) intended to build a wall. Around the same time John parted with a piece of land on the east to Edward Willis of King's Norton, Worcestershire, who had a scheme to convert two small houses into an inn, which he would call The Bell. These conveyances show that for almost half a century of his life John Shakespeare resided in Henley Street.

Thus settled, he took for his bride Mary Arden, the rich farmer's daughter. The Ardens boasted one of the most venerable names in Warwickshire; Dugdale describes them as 'that most antient and worthy Family'. They had been 'lords of Warwick' before the Norman Conquest, and not many families in England could trace back their descent so far. Some Ardens had enormous wealth. In the Domesday Book, Turchillus de Eardine — Turchill of the Forest of Arden — held lands that filled over four columns; nobody else possessed so much. Our Ardens were more ordinary folk, affluent yeomen shading into minor gentry. The precise branch to which Robert Arden belonged remains obscure, despite intense genealogical zeal;[2] perhaps he was descended from some younger son of the Ardens of Park Hall, which is in Castle Bromwich in the parish of

1 Edgar I. Fripp, *Shakespeare: Man and Artist* (1938), i. 73.
2 See G. R. French, *Shakespeareana Genealogica* (1869), pp. 416–524; EKC, ii. 28–32; and ME, 12–14.

12 EXTERIOR OF THE BIRTHPLACE, *c.* 1762. *Water-colour by Richard Greene, formerly owned by H-P and now in the Folger Shakespeare Library; shelfmark: Art Vol. d 75, no. 27c. H-P described it as 'the earliest representation of the house known to exist' (Calendar of the Shakespearean Rarities (1891), p. 132). The water-colour is the basis for the well-known engraving (item 13). The vicissitudes of the Henley Street house are recounted by Levi Fox in 'The Heritage of Shakespeare's Birthplace', Shakespeare Survey 1 (Cambridge, 1948), pp. 79–88.*

13 EXTERIOR OF THE BIRTHPLACE, 1769. *This, the first printed view of the house, was engraved by B. Cole, and appeared in* The Gentleman's Magazine, *xxxix (July 1769), facing p. 345. During the summer of 1769 interest in the Shakespeare monuments had been stimulated by the forthcoming Stratford Jubilee organized by David Garrick. 'I do not know whether the apartment where the incomparable Shakespeare first drew his breath, can, at this day, be ascertained, or not', 'T.B.' of Lichfield wrote to Sylvanus Urban; 'but the house of his nativity (according to undoubted tradition) is now remaining. My worthy friend Mr Greene, of this place, hath favoured me with an exact drawing of it (here inclosed) which may not possibly be an unacceptable present to such of your readers as intend to honour Stratford with their company at the approaching jubilee. . . .' This is the first reference to a tradition regarding the Birthplace. Garrick, assisted by intuition, identified the precise room of Shakespeare's nativity. For accounts of the Jubilee, see Christian Deelman,* The Great Shakespeare Jubilee *(1964), Johanne M. Stochholm,* Garrick's Folly *(1964), and Martha Winburn England,* Garrick's Jubilee *(Ohio State University Press, 1964); also SL, 154–62.*

Gent. Mag. July 1769.

R. Greene delin.   B. Cole sculp.

A House in Stratford upon Avon, in which the famous Poet Shakespear was Born.

14 JOHN SHAKESPEARE'S SALE OF LAND IN HENLEY STREET, 26 JANUARY 1597. Shakespeare Birthplace Trust Records Office, TTD 1/2. Transcript: H-P, Outlines, ii. 13; BRL, i. 222–4 (text and translation).

The document was first printed and analysed by H-P, Life, pp. 36–8. 'This deed', he writes, 'was found very recently in the office of a solicitor at Birmingham, who very kindly, at the request of Mr. Hunt, of Stratford, permitted me to take a transcript of it' (p. 36). As H-P notes, the deed shows that the Henley Street property was bounded on the north by the royal highway called the Gild Pits ('Gyll pyttes'). Here John Shakespeare signs with a cross; for his mark, the glover's compasses, see item 35. His sole use of an alternative mark, the glover's 'donkey', is to be found in item 36. Evelyn Philip Shirley of Ettington Park presented the document to the Birthplace.

15 MARY ARDEN'S HOUSE. *This sketch, made by John Jordan probably around 1795, is in the Shakespeare Birthplace Trust Records Office; shelfmark: ER/109, no. 39.*

Aston Cantlow, not far from Birmingham. His grandfather may have been Robert Arden, a bailiff of Snitterfield around the middle of the fifteenth century, and he was certainly the son of Thomas Arden of Wilmcote. This hamlet lies in Aston Cantlow parish, stretching across the valley of the Alne, bounded on the east by the low, partly wooded hills dividing it from the Avon. This Thomas bought lands in Snitterfield, and passed them on to his son. How extensive Robert Arden's Snitterfield holdings were we cannot say, but they included two farmhouses, one of which he let to Richard Shakespeare, and maybe a hundred or more acres of land.

When, on 21 April 1548, Arden married Agnes Hill, *née* Webbe, the widow of a substantial farmer of Bearley Grange, he was already well along in years, and had by previous marriage — or marriages — eight daughters. They must have been presentable young women, for at least six found husbands, and two of them married twice. Arden's new wife brought two sons and two daughters from her previous match, so it was a large family. The ménage lived in Wilmcote. Where precisely is not known; late in the eighteenth century, however, John Jordan, autodidact and self-appointed repository of Shakespearian lore, identified a timber-frame house in Featherbed Lane as Mary Arden's House, and by this name it is still visited by tourists. Jordan is never to be taken on faith ('one of those humble geniuses', a contemporary charitably sized him up, 'to whom a little learning, if not a dangerous thing, proved almost useless'), but Mary must have grown up, if not in these, in very similar surroundings. Situated near the village green, on the north side of the road to Stratford, the dwelling is a handsome big sixteenth-century farmhouse, two-storeyed, with stone foundation and two stone hearths on each floor (there is a large fireplace in the kitchen), inglenook in the sitting-room corner, roughly-hewn oak beams for the open-timbered ceilings, and gabled dormers to light the upper storey.[1]

1   For a more technically detailed description of the house, see *The Victoria History of the County of Warwick* (1904–69), iii. 32–3.

A number of years must have separated John and Mary — she was the youngest of numerous siblings, he an elder son; he would live to be past seventy, and she would outlast him by seven years. Mary must have seemed a desirable match; probably her father's favourite, and practically an heiress, although (it seems) she could neither read nor write, signing documents with her mark.

In the autumn of 1556 Robert Arden lay dying. By his will made on 24 November, when he was sick in body but 'good and perfett of rememberence', he bequeathed his soul 'to Allmyghtye God and to our bleside Ladye Sent Marye and to all the holye compenye of heven' — this loyal subject of Catholic Queen Mary held fast to the Old Faith. His wife he looked after prudentially, setting conditions on his bequest of ten marks (£6.13s.4d.). But his youngest daughter inspired fonder thoughts; Arden left her, besides the customary ten marks, all of his most valuable possession: the estate in Wilmcote, called Asbyes, 'and the crop apone the grounde sowne and tyllide as hitt is'.

Despite her youth, Mary was named one of the two executors, so she was present the next month for the inventory of goods and movables, which testifies to the comfortable circumstances of the deceased. His belongings included full eleven of the painted cloths in those days used in place of tapestries for wall decorations; on broad strips of canvas were rudely painted in tempera scenes Biblical or mythological, with appropriately sententious mottoes beneath. (Shakespeare remembered the mottoes in *The Rape of Lucrece*: 'Who fears a sentence or an old man's saw / Shall by a painted cloth be kept in awe.') Arden's house boasted two such cloths in the hall, five in the great adjoining chamber, and four more scattered through the upstairs bedrooms. Also cupboards and oak furniture (including a little table with shelves), and enough bed linen, as well as copper pots and brass pans, a chafing dish, small handmill, and kneading trough. The inventory also included the farmer's tools and agricultural gear, a barn filled with wheat and barley, store of livestock — oxen, bullocks, colts, swine, and weaning calves — as well as bees and poultry, wood in the yard, and bacon in the roof. The Ardens had sufficient.

His body Robert asked to have buried in the churchyard of Aston Cantlow. The widow kept on in Wilmcote (apparently, as Arden hoped, she did not make trouble because of her small inheritance, but suffered his daughter Alice to live quietly with her). In 1580, 'aged and impotent' (so she described herself), she died, and was buried in the churchyard. Some time between March 1556, when Mary Arden's father drew up his will, and September 1558, when her first daughter was born, she married John Shakespeare. Very likely the ceremony took place in Aston Cantlow, in the parish church of St. John the Baptist. The registers there commence only later, and probably for that reason there is no record of John Shakespeare's marriage.

3

Offspring

The Shakespeares proved fruitful; so the parish registers over a period of twenty years or so, from 1558 to 1580, testify. To be sure, they chronicle burials as well as christenings, but during these decades births in the family outnumber deaths. The Shakespeares' first-born was christened after the Catholic fashion, in Latin and with the anointing; for Mary still reigned. The rest — there were eight children in all — had Anglican baptism.

John Shakespeare's first offspring was a daughter, Joan, christened (the registers inform us) on 15 September 1558. The curate who officiated was Roger Dyos. The next year, with a new sovereign on the throne, Dyos's Romanist persuasion became unpalatable, and since he volunteered neither to resign nor to die — the usual grounds for replacement — the corporation ousted him by the simple expedient of withholding his stipend. John Shakespeare, then on the council, voted with the Protestant majority. Dyos retired to Little Bedwyn in Wiltshire, and for seventeen years nursed his grievances. Then, in 1576, he brought suit against the bailiff of Stratford for his 'yerelie annuitie', which he recovered with damages. Meanwhile the town managed for several years without a pastor — visiting preachers must have filled the gap — until, in January 1561, a new vicar was installed. Master John Bretchgirdle, who came from Witton, Northwich, was an M.A. of Christ Church, Oxford, and held impeccable Church of England principles. He was unmarried — a sister, perhaps two sisters, kept house for him — and bookish; his library (valued at about half his estate) included Tyndale's *New Testament in English*, Aesop, Sallust, Vergil, Horace, two works of Erasmus, a Latin–English dictionary, and *The Actes of the Apostles, translated into Englyshe Metre . . . by Christofer Tye, . . . wyth notes to eche Chapter, to synge and also to play upon the Lute, very necessarye for studentes after theyr studye, to fyle theyr wyttes, and also for all Christians that cannot synge, to read the good and Godlye storyes of the lyves of Christ hys Appostles.*[1] Master Bretchgirdle performed the christening of the Shakespeares' second child, Margaret, on 22 December 1562, and witnessed her burial a few months later. On 26 April 1564, 'discretely, and warely' (as the Prayer Book enjoins) he baptized William Shakespeare. The next spring the vicar died, leaving his dictionary to the scholars at Stratford grammar school, and was laid to rest in the parish church.

Thus we have the date of Shakespeare's baptism, but when was the poet born? Not a momentous question, perhaps, but a necessary one; for the biographer will wish to have, as his starting-point, the precise date of his hero's nativity. Traditionally, of course, we celebrate Shakespeare's birth on 23 April. That date is irresistibly attractive, coinciding as it does with the feast of St. George. Since 1222 his day has been celebrated as a national festival in Britain, and he has been patron saint of England since the time of John de Stratford. How fitting that St. George's Day should also mark the birth-date of the National Poet! We are almost tempted to forget that the wish is father of many a tradition.

This particular one goes back two centuries. In a note to his copy of Gerard Langbaine's *Account of the English Dramatick Poets* (1691), the eighteenth-century antiquary William Oldys is apparently the first to declare 23 April as Shakespeare's date of birth, although Oldys has the year wrong (1563). His contemporary Joseph Greene, Curate of Stratford and master of the grammar school there, passed along to the great Shakespearian scholar George Steevens an extract from the parish register with the note 'Born April 23, 1564'. Steevens adopted this date in his 1773 edition of Shakespeare, and he has been followed by editors and biographers ever since.

1   Bretchgirdle's will and inventory were transcribed by Richard Savage and printed by Edgar I. Fripp, *Shakespeare Studies, Biographical and Literary* (1930), pp. 23–31. On Dyos and Bretchgirdle, see *MA*, i, pp. xlvii–xlviii, 101–2; ii. 110; Fripp, *Shakespeare: Man and Artist*, i. 37–8, 41–2.

Baptismes

WILLIAM SHAKESPEARE CHRISTENED, 26 APRIL 1564. *The entry appears on f. 5 of the baptismal register. The page is here reduced.*

17-28 Stratford Parish Register Entries

17   JOAN SHAKESPEARE CHRISTENED, 15 SEPTEMBER 1558. *Baptismal register, f. 1.*

18   MARGARET SHAKESPEARE CHRISTENED, 2 DECEMBER 1562.   *Baptismal register, f. 3.*

19   MARGARET SHAKESPEARE BURIED, 30 APRIL 1563. *Burial register, f. 4.*

20   THE PLAGUE BEGINS IN STRATFORD, 11 JULY 1564. *Burial register, f. 5.*

21   GILBERT SHAKESPEARE CHRISTENED, 13 OCTOBER 1566. *Baptismal register, f. 7.*

22   JOAN SHAKESPEARE CHRISTENED, 15 APRIL 1569. *Baptismal register, f. 9.*

23   ANNE SHAKESPEARE CHRISTENED, 28 SEPTEMBER 1571. *Baptismal register, f. 10.*

24   RICHARD SHAKESPEARE CHRISTENED, 11 MARCH 1574. *Baptismal register, f. 11ᵛ.*

1579

April 4   Anne daughter to mr John Shakspere ✕

25 ANNE SHAKESPEARE BURIED, 4 APRIL 1579. *Burial register, f. 15.*

May 2   Elizabeth, daughter toe William Byddull
3   Edmund sonne to mr John Shakspere ✕

26 EDMUND SHAKESPEARE CHRISTENED, 3 MAY 1580. *Baptismal register, f. 17.*

27 GILBERT SHAKESPEARE BURIED, 3 FEBRUARY 1612. *Burial register, f. 41ᵛ.*

28 RICHARD SHAKESPEARE BURIED, 4 FEBRUARY 1613. *Burial register, f. 42ᵛ.*

STRATFORD PARISH REGISTER ENTRIES. *Shakespeare Birthplace Trust Records Office, DR 243/1. Richard Savage transcribed the early* Registers of Stratford-on-Avon, in the County of Warwick *in full for the Parish Register Society, which published them in three volumes:* Baptisms, 1558–1652 (*1897*), Marriages, 1558–1812 (*1898*), *and* Burials, 1558–1652–3 (*1905*). *The christening, marriage, and burial entries for the Shakespeares are given, with commentary, by EKC, ii. 1–13; also, passim, by BRL and TB.*

The Stratford registers were first consulted for Nicholas Rowe's Some Account of the Life &c. of Mr. William Shakespear *prefacing his 1709 edition of* The Works of Shakespear. *Rowe did not himself examine these records but employed the actor Thomas Betterton, 'his Veneration [Rowe tells us] for the Memory of* Shakespear *having engag'd him to make a Journey into* Warwickshire, *on purpose to gather up what Remains he could of a Name for which he had so great a Value'. Then in his seventies (he died in 1710), and untrained for his task, Betterton led Rowe into error. The latter in his* Account *credits John Shakespeare with ten children, and the poet with three daughters, of whom Judith is made senior to Susanna.*

The Revd. Joseph Greene first compiled relevant extracts from the registers, and transmitted them, via the Hon. James West, to George Steevens, who included them in the preliminaries to the Johnson–Steevens edition of* The Plays of William Shakespeare *in 1773 (i. sigs. N1ᵛ–N2). In his extracts, which Malone censured as 'inaccurate and very imperfect', Greene misread the name of Shakespeare's son Hamnet as Samuel, and made John Shakespeare the thrice-married father of eleven children. Subsequent editors, including for a time Malone, passed down Greene's errors. But, his suspicions aroused by the long interval separating the baptismal entries for 'Jone Shakspere daughter to John Shakspere' in 1558, and 'Humphrey sonne to John Shakspere' in 1590, Malone first distinguished between the two John Shakespeares (see above, p. 12). He discovered that the christening records carefully discriminate between plain John Shakespeare, the shoemaker, and Mr. John Shakespeare, the respected townsman. (The honorific* Master *was reserved for those who had achieved aldermanic status or otherwise merited deferential address.) Malone's findings appear in his posthumous* Life, *included in the 1821 Variorum edition of* The Plays and Poems of William Shakspeare, *ii. 51–62.*

But what is the evidence? We have the christening date. In Victorian times the learned Halliwell (later Halliwell-Phillipps) remarked in passing that three days often elapsed between birth and baptism. This casual suggestion hardens into positive assertion in Sir Sidney Lee's *Life of William Shakespeare*, for long regarded as standard: '. . . it was a common practice at the time', Lee says, 'to baptise a child three days after birth.'[1] Actually no evidence demonstrates that such a customary interval ever existed. The Prayer Book of 1559 offers sounder guidance. It instructs parents not to postpone christening beyond the first Sunday or Holy Day following birth, 'unless upon a great and reasonable cause declared to the Curate, and by hym approved'. In the latter weeks of April 1564, Sundays fell on the 16th, 23rd, and 30th, and festivals were kept on Wednesday the 19th (for Alphege, Archbishop and Martyr of blessed memory) and on Tuesday the 25th (St. Mark the Evangelist's Day); these in addition to St. George's feast. So, if Shakespeare was born on the 23rd, he should, according to the Prayer Book, have been baptized by the 25th. But perhaps superstition intervened — people considered St. Mark's Day unlucky. 'Black Crosses', it was called; the crosses and altars were almost to Shakespeare's day hung with black, and (some reported) the spectral company of those destined to die that year stalked the churchyard. Observing that Shakespeare's granddaughter Elizabeth Hall married on 22 April, De Quincey wondered whether she chose that day in honour of her famous relation. On the tablet in the poet's monument in Stratford Church, the inscription reads, '*obiit anno . . . ætatis 53*'. As he was buried on 25 April 1616, these words seemingly imply that his birth took place no earlier than 24 April 1563, or later than 23 April 1564; if not, Shakespeare would have expired in his fifty-second or fifty-fourth year. But this assumes that the anonymous author of the epitaph had in mind a current rather than a completed year, and that he regarded a new year as commencing with the anniversary of birth (the present legal convention) rather than with the first moment of life, if that was known. In fact we do not know what he thought. What we can reasonably assume is that Shakespeare was born on either the 21st, 22nd, or 23rd — Friday, Saturday, or Sunday — of April 1564. As well to celebrate his birthday on the 23rd as on either of the others.[2]

That summer the plague struck Stratford. In the burial register, alongside the entry on 11 July for Oliver Gunne, an apprentice, appears the ominous phrase, 'hic incepit pestis'. We associate pestilence in that period mainly with the capital, with its concentrated population, huddled dwellings, and narrow back lanes; but travellers carried the bacillus into the purer air of pleasant market towns like Stratford. When in the eighteenth century Malone studied the burial register for the fatal summer of 1564, he calculated that the plague had carried off more than two hundred souls — from one-sixth to one-seventh of the entire population — of whom only one resided not in Stratford proper but in the nearby village of Welcombe.

'Let us be thankful that "this sweetest child of Fancy" did not perish while he yet lay in the cradle . . . ,' exclaimed Malone. 'Fortunately for mankind it [the plague] did not reach the house in which the infant Shakspeare lay; for not one of that name appears in the dead list. — May we suppose, that, like Horace, he lay secure and fearless in the midst of contagion and death, protected by the Muses to whom his future life was to be devoted . . . .'[3] Such rhetorical extravagance is unusual for Malone, but one can scarcely overestimate the danger to which the infant was exposed. In plague time the bell tolled most often for the very young and enfeebled old. Richard Symons, the town clerk, buried two sons and a daughter; in Henley Street, where the Shakespeares lived, Roger Green lost four children. In August the council held an emergency session. To avoid contagion they sat in sunshine in the chapel garden, fragrant with pears and

1   Sidney Lee, *A Life of William Shakespeare* (4th ed. of revised version, 1925), p. 8.

2   On the birth-date I am principally indebted to EKC (ii. 1–2), who authoritatively recapitulates and analyses preceding scholarship, but I have also consulted Fripp, *Shakespeare: Man and Artist* (1938), i. 38; and Charles Isaac Elton, *William Shakespeare: His Family and Friends* (1904), pp. 22-5, is still too useful to be ignored.

3   William Shakespeare, *Plays and Poems*, ed. Edmond Malone (1790), vol. i, pt. i, p. 124n. Malone's flight proved too much for one contemporary reader, the Revd. John Horne Tooke; in his copy he scrawled alongside the passage, 'Alack aday Mr Malone!', and after it expressed his distaste with a single forcible expletive: 'Boh!' (Folger Shakespeare Library, PR 2752.1790c. Sh. Col., copy 4).

apples, rather than in the close confines of the Guild Hall, and discussed the organization of relief for the victims of pestilence. John Shakespeare attended; he was then a burgess. By December, with the coming of cold weather, the plague abated.

On 13 October 1566 the Shakespeares' second son, Gilbert, was baptized at Holy Trinity. He may have been named for Gilbert Bradley, who lived a few houses down in Henley Street, and was, like John, a glover and a member of the corporation — Bradley had become a burgess in 1565. Trade and municipal government: Gilbert Shakespeare was born into impeccably bourgeois circumstances, and his life would follow a middle-class pattern. In that respect, if no other, he resembled his brother William, who became not only a poet but also successful as the world measures success. In 1597 one 'Gilbert Shackspere' is described as a haberdasher of St. Bride's. That year, with a shoemaker from the same parish, he stood bail in Queen's Bench for £19, for William Sampson, a clock-maker of Stratford. St. Bride's is in London, but Gilbert lived in Stratford as well.[1] He was there on 1 May 1602, when he took delivery of a conveyance of land in Old Stratford on behalf of his brother William.

In November 1609 Gilbert Shakespeare was summoned to appear in the Court of Requests with Peter Ruswell, Richard Mytton, and others. What prompted the action we do not know, but feelings ran high, for when Elionor Varney, a twenty-one-year-old Stratford serving girl, presented Ruswell with the subpoena, he 'did vyolently snatche from her the said writt and refused to redeliver it unto her, and delivered his staffe he then had in his hand to a stander by who therewith did assault & beate this deponent out of the house'.[2] This Ruswell (or Rosswell) is mentioned along with Mytton in the only extant letter addressed to William Shakespeare:[3] we are dealing with a small town, and a limited circle of neighbours and acquaintances.

The next year, on 5 March, 'Gilbart Shakesper' witnessed a leasing of property in Bridge Street, signing his name in a fair Italian hand. Gilbert died in his forty-fifth year. On 3 February 1612 the Stratford register records the burial of 'Gilbertus Shakspeare adolescens'. The term *adolescens* has occasioned puzzlement, but probably means 'single', for *adolescentulus* and *adolescentula* appear more than once in the registers to describe bachelors and spinsters.[4]

In April 1569 the Shakespeares gained another daughter. She was christened Joan on the 15th; so apparently the first Joan had died, probably while still an infant, in 1559 or 1560, when burial entries are sparse in the register. Of the family's four daughters, only the second Joan survived childhood, and of the eight siblings, only she — apart from William — took a spouse. Her husband was an obscure hatter, William Hart, and their marriage, some time before 1600, is not recorded in the register; perhaps he moved to Stratford after the wedding. In 1600, and also the next year, Hart was sued for debt. His principal accomplishment seems to have been the begetting of four children: William (1600–39), Mary (1603–7), Thomas (1605–61), and Michael (1608–18). The hatter was buried on 17 April 1616, a week before his brother-in-law the dramatist. Shakespeare looked after his sister, a poor relation, in his will, for he bequeathed the widow (in addition to £20 and all his wearing apparel) a life-tenancy in the western wing of the double house in Henley Street, 'wherein she dwelleth', for the nominal yearly rent of one shilling. Joan Hart outlived her husband and her brother by thirty years. Eventually her grandson Thomas came into possession of the old homestead, both the eastern and western houses, by the terms of the testament of Lady Bernard, Shakespeare's granddaughter and last lineal descendant. The story of the Birthplace then becomes synonymous, for a long period, with that of the Harts.[5]

Of the Shakespeares' next two children we know almost nothing. One died young. The last daughter, Anne, was baptized on 28 September, and buried before her eighth birthday, on 4 April

1 H-P (*Outlines*, ii. 298) found this suit in the Coram Rege rolls. Unable to locate Gilbert Shakespeare in the St. Bride's register or in the books of the Worshipful Company of Haberdashers (which however contain a Gilbert Shepheard, who took up his freedom in 1579), and unprepared 'to wade through the six volumes of closely-written contracted Latin cases that make up the Coram Rege Roll of 1597', Mrs. C. C. Stopes concluded that H-P must have erred (*Shakespeare's Environment* (1914), pp. 64–5). But she is wrong, and he is right.

2 ME, 108.

3 See below, pp. 179–81.

4 Stopes, *Shakespeare's Environment*, pp. 333–4, brings together a number of such entries.

5 See above, caption 12, p. 16, and below, p. 261.

1579. The Chamberlain's Account shows that John Shakespeare paid a fee of 8*d*. 'for the bell & paull'. A son, Richard, was christened on 11 March 1574. He lived almost forty years but left no trace of where he dwelt or how he fared. Richard was buried on 4 February 1613.

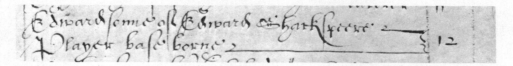

29 EDWARD SHAKESPEARE BURIED, 12 AUGUST 1607. *Parish register, St. Giles Church without Cripplegate, London, now in the Guildhall Library; shelfmark: MS. 6419/2. Transcript: EKC, ii. 18; BRL, ii. 386. The entry was first printed by J. Payne Collier in his* Memoirs of the Principal Actors in the Plays of Shakespeare *(1846), p. xv. It does not occur to Collier to identify Edward senior with the playwright's brother Edmund.*

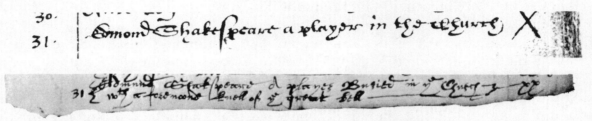

30, 31 EDMUND SHAKESPEARE BURIED, 31 DECEMBER 1607. *Parish register and fee book, St. Saviour's Cathedral, Southwark, now in the Greater London Record Office; shelfmarks: P92/SAV/3001 (register) and P92/SAV/370/10 (fee book). Transcript: TB, 56; EKC, ii. 18; BRL, ii. 387. First published by Collier in* Memoirs, *p. xiv. He does not claim to have discovered these items.*

When John Shakespeare stood at the font in Holy Trinity with his own infant for the last time on 3 May 1580, he was getting on — in just three years he would become a grandfather — and in reduced circumstances. The Shakespeares christened their last child Edmund, possibly (although the name is familiar enough) after his uncle, Edmund Lambert, to whom they had lately mortgaged part of an inheritance — a house and land in Wilmcote. (Aunt Joan, Lambert's wife, was probably godmother to the two daughters of that name.) More than anyone else in the family, Edmund seems to have taken after his playwright brother; for, when he was old enough, he followed William to London, and became a professional actor, with which company is not recorded. In his profession he does not seem to have achieved any special eminence, but he was only twenty-eight when he died. In London he appears to have fathered an illegitimate child, buried in the cemetery of St. Giles Church without Cripplegate on 12 August 1607. The register cites 'Edward sonne of Edward Shackspeere Player base borne'; thus the christian name is wrong, but the parish clerk showed himself disinclined to make nice distinctions between similar-sounding appellations like Joan and Joanna or Orton and Horton — or Edmund and Edward.[1] Just a few months later, on New Year's Eve, the actor himself was interred in St. Saviour's Cathedral, Southwark, 'with a forenoone knell of ye great bell'. This was an expensive funeral, costing twenty shillings; burial in the churchyard could be had for only two shillings, and the lesser bell tolled for a shilling. Evidently somebody of means cared about Edmund; probably his prosperous brother William. St. Saviour's stood near London Bridge, a stone's throw from the Globe Theatre; in time to come, John Fletcher and Philip Massinger, principal dramatists for the King's men, would be buried there. Did Shakespeare arrange for a morning rather than (as customary) afternoon service so that his fellows could attend on that bitterly cold day, when children played on the frozen Thames?[2]

These were John Shakespeare's offspring — four sons and four daughters; seven ordinary mortals and one immortal — all christened and all but one buried in the collegiate church of the Holy Trinity in Stratford-upon-Avon.

---

1   G. E. Bentley, *Shakespeare: A Biographical Handbook* (New Haven, 1961), p. 81.
2   *The Great Frost; cold doings in London* (1608); cited by Fripp, *Shakespeare*, ii. 687.

4

Rise and Fall

When, in the winter of 1561, Richard Shakespeare died, his elder son was described as a husbandman (*agricola*) in the letters of administration of the estate. Perhaps this is a mistake — there are many slips in the Worcester records — but we cannot be sure. At any rate he came into his father's holdings; so we gather from a fine levied against John Shakespeare the following October for neglecting his hedges in Snitterfield. He kept the farm for only a few months, however, before giving over the lease to his brother-in-law Alexander Webbe, who came from Bearley to live in Snitterfield with his wife Margaret (*née* Arden) and their four small children. Husbandry did not, evidently, much appeal to John.

More than once he is described in Stratford records as a glover: in 1556 Thomas Siche, a husbandman of Armscote, unsuccessfully sued 'Johannem Shakyspere de Stretforde . . ., glover' for £8; in 1586 'Johannes Shakespere . . ., glover' stood bail for a local tinker indicted for felony; another record, in 1573, describes John as a 'whyttawer'. Our only traditional anecdote about him, set down around 1657 by Thomas Plume, Archdeacon of Rochester, refers to John Shakespeare as a glover. Plume recalls that Sir John Mennis once saw the 'merry cheekd old man' in his shop; 'Will was a good Honest Fellow', the dramatist's father allowed, 'but he durst have crackt a jeast with him at any time.' Sir John Mennis was born in 1599, two years before John Shakespeare's death, so the two could scarcely have exchanged jests together. Maybe Plume has confused this Mennis with an older brother, Matthew, born around 1593 (although that is not too much help); or perhaps somebody told Sir John the anecdote. No matter; it shows that in the next century John Shakespeare was remembered as a glover, and associated even in old age with his shop.

That shop must have occupied the western wing of the double house in Henley Street, the part known, from far back, as the Woolshop. But why wool, when John Shakespeare worked in leather? There is a Stratford tradition, first reported by Rowe in 1709, and confirmed by the ever-helpful Jordan, that John was 'a considerable Dealer in Wool'. Early in the nineteenth century, long after the house had become an inn, the landlord of the Swan and Maidenhead assured a visitor that, 'when he re-laid the floors of the parlour, the remnants of wool, and the refuse of wool-combing, were found under the old flooring, imbedded with the earth of the foundation'.[1] The early biographers persistently refer to John Shakespeare as a wool-stapler, but only in the present century has documentary evidence of his subsidiary fleece dealings turned up: a suit in the Court of Common Pleas shows that, in Trinity Term 1599, John Shakespeare sued John Walford, clothier and thrice mayor of Marlborough in Wiltshire, for failing to pay on demand £21 for twenty-one tods of wool, a bargain agreed to thirty years earlier; a debt is a debt. Since a tod weighed twenty-eight pounds, the transaction was not trifling. How the action was resolved we cannot say, for, although its continuation is noted in the docket for the following term, the relevant plea roll has disappeared.[2] This discovery holds a salutary lesson. Tradition, often discredited and always to be regarded with scepticism, may yet conceal a kernel of truth.

On other occasions John Shakespeare sold the corporation of Stratford-upon-Avon a piece of timber for three shillings, and brought an action against Henry Field, a tanner in Bridge Street, for eighteen quarters of barley — a lot of barley, for a quarter equalled eight bushels, or sixty-four gallons. Barley was used for what has been, until very recently, Stratford's principal industry, the manufacture of beer and ale. (Otherwise John seems to have got along amicably

---

1 Sir Richard Phillips, in *The Monthly Magazine; or British Register*, xlv (1818), 2; EKC, ii. 299.
2 Leslie Hotson, 'Three Shakespeares', *Shakespeare's Sonnets Dated and Other Essays* (1949), p. 231. Hotson discovered the action.

32   JOHN SHAKESPEARE IDENTIFIED AS A GLOVER, 17 JUNE 1556. *Shakespeare Birthplace Trust Records Office, Corp. Rec., Proceedings of the Court of Record, 29 Nov. 1553 – 7 Oct. 1601, f. 3ᵛ. Transcript: H-P, Outlines, ii. 215; BRL, i. 53. The identification occurs in a suit brought against John Shakespeare by Thomas Siche of Armscote to recover a debt of £8. Judgement with costs was returned in favour of the defendant.*

The Stratford archives were first systematically investigated by Edmond Malone. For his 1790 edition of Shakespeare, he had the vicar of Stratford, the Revd. James Davenport, furnish him with extracts from the corporation books. These show John Shakespeare passing the chamberlain's accounts, presiding in the Hall as High Bailiff, being excused from his weekly tax of 4d., and finally, in 1586, being replaced as alderman. The information appears in Malone's first note to his reprint of Rowe's Account in vol. i, pt. 1, pp. 102-3, of The Plays and Poems of William Shakspeare.

Malone devotes several sections to the poet's father in the posthumous Life of William Shakspeare which his friend James Boswell the younger tidied, arranged, and saw through the press as vol. ii of the 1821 Variorum Shakspeare. Here Malone describes meeting with the entry for the Siche–Shakespeare suit 'in a very ancient manuscript, containing an account of the proceedings in the bailiff's court, which furnished me with the long sought-for information, and ascertains that the trade of our great poet's father was that of a glover' (p. 78). Malone chronicles John Shakespeare's career from 30 April 1556, when John served on the jury of the court leet, through his various civic promotions and subsequent decline. To information about this last phase, Malone adds the fact, previously unknown, that John Shakespeare defaulted in 1579, when the corporation was levying taxes for the musters. Malone also gives an account of the Shakespeare properties: the freehold estate brought by Mary Arden, the two houses in Henley Street, and the dwelling in Greenhill Street. The outlines of John Shakespeare's career were thus documented by 1821. Joseph Hunter and H-P made minor augmentations, and the latter brought together the texts of all the documents in chronological order in 'John Shakespeare. — Annals.' in his Outlines, ii. 215-48. H-P includes a number of line-block facsimiles.

The pertinent documents have been re-transcribed by Richard Savage, formerly Deputy Keeper of the town archives, in MA, with introduction and notes by Edgar I. Fripp; published by the Dugdale Society, 1921-9. The ambitious plan was abandoned after the fourth volume, which brought the story to 1592. The records for 1553 to 1566 are published verbatim; in subsequent volumes the editors include 'every document in the Borough records which contains the name or bears directly on the life of John Shakespeare'. Lewis's chapter, 'The Business and Municipal Career of John Shakespeare', gives extracts from a number of the relevant records (BRL, i. 51-80; documents 5-27).

33   PLUME'S ANECDOTE OF JOHN SHAKESPEARE. *MS. 25, f. 161, in the Plume Library at Maldon, Essex, bequeathed by Thomas Plume (1630-1704), Archdeacon of Rochester. Transcript: EKC, ii. 247; The Shakspere Allusion-Book, ed. John Munro (1932), ii. 68; BRL, i. 54. Most of Plume's Shakespeare memoranda, including this note, were first printed by F. J. Furnivall, from transcripts supplied by Andrew Clark, in the Westminster Gazette, xxiv (31 October 1904), p. 4. Plume compiled the notes of contemporary gossip that comprise MS. 25 at various intervals between 1657 and 1680; EKC dates the Shakespeare entries c. 1657 (ii. 247). For other Plume anecdotes, see below, item 169.*

enough with Field; when the latter died, in the summer of 1592, John helped to appraise his goods. Field had a son Richard, with whom, as we shall see, the poet had dealings in the metropolis.) Probably John Shakespeare dealt in other agricultural commodities as well, storing them, along with his hides, in the Woolshop.

He also bought houses and let them. In October 1575 John paid Edmund and Emma Hall from Hallow in the parish of Grimley, near Worcester, £40 for two houses, with gardens and orchards, in Stratford. Some time before 1582 he leased one of his houses to a William Burbage — was he related to the theatrical Burbages? — who later sought release from his bargain and the return of £7 he had put down. Arbitrators instructed John to return the money, but Burbage had trouble collecting it (he was still trying a decade later), and perhaps never got his deposit back. John had acquired, from one of the powerful Cloptons, the lease of fourteen acres in Over Ingon meadow, in Hampton Lucy, where his brother Henry farmed. When Joyce and Alice, Mary Shakespeare's sisters, died, the Shakespeares inherited a ninth share in two houses and a hundred acres in Snitterfield.

Like others of his class John Shakespeare more than once entered the courtroom to sue and be sued. Sometimes considerable sums were at stake. In 1572 the Court of Common Pleas at Westminster awarded him the £50 he claimed a glover of Banbury owed him. The next year, in the same court, he was ordered to pay his £30 debt to Henry Higford of Solihull, a former steward of Stratford; five years later he was still being asked to pay up. So it went. These were good years, most of them, for the son of the Snitterfield tenant farmer.

In 1553, just about the time that John Shakespeare settled in Stratford, the borough (as we have seen) received its Charter of Incorporation from the Crown. Now, vested with the Guild's property and authority, and possessing the power to make by-laws, a common council of burgesses and aldermen set about managing local affairs, although the Earl of Warwick, lord of the manor, retained the nomination of the vicar and the schoolmaster, and could, if he wished, veto the corporation's choice of a bailiff. Into this new Establishment the up-and-coming John Shakespeare was quickly absorbed, and by degrees he rose in the hierarchy. In September 1556 he was chosen one of the two ale-tasters, an office reserved for 'able persons and discreet'. By 'weekly and diligent search', these tasters saw that bakers made full-weight loaves, and that brewers vended wholesome ale and beer at the prescribed price in sealed pots. Offenders were summoned before the manorial court, or Leet, held twice yearly, and punished by fine, whipping, or humiliation in the stocks or pillory or on the cucking stool.[1] This was a regulated economy. The June after his appointment, John himself was fined for having missed, as taster, three sittings of the Court of Record, which met fortnightly. But that spring more importunate personal affairs drew him from Stratford to Mary Arden's house in Wilmcote.

34 JOHN SHAKESPEARE CHOSEN CONSTABLE, 30 SEPTEMBER 1558. *Shakespeare Birthplace Trust Records Office, Misc. Doc. VII, 57. Transcript:* MA, *i. 90;* BRL, *i. 55. This extract is slightly reduced.*

In the autumn of 1558 John was sworn one of the four constables: able-bodied citizens charged with preserving the peace. The Elizabethans made a standing joke of constables, their stupidity being literally proverbial — 'You might be a constable for your wit', ran the familiar saying. From this easy source of risibility the constable's son does not dissociate himself. Constable Dull in *Love's Labour's Lost* — 'Most dull, honest Dull', who offers to dance and play on the tabor in the pageant of the Nine Worthies — is the slightest of preliminary sketches for the immortal Dogberry of *Much Ado About Nothing*. In his charge to Hugh Oatcake and neighbour Seacoal, stalwarts of the watch, the essential duties of the constable's office may be glimpsed through a

---

1 *MA*, i, pp. xxi–xxii, xxxiv–xxxv; see also *The Taming of the Shrew*, Induction, sc. ii, 83–6.

D

haze of malapropism: to 'comprehend all vagrom men . . . to bid any man stand, in the Prince's name. . . . [to] make no noise in the streets; for for the watch to babble and to talk is most tolerable and not to be endured. . . . to call at all the ale-houses, and bid those that are drunk get them to bed. . . . If you meet a thief, you may suspect him, by virtue of your office, to be no true man; and, for such kind of men, the less you meddle or make with them, why, the more is for your honesty.' Despite the prudential character of Dogberry's advice, however, these guardians of law and order were entrusted with a serious enough responsibility during a volatile period in the town's history. They had to deprive angry men of their weapons, and hale into court quarrelsome types who had started bloody street brawls. This happened more than once during John Shakespeare's tenure. Constables were also responsible for fire-prevention measures in a community vulnerable to conflagration.[1]

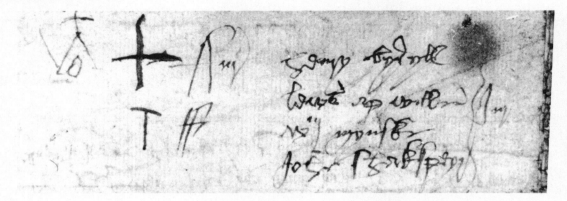

35 JOHN SHAKESPEARE, AFFEEROR, WITNESSES THE COURT LEET, 4 MAY 1561. *Shakespeare Birthplace Trust Records Office, Misc. Doc. VII, 56. Transcript: MA, i. 119. John Shakespeare here uses, as his mark, a pair of glover's compasses. The mark of Lewes ap Williams may be a church gable.*

Other promotions quickly followed for John. The next year, in 1559, he was witnessing the minutes of the Leet as an affeeror, whose task it was to assess fines not prescribed by the statutes. Shortly afterwards — just when is uncertain — the town fathers elected him one of the fourteen principal burgesses, who sat monthly at 'nine o'clock of the forenoon' in the Guild Hall. Now he was privileged to educate his children without charge at the King's New School of Stratford-upon-Avon.

From 1561 to 1563 the burgess served as one of the two chamberlains who administered borough property and revenues. John Taylor, a shearman of Sheep Street, was his senior colleague. At the year's end Richard Symons, the deputy steward, drew up the official audit — a bare listing of receipts and outlays — and Taylor duly endorsed it on the back with his cross. John Shakespeare must have discharged this office well, for after the expiration of his term, he stayed on as acting-chamberlain; nobody in Stratford held the job for so long. The accounts presented in 1565 are described as 'made by John Shakspeyr & John tayler'; those in 1566, as made

36 THE ACCOUNT OF JOHN TAYLOR AND JOHN SHAKESPEARE, CHAMBERLAINS, MADE BY JOHN TAYLOR, 24 JANUARY 1563. *Shakespeare Birthplace Trust Records Office, Misc. Doc. III, 21. Transcript (entire record): MA, i. 120–2. The preamble (reduced) and John Shakespeare's mark, a glover's 'donkey', are reproduced.*

1 Edgar I. Fripp, *Shakespeare: Man and Artist* (1938), i. 34; *The Victoria History of the County of Warwick* (1904–69), iii. 254.

by John Shakspeyr alone. These were stirring years for the custodians of Stratford's purse-strings. The chapel was being Protestantized — workmen whitewashed the frescoes and took down the rood-loft; they installed seats for the priest and his clerk, and perhaps a communion-board where formerly the altar stood. Vicar Bretchgirdle's house in Church Street underwent needed repair. A new classroom in the upper storey of the Guild Hall replaced the old schoolhouse in the quad. Meanwhile the pestilence came and spent itself. Through it all the acting-chamberlain kept the books, although he was slightly tardy in presenting his account for the plague year.

37 THE ACCOUNT OF JOHN TAYLOR AND JOHN SHAKESPEARE, CHAMBERLAINS, MADE BY JOHN SHAKESPEARE, 10 JANUARY 1564 (first page). *Shakespeare Birthplace Trust Records Office, Corp. Rec., Council Book A, pp. 1–3. Transcript (entire record): MA, i. 126–9; BRL, i. 56–7.*

38 THE ACCOUNT OF WILLIAM TYLER AND WILLIAM SMITH, CHAMBERLAINS, MADE BY JOHN SHAKESPEARE, 15 FEBRUARY 1566 (first page). *Shakespeare Birthplace Trust Records Office, Council Book A, pp. 11–14. Transcript: MA, i. 148–52 (entire record).*

39 JOHN SHAKESPEARE, BURGESS, WITNESSES A CORPORATION ORDER, 27 SEPTEMBER 1564. *Shakespeare Birthplace Trust Records Office, Corp. Rec., Council Book A, p. 5. Transcript: MA, i. 133–4 (entire record). The bailiff, aldermen, and burgesses comprise the witnesses to the order.*

40 JOHN SHAKESPEARE, BURGESS, ATTENDS A CORPORATION MEETING, 20 DECEMBER 1564. *Shakespeare Birthplace Trust Records Office, Corp. Rec., Council Book A, p. 355. Transcript: MA, i. 135–6. The word 'Syxt' in the preamble is a slip for 'seventh' (MA, i. 135n).*

41 JOHN SHAKESPEARE ELECTED AN ALDERMAN, 4 JULY 1565. *Shakespeare Birthplace Trust Records Office, Corp. Rec., Council Book A, p. 358. Transcript (entire record)*: MA, i. 145–6; BRL, i. 59.

42 JOHN SHAKESPEARE A CANDIDATE FOR BAILIFF, 4 SEPTEMBER 1568. *Shakespeare Birthplace Trust Records Office, Corp. Rec., Council Book A, p. 368. Transcript (entire record)*: MA, ii. 12–13; BRL, i. 61. *John Shakespeare won the election by defeating his two rivals, Robert Perrot and Robert Salusburye. The latter eventually served three times as bailiff.*

John Shakespeare attended the session in the chapel garden when the council met to consider ways of relieving those rendered destitute by the plague. The garden stood a few yards from the door of Alderman William Bott. In May 1564 this Bott was 'expulsed' by the brethren after failing to appear before them to answer the charge of using abusive terms of the council and bailiff. On 4 July 1565 they elected John Shakespeare to replace Bott as one of the fourteen aldermen. Installation took place on 12 September. Henceforth he would be respectfully addressed as Master Shakespeare. At hall and in church — indeed on all public occasions — he was entitled to wear a black cloth gown faced with fur, as well as the aldermanic thumb ring ('When I was about thy years, Hal', Falstaff boasts at the Boar's Head, 'I was not an eagle's talon in the waist: I could have crept into any alderman's thumb-ring').

Each September, on the first Wednesday, the corporation elected its bailiff by majority vote. In 1567 John Shakespeare was entered as one of the three nominees, and the next year the council chose him. On 1 October he took office, exchanging his black gown for one of scarlet. Master Shakespeare, now a justice of the peace, presided at the sessions of the Court of Record, which was a court of the Crown, and at council meetings. For his borough the bailiff was almoner, coroner, escheater, and clerk of the market. Together with one alderman annually elected to the office, he served the borough as justice of the peace. He issued warrants, dealt with cases of debt and violations of the by-laws, and carried on negotiations with the lord of the manor. Every Thursday night, when the market stalls had shut down, the bakers and brewers danced attendance on him, for it was the bailiff's prerogative to decree the weekly price of corn, and hence of bread and ale. Appropriate ceremony accompanied his exalted station. He and his deputy

wore their furred gowns in public, were escorted from their houses to the Gild Hall by the serjeants bearing their maces before them. They were waited on by these buff-uniformed officers once a week to receive instructions, and accompanied by them through the market on Thursdays, through the fair on fair-days, about the parish-bounds at Rogation, and to and from church on Sundays. At church they sat with their wives in the front pew on the north side of the nave. At sermons in the Gild chapel they had their seats of honour. At plays in the Gild Hall they probably sat in the front row.[1]

1 Fripp, *Shakespeare*, i. 43. I am chiefly indebted to Fripp for the details of corporate life.

43 JOHN SHAKESPEARE, ALDERMAN, ATTENDS A CORPORATION MEETING, 5 SEPTEMBER 1571. *Shakespeare Birthplace Trust Records Office, Corp. Rec., Council Book A, p. 146. Transcript: MA, ii. 52–3 (entire record).*

44 ADRIAN QUINEY AND JOHN SHAKESPEARE COMMISSIONED BY THE CORPORATION, 18 JANUARY 1572. *Shakespeare Birthplace Trust Records Office, Corp. Rec., Council Book A, p. 150. Transcript: MA, ii. 60–1 (entire record).*

When John Shakespeare stepped down after his year in office and thirteen sessions of the council, he was in 1571 appointed deputy to the new bailiff — Adrian Quiney, a mercer and neighbour in Henley Street. The following January the two men rode to London together on borough business, with permission from the aldermen and burgesses to proceed 'according to theire discrecions'.

The public man who enjoyed such unqualified trust witnessed corporation minutes with his mark. Usually he employed as his sign a gracefully drawn pair of compasses, the instrument used for measuring and making ornamental cuttings in the backs of gloves. Once he appended a different sign, which has been interpreted as a glover's stitching clamp, or 'donkey'.[1] Legal documents (such as the inventory of Henry Field's goods and movables) he signed with a cross. It is therefore natural to infer that he was illiterate. But is this necessarily the case? Literate persons, as some authorities have pointed out, preferred on occasion to use a mark — Adrian Quiney, for example, whose mark or sign (an inverted upper-case *Q*) embellishes the same page as John Shakespeare's in the council records; that Quiney could sign his name we know, for letters written by him have come down. A cross on a document symbolized the Holy Cross, and avouched the piety of the signer; it was, in other words, equivalent to an oath. It has been suggested that the compass sign meant 'God Encompasseth Us', and the clamp had some other, undeciphered allegorical significance; but to this admittedly sceptical writer John Shakespeare's signs symbolize his trade and no more. It is true that he handled complicated municipal business, and that literacy is an asset to a book-keeper. It is also true that unlettered men may have shrewd business acumen. Possible light on the problem is shed by a teasing memorandum of 1596. It concerns the suit of Widow Margery Young (she was Richard Field's sister) against another widow, Joan Perritt, over some 'deceitfully' appropriated goods, and among the items appears 'm^r Shaxpere one boke'. Probably the entry refers to John Shakespeare rather than William, but one cannot tell for certain; and although possession of a book points to a capacity to read, it does not necessarily carry that presumption: some owners are no users. To sum up: John Shakespeare may have mastered reading and writing — there is some force to the arguments supporting that conclusion. But not a single autograph by him is extant, his civic responsibilities did not absolutely require such knowledge (a professional scrivener always stood at the ready, pen in hand), and raised as he was, a humble tenant farmer's son in a country village without a school, his educational opportunities were strictly limited.

We do know that after attaining the highest elective office that Stratford had to offer, Master Shakespeare contemplated applying to the Heralds' College for a coat of arms. As bailiff of an incorporated town he held one of those 'divers offices of dignitie and worship, [that] doe merite coats of Armes, to the possessour of the same offices'. Thus wrote Sir John Ferne in *The Blazon of Gentrie* in 1586; and further: 'If any person be advaunced, into an office or dignity, of publique administration, be it eyther Ecclesiasticall, Martiall, or Civill . . . the Herealde must not refuse, to devise to such a publique person, uppon his instant request, and willingnes to beare the same without reproche, a coate of Armes: and thenceforth, to matriculate him, with his intermariages, and issues discending, in the register of the Gentle and Noble.'[2] But nothing came of the application, although John presented the College with a 'pattern', or sketch, for his arms. Years later, when his son applied (as it seems) in his father's behalf, the Clarenceux King-of-Arms noted: 'And the man was A magestrat in Stratford upon Avon. A Justice of peace he maryed A Daughter and heyre of Ardern. and was of good substance and habelite'.[3]

What happened? The evidence suggests that John Shakespeare had fallen on hard times. Formerly punctilious about attending council meetings, he stopped coming after 1576, missing all but one session for which attendance records exist. His brother aldermen evidently kept hoping he would return, for year after year they included his name on the roster, even though they could not put a prick alongside to denote his presence. They showed consideration in other ways. When a levy for equipping soldiers was passed by the council, they asked John to pay only 3*s*.4*d*., the assessment on burgesses, rather than the double amount levied on aldermen. But, over a year later, he still owed even this reduced sum. On election day, 1578, the corporation fined one absentee, John Wheeler, stiffly (20*s*.) but let Master Shakespeare off. The following November they voted to have every alderman pay 4*d*. weekly towards poor relief, except 'm^r John shaxpeare and m^r Robert bratt who shall not be taxed to pay any thinge'. Bratt was old and infirm, and anyway no longer an alderman; he would die the next year. Finally, in September 1586, the council elected two new aldermen; 'for that m^r wheler dothe desyre to be put out of

1 The Shakespeare Birthplace Trust preserves a specimen of a glover's 'donkey' in the museum collection at Mary Arden's House.

2 John Ferne, *The Blazon of Gentrie* (1586), the first part, *The Glorie of Generositie*, pp. 58–60; cited (in part) by EKC, ii. 25.

3 See below, item 133, p. 172.

the Companye & m^r Shaxspere dothe not Come to the halles when they be warned nor hathe not done of Longe tyme'.

The picture is of a piece; John Shakespeare incurred debts and exchanged land for ready money. On 14 November 1578 he borrowed £40 by mortgaging part of his wife's inheritance — a house and fifty-six acres in Wilmcote — to her brother-in-law Edmund Lambert of Barton on the Heath, to whom he already owed money. On that very day Roger Sadler, a baker in Sheep Street, drew up his will, and noted in it that Edmund Lambert and another owed him £5 for the debt of John Shakespeare. When the borrowed £40 fell due at Michaelmas 1580, John could not pay it, so Lambert held on to the property. He was still in possession when he died seven years later. There followed litigation in the court of Queen's Bench in Westminster, as the Shakespeares (John and Mary, joined by their eldest son William) tried to recover their holding from Lambert's son and heir John. The plaintiffs claimed that John Lambert had promised an additional £20 in return for full title to the parental estate. Lambert denied making any such promise. In another suit ten years later, this time in Chancery, the Shakespeares insisted that they had offered Lambert the £40 for the property, only to be spurned — he wanted other money which they owed him. They never did get back this land, part of the Asbyes estate. In November 1578 John and Mary Shakespeare conveyed eighty-six more acres in Wilmcote, including meadows and pasture, to a Webbe relative for a period of years, after which the land would revert to the original possessors and their heirs; again a need for cash — immediate cash — seems to have motivated the transaction. The Shakespeares were also obliged to let go their ninth part in the two houses and hundred acres in Snitterfield, the property leased to Alexander Webbe. This they sold in 1579 to Webbe's son Robert for the mean sum of £4.

Troubles multiplied. In Trinity term, 1580, John was fined £20 for not appearing in the court of Queen's Bench to find surety for keeping the peace towards the Queen and her subjects. (At this time the Crown similarly penalized many others, more than 140 throughout England; why is not known.) The same court also fined him another £20 as pledge for a hatmaker of

47 JOHN AND MARY SHAKESPEARE WITNESS THE SALE OF THEIR SNITTERFIELD PROPERTY, 15 OCTOBER 1579. *Shakespeare Birthplace Trust Records Office, ER 30/1. Mary Shakespeare took part in the transaction presumably as a bar to dower, 'the terms of the warranty proposed for the covenanted fine being inconsistent with the supposition that she was joining in a conveyance of her own property'* (*H-P*, Outlines, *ii. 179*). *H-P gives a transcript of the indenture (ii. 179–82). This item is slightly reduced.*

Nottingham who failed to appear to find surety for good behaviour. Together the two fines amounted to the whole of the Lambert mortgage. If they were ever collected after being turned over to the Exchequer for that purpose, no record is extant to show it. Evidently John Shakespeare did not always judge well the character of those for whom he vouched. Thus the £10 bail he stood for Michael Price, the felonious Stratford tinker, was forfeited. So too was his surety for £10 of a debt of £22 incurred by his brother Henry. On that occasion a suit followed; to escape jail John turned to his friend Alderman Hill for bail, and even swore out a writ of habeas corpus to remove the case to another court.

Adversaries, as well as adversities, oppressed him. In the summer of 1582 he petitioned for sureties of the peace against four men — Ralph Cawdrey, William Russell, Thomas Logginge, and Robert Young — 'for fear of death and mutilation of his limbs'.[1] Old Cawdrey, a butcher of Bridge Street, was then bailiff, but in his younger days he had been fined more than once for frays. He and John Shakespeare did meet again on the last occasion when the latter attended a council meeting, on 5 September 1582. Together they helped to elect a new bailiff, so the two men had most likely patched up their differences, whatever these were.

In the autumn of 1591 the Privy Council, spurred on by the zeal of the Archbishop of Canterbury, launched one of its periodic inquisitions into the spiritual health of the realm. This time the Council ordered commissioners in every shire to ferret out and report all those who gave sanctuary to seminary priests, Jesuits, or 'fugitives', and 'all such as refused obstinately to resort to the church'. At Stratford the following March or thereabouts, the presenters (probably the churchwardens) duly drew up a list of recusants who did not come monthly to church, as her Majesty's laws required, and they added: 'Wee suspect these nyne personns next ensuinge absent themselves for feare of processes.' Among the names appears that of 'm^r John Shackspeare'. On 25 September following, the commissioners — Sir Thomas Lucy and other justices — had the satisfaction of reporting the names of Catholics who had since conformed or undertaken to conform. The commissioners went on to repeat what the presenters had said about the other nine: 'It is sayd that these laste nine, coom not to Churche for feare of processe for Debtte.'[2]

Some have viewed this episode as evidence that John Shakespeare's plight derived not from pecuniary embarrassment but his ideological waywardness. They see him as a nonconformist hero of the faith, Catholic or Puritan, valiantly — or cunningly — defying authority and partaking

1 ME, 31.
2 Curiously, three names used by Shakespeare in *Henry V* — Fluellen, Bardolph, and Court — appear among the nine.

48 JOHN SHAKESPEARE ABSENT FROM CHURCH, 25 SEPTEMBER 1592. *Public Record Office, State Papers Domestic, Elizabeth I, S.P. 12/243, no. 76. Transcript:* MA, *iv. 161.*

in forbidden ceremonies with the tacit support of other malcontents in the corporation; or as a man broken in body and spirit by that authority, and therefore retreating from the public arena. These interpretations have a romantic appeal, but John Shakespeare was a tradesman, not an ideologue. His religious views (whatever they were) need not have forced him away from the halls where his brethren — Puritans like Nicholas Barnhurst, and Catholics like George Badger — kept their faith and (unless 'expulsed' for opprobrious conduct) their posts. The presenters and commissioners clearly stated on two occasions that John Shakespeare feared process for debt. None of the Stratford Nine appears in the recusant rolls of 1593, and most of them were in financial difficulty — poor John Wheeler, Jr., for example: we hear several years later that his house was 'very ruinous' and his barn 'readie to fall for rottennes'. In those days sheriff's officers could make arrests on Sundays, and the church was a likely place in which to track down one's man. Did they come there to seek out John Shakespeare at the behest of William Burbage, for years frustrated in his efforts to collect the £7 plus damages due him?[1]

If the records are silent about the causes of John Shakespeare's financial difficulties, other townsmen experienced similar problems. Travellers in the west Midlands commented on what today we would describe as an economic recession. As the century wore on, conditions worsened rather than improved; in the year of John Shakespeare's death the poor of Stratford numbered over 700, young and old: approximately half the population. Poverty breeds other miseries. Illegitimate births, violence, and disorder increased in the borough, and the corporation duly reprimanded the ale-house keepers for contributing, 'thorough their unreasonable strong drink, to the increase of quarrelling and other misdemeanours in their houses, and the farther and greater impoverishment of many poor men haunting the said houses, when their wives and children are in extremity of begging'.[2]

1 ME, 33–4. I have found ME invaluable throughout on John Shakespeare's career.
2 Council Book, cited by Fripp, *Master Richard Quyny* (Oxford, 1924), p. 132.

Viewed against this background, John Shakespeare's misfortunes take on a less dramatic aspect. He could still raise £10 for somebody's bail, and the court that imposed £40 in fines on him must have considered him a fairly substantial citizen. That he did not forfeit the esteem of fellow townsmen is suggested by the fact that twice during the summer of 1592 he was called upon to assist in the responsible task of making inventories of the goods of deceased neighbours — the wool-driver Ralph Shaw and Henry Field the tanner. In some ways John might count himself lucky. The wet summer of 1594 — 'wonderful cold, like winter', a diarist noted — was followed by a great fire that swept through Stratford. Within the twelvemonth, on a Sunday, the town was again laid waste by conflagration, 'chiefly [as a Puritan gospeller remarked with satisfaction] for prophaning the *Lords Sabbaths*, and for contemning his Word in the mouth of his faithfull *Ministers*'.[1] One hundred and twenty dwellings, as well as eighty other buildings, went up in flames; on the south side Wood Street blazed from end to end. In Henley Street the cottage where Price the tinker lately lived burnt to the ground. It stood two doors above the Birthplace, which escaped. If during these troubled years inexorable pressures forced John Shakespeare to part with properties, they were mostly inherited. His double house in Henley Street, where he conducted his business and raised his family, he kept intact to his dying day and passed on to his playwright son.

In 1601, the last year of his life, the corporation was busy guarding established privileges, like the bestowing of the office of market toll-gatherer, which were being challenged by Sir Edward Greville, the grasping lord of the manor. That summer, in Trinity Term, Richard Quiney (Adrian's son) rode to London to plead the borough's cause. With him he carried a declaration he had drawn up naming 'm^r John Sackspere' along with other local worthies — including such elders as Simon Biddle the cutler and Thomas Barber, tenant of the Bear Inn, opposite the Swan in Bridge Street — as able to speak in behalf of borough rights. But John Shakespeare did not live to defend the interests of the town he had served for half a century. In early September he died at what was, for those times, a great age: he must have been in his early seventies. On the 8th he was buried in the churchyard of Holy Trinity. The stone marking his grave has long since vanished.

49 JOHN SHAKESPEARE BURIED, 8 SEPTEMBER 1601. *Stratford parish register, burials, f. 34^v. Shakespeare Birthplace Trust Records Office, DR 243/1. Transcript: TB, 38; EKC, ii. 4; BRL, i. 316.*

1 Lewis Bayly, *The Practise of Pietie* (1613 ed.), p. 551; cited (in 1699 ed.) by Fripp, *Quyny*, p. 101. By 1842 this edifying treatise had gone through seventy-five editions.

5

John Shakespeare's Spiritual Testament

If John Shakespeare drew up a last will and testament, it would have been proved in the vicar's court; provided, that is, that his property all lay in the parish.[1] Wills and inventories from this court now rest in the Birthplace archives, but these include no testament by the elder Shakespeare. Probably he left none, and his widow or one of their five surviving children administered the estate. More than a century and a half after his death, however, another sort of testament associated with John's name mysteriously came to light in the western house in Henley Street.

In April 1757 the then owner, Thomas Hart, fifth lineal descendant of the poet's sister Joan, was employing labourers to retile his roof. On the 29th Joseph Moseley, a master bricklayer described as of 'very honest, sober, industrious' character, found, while working with his men, a small paper-book between the rafters and the tiling. This book, or (more properly) booklet, consisted of six leaves stitched together. A Catholic profession of faith in fourteen articles, it has come to be known as the Spiritual Last Will and Testament of John Shakespeare.

With the knowledge of Hart, Moseley some time later gave the document to Mr. Payton of Shottery, a Stratford alderman. Years passed. In 1784 the ubiquitous cicerone of the Shakespeare shrines, John Jordan, was allowed to copy the manuscript, which by then lacked the first leaf. He tried to place his transcript in the *Gentleman's Magazine*. The original, Jordan informed the editor, 'is wrote in a fair and legible hand, and the spelling exactly as I have sent it you.'[2] But, unimpressed, the magazine rejected it. Meanwhile the greatest Shakespearian scholar of the day had heard of the discovery, and through the inquiries of the Revd. James Davenport, vicar of Stratford, traced it down to Payton. The latter willingly permitted Davenport to send the relic on to Edmond Malone.

In his study, surrounded by sixteenth- and seventeenth-century documents, Malone perused the testament. 'The handwriting is undoubtedly not so ancient as that *usually* written about the year 1600', Malone concluded; 'but I have now before me a manuscript written by Alleyn the player at various times between 1599 and 1614, and another by Forde, the dramatick poet, in 1606, in nearly the same handwriting as that of the manuscript in question.'[3] And so he pronounced himself 'perfectly satisfied' of its genuineness. This fragment Malone published in his 'Historical Account of the English Stage' in volume i, part 2, of his 1790 edition of *The Plays and Poems of William Shakspeare*.

III.
" * * * * at leaſt ſpiritually, in will adoring and moſt humbly beſeeching my ſaviour, that he will be pleaſed to aſſiſt me in ſo dangerous a voyage, to defend me from the ſnares and deceites of my infernall enemies, and to conduct me to the ſecure haven of his eternall bliſſe.

IV.
" *Item*, I John Shakſpear doe proteſt that I will alſo paſſe out of this life, armed with the laſt ſacrament of extreme unction: the which if through any let or hindrance I ſhould not then be able to have, I doe now alſo for that time demand and crave the ſame; beſeeching his divine majeſty that he will be pleaſed to anoynt my ſenſes both internall and externall with the ſacred oyle of his infinite mercy, and to pardon me all my ſins committed by ſeeing, ſpeaking, feeling, ſmelling, hearing, touching, or by any other way whatſoever.

V.
" *Item*, I John Shakſpear doe by this preſent proteſt that I will never through any temptation whatſoever deſpaire of the divine goodneſs, for the multitude and greatneſs of my ſinnes; for which although I confeſſe

1 ME, 36–7.
2 Letter, dated 14 June 1785, cited in H-P, *Outlines*, ii. 399.
3 William Shakespeare, *Plays and Poems*, ed. Edmond Malone (1790), vol. i, pt. 2, pp. 161–2.

that I have deserved hell, yet will I stedfastly hope in gods infinite mercy, knowing that he hath heretofore pardoned many as great sinners as my self, whereof I have good warrant sealed with his sacred mouth, in holy writ, whereby he pronounceth that he is not come to call the just, but sinners.

VI.

" *Item,* I John Shakspear do protest that I do not know that I have ever done any good worke meritorious of life everlasting: and if I have done any, I do acknowledge that I have done it with a great deale of negligence and imperfection; neither should I have been able to have done the least without the assistance of his divine grace. Wherefore let the devill remain confounded; for I doe in no wise presume to merit heaven by such good workes alone, but through the merits and bloud of my lord and saviour, jesus, shed upon the crose for me most miserable sinner.

VII.

" *Item,* I John Shakspear do protest by this present writing, that I will patiently endure and suffer all kind of infirmity, sicknes, yea and the paine of death it self:

wherein if it should happen, which god forbid, that through violence of paine and agony, or by subtility of the devill, I should fall into any impatience or temptation of blasphemy, or murmuration against god, or the catholike faith, or give any signe of bad example, I do henceforth, and for that present, repent me, and am most heartily sorry for the same: and I do renounce all the evill whatsoever, which I might have then done or said; beseeching his divine clemency that he will not forsake me in that grievous and paignefull agony.

VIII.

" *Item,* I John Shakspear, by virtue of this present testament, I do pardon all the injuries and offences that any one hath ever done unto me, either in my reputation, life, goods, or any other way whatsoever; beseeching sweet jesus to pardon them for the same: and I do desire, that they will doe the like by me, whome I have offended or injured in any sort howsoever.

IX.

" *Item,* I John Shakspear do heere protest that I do render infinite thanks to his divine majesty for all the benefits that I have received as well secret as manifest, & in particular, for the benefit of my Creation, Redemption, Sanctification, Conservation, and Vocation to the holy knowledge of him & his true Catholike faith: but above all, for his so great expectation of me to pennance, when he might most justly have taken me out of this life, when I least thought of it, yea even then, when I was plunged in the durty puddle of my sinnes. Blessed be therefore and praised, for ever and ever, his infinite patience and charity.

X.

" *Item,* I John Shakspear do protest, that I am willing, yea, I doe infinitely desire and humbly crave, that of this my last will and testament the glorious and ever Virgin mary, mother of god, refuge and advocate of sinners, (whom I honour specially above all other saints,) may be the chiefe Executresse, togeather with these other saints, my patrons, (saint Winefride) all whome

I invocke and beseech to be present at the hour of my death, that she and they may comfort me with their

desired presence, and crave of sweet Jesus that he will receive my soul into peace.

XI.

" *Item,* In virtue of this present writing, I John Shakspear do likewise most willingly and with all humility constitute and ordaine my good Angel, for Defender and Protectour of my soul in the dreadfull day of Judgement, when the finall sentance of eternall life or death shall be discussed and given; beseeching him, that, as my soule was appointed to his custody and protection when I lived, even so he will vouchsafe to defend the same at that houre, and conduct it to eternall bliss.

XII.

" *Item,* I John Shakspear do in like manner pray and beseech all my dear friends, parents, and kinsfolks, by the bowels of our Saviour jesus Christ, that since it is uncertain what lot will befall me, for fear notwithstanding least by reason of my sinnes I be to pass and stay a long while in purgatory, they will vouchsafe to assist and succour me with their holy prayers and satisfactory workes, especially with the holy sacrifice of the masse, as being the most effectuall meanes to deliver soules from their torments and paines; from the which, if I shall by gods gracious goodnesse and by their vertuous workes be delivered, I do promise that I will not be ungratefull unto them, for so great a benefitt.

XIII.

" *Item,* I John Shakspear doe by this my last will and testament bequeath my soul, as soon as it shall be delivered and loosened from the prison of this my body, to be entombed in the sweet and amorous coffin of the side of jesus Christ; and that in this life-giveing sepulcher it may rest and live, perpetually inclosed in that eternall habitation of repose, there to blesse for ever and ever that direfull iron of the launce, which, like a charge in a censore, formes so sweet and pleasant a monument within the sacred breast of my lord and saviour.

XIV.

" *Item,* lastly I John Shakspear doe protest, that I will willingly accept of death in what manner soever it may befall me, conforming my will unto the will of god; accepting of the same in satisfaction for my sinnes, and giveing thanks unto his divine majesty for the life he hath bestowed upon me. And if it please him to prolong or shorten the same, blessed be he also a thousand thousand times; into whose most holy hands I commend my soul and body, my life and death: and I beseech him above all things, that he never permit any change to be made by me John Shakspear of this my aforesaid will and testament. Amen.

" I John Shakspear have made this present writing of protestation, confession, and charter, in presence of the blessed virgin mary, my Angell guardian, and all the Celestiall Court, as witnesses hereunto: the which my meaning is, that it be of full value now presently and for ever, with the force and vertue of testament, codicill, and donation in cause of death; confirming it anew, being in perfect health of soul and body, and signed with mine own hand; carrying also the same about me; and for the better declaration hereof, my will and intention is that it be finally buried with me after my death.

" Pater noster, Ave maria, Credo.
" jesu, son of David, have mercy on me.
Amen."

50 WILLIAM SHAKESPEARE, *PLAYS AND POEMS*, ED. EDMOND MALONE (1790), vol. i, pt. 2, pp. 162–6.

Before the volume was printed off, Davenport forwarded to Malone a small quarto notebook belonging to Jordan, and containing the complete text of the spiritual testament. Puzzled by the sudden resurfacing of the missing first leaf, Malone put pointed questions to Jordan, whose replies, evasive and contradictory, were not calculated to allay suspicion. Nevertheless Malone went ahead and published the supplementary articles in his 'Emendations and Additions' included in the same volume.

I.

" In the name of God, the father, sonne, and holy ghost, the most holy and blessed Virgin Mary, mother of God, the holy host of archangels, angels, patriarchs, prophets, evangelists, apostles, saints, martyrs, and all the celestial court and company of heaven, I John Shakspear, an unworthy member of the holy Catholick religion, being at this my present writing in perfect health of body, and sound mind, memory, and understanding, but calling to mind the uncertainty of life and certainty

of death, and that I may be possibly cut off in the blossome of my sins, and called to render an account of all my transgressions externally and internally, and that I may be unprepared for the dreadful trial either by sacrament, pennance, fasting, or prayer, or any other

purgation whatever, do in the holy presence above specified, of my own free and voluntary accord, make and ordaine this my last spiritual will, testament, confession, protestation, and confession of faith, hopinge hereby to receive pardon for all my finnes and offences, and thereby to be made partaker of life everlafting, through the only merits of Jefus Chrift my faviour and redeemer, who took upon himfelf the likenefs of man, fuffered death, and was crucified upon the croffe, for the redemption of finners.

II.

" *Item*, I John Shakfpear doe by this prefent pro-teft, acknowledge, and confefs, that in my paft life I have been a moft abominable and grievous finner, and therefore unworthy to be forgiven without a true and fincere repentance for the fame. But trufting in the manifold mercies of my bleffed Saviour and Redeemer,

I am encouraged by relying on his facred word, to hope for falvation and be made partaker of his heavenly kingdom, as a member of the celeftial company of angels, faints and martyrs, there to refide for ever and ever in the court of my God.

III.

" *Item*, I John Shakfpear doe by this prefent proteft and declare, that as I am certain I muft paffe out of this tranfitory life into another that will laft to eternity, I do hereby moft humbly implore and intreat my good and guardian angell to inftruct me in this my folemn preparation, proteftation, and confeffion of faith, at leaft fpiritually," &c.

51 WILLIAM SHAKESPEARE, *PLAYS AND POEMS*, ED. EDMOND MALONE (1790), vol. i, pt. 2, pp. 330–1.

Later Malone was assailed by misgivings, and in his *Inquiry into the Authenticity of Certain Miscellaneous Papers and Legal Instruments*, his celebrated exposure in 1796 of William Henry Ireland's forged Shakespeare papers, he retracted his earlier faith in John Shakespeare's attestation of faith. 'In my conjecture concerning the writer of that paper, I certainly was mistaken', he announced; 'for I have since obtained documents that clearly prove it could not have been the composition of any one of our poet's family; as will be fully shewn in his Life.'[1] But Malone never lived to complete the great biography to which all his previous researches comprised a prelude, and his literary executor, James Boswell the younger, could not find among Malone's papers the documentary evidence to which he had alluded. Perhaps, Boswell speculated, Malone had uncovered information to associate the testament with the other John Shakespeare. But what could the Catholic declaration of a shoemaker of Warwick be doing in the roof of the house in Henley Street?

The note-book of five leaves that Malone held in his hands has since vanished. A pity, for the techniques of modern scholarship might have answered several intriguing questions. Was the text transcribed in England (where the secretary script was favoured) or on the Continent (where the italic hand held sway)? Where was the paper manufactured? The watermark would have revealed that, and also provided a clue as to date. Was John Shakespeare's name entered in the same hand as the rest? The answer to that question would have indicated whether the copy was made locally or imported. Did the document (signed, as the last paragraph says, with the testator's own hand) bear a cross or John Shakespeare's characteristic mark of the glover's compass? These questions must remain unanswered.[2]

Another broader issue has in this century been settled. Was the whole document an invention — Jordan's invention? So that eminent Victorian Halliwell-Phillipps suspected, and in Sir Sidney Lee's biography, for long regarded as standard, this possibility has assumed the status of fact. 'Much notoriety', Lee informs us, 'was obtained by John Jordan (1746–1809), a resident at Stratford-on-Avon, whose most important achievement was the forgery of the will of Shakespeare's father. . . .'[3] Certainly Jordan was a rogue, and more than once he led Malone up the garden path; but that does not mean that the testament was a piece of his roguery.

The earlier commentators, whatever their misgivings, had no doubt that the formulary itself was authentic. Now we know that they were right. Around 1923 a Jesuit scholar, Father Herbert Thurston, found in the British Museum a Spanish version of the spiritual testament printed in 1661 in Mexico City. This 'Last Will of the Soul, made in health for the Christian to secure himself from the temptations of the devil at the hour of death',[4] was drawn up by Carlo Borromeo, the Cardinal Archbishop of Milan who died in 1585 and was canonized in 1610. His celebrated piety was fearfully tested in the late seventies, when the plague gripped Milan, carrying off (it is said) 17,000 souls. During this emergent occasion Borromeo composed the devotion which became a favoured instrument of Counter-Reformation, and which, two centuries later, was extricated from the roof-tiles of John Shakespeare's house in Stratford.

1 Malone, *An Inquiry into the Authenticity of Certain Miscellaneous Papers and Legal Instruments* (1796), pp. 198–9.
2 The questions are put by James G. McManaway in 'John Shakespeare's "Spiritual Testament" ', *Shakespeare Quarterly*, xviii (1967), 197–205; reprinted in McManaway, *Studies in Shakespeare, Bibliography, and Theater*, ed. Richard Hosley, Arthur C. Kirsch, and John W. Velz (New York, 1969), pp. 293–304.
3 Sidney Lee, *A Life of William Shakespeare* (4th ed. of revised version, 1925), p. 647.
4 *Testamento o Ultima Voluntad del Alma hecho en Salud para assegurarse el christiano de las tentaciones del Demonio, en la hora de la muerto*; Herbert Thurston, 'A Controverted Shakespeare Document', *The Dublin Review*, clxxiii (1923), 165. I give Thurston's translation.

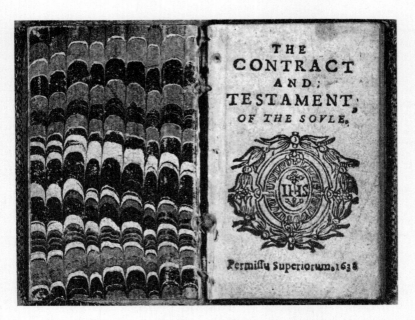

THE
CONTRACT
AND
TESTAMENT,
OF THE SOVLE.

Permissu Superiorum. 1638

THE TESTAMENT OF THE SOVLE.
Made by S. *Charles Borrom. Card. & Arch. of Millan.*

An Aduertisement to the deuout Reader.

1. THe deuout Person who will make vse of this spirituall Writing, for the good of his soule, let him read, or heare it read often, especially when he hopes he is in state of Grace, after Confession &

& Cōmunion. And let him keep it in some place of note, & neere vnto him: & when he goeth any iourney, let him carry the same always with him to haue it ready vpon all occasions. And whē he shall fall sicke, after Cōfession let him renew, by reading, or hearing read, this Testamēt, in presence of others, confirming finaly what he hath formerly at other times promised, & bequeathed for the good of his Soule.

2. This Testament may be made by all sorts of Persons, & at al times, writing

---

or causing to be written their Names, at the end of the Protestations following, in manner of subscription, or sea.ing. And he that cannot write, let him make a Crosse (†) thus, or some such marke.

---

† *Kneeling, standing, or sitting in deuout manner, before some Altar, or Oratory, say as followeth*
In the Name of the Father, & of the Sonne, and of the holy Ghost. Amen.

IN. N. a most miserable Sinner, knowing my selfe

selfe to be mortal, & borne to dye, without knowing the houre, where, when, or how; to the end that I be not surprised vpō a sudaine am resolued through the help, and aide of my sweet Sauiour, to make my selfe ready for this vncertaine Houre, seeing he vouchsafeth me now a fit time; Wherfore sincerely from the bottom of my Hart, I giue the world to vnderstād of this my last Wil, & testament, in māner following.

I.
FIrst, I heere protest, and declare in the sight, &

---

presence of Almighty God, Father, Sonne, and holy Ghost, three Persons, & one God; and of the B. V. Mary, and of all the holy Court of Heauen, that I will liue and dye obedient vnto the Catholike, Rōmaine, & Apostolicke Church, firmely belieuing all the twelue Articles of the Fayth taught by the holy Apostles, with the interpretation, & declaration made thereon by the same holy church, as taught defined & declared by her. And finally I protest, that I do belieue all that, which a good & faithfull Christian

ought to belieue: In which faith I purpose to liue & die. And if at any time (which God forbid) I should chāce by suggestion of the diuell to do, say, or thinke cōtrary to this my beliefe, I do now for that time, in vertue of this present act, reuoke, infring, & annull the same, & will that it be held for neither spokē, or done by me.

II.
SEcondly. By this my last Will I protest, that, at my death I will receiue the Sacramēts of Pennance, & Confession, the which if by any accident I should not

---

be able to haue, or make, I do in vertue of this present, resolue from this instant, for that time, to make it frō my hart, accusing my selfe of all my sins cōmitted in Thought, Word, & Worke, as wel against God as against my selfe and my neighbour, wherof I do repent me with infinite sorrow, & desire time of pennance, bitterly to bewaile the same, for that I haue offēded my Soueraigne Lord & God, whome I ought to loue and serue aboue all things. The which I now firme-

firmely purpose, with his grace, to do as lōg as I shall liue, without euer more offending him.

III.
ITem, I do protest, that at the end of my life, I will receiue the most Blessed Sacrament for my *Viaticum*, or last iourney, that by meanes of so diuine a Pledge, I may perfectly recōcile & vnite my selfe vnto my Lord. The which if through any accidēt, I should not then be able to performe, I do now for that time, declare, that I will receiue
D it,

---

it, at least (spiritually in wil, adoring & most hūbly beseeching my Sauiour, that he will be pleased to assist me in so dāgerous a voyage & defend me from the snares, & deceits of my infernal Enemies, & to conduct me to the secure Hauen of his Eternall Blisse.

IV.
ITem. I protest that I will also passe out of this life, armed with the last Sacrament of Extreme Vnction: the which if through any let, or hinderance, I should not then be able to haue, I do

do now also, for that same time, demaūd, & craue the same, beseeching his diuine Maiesty that he wil be pleased to anoint my Senses both internall and external, with the sacred oile of his infinit Mercy, & to pardō me al my sins committed, by Seeing, Speaking, Tasting, Touching, Smelling, Hearing, or any other way whatsoeuer.

V.
ITem. I do by this present protest, that I will neu.r through any temptation whatsoeuer, despaire of the diuine Goodnes, for the
D 2 mul-

---

multitude and greatnes of my sinnes, for which although I cōfesse, that I haue deserued Hel, yet wil I stedfastly hope in Gods infinit Mercy, knowing that he hath hertofore pardoned many grieuous sinners, wherof I haue good warrant, sealed with his sacred mouth, in holy Writ, wherby he pronounceth, *that he is not come to call the iust, but sinners.*

VI.
ITem. I protest that I do not know, that I haue euer done any good worke meri-

meritorious of life euerlasting: & if I haue done any, I acknowledge that I haue done it with a great deale of negligence, & imperfection; neither should I haue bin able to haue done the least, without the assistance of his diuine grace. Wherfore let the diuell remaine confounded, for I do in no wise presume to merit heauen by such good Workes alone: but through the merits, & bloud of my Lord and Sauiour *Iesus*, shed vpon the Crosse for me most miserable sinner.
D 3 VII.

54 *The Testament*

VII.

Item, I protest by this present Writing, that I will patiëtly endure, & suffer all kind of infirmity, sicknesse, yea & the paine of death it selfe: wherin if it should happë, which God forbid, that through violence of paine & agony, or by subtility of the Diuell, I should fall into any impatience, or tëptation of blasphemy, or murmuration against God or the Catholike Fayth, or giue any signe of bad exäple, I do henceforth, & for that present, repent

of the Soule. **55**

repent me, & am most hartily sorry for the same: & I do renounce all the euill whatsoeuer, which I might haue then done, or said, beseeching his diuine Clemëcy, that he will not forsake me in that grieuous & painefull Conflict.

VIII.

Item. By vertue of this present Testament, I do pardon all the iniuries and offences that any one hath euer done vnto me, either in my reputatiö, life, goods or any other way whatsoeuer; beseeching sweet Iesus

D 4 to

56 *The Testament*

to pardon thë for the same: & I desire, that they wil doe the like by me, whome I haue offended, or iniured in any sort howsoeuer.

IX.

Item. I heere protest, that I do render infinit thankes to his diuine Maiesty, for all the benefits that I haue receiued, as wel secret as manifest, & in particular, for the benefit of my Creation, Redemption, Sanctification, Conseruation, & Vocation to the holy knowledge of him, and his true Catholike fayth: but aboue all, for his so great expecta-

of the Soule. **57**

tion of me to pennance, when he might most iustly haue taken me out of this life, when I least thought therof: yea euë then, when I was plüged in the durty puddle of my sins. Blessed be therfore & praysed, for euer & euer, his infinite Patience and Charity.

X.

Item, I protest, that I am willing, yea I do infinitly desire, & humbly craue, that of this my last Will & Testament the glorious, & euer Virgin Mary mother of God, Refuge and Aduocate

D 5 cate

58 *The Testament*

cate of sinners (whome I honour specially aboue all other Saints) may be the chiefe Executresse, together with these other saints my Patrons, [   ] all whom I inuoke, and beseech to be present at the houre of my death, that she & they may cöfort me with their desired presence, and craue of sweet Iesus, that he will receiue my soule into peace.

XI.

Item. In vertue of this presët writing I do likewise most willingly, & with all humility cöstitute, & ordaine my good Angell, for

of the Soule. **59**

for Defender & Protectour of my Soule in the dreadfull day of iudgment, when the finall sentence of eternall life or death shalbe discussed, & giuen: beseeching him, that as my soule was by my Creatour cömitted to his custody, & protection when I liued; euen so he wil vouchsafe to defëd the same at that houre, & conduct it to eternall Blisse.

XII.

Item. I do in like manner pray, & beseech all my deare friends, Parëts, & kinsfolks, by the bowels of our Sauiour Iesus Christ,

60 *The Testament*

that, since it is vncertaine what lot will befall me, for feare notwithstanding least by reason of my sinnes, I be to passe, & stay a lög while in Purgatory, they will vouchsafe to assist and succour me with their holy praiers, & satisfactory workes, especially with the holy Sacrifice of the Masse, as being the most effectuall meanes to deliuer Soules from their tormëts & paines; frö the which, if I shall by Gods gracious goodnes, & by their vertuous works be deliuered, I do promise that I wil not be vngratefull

of the Soule. **61**

vnto thë, for so great a benefit.

XIII.

Item. By this my will & Testament, I bequeath my soule assoone as it shall be deliuered, & loosned frö the prison of this my body, to be entöbed in the sweet & amorous Coffin of the Side of Iesus Christ: & that in this life-giuing-Sepulcher it may rest, & liue perpetually inclosed in that eternall habitatiö of Repose, there to blesse for euer and euer, that dreadfull Iron of the Launce, which like a sharp cutting Rasour, formed to sweet and pleasant

62 *The Testament*

a monument, within the sacred breast of my Lord & Sauiour.

XIV.

Lastly, I do protest, that I will willingly accept of death, in what manner soeuer it may, or shall befal me, conforming my wil vnto the will of God; accepting of the same in satisfaction for my sinnes, & giuing thankes vnto his diuine Maiesty for the life he hath bestowed vpon me: & if it please him to prolong, or shorten the same, blessed be he also a thousand thousand times; into whose most

of the Soule. **63**

most holy hands I cömend my soule, my body, my life, & my death: and I beseech him aboue all things, that he neuer permit any change to the made by me, of this my foresaid Will, and Testament. Amen.

§. *Heere let him write his Name and Quality, as followeth:*

I [   ] haue made this present Writing of Protestation, Confession and Charter, in presence of the Blessed V. Ma. my Angell guardian, & all the celestiall Court as Witnesses heerunto: the

64 *The Testament*

which, my meaning is, that it be of full value, now presently, & for euer, with the force and vertue of Testament, Codicil, & Donation, in case of death; confirming it a new, being in perfect health of soule and body, & signed with mine owne hand, carrying also the same continually about me: and for the better declaration herof, my Will & intention is, that it be finally buried with me, after my death.

Hauing made this protestation, let him say denoutly, Pater, A[ve]. & Creed.

FINIS.

52 CARLO BORROMEO, *THE TESTAMENT OF THE SOULE* (1638). *Folger Shakespeare Library; shelfmark: STC 5645.5. This unique copy of the tiny 32mo volume, here reproduced in facsimile for the first time, was acquired by the Folger in 1966. James G. McManaway, then Consultant in Literature and Bibliography at the Library, at once recognized the significance of the book. 'This is the earliest surviving text of the Testament, as well as the only authentic English Text,' he wrote in* Shakespeare Quarterly. *'For the first time we can know what should have appeared on the missing first leaf of the manuscript sent to Edmund Malone' ('John Shakespeare's "Spiritual Testament"', xviii (1967), 197-205). This essay, in which the Borromeo formulary is described, analysed, and reprinted, is included in McManaway,* Studies in Shakespeare, Bibliography, and Theater, *ed. Richard Hosley, Arthur C. Kirsch, and John W. Velz (New York, 1969), pp. 293-304.*

E

In the spring of 1580 a team of British Jesuit missionaries, led by Fathers Edmund Campion and Robert Parsons, stopped in Milan on their way to England from Rome, and there enjoyed the hospitality of the famous cardinal. His emaciated frame and zealous preaching in contempt of the world left a deep impression on his English guests. When they moved on, they apparently took with them copies of Borromeo's Last Will of the Soul. So we may gather from a letter written on 23 June 1581 by the rector of the English College in France to his counterpart in Rome, where the mission originated. 'Father Robert [Parsons] wants three or four thousand or more of the Testaments', Dr. William Allen remarks, 'for many persons desire to have them.'[1] These persons were Catholics or likely converts in England. Into their houses the missionaries insinuated themselves, and, once lodged, they donned the priest's vestments they always carried with them. They held secret conference, listened to confession, and performed the mass. They secured signatures on the testaments. Then they departed. Wandering their separate ways, both Campion and Parsons passed through the Midlands. At his house, Bushwood, in Lapworth, only twelve miles from Stratford, Sir William Catesby put up Campion, and for his indiscreet hospitality was arrested and imprisoned in the Fleet. One ran a dangerous risk in harbouring popish priests, for the offence was a felony and could be punished by death. During Elizabeth's reign almost 200 Catholics suffered execution under the penal laws.

Not until 1966 did an early edition in English of the formulary come to light. *The Contract and Testament of the Soule*, printed in 1638 (probably on the Continent), closely follows Malone's text, except for the first two articles and part of the third. So the document is genuine — there can be no question of that — except for the fabricated first leaf supplied by Jordan. But did John Shakespeare, a miserable sinner, kneel devoutly before some improvised altar, and subscribe to the profession? If he did, it is curious that after 1580 (for the document could not have had English dissemination earlier) he should, in Article XII, beseech not only dear friends and kinsfolk, but also his parents, to pray for his soul's delivery from the torments of Purgatory. His parents were then both dead. It has been suggested that the testator was using *parents* in the root sense of 'relations', the equivalent of *parientes* in the Italian and Spanish versions. A simpler explanation holds that John Shakespeare signed a standardized form rather than one adapted to particular circumstances. It has also been suggested that he hid the testament in his rafters in 1583, after the attempt of a deranged local Catholic youth to assassinate the Queen had instigated a wave of persecution; then did prudent Warwickshiremen 'greatly work upon the advantage of clearing their houses of all shows of suspicion'.[2]

But did he in fact make such a Catholic affirmation? The faith in which William Shakespeare was raised is, after all, a matter of no small moment, to ordinary readers as well as to theologians. But Malone's paper has disappeared, and too many questions remain teasingly unanswered. For clues to Shakespeare's religion we must turn to other sources, and as regards his father's Spiritual Last Will and Testament, settle (as on other occasions) for a secular agnosticism.

1   Cited by John Henry de Groot, *The Shakespeares and 'The Old Faith'* (New York, 1946), p. 88.
2   Thomas Wilkes, Clerk of the Council, quoted by Peter Milward, *Shakespeare's Religious Background* (Bloomington and London, 1973), p. 21.

6

Faith and Knowledge

If the form of faith instilled in the young William Shakespeare remains mysterious, no similar uncertainty attaches to what he experienced in church. That he worshipped at Matins and Evensong, participated at least three times a year in Communion, and was instructed by the parish priest in his catechism, we need not doubt. In Shakespeare's Stratford, on Sundays and Holy Days, shops and ale-houses shut their doors; all fairs and markets ceased. The law of the realm compelled church-going, and infractions were punishable by fine. More than half a century after the dramatist's death Richard Davies, then chaplain of Corpus Christi College, Oxford, added this terse declaration to some memoranda on Shakespeare: 'He dyed a papist.' However intriguing, such reports belong to tradition rather than to the factual record. The religious training provided for Shakespeare by his community was orthodox and Protestant.

The moderate Protestantism of the parish churches was set forth by Queen Elizabeth's Book of Common Prayer, which her first Parliament ordered into use by the Act of Uniformity on 24 June 1559. Besides the Prayer Book, churches were instructed to furnish themselves with 'the new Kalendar, a Psalter, the English Bible in the largest volume, the two tomes of the Homilies, and the Paraphrases of Erasmus translated into English'.[1] The large Bible authorized for the churches by the episcopate was the Bishops' Bible of 1568, a not very satisfactory revision of the Great Bible of 1539–41. Some churches, however, clung to the Genevan Bible, despite its association with Calvin, and this version, cheaply available in legible roman type, was favoured in most middle-class homes. Shakespeare knew it.

At services the minister appeared in 'a comely surplice with sleeves'. (This seemingly innocuous vestment occasioned distress in some quarters, where it was dispensed with as a manifesto of nonconformity. 'Though honesty be no puritan', the Clown chides the Countess in *All's Well that Ends Well*, 'yet it will do no hurt; it will wear the surplice of humility over the black gown of a big heart.'[2]) For Holy Communion, administered upon the first or second Sunday of each month, there was placed 'a comely and decent table standing on a frame, . . . with a fair linen cloth to lay upon the same, and some covering of silk, buckram, or other such-like for the clean keeping thereof'. Morning Prayer commenced early, at 7 a.m., and Evening Prayer was over by 3 p.m. In those days candles lit up the churches only at Christmas, and so services had to be conducted during daylight hours.

A passage from Scripture opened both Morning and Evening Prayer. In the course of a year all such portions of the Old Testament as were deemed 'edifying' were read; so the Prayer Book prescribed. The reading of the Old Testament was, then, selective, an appropriate passage being chosen for each service. The Apocrypha received the same treatment. Each month, however, the congregation (that is, all who attended daily) sang or said the whole of the Psalms, which in the Prayer Book appeared according to the Great (not Bishops') Bible, with the opening words of the Latin Vulgate for their titles. Over the year the whole of the New Testament was read three times, the Gospels and the Acts at Matins, the Catholic and Pastoral Epistles at Evensong. Proper Lessons from the New Testament were set only for the Holy Days and a few special Sundays. For the daily offices Canticles were appointed, and the choir sang the *Te Deum*, *Benedictus*, and *Magnificat*, and (in Lent) the *Benedicite*.

---

1 Articles of Grindal and Sandys, issued in 1571; quoted by the Revd. Ronald Bayne in his chapter, 'Religion', in *Shakespeare's England* (Oxford, 1916), i. 63. Bayne furnishes a compendious survey of the subject.
2 On this passage Bayne remarks, 'The words seem to recognize some pride in the refusal to don the surplice and yet to imply a respect for the zeal which distinguished the wearers of the black gown' ('Religion', i. 56).

After the reading and singing, a sermon; but if the priest lacked 'the gift of preaching sufficiently to instruct the people', he could instead read some of the Homilies 'distinctly and plainly'.[1] No matter how eloquent in the pulpit, however, the vicar could only defer the reading, not avoid it altogether. The Homilies were official sermons 'appointed by the Queenes Majestie [so reads the title-page of the 1582 edition] to be declared and read, by all Parsons, Vicars, and Curates, every Sunday and Holy day in their churches . . . for the better understanding of the simple people'. These *Certaine Sermons* included appropriate set discourses for Good Friday, Easter Sunday, and Rogation week; also for the marriage service. They expounded the right use of the church, the efficacy of prayer, and the peril of idolatry. After the suppression of the rebellion in the North in 1569 and the excommunication of Elizabeth by Pope Pius V the next year, the collection was enriched by 'An Exhortation to Obedience' in three parts, and 'An Homilie against Disobedience and Wilfull Rebellion' in six. Each instalment of the latter appropriately ended with a prayer for the Queen and the security of the realm. These Homilies on obedience and rebellion, delivered over nine Sundays and Holy Days, instilled political submissiveness in the simple people.

Before Evensong on each Sunday and Holy Day, the vicar instructed the children of both sexes in their catechism. He called on them by name, and listened while they recited. That was in English. At school the boys learnt their catechism in Latin.

Thus inculcated from the formative years of early childhood, the Bible and Book of Common Prayer and Homilies profoundly nourished Shakespeare's imagination. One learned Biblical scholar, ranging through all the works with the exception of *Pericles* and the non-dramatic poems, has identified quotations from, or references to, forty-two books of the Bible — eighteen each from the Old and New Testaments, and six from the Apocrypha.[2] Scarcely a phrase from the first three chapters of Genesis escapes allusion in the plays. Job and Ecclesiastes were favourite books, but the story of Cain left an especially powerful impression — Shakespeare refers to it at least twenty-five times. Evidently Shakespeare continued to consult the Bible long after his youthful indoctrination; so we may gather from certain details in the texts of *Henry V* (where he seems to have used, for the Dauphin, the de Tournes *Testament*, printed at Lyons in 1551) and *Measure for Measure*, in which the Provost's description of Barnadine —

> As fast lock'd up in sleep as guiltless labour
> When it lies starkly in the traveller's bones

— has as its source Ecclesiastes 5:11, apparently as rendered in certain revised Genevan Bibles of 1595 or later: 'The sleepe of him that travelleth is sweete.'[3] He refers more often to earlier than to later parts of books — chapters 1–4, for example, of the fifty chapters of Genesis — and shows greater familiarity with Genesis and Matthew than with any subsequent book from the Old or New Testament.[4] Not surprisingly he makes mistakes. He confuses Lucifer with Satan, and the Sabaoth — the hosts of the Lord of the *Te Deum* — with the Holy Sabbath of Shylock and his brethren. But an apparent slip may, upon closer study, merely illustrate Shakespeare's complex way with sources. Richard II, fetched forth to surrender his crown, asks, 'Did they not sometime cry "All hail!" to me?/So Judas did to Christ.' In Matthew's Gospel and Mark's, Judas salutes Jesus with 'Hail Master', and the variant has been cited as a defect in Shakespeare's Biblical knowledge. There is, however, precedent for it in Judas's greeting, 'All hayll', in the play of the Agony and the Betrayal in the medieval York cycle of Mystery Plays.

Shakespeare's range of religious reference is not limited to the Bible. Sometimes he quotes Scripture by way of the Prayer Book, as when the Fifth Commandment becomes 'thou shalt do no murder', and the words of the Psalmist, 'we bring our years to an end, as it were a tale that is told' ('we have spent our yeeres as a thought', in the Genevan Bible), metamorphose into the tale told by an idiot. Nor did Shakespeare forget his catechism: in *Love's Labour's Lost* Berowne

1   Articles of Grindal and Sandys, quoted by Bayne, 'Religion', i. 63.
2   Richmond Noble, *Shakespeare's Biblical Knowledge and Use of the Book of Common Prayer as Exemplified in the Plays of the First Folio* (1935), p. 20. On Shakespeare's use of the Bible I am especially indebted to Noble.
3   Ibid., pp. 69, 86–7.
4   Edgar I. Fripp, *Shakespeare: Man and Artist* (1938), i. 85–6.

reminds the King that every man is mastered not by might but by 'special grace'; Hamlet shows his hands, 'these pickers and stealers', to Rosencrantz ('keep my hands from picking and stealing'). Our most thorough student of the Homilies takes them to be 'A New Shakespearean Source-Book', and concludes that the dramatist derived his ideas of the divine right of kings, the subject's duty to obey, and the mischief and wickedness of rebellion — ideas that so powerfully inform the English History plays — not from his narrative sources, Holinshed and the rest, but either directly or indirectly from the politico-religious creed set forth in the Homilies.[1] The services at Holy Trinity, Morning Prayer and Evening Prayer, Baptism and Holy Communion — indeed all the occasions of worship — remained with Shakespeare, and echo through the plays.

Was it, then, the Anglican faith that he embraced? Many have so concluded. One recent biographer, Dr. Rowse, is firm on this matter as on others: 'He was an orthodox, conforming member of the Church into which he had been baptised, was brought up and married, in which his children were reared and in whose arms he at length was buried.'[2] As Rowse sees it, there were for Shakespeare only two sacraments, Baptism and Holy Communion, rather than the Catholic seven. His chief exhibit of evidence is the preamble to the dramatist's will. This employs 'the regular Protestant formula', and 'one can always tell from the formula in these contemporary wills whether the person is dying a Protestant or a Catholic'.[3] But the confidence is here misplaced: testators, whether Catholic or Protestant, could use the same exordium (or their lawyers used it for them) without necessarily regarding it as an avowal of sectarian faith.[4] The baptisms and marriages and burials all within the bosom of Holy Trinity are, however, not guesses. No doubt Shakespeare did conform to the rituals of the Established Church, and attend its services. Had he neglected to do so, as a well-known theatrical figure he would with difficulty have escaped the notice of municipal authorities hostile to the stage on religious grounds. Certainly Ben Jonson's recusancy did not go unremarked. Still, the Church of England encompassed a breadth of religious experience, and to either side of the *via media* stood Puritan and neo-Catholic extremists. Moreover, one may conform outwardly as a matter of convenience, to avoid the law's importunities, and still privately nourish heterodoxy or indifference. Thus the scattering of Jews in Elizabethan London survived by conforming to the Anglican Church, but for some at least the conversion must have been prudential.

We remember the testament in the tiles, and it is a fact that Shakespeare's daughter Susanna was reported in a list of those, popishly affected, who failed to receive the Communion on an Easter Sunday.[5] But of course, even if we could definitively ascertain the religious convictions of Shakespeare's father and daughter, we would still not possess a sure clue to the poet's own faith. Thus it is that theologically minded students have so industriously searched the plays for evidences of Catholic sympathies. Does not the dramatist treat his lesser Romanist clergy, a Friar Lawrence or Abbess Æmelia, more respectfully than his Protestant vicars of the villages, the Martexts and the Nathaniels? Surely his imagination did not stand aloof from the vessels and vestments of Catholicism. Nor was he unmoved by the abandoned abbeys and monasteries left crumbling in the wake of Reformation; in his 73rd Sonnet these are evoked by the poignant metaphor of the bare ruined choirs where late the sweet birds sang. In *King John*, the historical matter of which deals directly with the clash between English crown and papal authority, Shakespeare lets pass the invitation to anti-Catholic polemics, an invitation eagerly seized by his two predecessors, the renegade monk John Bale and the anonymous author of *The Troublesome Reign of King John*. Interested readers have discerned echoes here and there of the disused prayers and hymns of the Catholic liturgy; also a grasp of the fuller meaning of such Catholic practices as fasting and confession, and even of technical terminology. Thus, when Julia in *The Two Gentlemen of Verona* speaks of a 'month's mind', the phrase has been glossed as 'the name first used for the month of remembrance during which daily Masses were offered for the souls of the dead,

---

1 Alfred Hart, *Shakespeare and the Homilies* (Melbourne, 1934), pp. 9–76; see, esp., p. 67.
2 A. L. Rowse, *William Shakespeare: A Biography* (1963), p. 43.
3 Ibid., p. 451.
4 See BRL, ii. 481–2; also below, p. 246.
5 See below, pp. 234–5.

E*

and now applied to the Mass said for them a month after death'.[1] But by the late sixteenth century a 'month's mind' could signify merely a longing, such as might take a pregnant woman. Still, the Ghost of Hamlet's father uses the term *unaneled* ('Unhous'led, disappointed, unanel'd'), a reference to the Catholic Sacrament of Extreme Unction. And, if the word *purgatory* occurs only twice in the whole corpus, the concept itself is powerfully evoked by the same ghost,

> Doom'd for a certain term to walk the night,
> And for the day confin'd to fast in fires,
> Till the foul crimes done in my days of nature
> Are burnt and purg'd away.

To be sure, Shakespeare seems to err in his only overt reference to the sacrifice of the Mass — when Juliet asks the Friar whether she should come to 'evening mass' — for Pope Pius V and the Council of Trent had in 1556 done away with evening mass; but twelve years later, recusants in the Welsh Marches were still celebrating it, and anyway the allusion appears in Shakespeare's source.[2] The facts are ambiguous: too ambiguous to justify a recent Jesuitical commentator's conclusion that Shakespeare felt a positive nostalgia for England's Catholic past, although the same writer is on safer ground when he claims that Shakespeare shows much familiarity but little awkwardness in his treatment of Catholic customs and beliefs.[3]

What remains clear is that the artist takes precedence over the votary, and resists efforts on the part of sectarian apologists to put him in a convenient theological pigeon-hole. Probably Shakespeare remained a tolerant Anglican — after all, he could imaginatively comprehend, if not condone, a Shylock — but we need not find too puzzling chaplain Davies's claim that he died a Papist.

His schooling, if it faithfully adhered to the law of the realm, would have inclined him to the Church of England. The forty-first item of the Royal Injunctions of Queen Elizabeth in 1559 decreed 'That all teachers of children shall stir and move them to love and do reverence to Gods true Religion, now truly set forth by publick Authority'. A noted educator of the day, headmaster of Westminster School and afterwards Dean of St. Paul's, has his ideal pedagogue thus address one of his younger charges:

Forasmuch as the maister ought to be to his scholars a second parent and father, not of theyr bodyes but of their myndes, I see it belongeth to the order of my dutie, my dere child, not so much to instruct thee civilly in learnyng and good maners, as to furnish thy mynde, and that in thy tender yeres, with good opinions and true Religion. For this age of childhode ought no lesse, yea also much more, to be trayned with good lessons to godlinesse, than with good artes to humanitie.[4]

This dear child was a boy; girls from comfortable families learned to sew and sing and play upon the virginals; with luck, they mastered the rudiments of reading and writing. Warwickshire bred few Rosalinds.

The curriculum of Stratford grammar school has not come down, but we can reconstruct it with some confidence on the basis of what we know of similar foundations in other parts of England. Fortunately the 'good arts' thrived better than some theorists thought sufficient. The parchment registers for Stratford pupils of this period have also, not surprisingly, perished. More than a century later, in 1709, Nicholas Rowe remarked that John Shakespeare had bred his poet son 'for some time at a Free-School, where 'tis probable he acquir'd that little *Latin* he was Master of'. This is our earliest allusion to Shakespeare's formal education, and may either record a tradition or reflect Rowe's natural inference. If an inference, it seems valid enough: we need not doubt that Shakespeare received a grammar school education, and the only likely place for it was the King's New School of Stratford-upon-Avon. The schoolroom stood in Church Street,

1   Frank Mathew, *An Image of Shakespeare* (1922), p. 391; cited by John Henry de Groot, *The Shakespeares and 'The Old Faith'* (New York, 1946), p. 170. I am mostly obliged to de Groot for, in his phrase, 'positive indications of Shakespeare's esteem for the Old Faith', but I have also profitably consulted the more recent study by Peter Milward, *Shakespeare's Religious Background* (Bloomington and London, 1973).

2   Roland Mushat Frye, *Shakespeare and Christian Doctrine* (Princeton, 1963), pp. 262–3.

3   Milward, *Shakespeare's Religious Background*, pp. 24, 78.

4   Alexander Nowell, *A Catechisme, or first Instruction and Learning of Christian Religion*, transl. T. Norton (1570), sig. B1.

53 A SEVENTEENTH-CENTURY HORNBOOK. *This hornbook, which dates from the time of Charles I, is in the Bodleian Library; shelfmark: Arch. A. f. 11.*

behind the Guild Chapel, and only a quarter-mile distant from the family house in Henley Street.

A child's education began at the age of four or five, not in the grammar school proper but in an attached petty school, under the tuition of an usher, or *abecedarius*, who also looked after the lower forms.[1] He thus spared the master 'that tedious trouble', as the council described it, of teaching the 'young youth' of the town. These ushers were not as a rule themselves especially well educated, and if the dramatist fell into the hands of a pedagogue as accomplished as his own creation Holofernes he might have accounted himself lucky.

The scholars came to class equipped with their hornbook: a leaf of paper or parchment framed in wood and covered, for protection, with a thin layer of transparent horn. On the paper was set forth the alphabet, both small letters and capitals; combinations of the five vowels with *b*, *c*, and *d* — the elements of syllabication; and the Lord's Prayer. The mark of the cross preceded the alphabet, which was hence called the 'Christ cross row'. So Clarence, in *Richard III*, frets about the dying King Edward's superstitious behaviour:

> He hearkens after prophecies and dreams,
> And from the cross-row plucks the letter G,
> And says a wizard told him that by G
> His issue disinherited should be;
> And, for my name of George begins with G,
> It follows in his thought that I am he.

Shakespeare also remembered his hornbook in *Love's Labour's Lost*. 'Monsieur, are you not lett'red?', Armado asks Holofernes, and Moth answers for the pedant: 'Yes, yes; he teaches boys the hornbook. What is a, b, spelt backward with the horn on his head?' — thus labelling Holofernes as a muttonhead.

Having mastered their hornbooks, the children moved on to *The ABC with the Catechism*, which reprinted the hornbook leaf, and followed it with the catechism from the Book of Common

1 The comprehensive account is T. W. Baldwin, *William Shakspere's Petty School* (Urbana, Ill., 1943).

54 AN ELIZABETHAN SCHOOLROOM. *Engraving on verso of title-page of Alexander Nowell*, Catechismus parvus . . . Latinè & Græcè *(1574 ed.)*. *Copy in the British Library; shelfmark: 843. c. 21 (2).* STC *18711ᵃ. The engraving is reproduced by T. W. Baldwin,* William Shakspere's Petty School *(Urbana, Ill., 1943), p. 8. Baldwin asks readers not to overlook 'Launce's dog and his bone'.*

Prayer and a set of graces for praising God before and after meals. ('That is question now', catechizes the satirical Bastard in *King John*; 'And then comes answer like an Absey [i.e. ABC] book.') The third and last textbook, *The Primer and Catechism* — amounting to only two octavo gatherings — included the Calendar and Almanac, as well as the seven penitential psalms and other devotional matter. Armed with these models, the pupils were introduced to the mysteries of *prosodia* — the 'pronouncing of letters, syllables, and words with the mouth' — and *orthographia*, the 'writing of them with the hands'. In addition to reading and writing, some petty schools provided elementary instruction in the third R: numeration, the first part of arithmetic; and perhaps also the casting of accounts. *The ABC with the Catechism* furnished the nine figures 'and this circle (o) called a Cypher'. After two years the scholars were ready for grammar school.

Shakespeare does not seem to have cherished especially tender memories of these days, if we may judge from the references to schools and schoolboys scattered through the plays. 'Love goes toward love, as schoolboys from their books', sighs Romeo beneath Juliet's balcony; 'But love from love toward school with heavy looks.' In *The Taming of the Shrew* Gremio returns from Petruchio's disconcerting wedding 'As willingly as e'er I came from school'. Schoolboys (in *Much Ado About Nothing*) take less delight in their lessons than in finding birds' nests. Jack Cade, in *2 Henry VI*, condemns Lord Say to immediate beheading for having, among other enormities, 'most traitorously corrupted the youth of the realm in erecting a grammar school'. In the second of Jaques's Seven Ages of Man, we encounter

> the whining school-boy, with his satchel
> And shining morning face, creeping like snail
> Unwillingly to school.

A less than seductive picture. All these allusions are, to be sure, made in character: Cade is the rebel leader of an ignorant and anarchic rabble; taken together, Jaques's Ages comprise, without exception, a set-piece progress of human futility. Still, these recollections of schooldays are not counterpoised in the *oeuvre* by any more sympathetic opposing voice.

Nevertheless, Shakespeare was lucky to have the King's New School at Stratford-upon-Avon. It was an excellent institution of its kind, better than most rural grammar schools. According to the 1553 charter the Stratford school was to have one teacher who would receive £20 per annum and enjoy a house rent-free. This was good remuneration by the standards of the day: at Gloucester the schoolmaster, 'an ancient Citizen of no great learning', drew £10, and other provincial pedagogues fared no better. Enthusiasts of Stratford have pointed out that the master there commanded a higher salary than his counterpart at Eton College. Although, strictly speaking, this is true, such comparisons are not very illuminating; for the Eton master had special perquisites (such as lodgings and meals in college), whereas in Stratford the schoolmaster had to pay out of his own pocket for the services of an usher, and for repairs to the schoolhouse. In the fifties an usher was getting £4 a year 'for techyng of ye chylder'. There can be no question, however, that the masters during Shakespeare's boyhood were well qualified. They held university degrees, and when they resigned their posts, the town authorities had no difficulty in attracting able replacements.

Patient inquiry has rescued from oblivion the names and careers of the five masters who came and went while Shakespeare was growing up.[1] Vicar Bretchgirdle in 1565 fetched from Warwick John Brownsword, his friend and former pupil from the Witton days (for Bretchgirdle had taught there). Brownsword wrote and published Latin verses, and was described by a contemporary educator as 'that auncient Schoolemaster . . . so much commended for his order and Schollars'.[2] He remained in Stratford only three years before being replaced briefly by John Acton, a Brasenose scholar. In 1569 Acton was succeeded by Walter Roche, a Lancashire man and a fellow of Corpus Christi College, Oxford. He had taken holy orders, and, around the same time that he was offered the Stratford post, came into a living, the rectory of Droitwich, which he held on to. Roche resigned as schoolmaster in 1571 to practise law (he on one occasion served as lawyer to Shakespeare's cousin, Robert Webbe of Snitterfield), so it is doubtful whether he taught Shakespeare, who would have been supervised in the Lower School by the usher in the same room with the older boys. The next master, Simon Hunt, served from 1571 until 1575, and probably had Shakespeare as his pupil. There was a Simon Hunt who matriculated at the University of Douai, that continental outpost for the education of English Catholics; he became a Jesuit in 1578, and succeeded the notorious Father Parsons as confessor at St. Peter's. This Hunt died in Rome in 1585. He may have been the Stratford schoolmaster, but there was another, more obscure, Hunt who died in Stratford in 1598, leaving an estate valued at £100. About the identity of the next master — Shakespeare's principal instructor — we can speak with greater certainty. Thomas Jenkins was of humble origin, the son of 'a poor man', an 'old servant' to Sir Thomas White, who was the founder of St. John's College, Oxford. At St. John's, Jenkins received his B.A. and M.A.; he was a fellow from 1566 to 1572, when the College granted him the lease of Chaucer's House in Woodstock. Meanwhile Jenkins had taken orders. In 1575 the Stratford burgesses paid for his removal expenses from Warwick, where he was schoolmastering. Jenkins was married: the Holy Trinity registers record the burial of his daughter Joan and the baptism of his son Thomas. With the consent of the corporation, Jenkins resigned as schoolmaster in 1579, but not before finding a replacement, John Cottom, 'late of London' and a Brasenose graduate. Cottom's younger brother was a missionary priest who was arraigned (along with Edmund Campion), tortured on the rack, and in 1582 put to death, a Catholic martyr. His schoolmaster brother resigned in the previous year. Did the authorities ask him to leave? Cottom retired to Lancashire, where he inherited his father's lands and became a Catholic recusant.

Thus it was possible, in Elizabethan grammar schools, to receive tuition from Catholics or Catholic sympathizers, despite the severe penalties to which recusant schoolmasters were subject. Presumably they maintained an outward conformity.

The next master, Alexander Aspinall, M.A., arrived on the scene too late to be Shakespeare's master, but he has a curious Shakespearian connection. In 1594 Aspinall, for many years a widower, married the Widow Shaw. The Shaws were friends and neighbours of the Shakespeares in Henley Street. John Shakespeare (it will be recalled) helped to appraise Ralph Shaw's goods, and some twenty years later Shaw's son July was one of the witnesses to the will of William Shakespeare. Long afterwards Sir Francis Fane of Bulbeck (1611–80) recorded in his manuscript commonplace book this posy:

> The gift is small
> The will is all:
> A shey ander [i.e. Alexander] Asbenall.
> Shaxpaire upon a peaire of gloves that master sent to his mistris.[3]

1 The most convenient and reliable account of these pedagogues is in ME, 54–8.
2 John Brinsley, *Ludus Literarius: or, The Grammar Schoole* (1612), p. 88; cited (from 1627 ed.) by Baldwin, *William Shakspere's Small Latine & Lesse Greeke* (Urbana, Ill., 1944), i. 567.
3 Fane MS., f. 177, printed by E. M. Martin, 'Shakespeare in a Seventeenth Century Manuscript', *English Review*, li (1930), 484–9; see also Fripp, *Shakespeare*, i. 401–2, and ME, 57.

It has been suggested, with more fancy than plausibility, that Aspinall bought the gloves for Mrs. Shaw in the Shakespeare shop, and that the glover's son, his brain on fire with *Romeo and Juliet*, did not disdain to assist a middle-aged schoolmaster in his courtship of a Stratford wool-driver's widow.

About the sort of education that Shakespeare enjoyed — if that is the right word — under his schoolmasters, conjecture may be less waywardly pursued. The children began their long school-day by six or seven in the morning. Lessons went on until eleven, with a short recess for breakfast; then resumed after lunch at one, and continued until five in the afternoon, interrupted only by a fifteen-minute respite for recreation. The day's instruction began and ended with devotions. In between, the scholars plied their Latin grammar. Ornamented with a woodcut showing little boys aspiring for the tempting bidden fruit of the tree of knowledge, the authorized textbook was William Lily's *Shorte Introduction of Grammar*. It consisted of two parts: the first setting forth the 'accydence & princypalls of gramer' in English; the second, the *Brevissima Institutio*, entirely in Latin. This book the scholars memorized by rote, and thus mastered declensions and conjugations.

His own experience Shakespeare recalled with rueful amusement in Act IV of *The Merry Wives of Windsor*. There the bumbling parson-pedagogue Sir Hugh Evans — he speaks Welsh flannel, according to Falstaff, and 'makes fritters of English' — catechizes the unfortunate Master William in his accidence for the benefit of the lad's disgruntled mother. 'Sir Hugh', Mistress Page complains, 'my husband says my son profits nothing in the world at his book.' The tutor's triumphal disproof of the charge follows Lily's *Grammatica Latina* step by step, and sometimes word for word. Some have assumed, from the name, that Shakespeare's schoolmaster Thomas Jenkins was a Welshman, and they have seen Sir Hugh as a gently satiric portrait of that pedagogue; but Jenkins was (despite his presumed ancestry) a Londoner. It is always dangerous to read Shakespeare's plays as *pièces à clef*.

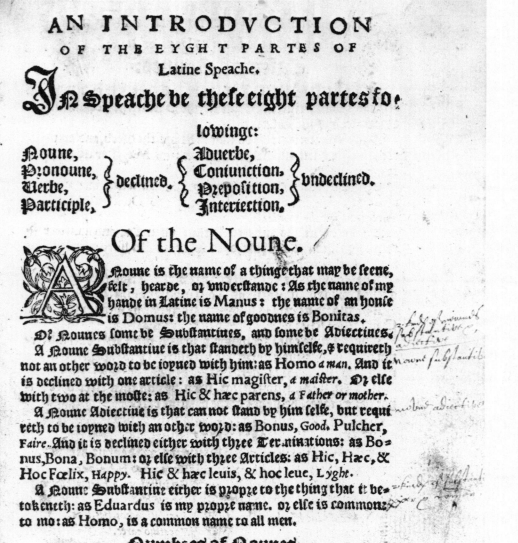

AN INTRODVCTION OF THE
numbre speaketh of mo then one: as Lapides, stones.

Cases of Nounes.

Nounes be declined with six cases, Singularly and Plurally the Nominative, the Genitive, the Dative, the Accusative, the Vocative, and the Ablative.

The Nominative case commeth before the Verb, and answereth to this question, Who or What: as Magister docet, The Maister teacheth.

The Genitive case is knowen by this token Of, and answereth to this question, Whose or wherof: as Doctrina Magistri, The learning of the Maister.

The Dative case is knowen by this token To, and answereth to this question, To whom, or to what: as Do librum magistro, I giue a booke to the Maister.

The Accusative case foloweth the verbe, & answereth to this question, whome, or what: as Amo magistrum, I loue the Maister.

The Vocative case is knowen by calling or speakinge to: as O magister, O Maister.

The Ablative case is commonly ioyned with Prepositions seruing to the Ablative case: as De magistro, Of the Maister. Coram magistro, Before the Maister.

Also In, with, through, for, from, by and then, after the comparative degree, be signes of the ablatiue case.

Articles.

Articles are borowed of the Pronoune, and be thus declined.

Singulariter:
Nominatiuo hic, hæc, hoc.
Genitiuo huius.
Datiuo huic.
Accusatiuo hūc, hanc, hoc.
Vocatiuo caret.
Ablatiuo hoc, hac, hoc.

Pluraliter:
Nominatiuo hi, hæ, hæc.
Genitiuo horum, harum, horum.
Datiuo his.
Accusatiuo hos, has, hæc.
Vocatiuo caret.
Ablatiuo his

55   WILLIAM LILY, *A SHORTE INTRODUCTION OF GRAMMAR . . .* (1567 ED.), sig. A5[r-v]. *Copy in the Bodleian Library; shelfmark: 4°. A. 17. Art. BS. STC 15614. Compare* The Merry Wives of Windsor, *Act IV, sc. 1 :*

Evans. *William, how many numbers is in nouns?*

William. *Two. . . .*

Evans. *What is 'lapis', William?*

William. *A stone.*

Evans. *And what is 'a stone', William?*

William. *A pebble.*

Evans. *No, it is 'lapis'; I pray you remember in your prain.*

William. *Lapis.*

Evans. *That is a good William. What is he, William, that does lend articles?*

William. *Articles are borrowed of the pronoun, and be thus declined: Singulariter, nominativo; hic, haec, hoc.*

Evans. *Nominativo, hig, hag, hog; pray you, mark: genitivo, hujus. Well, what is your accusative case?*

William. *Accusativo, hinc.*

Evans. *I pray you, have your remembrance, child. Accusativo, hung, hang, hog.*

Quickly. *'Hang-hog' is Latin for bacon, I warrant you.*

Evans. *Leave your prabbles, oman. What is the focative case, William?*

William. *O—vocativo, O.*

Evans. *Remember, William: focative is caret.*

Quickly. *And that's a good root.*

Evans. *Oman, forbear.*

Mrs. Page. *Peace.*

Evans. *What is your genitive case plural, William?*

William. *Genitive case?*

Evans. *Ay.*

William. *Genitive: horum, harum, horum.*

Quickly. *Vengeance of Jenny's case; fie on her! Never name her, child, if she be a whore.*

As year in and year out the children toiled at their Latin, they found the precepts they needed in Lily's grammar. For examples they had to be directed elsewhere; first to a manual of brief sentences from Latin authors, such as the famous *Sententiae Pueriles* gathered together by Leonhardus Culmannus — 'a Parcel of dry, moral Sayings . . .', one early educator describes it, that 'might more properly be called *Sententiae Seniles*'.[1] Further moral maxims followed in Erasmus's *Cato*. This was read in the second form, along with Aesop latinized and morally interpreted. To some these texts ranked in educational value second only to Scripture. 'So far as I am able to understand, next unto the Bible, wee have no better books then *Catonis scripta*, & *fabulas Æsopi*, the Works of Cato, and the Fables of Esop'; thus Martin Luther.[2] Terence joined the curriculum next. Plautus was read too, although less often, and in some schools the children acted a scene from either as a weekly exercise. Thus was Shakespeare introduced to classical comedy and the five-act structure of plays.

In the third form the pupils encountered modern Latin moral poets. There was Palingenius, whose *Zodiacus Vitae* acquainted Shakespeare with the great commonplace that all the world's a stage. He also read Baptista Spagnuoli, called Mantuanus, the Carmelite whose bucolic eclogues, fruits of his retirement, became a set text for the English grammar schools. In Mantua the Duke extolled Baptista's memory with a marble statue, crowned with laurel, which he placed alongside the monument to Vergil. Shakespeare praises Baptista in *Love's Labour's Lost*. 'Ah, good old Mantuan!' exclaims Holofernes, and he goes on to quote the opening lines from the *Bucolica*:

I may speak of thee as the traveller doth of Venice:
   Venetia, Venetia,
   Chi non ti vede, non ti pretia.
Old Mantuan, old Mantuan! Who understandeth thee not, loves thee not.

But, as these commendations are voiced by a pedant, they may not be untinged by irony, and quite possibly his creator never got beyond the first eclogue. With these models the boys learned to construe. Their vocabularies they enriched by memorizing Withals's *Short Dictionary* or some similar compilation. This preparation enabled them to proceed to make their own Latins, which they began by translating passages from the Geneva Bible. For Latin speaking they were guided by the conversational colloquies of Corderius, Gallus, or Vives, or the literary dialogues of Castilo and Erasmus: continental humanists all today forgotten, except for Erasmus and (in England, at least) Vives. This was the work of the first three or four years.

Around 1574 or 1575 Shakespeare would have passed from the usher to the master, and entered upon the advanced curriculum of the Upper School. Now the students were taught rhetoric, with enough logic to make it intelligible. For texts they used Cicero's *Ad Herennium* (for general information) and *Topica* (for *inventio*), Susenbrotus (for *elocutio*, the tropes and figures of speech), Erasmus's *Copia* (for *elocutio* applied), and Quintilian, the supreme rhetorician. With these models before them, the children composed epistles, then formal themes, and ultimately — the pinnacle of grammar-school rhetoric — orations and declamations. After prose, verse. 'Though Poetry bee rather for ornament then for any necessary use', conceded one contemporary authority, ' . . . it is not amisse to traine up schollars even in this kinde also. And the rather because it serveth very much for the sharpning of the wit, and is a matter of high commendation, when a schollar is able to write a smooth and pure verse, and to comprehend a great deale of choise matter in a very little roome.'[3] So the scholars were introduced to Ovid, Vergil, and Horace. Ovid, especially the *Metamorphoses*, was the favourite of the schools, and would remain the dramatist's

---

1   John Clarke, *An Essay upon the Education of Youth in Grammar-Schools* (1720), pp. 86–7; cited by Baldwin, *Shakspere's Small Latine*, i. 594n.

2   *Colloquia Mensalia: or, Dr Martin Luther's Divine Discourses . . .*, trans. Henry Bell (1652), p. 532; cited by Baldwin, *Shakspere's Small Latine*, i. 609.

3   Brinsley, *Ludus Literarius*, p. 191; cited (from 1627 ed.) by Baldwin, *Shakspere's Small Latine*, i. 380. In the next century Clarke (also quoted by Baldwin, i. 462–3) takes a more philistine view of versifying: ' . . . the best you can make of it is but a Diversion, a Degree above Fidling . . . . If I might advise therefore, I would have Boys kept wholly from this Sort of Exercise. . . . The Scribbling of paultry, wretched *Verse*, is no Way for them to improve their Parts in' (*Essay upon the Education of Youth in Grammar-Schools* (1720), pp. 65–7).

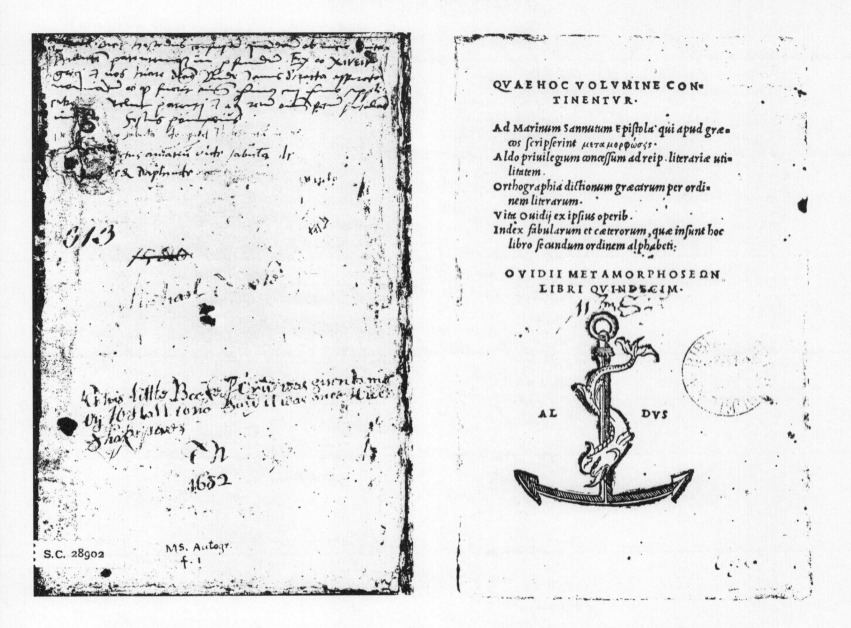

56 OVID, *METAMORPHOSES* (VENICE, 1502). *Bodleian Library, MS. Autogr. f. 1. This small octavo Aldine edition of the* Metamorphoses *was acquired by the Bodleian in the tercentenary year of Shakespeare's birth, and announced in* The Athenæum *for 28 January 1865 ('A New Shakespeare Autograph', pp. 126–7). The abbreviated signature, 'W.ᵐ Sh.ᵉ', is no longer generally accepted as authentic. Sir Edward Maunde Thompson, the distinguished palaeographer, dismissed it as an amateurish forgery based on the shaky third signature to the will, as reproduced in facsimile in the Johnson–Steevens* Plays of William Shakspeare, *2nd ed., 1778 ('Two Pretended Autographs of Shakespeare',* The Library, *3rd Ser., viii (1917), 208–17). Maunde Thompson's article elicited a cautious rejoinder from the Bodleian Librarian, Falconer Madan, who admitted that 'the probabilities are against' authenticity ('Two Lost Causes and What May Be Said in Defence of Them',* The Library, *3rd Ser., ix (1918), 97–105). Madan is, however, surely right in reading the date of the note as 1682 (Maunde Thompson takes it as 1602). The W. Hall referred to cannot be the William Hall of Lichfield cited below (see item 205), for the latter did not take his B.A. at Queen's College, Oxford, until 1694.*

favourite as well. To these poets were sometimes added Juvenal (Hamlet's 'satirical rogue') and Persius. For history the boys read Sallust and Caesar; the *De Officiis* of Cicero gave them moral philosophy. Thus did Shakespeare acquire the small Latin — not so small by the standards of a later age — with which Jonson credits him. In the Upper School he would also attain his less Greek, with the Greek New Testament his first source for constructions.

This then, in outline, is the education that an Elizabethan grammar school provided. It offered about as much formal belletristic instruction as was available in those days for an incipient

Mr William Shakespear.

was borne at Stratford upon Avon in the County of Warwick
his father was a Butcher, & I have been told heretofore by some
of the neighbours, that when he was a boy he exercised his fathers
Trade, but when he kill'd a Calfe, he would doe it in a high style, &
make a Speech. There was at that time another Butchers son in
this Towne, that was held not at all inferior to him for a naturall
witt, his acquaintance & coaetanean, but dyed young. This Wm
being inclined naturally to Poetry and acting, came to London
I guesse about 18: and was an Actor at one of the Play-houses
and did act exceedingly well: now B. Johnson was never a
good Actor, but an excellent Instructor. He began early to
make essayes at Dramatique Poetry, which at that time was very
lowe; and his Playes tooke well: He was a handsome well
shap't man: very good company, and of a very readie and
pleasant smooth Witt. The Humor of .... the Constable
in a Midsomernights Dreame, he happened to take at
Grendon in Bucks wch is the roade from London to Stratford
and there was living that Constable about 1642 when I
first came to Oxon: Mr Jos: Howe is of that parish and knew him.
Ben Johnson and he did gather Humours of men dayly
where ever they came. One time as he was at the Taverne
at Stratford super Avon, one Combes an old rich Usurer
was to be buryed, he makes there this extemporary Epitaph

Ten in the Hundred the Devill allowes
But Combes will have twelve, he sweares & vowes:
If any one askes who lies in this Tombe:
Hoh! quoth the Devill, 'Tis my John o Combe.

He was wont to goe to his native Countrey once a yeare.
I thinke I have been told that he left 2 or 300 li per annum there
and thereabout: to a sister. I have heard Sr Wm Davenant and Mr Thomas Shadwell (who is counted the best Co-
median we have now) say, that he had a most prodigious Witt,
and did admire his naturall parts, beyond all other Dramaticall
writers. He was wont to say, That he never blotted out a line
in his life: sayd Ben: Johnson, I wish he had blotted out a thousand. His Comedies will remaine witt, as long as the English
tongue is understood; for that he handles mores hominum; now
our present writers reflect so much upon particular persons, &
coxcombeities, that 20 yeares hence, they will not be understood.
Though as Ben: Johnson says of him, that he had but little Latine and
lesse Greek, He understood Latine pretty well: for he had been in his younger
yeares a Schoolmaster in the Country.

* I thinke it was Mid-
somer night that he
happened to lye there.

v: his Epitaph
in Dugdales Warw:

B: Johnsons Vnder-
wood.

from Mr ... Beeston.

man of letters. The universities had little to add, for their task was to train up men for the professions: medicine, law, above all divinity. The literary profession, as we know it, did not then exist. 'What of It?' asks T. W. Baldwin in the title of the last chapter of his monumental study, *William Shakspere's Small Latine & Lesse Greeke*, and he offers this summing up:

> If William Shakspere had the grammar school training of his day — or its equivalent — he had as good a formal literary training as had any of his contemporaries. At least, no miracles are required to account for such knowledge and techniques from the classics as he exhibits. Stratford grammar school will furnish all that is required. The miracle lies elsewhere; it is the world-old miracle of genius.[1]

That miracle found expression in London, not Stratford, and its dimensions were apprehended not then but by succeeding generations. In schoolmaster Jenkins's eyes other pupils then in his charge may have held more conspicuous promise. Certainly none fulfilled academic expectations better than William Smith, christened half a year after Shakespeare, on 22 November 1564, the sixth son of Alderman William Smith. The Smiths were evidently favourites of Vicar Bretchgirdle, who, as he lay 'visited with the hand of God', bequeathed books from his library to five of the boys, and left a shilling to young William. (Bretchgirdle did not remember any of the Shakespeares.) Of the twenty-six male children christened in Stratford in the year of Shakespeare's birth, only one, this William Smith, would receive a university education. He was enrolled in Winchester College, and went on to matriculate from Exeter College, Oxford, in 1583. By then the family had removed to Worcester. Having taken his B.A., William Smith lived for a time in Waltham Cross before settling down as a schoolmaster in Loughton, Essex. This was the aptest scholar of Shakespeare's class. In the next century we hear of another exceptional Stratford lad contemporary with the dramatist. The gossip Aubrey, who obtained his information from 'some of the neighbours', informs us that 'There was at that time another Butchers son in this Towne, that was held not at all inferior to him [Shakespeare] for a naturall witt, his acquaintance & coetanean, but dyed young.' Perhaps this extraordinary natural wit graced Adrian Tyler, son of a Sheep Street butcher who had served as constable with John Shakespeare — the dramatist thought of Adrian's brother Richard in his will, so the families evidently remained friendly.[2] Aubrey's anecdote, however, belongs not to the biographical record proper but to the mythos: that accretion of legend and lore which comes to surround the names of famous men. As to whether Stratford indeed nursed a second Bard who died young, history is mute, and posterity has had, perforce, to content itself with one Shakespeare.

Opposite:

57 JOHN AUBREY, BRIEF LIFE OF SHAKESPEARE, 1681. *Bodleian Library, MS. Arch.F.c.37 (formerly Aubrey MS. 6, f. 109). The leaf has been removed from its place in Part I of Aubrey's* Brief Lives *and separately mounted. Transcript: EKC, ii. 252–4;* Aubrey's Brief Lives, *ed. Oliver Lawson Dick (1949), pp. 275–6. In 1792 Malone undertook to edit the* Brief Lives, *but abandoned the project after transcribing 174 lives. He had, however, already printed, for the first time, Aubrey's sketch of Shakespeare in the 1790 edition of the* Plays and Poems, *vol. i, pt. 2, pp. 172–3.*

Aubrey embellishes his lives of several poets — e.g. Marvell, Jonson, Waller — with laureate bays, but he includes no garlands for (among others) Spenser, Beaumont, and Taylor the Water Poet. For another Aubrey entry respecting Shakespeare, see below, item 166.

---

1   Baldwin, *Shakspere's Small Latine*, ii. 663. Baldwin must be reckoned the principal authority for any account of grammar-school education in this period.
2   The possibility is tentatively suggested by ME, 62.

Early Employment and Marriage

How long Shakespeare remained at the King's New School of Stratford-upon-Avon we cannot reliably say. A report from early in the eighteenth century holds that he did not complete the course: the narrowness of John Shakespeare's circumstances, 'and the want of his [i.e. William's] assistance at Home, forc'd his Father to withdraw him from thence'. Thus wrote Nicholas Rowe.[1] Even if permitted to finish his schooling, William would have found himself, at the age of fifteen or thereabouts, confronted with the necessity of earning his living.

The 'aptist and moste propre scholers', wrote Sir Thomas Elyot in his celebrated treatise on the education of the governing classes, 'after they be well instructed in speakyng latine, and understanding some poetes, beinge taken from theyr schole by their parentes', they '. . . either be brought to the courte, and made lakayes [i.e. lackeys] or pages: or els are bounden prentises.'[2] As regards Shakespeare, the first possibility has appealed irresistibly to those biographers who yearn to furnish the prince of poets with noble connections; usurping parental privilege, they place him for adoption in some aristocratic household, as though the sublimities of literary creation could ill spring from prosaic bourgeois soil. The second possibility — that he was bound prentice — probably comes closer to the reality, and has the support of the earliest authorities. Rowe says that the father took his eldest son into 'his own Employment'. In the previous century Aubrey had jotted in his notes: '. . . his father was a Butcher, & I have been told heretofore by some of the neighbours, that when he was a boy he exercised his fathers Trade, but when he kill'd a Calfe, he would doe it in a *high style*, & make a Speech.' Genius will out, even from the mouths of butcher boys.

Although (as he indicates) Aubrey was in touch with local Stratford tradition, his confusion here runs deep. Glovers, as we have seen, were restrained from looking after their own slaughtering; and the picture of a poetical prodigy moved to extempore effusions in the shambles is sufficiently ludicrous. It is true that in an early play, *2 Henry VI*, Shakespeare does indeed recall, with characteristic sympathy, the cruelty of the abattoir:

> And as the butcher takes away the calf,
> And binds the wretch, and beats it when it strays, . . .
> And as the dam runs lowing up and down,
> Looking the way her harmless young one went,
> And can do nought but wail her darling's loss. . . .

But for a lad growing up in a rural community such experience would be natural enough. He might have obtained it in Snitterfield, where his Uncle Henry farmed. Walking down to the Avon from Henley Street, he would have passed the Shambles in Middle Row, behind which the quarrelsome Ralph Cawdrey had his butcher shops. Another interpretation of the Aubrey passage has, however, suggested itself. Does there lurk in his account an obscurely disguised recollection of the boy Shakespeare taking part — with basin, carpet, horns, and butcher's knife and apron — in the Christmas mumming play of the killing of the calf? This traditional pantomime lingered into the present century in some English villages.[3] No matter. It seems a reasonable enough supposition that William was apprenticed in his father's shop.

Reminiscences from this phase of the dramatist's career have been sought, not in vain, in the

---

1 Nicholas Rowe, *Some Account of the Life, &c. of Mr. William Shakespear*, in Shakespeare, *Works*, ed. Rowe (1709), i, pp. ii–iii.
2 Thomas Elyot, *The Boke Named the Governour* (1531 ed.), f. 60ᵛ. Quoted (in 1533 ed.) by Joseph Quincy Adams, *A Life of William Shakespeare* (Boston and New York, 1923), pp. 61–2.
3 I am here obliged to Douglas Hamer's review of *SL* in *Review of English Studies*, N.S., xxxii (1971), 484.

Sam. Ireland del.

58 ANNE HATHAWAY'S COTTAGE. *From Samuel Ireland*, Picturesque Views on the Upper, or Warwickshire Avon, from its Source at Naseby to its Junction with the Severn at Tewkesbury *(1795), facing p. 206. When Ireland and his son William Henry toured the Shakespeare country in the summer of 1794, the Hathaway house was one of the shrines pointed out to them by John Jordan. 'The cottage in which she is said to have lived with her parents is yet standing', Ireland writes, 'and although I have doubts as to the truth of the relation, I have yet given a faithful representation of it in the annexed view. It is still occupied by the descendants of her family, who are poor and numerous. To this same humble cottage I was referred when pursuing the same inquiry, by the late Mr. Harte, of Stratford . . .' (pp. 206–7). This Harte, a butcher, was a descendant of Shakespeare's sister Joan.*

corpus; most lovingly by the Warwickshire antiquary Edgar I. Fripp:

William Shakespeare refers to the hides of oxen and horses, to calf-skin, sheep-skin, lamb-skin, fox-skin, and dog-skin, deer-skin and cheveril. He knew that 'neat's-leather' was used for shoes, sheep's leather for a bridle. 'Is not parchment', asks Hamlet, 'made of sheep-skins?' Horatio replies, 'Ay, my lord, and calf-skins too.' . . . The poet was aware that horsehair was used in bowstrings and 'calves' guts' in fiddle-strings. He notices leathern aprons, jerkins, and bottles, the 'sow-skin bowget' or bag carried by tinkers, and he comments humorously on the capacity of tanned leather to keep out water. He alludes to 'flesh and fell', to the 'greasy fells' of ewes, and, with evident pleasure, to the lamb's 'white fleece'. He knew that the deer's hide was the keeper's perquisite, and we may believe that his father made purchases from the keepers round Stratford. References to cheveril (kid-skin) are much to the point. On account of its softness and flexibility it was used in the making of finer qualities of gloves. Shakespeare speaks of 'a wit of cheveril, that stretches from an inch narrow to an ell broad'. This is technical language, borrowed from his father's business. He mentions also a 'soft cheveril conscience', capable of 'receiving gifts' if the owner will 'please to stretch it', and 'a cheveril glove, . . . how quickly the wrong side may be turned outward'.[1]

If his apprentice days were cluttered with the merchandise of his father's shop, pungent with the aroma of leather, he nevertheless found time — and occasion — for other pursuits. During the long summer twilights of 1582 he must more than once have found his way along the narrow footpath that led west from his home, through green fields, to a clump of farmhouses called Shottery, a mile distant, where the large Hathaway family dwelt. Shakespeare wooed and bedded the farmer's eldest daughter — or did she seduce her boy lover? — and in November they married. Visitors today follow the same path to the house known since 1795 as Anne Hathaway's Cottage, but creeping suburbia, deadlier than any weed, has blighted the pastoral loveliness of the walk.

1 Edgar I. Fripp, *Shakespeare: Man and Artist* (1938), i. 79–80.

F

Marriage is no doubt a crucial event in the histories of most men, but when it occurs in the life of the National Poet it assumes a fateful significance.[1] The episode has given rise to strange reveries of biography — romantic, sentimental, misogynistic — resembling nothing so much as 'those laborious webbes of Learning' which, according to Francis Bacon, the scholastic philosophers spun out of 'no great quantitie of matter, and infinite agitation of wit'. The task of the responsible biographer is to clear away the cobwebs, and sift, as disinterestedly as he may, the facts that chance and industry have brought to light. Those facts are admittedly sometimes perplexing.

Shakespeare's marriage required the official attention of the diocesan consistory court of Worcester, and the relevant records may still be examined by the curious in the muniment room there. The mere existence of such documents is itself of interest, for in Shakespeare's day a marriage certificate, as we know it, did not exist. All that was needed for a legally binding union — one which insured rights of dower and inheritance — was the proclamation of the banns three times in church on successive Sundays or Holy Days, so that anybody with knowledge of an impediment to matrimony might come forward and protest. After that, a ceremony before family, friends, and neighbours. Customarily the setting was the bride's parish, and the wedding was duly entered in the church register. But special circumstances attended this match. The groom was a minor, and his lady pregnant. Anne Hathaway's interesting condition had only lately become evident — she would not deliver until May — but haste in tying the knot was demanded anyway; for the canon law prohibited the asking of the banns during certain seasons. These included the interval from Advent Sunday until the Octave of Epiphany; in 1582, from 2 December until 13 January. That November the last three available days for publishing the banns were the Sundays of 18 and 25 November and St. Andrew's Day, the 30th. This opportunity the couple missed. Did the youth require more time to overcome his father's resistance? In any event, not until the 27th did two friends of the bride's family make the journey to Worcester, twenty-one miles to the west, there to secure the common licence required on such occasions from the consistory court, which was held at the western end of the south aisle of the cathedral. William may have come along also — 'possibly with Anne on his horse behind him', one biographer helpfully suggests — but, being a minor, he had little to contribute by his presence. The then Bishop of Worcester was John Whitgift, shortly to be translated to the see of Canterbury; he was a zealous reformer of ecclesiastical abuses, and in matters of canon law a strict constructionist. Over his consistory court there presided his officers: a chancellor (Richard Cosin in 1582), assisted by a registrar, Robert Warmstry, who acted as executive officer. By the power vested in them, they could authorize exemptions from the usual regulations governing matrimony.

Such dispensations took the form of a licence addressed to the minister (sometimes named) of the church in which the wedding was to take place — this need not have been in the parish where the couple dwelt — and setting forth the special conditions as to banns. In some cases they were to be 'twyst [i.e. twice] lawfully first asked and proclaymed'; sometimes just once, perhaps at the church door at the time of the ceremony. There is even extant one licence in which the banns are dispensed with altogether. These licences were not at all uncommon; in 1582 the Worcester court granted ninety-eight. To secure one, the applicants had to arm themselves with several documents attesting that there were no irregularities of the sort which the banns were intended to discourage. These papers consisted of (1) a sworn allegation, giving the name, address, and occupation of the parties and of the consenting parents or guardians, and the reasons for dispensing with full publication; (2) a letter from the same parents or guardians, or from an intermediary known to the court, certifying — sometimes on oath — that no lawful impediment existed; and (3) a bond, or obligation, to indemnify the bishop and his officers should any legal action arise out of the grant of licence. These documents having been accepted, the petitioners paid a fee, anywhere from around 3s.8d. to 10s.4d., depending upon the nature of the dispensation. In return they were given a licence which was presumably kept by the vicar or curate to whom it was addressed. The clerk of the court recorded the licence in the Bishop's Register. Now the

---

1 Joseph William Gray, *Shakespeare's Marriage* (1905), remains the most authoritative treatment of the subject, although EKC (ii. 43–52) is also especially helpful. On this episode the biographer is well served.

couple were free to marry. Of these several papers most biographical interest would be attached to the first, but unfortunately no sixteenth-century allegations have been preserved for Worcester diocese. Nor have any licences from this period survived. For Shakespeare's marriage we have only the bond and the entry of licence. They answer some questions and pose others.

Couched in the dry legalistic terminology of such documents, the bond (dated 28 November) specifies that William Shagspere and 'Anne hathwey of Stratford in the Dioces of worcester maiden' may, with the consent of the bride's family, lawfully solemnize matrimony, and thereafter live together as man and wife, after one asking of the banns — that is, they may do so, barring any obstacle of precontract, consanguinity, or the like. Should the validity of the union be later impeached, then the bond of £40 posted by the two sureties would be forfeited to 'save harmles the right Reverend father in god Lord John bushop of worcester and his offycers'. In those days £40 was a good sum of money, and would not be lightly risked. The description of Anne as a maiden has interest; some Worcester bonds make an invidious distinction between a 'maiden' and a 'singlewoman', but the Bishop's officers appear not to have enquired too curiously into this bride's virginity or lack thereof.

The sureties, Fulke Sandells and John Rychardson, are described in the bond as husbandmen of Stratford ('. . . ffulconem Sandells de Stratford in Comitatu warwicensi agricolam et Johannem Rychardson ibidem agricolam'). Actually they farmed in Shottery, which formed part of Stratford parish, and were friends of the bride's father. So much we gather from Richard Hathaway's will, in which he names his 'trustie friend and neighbour' Sandells as one of his two supervisors (trustees, we would say), and asks Rychardson to witness the covenant. That no spokesmen for the Shakespeares are named in the bond has aroused dark suspicions in the suspicious. 'The prominence of the Shottery husbandmen in the negotiations preceding Shakespeare's marriage suggests the true position of affairs', writes Sir Sidney Lee magisterially:

Sandells and Richardson, representing the lady's family, doubtless secured the deed on their own initiative, so that Shakespeare might have small opportunity of evading a step which his intimacy with their friend's daughter had rendered essential to her reputation. The wedding probably took place, without the consent of the bridegroom's parents — it may be without their knowledge — soon after the signing of the deed.[1]

Moreover, the clergyman who officiated was 'obviously' of an 'easy temper'. Confident words, 'doubtless' and 'obviously', and here used to imply fraud and collusion for which no evidence exists. As we have seen, William could not have obtained a licence without the knowledge or consent of his father. If the latter wished to prevent the match, he had only to complain to the consistory court. The minister who followed his bishop's instructions, as set forth in a licence, was not demonstrating an easy temper; he was performing his duty. At that time it was the custom for the bondsmen to be friends or kinsmen of the bride, for an unmarried heiress — not her suitor — stood most in need of the law's protection against fortune-hunters.

An heiress she was. So one may gather, even today, from the spaciousness and solidity of Anne Hathaway's Cottage; rather more than a cottage, truly — this twelve-roomed rectangular farmhouse that stands, partly concealed, round the corner of the narrow lane leading from Stratford, and a few yards up from the little brook which glides through Shottery. In Shakespeare's day the house must have stood almost at the edge of the Forest of Arden. It is such a setting as Celia describes in *As You Like It*; the dwelling 'in the purlieus of this forest':

> West of this place, down in the neighbour bottom.
> The rank of osiers by the murmuring stream
> Left on your right hand brings you to the place.

— although the olive trees of Celia's Arden find no counterpart in Anne's.

The house was soundly built on stone foundations, with timber-frame walls filled in with wattle and daub, and open-timbered ceiling. A pair of curved oak timbers, called 'crucks', reach from ground level to the top, where, pegged together, they support the high-pitched roof of thatch. The earliest part of the house, dating from at least the fifteenth century, consists of a

---

1 Sidney Lee, *A Life of William Shakespeare* (4th ed. of revised version, 1925). Lee allowed this passage to remain intact in this last edition during his lifetime, despite the fact that twenty years earlier Gray had refuted Lee's inferences in *Shakespeare's Marriage*, pp. 48–57.

hall or living-room of two twelve-foot bays, and a two-storey east wing. The stone fire-places with oak bressummers — one eight feet wide, the other eleven — were installed in the next century, when an upper floor was added to provide chambers over the hall. The massive old bake-oven in the kitchen still remains, and at the top of the narrow staircase stands the Hathaway bedstead with its elaborately carved posts (in his will Richard speaks of 'twoe joyned beddes in my parlor'). So too the dairy or buttery has been preserved intact. This was a farmhouse, and in former times other farm buildings stood nearby. To the Hathaways this property was known as Hewlands Farm and sheep grazed on its half-yardland — anywhere from ten to twenty-three acres — of pasture and meadowland. The pasturage is gone now, but the garden, with its herbs and roses and posy peas, still flourishes, as does the orchard fragrant with wild flowers and apple trees, while jasmine clings to the Cottage walls.[1]

The Hathaways were substantial Warwickshire yeomen who had dwelt in Shottery for more than one generation. Anne's grandfather John appears as an archer in the muster-rolls, and served his parish as beadle, constable, affeeror, and one of the Twelve Men of Old Stratford (the leading townsmen, actually fifteen, who presided twice a year at the Great Leet). In the subsidy of 1549 his goods were valued at £10, a high assessment. When he died, his son Richard carried on with the farming on the half-yardland called 'Hewland', and also on a toft and half-yardland called 'Hewlyns', as well as on a yardland (with house) late in the tenure of one Thomas Perkyns; in all, the holdings must have come to between fifty and ninety acres. Richard employed a shepherd, Thomas Whittington, and in his will did not forget to pay him the £4.6s.8d. he owed him; we shall be hearing again about this Whittington. The Hathaways and the Shakespeares knew one another, for in 1566 John Shakespeare stood surety for Richard, and was called on to pay debts for him to John Page and Joan Biddle. Richard Hathaway seems to have married twice, and to have had children by both wives, seven altogether. His second wife, Joan, survived her husband by many years; in the spring of 1601 she is described as 'the late decessed Jone Hathaway'. By then Richard lay almost twenty years in his grave.

In the will that he drew up on 1 September 1581, when he was 'sicke in bodye but of perfecte memorye (I thancke my lord God)', Hathaway itemizes bequests for his three daughters and four sons. But he mentions no Anne. Yet that Shakespeare's wife had that Christian name we may hardly doubt: it appears thrice in the marriage licence bond and is inscribed on her gravestone.[2] Richard Hathaway does, however, leave ten marks — £6.13s.4d. — to his daughter Agnes, to be paid out to her on her wedding day. In this period the names Anne and Agnes were interchangeable (the latter being pronounced *Annes*), and in the same will Richard bequeathes one sheep to Agnes, Thomas Hathaway's daughter, although she was christened as Annys. There are many other examples of the same conversion; thus the great theatrical entrepreneur Philip Henslowe calls his wife Agnes in his will, but she was buried as Anne.[3]

The Victorian Shakespeare scholar Halliwell-Phillipps, examining the marriage licence bond, thought that the letters on the seal were R.H., for Richard Hathaway. The seal has long since disintegrated, but (if we may judge from a surviving sketch) the second letter was more likely a *K*, and this seal bearing the letters R.K. closely resembles one in common use in the Registry in the 1580s.[4] Anyway Richard Hathaway was dead when Anne married, as demonstrated by his will, which Halliwell-Phillipps discovered while his life of Shakespeare was printing. That a daughter of Richard Hathaway became Shakespeare's wife is confirmed by Rowe; he never saw the bond, yet says that 'His Wife was the Daughter of one *Hathaway*'. But the matter is clinched by the last will and testament of the faithful Hathaway shepherd. 'Item', declared Thomas Whittington on 25 March 1601, 'I geve & bequeth unto the poore people of Stratford xl⁵ that is in the hand of Anne Shaxspere Wyf unto mʳ Wyllyam Shaxspere & is due dett unto me beyng payd to myne executor by the sayd Wyllyam Shaxspere or his assigns accordyng

1 For a more detailed description of Anne Hathaway's Cottage, see *The Victoria History of the County of Warwick* (1904–69), iii. 235; less technical but no less reliable are the descriptions by Levi Fox in his 'Pictorial Guide', *Anne Hathaway's Cottage* [1964], and *The Shakespearian Properties* (1964).
2 H-P refers to a 'Mʳˢ Ann Shakespeare' as cited in 'a contemporary transcript' of the burial entry (*Outlines*, ii. 372).
3 See ME, 63, for these and other examples.
4 The Worcester seals are studied by Gray in *Shakespeare's Marriage*, pp. 33–5.

60 RICHARD HATHAWAY'S LAST WILL AND TESTAMENT, EXECUTED 1 SEPTEMBER 1581. *Public Record Office, Prob. 11/64/31; formerly among the records of the Prerogative Court of Canterbury in Somerset House. Transcript: H-P, Outlines, ii. 195–6; Joseph William Gray, Shakespeare's Marriage (1905), pp. 221–3; MA, iii. 86–90; E. Vine Hall, Testamentary Papers (1931–3), ii. 15–17. H-P discovered the register with the will in the Prerogative Office, and printed it in the Life, pp. 292–3. BRL (i. 156–7) reproduces and transcribes another contemporary copy (Prob. 10/Box 107). The will is here reduced.*

F*

In the name of god Amen the [...]th day of march anno dm 160[0]2 in the [xliiij]th yeare of the Rayne of oure
soveraigne Lady Elizabeth by the grace of god Quene of England, ffraunce, & Ireland defender of
[...] I Thomas Whittington of Shottery the priest of Stratford vpon Avon [...] the Countie
[...] standinge [...]cke [...] body but of perfect memorye I thanke my lord god ordayne & make
this my last will & testament in maner & forme followinge/ ffirst I begyn the my soull vnto Almighty
god trustinge to be saved by the meritts of Christes passion/ & my body to be buryed in the church yard
of Stratford aforesayd/ It I gyve & bequeth vnto the poore people of Stratford [...]
that is in the hand of Anne Shaxspere wyf vnto [...] William Shaxspere & is due dett vnto me
[...] payd to myne executor by the sayd William Shaxspere or his assignes according to the true
meaninge of this my will/ It I gyve vnto the sayd poore of Stratford iij li to be distributed vnto [...]
theire most nede shall requyre at the discretion of my [...]
distributed to them where most nede shall requyre [...] Order [...]
It I gyve & bequeth vnto the poore of [...]
[...] It I gyve to Marg[ar]et [...] It I gyve to Joan [...]
the elder iij s It I gyve vnto Thomas boye sonne to [...] bore my godson [...] that
[...] to mother Cole iiij d It I gyve to Thomas sonne to Edward Cottell my godson iij s It I gyve
& bequeth toward the repair of the church of Stratford aforesayd iij s iiij d It I gyve & bequeth [...]
[...] part of the Cottre the elder [...]
[...] his children of the sayd Joan [...] Stratford iij s [...] bequest done [...]
[...] my godd [...]
[...] honestly buryed then I gyve & bequeth all the rest of my goodds [...]
[...] whole executors [...] be vnto William Whittyngton my kynsma Thomas Jordayne & make
my full & whole executors of this my last will & testament. And I desire my trusty friends
[...] afore named & John Barber of the same Cottre to be my overseers of this my last will and
Testament & for to [...] for theyr paynes therin to be taken iij s iiij d a piece of them

It I gyve to Thomas Hatheway sonne to the late deceased margret Hathway late of old Stratford
iij s

Detts due to me the sayd testator/

It is John Hathway & William Hathway executors vnto the late deceassed Joan Hathway theyr mother
do owe me that is due to me by there last will iiij markes iij s iiij d
It the sayd John & William Hathway owe me more [xx]s vij d
It John Barber of the Cottre oweth me lij s [...]
It Thomas ffletcher of Lightthorne oweth me [...] iij li xv s iiij d but if the sayd Thomas do [...]
van the sayd sonne the my will is that he shall save back agayne [...] iij s iiij d
It Rychard [...] of Stratford oweth me [...]
It the forsayd John Hathway oweth me more iij s iiij d
It the sayd William Hathway oweth me iiij s
It William [...] of Stratford oweth me iiij s iij s
It one Leonard of [...]ford oweth me ij s
It I owe the sayd John & William Hathway for a quarter of an yeares bord

Wytnesses/. William Gilbard alt higges stripter
John Barber/ Rychard [...]are

Thomas Whittyngton/

his marke/ testator/.

to the true meanyng of this my wyll.' That this is the same Whittington is apparent from the schedule of debts attached to the will, in which several Hathaways are mentioned, including John and William — Anne's brothers or half-brothers — to whom the shepherd owed money for 'a quarter of an yeares bord'.

Of the three daughters remembered in Richard Hathaway's will, Agnes-Anne, being the first mentioned, was probably eldest. No record of her christening has come down, for she was born, it seems, before 1558, when the baptismal registers commence. On the brass marker affixed to Anne Shakespeare's gravestone in the chancel of Stratford Church, she is described as having 'DEPARTED THIS LIFE . . . BEING OF THE AGE OF · 67 · YEARES'. That was on 6 August 1623. Tombstone inscriptions from this period are not invariably reliable — could the engraver have misread a carelessly formed *1* for a *7* in his script, and thus added six years to Anne's lifespan? But in the absence of other evidence we are obliged to accept this unambiguous testimony. Anne was, then, seven or eight years her husband's senior, and twenty-six in 1582; by the standards of those days, growing a bit long in the tooth for the marriage market. She took a teenaged lover, became pregnant, and married him. Did he reluctantly submit, to salvage the reputation of a fading siren of Shottery with whom he had lain in an interlude of midsummer passion? Scholars (as one might expect) have ransacked the corpus for intimations of retrospective regret, and their searches have not gone unrewarded. Thus, Lysander and Hermia in *A Midsummer-Night's Dream*:

> *Lysander.* The course of true love never did run smooth;
> But either it was different in blood . . .
> Or else misgraffed in respect of years —
> *Hermia.* O spite! too old to be engag'd to young.

And, more forcibly, the Duke in *Twelfth Night* to the disguised Viola:

> Let still the woman take
> An elder than herself; so wears she to him,
> So sways she level in her husband's heart.
> For, boy, however we do praise ourselves,
> Our fancies are more giddy and unfirm,
> More longing, wavering, sooner lost and won,
> Than women's are.
> *Viola.*   I think it well, my lord.
> *Duke.* Then let thy love be younger than thyself,
> Or thy affection cannot hold the bent;
> For women are as roses, whose fair flow'r
> Being once display'd doth fall that very hour.

Who can deny the possibility that buried here lies wisdom purchased at the cost of personal *Angst*? Yet we do well to remind ourselves that these comments are spoken not by the author in his own voice, but by the shadows he has created, and that they have an immediate application to the dramatic context. The Duke after all is sentimental and more than a trifle foolish.

Opposite:

61 THOMAS WHITTINGTON'S LAST WILL AND TESTAMENT, 25 MARCH 1601. *Worcestershire Record Office; shelfmark: 008.7; 16/1601. Transcript: EKC, ii. 42–3, gives extracts from both will and schedule. The document is number 72 (i. 168) in BRL, who limits himself to extracts from Chambers's extracts. Whittington is omitted, presumably inadvertently, from BRL's index. On 4 April 1847 Sir Thomas Phillipps forwarded to the Society of Antiquaries his transcript of Whittington's will, which he had discovered at Worcester 'about ten years since', and which he presumed would hold interest, 'however trivial the memorial of so great a bard may be'. The text of the will, minus the schedule of debts, appeared the same year in the Society's journal,* Archaeologia *(xxxii, pp. 444–5). It was first discussed two years later by J. Payne Collier: 'The New Fact Regarding Shakespeare and His Wife, Contained in the Will of Thomas Whittington',* The Shakespeare Society's Papers, *iii (1847), 127–30. Collier infers, from the mention of Anne rather than William Shakespeare, that the playwright was in London at the time the testament was drawn up. Of Phillipps, Collier remarks, 'His name is now indissolubly connected with the biography of our great dramatist.' Joseph William Gray, in* Shakespeare's Marriage *(1905), first printed pertinent entries from the schedule of debts (p. 28). The will is here somewhat reduced.*

62 ENTRY OF MARRIAGE LICENCE 'INTER WILLELMUM SHAXPERE ET ANNAM WHATELEY DE TEMPLE GRAFTON'. *Bishop of Worcester's Register, Worcestershire Record Office; shelfmark: b716.093 BA 2648/10 (i). Transcript: TB, 3 (with Latin translated); MA, iii. 111–12 (Latin translated); EKC, ii. 41; BRL, i. 161. The entry was first published by H-P as an 'illustrative note' to his Outlines, ii. 396. H-P reports that the Revd. T. P. Wadley drew his attention to the record at Worcester some years previously. The subsequent stir is not anticipated by H-P, who concludes simply that 'the scribe must, through some exceptional accident, have mis-written the last four words, the bond itself being of course of infinitely higher authority than the entry, and Temple Grafton not being one of the hamlets of Stratford'.*

These perplexities are slight to those created by the second Shakespeare marriage record in the Worcester muniments. When the clerk of the court entered the grant of a licence in the Bishop's Register on 27 November 1582 (one day earlier than the date on the bond itself), he gave the bride's name as Anne Whateley of Temple Grafton. This second Anne appears here once, and nowhere else. Who is she? In the absence of any facts whatever, biographers have created a persona for the mysterious maiden from Temple Grafton, and made her a principal in a triangular drama — romantic, melodramatic, and moral — in which the passionate Will must choose between Love and Duty.

A version of the scenario full blown is to be found in Anthony Burgess's popular biography:

It is reasonable to believe that Will wished to marry a girl named Anne Whateley. . . . Her father may have been a friend of John Shakespeare's, he may have sold kidskin cheap, there are various reasons why the Shakespeares and the Whateleys, or their nubile children, might become friendly. Sent on skin-buying errands to Temple Grafton, Will could have fallen for a comely daughter, sweet as May and shy as a fawn. He was eighteen and highly susceptible. Knowing something about girls, he would know that this was the real thing. Something, perhaps, quite different from what he felt about Mistress Hathaway of Shottery.

But why, attempting to marry Anne Whateley, had he put himself in the position of having to marry the other Anne? I suggest that, to use the crude but convenient properties of the old women's-magazine morality-stories, he was exercised by love for the one and lust for the other. . . .

I consider that the lovely boy that Will probably was — auburn hair, melting eyes, ready tongue, tags of Latin poetry — did not, having tasted Anne's body in the spring, go eagerly back to Shottery through the early summer to taste it again. Perhaps Anne had already said something about the advantages of love in an indentured bed, away from cowpats and the prickling of stubble in a field, and the word *marriage* frightened Will as much as it will frighten any young man. But, with the irony of things, he fell in love with a younger Anne and himself began to talk about marriage. This Anne was chaste, not wanton and forward, and there was probably no nonsense in her family about allowing consummation of the betrothal. . . .

The special licence meant only two readings of the banns, not the three normally required. Anne, through brawny and powerful friends, is demonstrating that she hath a way.

The other Anne, along with the parents on both sides, must have found out about this. Will had gotten a girl (well, hardly a girl) in the family way and had been trying to evade the penalty. Will gave in, with bitter resignation, and was led to the slaughter, or the marriage bed. The role of honourable Christian gentleman was being forced upon him. This, anyway, is a persuasive reading of the documented facts, but no Shakespeare-lover is necessarily bound to accept it.[1]

Colourful, if a trifle tawdry, this 'persuasive reading' certainly is; but it is not so much biography as imaginative invention, and hence more appropriate to a novel, which Mr. Burgess, in *Nothing Like the Sun*, earlier gave us. Nor does it less strain credulity to surmise (with Sir Sidney Lee) that on that remarkable November day in Worcester a second William Shakespeare — no relation — was granted a licence to marry a second Warwickshire Anne.[2] There are no 'documented facts' about Anne Whateley, only one fact — the Register entry — and so we do not know whether she was 'chaste, not wanton and forward', or 'sweet as May and shy as a fawn'. We cannot even say with reasonable assurance that she ever actually existed.

1   Anthony Burgess, *Shakespeare* (New York, 1970), pp. 57–60. The banns were of course read once, not twice.
2   Lee, *Life of William Shakespeare*, p. 31.

The Worcester clerk appears to have been fairly incompetent — careless, at least — for he got a number of names wrong in the Register. He wrote 'Baker' for 'Barbar', 'Darby' for 'Bradley', 'Edgock' for 'Elcock'. But why 'Whateley' for 'Hathaway'? These names only vaguely resemble one another. The diocesan records show that on the day the Hathaways applied for their licence, on the 27th, the court dealt with forty cases, and one of these concerned the suit of the vicar of Crowle, William Whateley, in arms against Arnold Leight for non-payment of tithes. This Whateley must have been a familiar figure in the court, for his name appears in several records for 1582 and 1583. The clerk, one suspects, was copying from a hastily written temporary memorandum, or from an unfamiliar hand in an allegation; he had just been dealing with Whateley, and by a process of unconscious association made the substitution.[1] A prosaic as well as speculative interpretation, no doubt, of the single document, and a reading hostile to romantic yearnings. But that Anne Whateley, so nubile and blushingly chaste, should owe her very being to the carelessness of a bumbling scribe perhaps has a beauty of its own.

We still may wonder how Temple Grafton enters the picture. The village lies five miles west of Stratford, and three and a half miles in the same direction from Shottery, just south of the high road leading to Alcester. From Temple Grafton, perched on a hill, one can look across the valley to Bredon Hill and the Cotswolds. Only a few of the old houses now remain, an old barn too, and an ancient stone pigeon-house with quaint conical roof; but in Shakespeare's day husbandmen farmed in the four fields of Temple Grafton, and pastured their flocks in the open common or Cow Common, while quarriers and stonemasons earned their bread from the surrounding slate deposits and limestone pits. Perhaps in the early eighties Anne Hathaway was living in Temple Grafton — the Worcester licence entries usually give the bride's residence — or the wedding ceremony may have taken place there.

63 TEMPLE GRAFTON CHURCH. *Sketch by Capt. James Saunders, c. 1800. Shakespeare Birthplace Trust Records Office; shelfmark: ER 1/72, f. 60. The Temple Grafton sketch is on paper watermarked 1794.*

A Puritan survey of Warwickshire clergy, made four years later, describes the vicar of Grafton, John Frith, as 'an old priest & Unsound in religion, he can neither prech nor read well, his chiefest trade is to cure hawkes that are hurt or diseased, for which purpose manie doe usuallie repaire to him'. Bishop Whitgift's officers kept a wary eye on such wayward sympathizers with the Old Faith; in 1580 they had made Frith give bond not to marry without licence 'any persons at any times prohibited by the ecclesiasticall lawes', and to conduct no marriages at other times 'without axinge the bannes in the churche thre Soundayes or holidayes solemly'.[2] Did Shakespeare and his betrothed present their licence to this unsound priest? One recalls again the

---

1   This analysis, with the supporting evidence, is offered by Gray in his chapter, 'Hathaway or Whateley', in *Shakespeare's Marriage*, pp. 21–35. E. R. C. Brinkworth thinks such a clerical error unlikely 'because the Bishop's Register is a neat fair copy written up later from notes or from files of loose documents and not on the actual day when the licence was issued' (*Shakespeare and the Bawdy Court of Stratford* (1972), p. 88). But it is not certain that the Register in this period was copied from a rough draft (see Gray, pp. 24–5); nor, in view of other, demonstrable errors in the Register, is it clear why a mistake in this entry could not have been duplicated. Joseph Hill, in his edition of J. T. Burgess's *Historic Warwickshire* (1892), p. 102 (cited in *MA*, iii. 111), suggests that the clerk's slip was of sight rather than memory.

2   I quote from the transcription of ME, 66.

testament in the Birthplace rooftiles. The parish register of Temple Grafton affords no clue, for it survives only in an incomplete transcript of entries commencing in 1612.

If not in Temple Grafton, then where else might the couple have wed? St. Michael's stands hard by the registry in Worcester, but the marriage is not among those recorded there. Elsewhere in Stratford parish two other chapels (besides Holy Trinity) might have served. One was in Bishopton, slightly to the north of Shottery; the other in Luddington, three miles west of Stratford. The register for St. Peter's, Bishopton, however, begins only in 1591, and that for All Souls, Luddington, in the bishop's transcript, in 1612. In Victorian times S. W. Fullom visited Luddington in quest of information, and in his *History of William Shakespeare* in 1862 he has a curious tale to tell:

The [old parsonage] house is occupied by a family named Dyke, respected for miles round, and here the report of the marriage can be traced back directly for a hundred and fifty years. Mrs. Dyke received it from Martha Casebrooke, who died at the age of ninety, after residing her whole life in the village, and not only declared that she was told in her childhood that the marriage was solemnized at Luddington, but had seen the ancient tome in which it was registered. This, indeed, we found, on visiting the neighbouring cottages, was remembered by persons still living, when it was in the possession of a Mrs. Pickering, who had been housekeeper to Mr. Coles, the last curate; and one cold day burnt the register to boil her kettle![1]

Fullom is elsewhere an eccentric guide,[2] but he is unlikely to have created from whole cloth an account so disarming in its particularities. Still, if this is a true report, it is odd that local tradition did not seize upon it early on. The voluble Jordan, for example, who contemplated the ruins of Luddington chapel around 1780, is silent on the subject. However, Joseph Gray, visiting Stratford shortly after 1900, heard from Edward Flower of the great Warwickshire brewing family that Luddington as the scene of Shakespeare's marriage 'was generally accepted in the neighbourhood early in the last century'.[3] Here we may let the matter rest.

Wherever the rites took place, the fact of the bride's pregnancy agitated some of the earlier biographers, who shook their heads gravely over the Bard's presumed 'antenuptial fornication'. The delinquency, if such it is, will raise few eyebrows in the permissive society; but, in his art if not in life, Shakespeare seems to place a premium on premarital continence. Romeo and Juliet bring to their single night together 'a pair of stainless maidenhoods'. 'One turf shall serve as pillow for us both', Lysander tells Hermia in the wood outside Athens; 'One heart, one bed, two bosoms, and one troth'. But she rejects such proximity to the lover she will marry:

> Nay, good Lysander; for my sake, my dear,
> Lie further off yet; do not lie so near. . . .
> Such separation as may well be said
> Becomes a virtuous bachelor and a maid,
> So far be distant; and good night, sweet friend.

'If', Prospero warns Ferdinand,

> thou dost break her virgin-knot before
> All sanctimonious ceremonies may
> With full and holy rite be minist'red,
> No sweet aspersion shall the heavens let fall
> To make this contract grow; but barren hate,
> Sour-ey'd disdain, and discord, shall bestrew
> The union of your bed with weeds so loathly
> That you shall hate it both.

In *The Winter's Tale* Florizel likens his love to that of Jupiter and golden Apollo, whose

> transformations
> Were never for a piece of beauty rarer,
> Nor in a way so chaste, since my desires
> Run not before mine honour, nor my lusts
> Burn hotter than my faith.

1   S. W. Fullom, *History of William Shakespeare, Player and Poet: with New Facts and Traditions* (1862), p. 202.
2   For an account of Fullom's vagaries, see *SL*, 479–82.
3   Gray, *Shakespeare's Marriage*, p. 236.

The desires of Florizel's creator, it seems, burnt somewhat hotter. Are we to suspect that, sated before the ceremony, he lamented with his own despoiled Lucrece —

> The sweets we wish for turn to loathed sours
> Even in the moment that we call them ours

— and embraced the cynical folk wisdom of a Parolles: 'A young man married is a man that's marr'd'? Some, not a few, have so inferred.

To interpret the episode thus, however, is to be seduced again by selective quotation. An alternative view holds that Shakespeare, far from yielding sullenly to the importunities of kin or conscience, had in fact tied the knot informally before entering into the holy bond of matrimony. Elizabethan custom recognized a troth-plight before witnesses as having the force of a civil marriage. Into such a pre-contract 'by words of the present' — *per verba de praesenti* — Alice Shaw of Hatton and William Holder of Fulbrook entered in 1585. Before two witnesses in her father-in-law's house, she said, 'I do confess that I am your wief and have forsaken all my frendes for your sake, and I hope you will use me well'. With these words she gave William her hand, and he 'used the like words unto her, in effect, and toke her by the hand, and kissed together'. William and Alice used one another less well than this ritual presaged, for shortly thereafter he was suing her about the contract. There is, however, no question that in the eyes of the consistory court they had the status of man and wife.[1] Shakespeare understood these pre-contracts well enough. They figure importantly in *Measure for Measure*, where Claudio, accused of fornication with Julietta, says in his own defence:

> upon a true contract
> I got possession of Julietta's bed.
> You know the lady — she is fast my wife,
> Save that we do the denunciation lack
> Of outward order.

Whether Shakespeare in this fashion got possession of Anne Hathaway's bed we have, of course, no way of determining, and to pursue such speculation may be merely to indulge in (as one biographer puts it) a 'kindly sentiment'. But kindly sentiment has no less claim than unkindly, and troth-plight was common enough in Shakespeare's Warwickshire.

Some antecedent courtship must have gone on. In the third of his celebrated Seven Ages of Man, Jaques describes the lover as

> Sighing like furnace, with a woeful ballad
> Made to his mistress' eyebrow.

If as a young lover Shakespeare composed any woeful ballads for Anne Hathaway, they no longer exist, and into this vacuum the forgers have rushed with ballads of their own, woeful in another sense. In the spacious cycle of the *Sonnets*, however, stands one anomalous amatory poem which has little connection with what has gone before or with what follows, and which is sufficiently ungainly to suggest creative adolescence. It is Sonnet 145:

> Those lips that Love's own hand did make
> Breath'd forth the sound that said 'I hate'
> To me that languish'd for her sake;
> But when she saw my woeful state,
> Straight in her heart did mercy come,
> Chiding that tongue that ever sweet
> Was us'd in giving gentle doom;
> And taught it thus anew to greet:
> 'I hate' she alter'd with an end
> That follow'd it as gentle day
> Doth follow night, who like a fiend
> From heaven to hell is flown away:
>   'I hate' from hate away she threw,
>   And sav'd my life, saying 'not you'.

1 On Alice Shaw and William Holder, and the depositions in their action, see H-P, *Outlines*, i. 64–5; Gray, *Shakespeare's Marriage*, pp. 190–2; ME, 66.

This figure, that thou there seest put
It was for Shakespear's Consort cut
Wherein the Graver had a strife
With Nature to outdo the Life
O had he Her Complexion shewn
As plain as He's the outline Drawn
The plate, believe me, would surpass
All that was ever made in brass.

N C 1708.

D. J.

64 SHAKESPEARE'S CONSORT. *Third Folio (second issue, 1664) in Colgate University Library. A genuine sheet from the 1663 first issue, comprising the title-page and adjoining leaf with the Jonson verses, has been mounted in the Colgate copy. The drawing appears on the verso of the inserted title-page. The accompanying verses, apparently first written out in pencil and then gone over in ink, are not necessarily by the artist who drew the portrait. Drawing and verses were first mentioned publicly by Samuel A. Tannenbaum in the* Shakespeare Association Bulletin *for April 1942 ('A Portrait of Anne Hathaway?', p. 112). They are reproduced, described, and analysed by George M. Friend in 'A Possible Portrait of Anne Hathaway',* Philobiblon, *No. 9 (Spring 1972), 44–51.*

In the concluding couplet could 'hate away' conceivably be a pun — one of those strained word-plays in which the Elizabethans delighted — on 'Hathaway'? So Andrew Gurr has ingeniously suggested: 'Shakespeare's future wife, so the poet says, took the meaning out of "hate" by adding its proper ending, and by so doing made it clear that she did not dislike the poet. Hate-away.'[1] *Hate-away* is not precisely equivalent to *Hathaway*, but then not all the rhymes in this sonnet are all that precise either; and the pronunciation — regarded in the context of Warwickshire dialect of the sixteenth century — makes for a better pun than might at first strike the modern ear.[2] The poem may indeed be a young poet's love token.

Naturally we yearn to visualize the object of so much biographical attention. Was Anne such an Amazonian Venus as the goddess who pursues the lovely Adonis in Shakespeare's first narrative poem? Or was she (despite her years) all yielding maidenly femininity, like Mariana at the moated grange, who plighted *her* troth to the perfidious Angelo? If Jaques's lover celebrates his mistress's eyebrow, at least one biographer has been forthcoming enough to tell us of 'the dark eyebrow of Anne Hathaway, a lovely maiden of the picturesque hamlet of Shottery'. But the dusty vellum yielded by the muniment room vouchsafes no intelligence as to the shade of Anne's eyebrow, nor does it even confirm her loveliness. There survives, however, in a copy of the Shakespeare Third Folio of 1663 in the Colgate University Library in Hamilton, New York, a faded drawing of a young woman wearing an Elizabethan cap and ruff. Accompanying verses identify her as 'Shakespeare's Consort'. The drawing bears the date 1708, and it seems reasonable

1   Andrew Gurr, 'Shakespeare's First Poem: Sonnet 145 , *Essays in Criticism*, xxi (1971), 221–6.
2   See F. W. Bateson's postscript to Gurr, p. 226.

enough to suppose that it belongs to the eighteenth century. The artist, we learn from his great grandson, was Sir Nathaniel Curzon of Kedlestone, and his handiwork is described in the Colgate Folio as a tracing. Did Curzon copy a portrait — long since vanished — of a young, rather soberly attractive Tudor girl, and playfully offer it as an *imago vera* of Shakespeare's wife? That is more plausible (given the facetious tone of the verses) than a theory of deliberate imposition in the manner of the later fabricators; more plausible too than the infinitely more exciting hypothesis that Curzon had somehow stumbled upon an authentic portrait of Anne Hathaway. What remains certain, in the midst of so much that is questionable, is that a year before Nicholas Rowe informed the world that the poet's 'Wife was the Daughter of one *Hathaway*, said to have been a substantial Yeoman in the Neighbourhood of *Stratford*', Shakespeare-lovers had begun to wonder about the lineaments of Shakespeare's consort. That is, if one can trust Curzon's date.

About the next episode in his career the record is mercifully exact. On Sunday, 26 May 1583 — Trinity Sunday, the church's feast day — vicar Henry Heicroft christened the first grandchild of Alderman John Shakespeare. Her parents named the child Susanna. That spring, in April, two other infants had been baptized as Susanna, but the name, with its associations appealing

65 CHRISTENING OF SUSANNA SHAKESPEARE, 26 MAY 1583. *Stratford parish register, baptisms, f. 29. Shakespeare Birthplace Trust Records Office; shelfmark: DR 243/1. For a description of the register, see above, p. 12, and item 10.*

66 CHRISTENING OF HAMNET AND JUDITH SHAKESPEARE, 2 FEBRUARY 1585. *Stratford parish register, baptisms, f. 22ᵛ. Shakespeare Birthplace Trust Records Office; shelfmark: DR 243/1.*

to Puritans, was still rather novel in Stratford, first appearing in the parish register in 1574.[1] Less than two years later Anne gave birth to twins, a boy and a girl. The vicar had meanwhile removed to a richer benefice in Rowington, so the twins were christened by his successor on 2 February 1585. Richard Barton of Coventry, who officiated, is described in a Puritan survey as 'a precher, learned, zealous, & godlie, & fit for the ministerie'.[2] The Shakespeares named their offspring Hamnet and Judith, after their neighbours and lifelong friends the Sadlers, who lived in a house at the corner of the High Street and Sheep Street, next to the Corn Market. When in 1598 Judith and Hamnet Sadler produced a son, they called him William.

By 1585 the family of William Shakespeare was complete. Before achieving his majority he had acquired a wife and three children. They did not yet have a house of their own — that day lay a dozen years off — and the roof over their heads was probably provided by the capacious homestead in Henley Street. We do not know whether William felt, with Milton's Adam, that the world was all before him, but before long his wandering steps would take him from Stratford on his solitary way. His wife did not go with him hand in hand, but neither did he turn his back permanently on the Eden, if such it was, of his youth.

1 ME, 70.
2 Cited by ME, 51.

8

The Lost Years

From 1585, when the twins were born, until 1592, when we hear about Shakespeare in a quite different context, the documentary record presents a blank. This is the interval that scholarship has designated the Lost Years. They are not, however, barren of legend, which flourishes in such voids.

Legendary heroes have legendary thirsts. If we may trust the mythos, Shakespeare quaffed deep draughts of good Warwickshire brown ale. He may well have been on intimate terms with local taps and tapsters. In *The Taming of the Shrew* Christopher Sly, 'old Sly's son of Burton Heath', boasts:

Ask Marian Hacket, the fat ale-wife of Wincot, if she know me not; if she say I am not fourteen pence on the score for sheer ale, score me up for the lying'st knave in Christendom. What! I am not bestraught. [*Taking a pot of ale*] Here's —
    3 Servant. O, this it is that makes your lady mourn!

Certainly Shakespeare knew the little village of Barton on the Heath, situated in a stretch of barren ground fifteen miles south of Stratford, for there dwelt his prosperous uncle Edmund Lambert. He had married Joan Arden, Mary Shakespeare's eldest sister but one. As to whether William ever encountered a fat ale-wife in Wincot, a hamlet some five miles south-west of Stratford, history is discreetly silent; but Hackets then lived in the parish. In the eighteenth century Francis Wise of the Bodleian Library journeyed to Stratford and its environs in search of anecdotes about the poet. One of the places he visited was Wincot, and his enquiries there supplied Thomas Warton, the Professor of Poetry at Oxford, with a note for his glossary to Shakespeare: '*Wilnecote* is a village in *Warwickshire*, with which *Shakespear* was well acquainted, near *Stratford*. The house kept by our genial hostess still remains, but is at present a mill.'[1] *The Taming of the Shrew* teases with its local allusiveness.

A grateful public first learned of the toping exploits of the young Shakespeare from the *British Magazine* in 1762. In that year an anonymous correspondent composed a 'Letter from the Place of Shakespear's Nativity' while putting up at the White Lion Inn near the top of Henley Street. His 'chearful landlord', the correspondent reports, took him to the house where the great man was born.

From thence my landlord was so complaisant as to go with me to visit two young women, lineal descendants of our great dramatic poet: they keep a little ale-house, some small distance from Stratford. On the road thither, at a place called Bidford, he shewed me, in the hedge, a crab-tree, called Shakespear's canopy, because under it our poet slept one night; for he, as well as Ben Johnson, loved a glass for the pleasure of society; and he having heard much of the men of that village as deep drinkers and merry fellows, one day went over to Bidford, to take a cup with them. He enquired of a shepherd for the Bidford drinkers; who replied, they were absent; but the Bidford sippers were at home; and I suppose, continued the sheep-keeper, they will be sufficient for you: and so indeed they were. He was forced to take up his lodging under that tree for some hours:

67 'LETTER FROM THE PLACE OF SHAKESPEAR'S NATIVITY', *BRITISH MAGAZINE, OR MONTHLY REPOSITORY FOR GENTLEMEN AND LADIES*, iii (1762), 302. *Reprinted in EKC, ii. 286–7.*

The story surfaces too late to have more force than that of traditional anecdote. Once told, it was embroidered in the retelling. Around 1770 that doubtful repository of Stratford lore, John Jordan, furnished an account of the morning after the Bidford débâcle. Shakespeare's companions roused him, and entreated him to resume the contest, but, declining — he had had

---

1   William Shakespeare, *Works*, ed. Sir Thomas Hanmer (2nd ed., 1770), vi, *Glossary*, s.v. *Wincote*; EKC, ii. 288.

enough — the poet surveyed the adjoining hamlets, and delivered himself of an extemporaneous doggerel rhyme. 'I have drunk', he declaimed, 'with

> Piping Pebworth, Dancing Marston,
> Haunted Hillborough, Hungry Grafton,
> Dadgeing Exhall, Papist Wicksford,
> Beggarly Broom, and Drunken Bidford.'[1]

A quarter of a century later Samuel Ireland stood, overcome with emotion, before the tree which had spread its shade over Shakespeare, 'and sheltered him from the dews of the night'. The truth of the relation he did not doubt — 'it is certain that the Crab Tree is known all round the country by the name of Shakspeare's Crab; and that the villages to which the allusion is made, all bear the epithets here given them: the people of Pebworth are still famed for their skill on the pipe and tabor: Hillborough is now called Haunted Hillborough; and Grafton is notorious for the poverty of its soil.'[2]

68 SHAKESPEARE'S CRABTREE. *From Samuel Ireland,* Picturesque Views on the Upper, or Warwickshire Avon, from its Source at Naseby to its Junction with the Severn at Tewkesbury (*1795*), *p. 232.*

The splendid crabtree, which Ireland sketched for his *Picturesque Views,* is now long since gone, having been devoured by the souvenir hunters. On 4 December 1824 what remained was dug up and carted to the Revd. Henry Holyoakes of Bidford Grange. 'For several years previously', the Stratford antiquary Robert Bell Wheler commented mournfully, 'the Branches had entirely vanished from the further depradations of pious votaries; & the stock had mouldered to touchwood, the roots were rotten, & the time worn remains totally useless.'[3] No marker commemorates the spot for the modern pilgrim.

Perhaps it is just as well; Shakespeare's drinking exploits may have no more authoritative basis than (in Chambers's phrase) 'the inventiveness of innkeepers'. But, if we may give credence to another and much better established tradition, the Warwickshire lads amused themselves with more exciting — and dangerous — diversions than carousing tournaments. The story of Shakespeare the Deerslayer appears full blown in Nicholas Rowe's preface to his 1709 edition. It is a picturesque relation deriving, one expects, from local Stratford lore passed on to Rowe's informant, the actor Betterton. Having taken on the responsibilities of matrimony, Rowe writes,

---

1   John Jordan, from 'a manuscript written about the year 1770', printed by H-P, *Outlines,* ii. 326. The manuscript is now in the Folger Shakespeare Library (shelfmark: S.a. 118), but the text is incomplete.

2   Samuel Ireland, *Picturesque Views on the Upper, or Warwickshire Avon . . .* (1795), p. 233.

3   R. B. Wheler, *Collectanea de Stratford,* p. 202, in Shakespeare Birthplace Trust Records Office; shelfmark: MS. ER 1/8.

In this kind of Settlement he continu'd for some time, 'till an Extravagance that he was guilty of, forc'd him both out of his Country and that way of Living which he had taken up; and tho' it seem'd at first to be a Blemish upon his good Manners, and a Misfortune to him, yet it afterwards happily prov'd the occasion of exerting one of the greatest *Genius*'s that ever was known in Dramatick Poetry. He had, by a Misfortune common enough to young Fellows, fallen into ill Company; and amongst them, some that made a frequent practice of Deer-stealing, engag'd him with them more than once in robbing a Park that belong'd to Sir *Thomas Lucy* of *Cherlecot*, near *Stratford*. For this he was prosecuted by that Gentleman, as he thought, somewhat too severely; and in order to revenge that ill Usage, he made a Ballad upon him. And tho' this, probably the first Essay of his Poetry, be lost, yet it is said to have been so very bitter, that it redoubled the Prosecution against him to that degree, that he was oblig'd to leave his Business and Family in *Warwickshire*, for some time, and shelter himself in *London*.

69 NICHOLAS ROWE, *SOME ACCOUNT OF THE LIFE, &C. OF MR. WILLIAM SHAKESPEAR*, IN SHAKESPEARE, *WORKS*, ED. ROWE (1709), i, p. v.

7. William Shakespeare.

William Shakespeare was born at Stratford upon Avon in Warwickshire about 1563.4. much given to all unluckiness in Stealing venison & Rabbits, particularly from Sr Lucy who had him oft whipt & Sometimes Imprisoned & at last made Him fly his Native Country to his great Advancemt. but His reveng was so great that he is his Justice Clodpate and calls him a great many in allusion to his name bore three lowses rampant for his Arms

From an Actor of Playes, he became a Composer

Ætat. 53.

He dyed Apr. 23. 1616. probably at Stratford, for there he is buryed, and hath a Monument on wch He lays a Heavy curse upon any one who shal remoove his bones He dyed a papist.

Dugd. p. 520.

70 RICHARD DAVIES ON SHAKESPEARE, DEER-STEALER AND PAPIST. *Fulman MS. xv (Corpus Christi College, Oxford, MS. 309), no. 7, f. 22, now in the Bodleian Library. Transcript: EKC, ii. 257. Malone saw this manuscript in the Corpus Christi archives in 1792, when he mentions it in a letter to James Davenport, then the vicar of Stratford. The passage on the poaching is printed by Malone in the 1821 Variorum, and there ascribed by him to Davies (ii. 121–3), an ascription confirmed by Chambers on the basis of an examination of Davies's signed script (EKC, ii. 255–6). The memoranda to which Davies added his notes were set down by William Fulman, a scholar of Corpus Christi.*

Other versions of the story filtered down. One appears in a memorandum jotted down in Oxford late in the seventeenth century by an obscure clergyman, Richard Davies. He was perhaps then the chaplain of Corpus Christi College. Later he became parson of Sandford-on-Thames in Oxfordshire, and afterwards rector of Sapperton, Gloucestershire; he finished his days as Archdeacon of Coventry in the diocese of Lichfield. So he never strayed very far from the Shakespeare country. The antiquary Anthony Wood, not celebrated for his benevolence, knew Davies, and described him as looking 'red and jolly, as if he had been at a fish dinner at C[orpus] C[hristi] C[ollege], and afterwards drinking — as he had been'. We do not know if Davies was in his cups when he wrote that Shakespeare was 'much given to all unluckinesse in Stealing venison & Rabbits particularly from Sr Lucy who had him oft whipt & Sometimes Imprisoned & at last made Him fly his Native Country to his great Advancement'. The victim, however, took an artist's revenge by portraying his persecutor as Justice Clodpate, and identifying this 'great man' by the 'three lowses rampant for his Arms'. The jolly parson's memory is not functioning very well: he cannot recall Lucy's christian name, and he has confused Clodpate — 'a hearty true *English* Coxcomb' in *Epsom Wells*, a play by Davies's contemporary, Thomas Shadwell — with Justice Shallow in *The Merry Wives of Windsor*. Rowe, who cannot have known Davies's notes, gets the reference right in his passage on Falstaff:

> Amongst other Extravagances, in *The Merry Wives of* Windsor, he has made him a Dear-stealer, that he might at the same time remember his *Warwickshire* Prosecutor, under the Name of Justice *Shallow*; he has given him very near the same Coat of Arms which *Dugdale*, in his Antiquities of that County, describes for a Family there, and makes the *Welsh* Parson descant very pleasantly upon 'em.

71 NICHOLAS ROWE, *SOME ACCOUNT OF THE LIFE, &C. OF MR. WILLIAM SHAKESPEAR*, IN SHAKESPEARE, *WORKS*, ED. ROWE (1709), i, pp. xvii, xviii.

In the play Falstaff has 'committed disparagements' upon Shallow, a Gloucestershire justice of the peace. 'Knight', he upbraids the fat roisterer, 'you have beaten my men, kill'd my deer, and broke open my lodge.' In retaliation Shallow has come to Windsor to make a Star Chamber case out of the affair. In the opening lines of *The Merry Wives of Windsor*, Shallow's kinsman, Slender, speaks admiringly of the justice who can write himself 'Armigero', or esquire, in any bill:

Shallow. Ay, that I do; and have done any time these three hundred years.
Slender. All his successors, gone before him, hath done't; and all his ancestors, that come after him, may: they may give the dozen white luces in their coat.
Shallow. It is an old coat.
Evans. The dozen white louses do become an old coat well; it agrees well, passant; it is a familiar beast to man, and signifies love.
Shallow. The luce is the fresh fish; the salt fish is an old coat.
Slender. I may quarter, coz.

Luces and louses; it is a predictable Elizabethan pun. From Rowe onwards commentators have noted that the Lucys of Charlecote punningly adopted as their heraldic device the luce, a freshwater fish more familiarly known (in its fully grown state) as the pike. The Lucys bore the arms *Vair, three luces hauriant argent*, and on one of their tombs in Warwick the three luces on the coat are quartered, thus making up the dozen to which Slender refers. If this is what the passage in the play is about, Shakespeare, a decade or more after the event, is taking an obscurely allusive revenge upon the country justice who had invoked the rigours of the law for a venial offence indulged in by high-spirited youths of more elevated social position than the bailiff's son.

A third report furnishes the ballad Rowe mentions. This Malone found late in the century, in a manuscript 'History of the Stage', and published without attempting to conceal his scepticism:

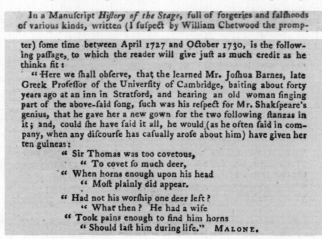

In a Manuſcript *Hiſtory of the Stage*, full of forgeries and falſhoods of various kinds, written (I ſuſpeᶜt by William Chetwood the promp-

ter) ſome time between April 1727 and Oᶜtober 1730, is the follow-ing paſſage, to which the reader will give juſt as much credit as he thinks fit:

"Here we ſhall obſerve, that the learned Mr. Joſhua Barnes, late Greek Profeſſor of the Univerſity of Cambridge, baiting about forty years ago at an inn in Stratford, and hearing an old woman ſinging part of the above-ſaid ſong, ſuch was his reſpeᶜt for Mr. Shakſpeare's genius, that he gave her a new gown for the two following ſtanzas in it; and, could ſhe have ſaid it all, he would (as he often ſaid in com-pany, when any diſcourſe has caſually aroſe about him) have given her ten guineas:

"Sir Thomas was too covetous,
"To covet ſo much deer,
"When horns enough upon his head
"Moſt plainly did appear.

"Had not his worſhip one deer left?
"What then? He had a wife
"Took pains enough to find him horns
"Should laſt him during life." MALONE.

72 WILLIAM SHAKESPEARE, *PLAYS AND POEMS*, ED. EDMOND MALONE (1790), vol. i, pt. 1, pp. 106-7n. *Malone printed the passage again in the Variorum, this time unequivocally labelling as spurious the verses of 'a songstress in Stratford' (ii. 144). The manuscript History of the Stage seems to have disappeared.*

Joshua Barnes, who lived from 1654 to 1712, was a Greek scholar and antiquary who belonged to Emmanuel College, Cambridge.

A different version of the ballad was set down, around the middle of the eighteenth century, by William Oldys in the notes he compiled for a life of Shakespeare which, in the general disorder of his life, he never got round to writing. The notes perished along with the scheme, but not before George Steevens had seen the 'several quires of paper' covered with Oldys's 'laborious collections', and made extracts from them for his 1778 *Shakspeare*:

Mr. William Oldys, (Norroy King at Arms, and well known from the ſhare he had in compiling the *Biographia Britannica*) among the colleᶜtions which he left for a *Life of Shakeſpeare*, ob-ſerves, that—"there was a very aged gentleman living in the neighbourhood of Stratford, (where he died fifty years ſince) who had not only heard, from ſeveral old people in that town, of Shakeſpeare's tranſgreſſion, but could remember the firſt ſtanza of that bitter ballad, which, repeating to one of his acquaintance, he preſerved it in writing; and here it is, neither better nor worſe, but faithfully tranſcribed from the copy which his relation very curteouſly communicated to me."

"A parliemente member, a juſtice of peace,
"At home a poor ſcare-crowe, at London an aſſe,
"If lowſie is Lucy, as ſome volke miſcalle it,
"Then Lucy is lowſie whatever befall it:
"He thinks himſelf greate,
"Yet an aſſe in his ſtate,
"We allowe by his ears but with aſſes to mate.
"If Lucy is lowſie, as ſome volke miſcalle it,
"Sing lowſie Lucy, whatever befall it."

73 SHAKESPEARE, *WORKS*, ED. GEORGE STEEVENS (1778), ii, *THE MERRY WIVES OF WINDSOR*, p. 223n.

Before the century was out, another eminent Shakespearian, Edward Capell, had identified the aged gentleman:

—Mr. Thomas Jo-nes, who dwelt at Tarbick a village in Worceſterſhire a few miles from Stratford on Avon, and dy'd in the year 1703. aged upwards of ninety, remember'd to have heard from ſe-veral old people at Stratford the ſtory of Shakeſpeare's robbing ſir Thomas Lucy's park; and their account of it agreed with Mr. Ro-we's, with this addition — that the ballad written againſt ſir Thomas by Shakeſpeare was ſtuck upon his park gate, which exaſperated the knight to apply to a lawyer at Wa-rwick to proceed againſt him: Mr.

Jones had put down in writing the firſt ſtanza of this ballad, which was all he remember'd of it, and Mʳ. Thomas Wilkes (my grandfather) tranſmitted it to my father by memory, who alſo took it in writing, and his copy is this;—"*A Parliamente member a Juſtice of Peace,| At Home a poore Scarecrow at London an Aſse.| If Lowsie is Lucy as ſome Volke Miſcalle it| Then Lucy is Lowsie whatever befalle it| He thinkes himſelfe greate| Yet an Aſse in his State | We allowe by his Eares but with Aſses to mate| If Lucy is Lowsie as ſome Volke miſcalle it| Sing [O] Lowsie Lucy whatever befalle it.*"— an exact tranſcript, bating the *O* ; to which is added a note, telling us—that the people of those parts

pronounce "Lowsie like Lucy:"— Sir Hugh's wit upon *luces* in the paſſage before us, and the deſcription of Shallow's *ſcare-crow* perſon in " 2. H. 4." p. 63, give (as was ſaid before) to this ſtanza the appearance of genuineneſs ; which as the Poet's *primitiæ*, and a ſort of comment beſides upon the laſt-mention'd paſſage in him, it was thought might be acceptable : Mʳ. Jones, of whom we had it originally, was alſo the hander-down of that anecdote which has been given you in a note upon "*a. y. l. i.*" at 40, 4; and of this anecdote, Mʳ. Wilkes (in the letter that brought the ſtanza) quotes another confirmer in the perſon of Mʳ. Oldys, a late ſtage-antiquarian.

74 SHAKESPEARE, *WORKS*, ED. EDWARD CAPELL; NOTE ON *THE MERRY WIVES OF WINDSOR*, IN *NOTES* (1780), iii. 75. *The passage is discussed by Malone, and reprinted as a note, with this prefatory comment: 'I have endeavoured to exhibit what Mr. Capel has left on this subject, in intelligible language; but am not sure that I understand him rightly. As a specimen of his style, I will add his own words, which the reader will interpret as he can' (ii. 138–41). The inelegancies of Capell's style did not escape remark by members of the Literary Club. 'If the man would have come to me', Dr. Johnson owned to his valued friend Bennet Langton, 'I would have endeavoured to "endow his purposes with words;" for, as it is, "he doth gabble monstrously"' (Boswell's Life of Johnson, ed. George Birkbeck Hill (rev. L. F. Powell; Oxford, 1934–40), iv. 5).*

There may be confusion here, for the burial register for Tardebigge, as the village is today known, lists no Thomas Jones in 1703, or around that time, although it does record the death of an Edward Jones that year.

Having once taken root, the deer-poaching legend would bear strange fruits of romantic elaboration. From a note to the memoir of Shakespeare in 1763, signed 'P', and identified as the contribution of Philip Nichols, a proprietor of the *Biographia Britannica*, we learn of the unrelenting hostilities between these mighty opposites, the glover's son and the justice of the peace, and the curious means by which conciliation at last came about:

[D] *He made a ballad upon the Knight.*] This ballad was not the only ſhaft which he let fly againſt his proſecutor, whoſe anger drove him to the extreme end of ruin, where he was forced to a very low degree of drudgery for a ſupport. How long the Knight continued inexorable is not known ; but it is certain, that Shakeſpeare owed his releaſe at laſt to the Queen's kindneſs.

75 'WILLIAM SHAKESPEARE', *BIOGRAPHIA BRITANNICA* (1747–66), vol. vi, pt. 1, p. 3628. *Reprinted in EKC, ii. 287. A manuscript note on the title-page of the Bodleian copy identifies 'P' as Philip Nichols, who contributed a number of articles to the* Biographia Britannica. *The shaft referred to in the passage is* The Merry Wives of Windsor.

Much later, in the next century, a descendant of the Lucys reported that not the Queen but her special favourite, Robert Dudley, Earl of Leicester, interceded to stay the vengeful Knight from prosecuting a crime punishable by death; subsequently Shakespeare wrote *The Merry Wives of Windsor* to please Leicester.[1] Such belated fancies, products of the myth-making imagination,

1 Mary Elizabeth Lucy, *Biography of the Lucy Family, of Charlecote Park, in the County of Warwick* (1862), pp. 12–13.

need no longer detain the sober biographer; but the essential story of poaching, capture, prosecution, and flight has come down in four separate versions — those of Davies, Rowe, Barnes, and Jones (*via* Oldys and Capell) — all presumably deriving from Stratford gossip of the late seventeenth century. Does this drama have the ring of truth?

The episode, we are told, took place in Charlecote park. Almost a century ago Henry James stood in summer twilight among the majestic oaks and ancient elms of that park, 'whose venerable verdure seems a survival from an earlier England and whose innumerable acres, stretching away, in the early evening, to vaguely seen Tudor walls, lie there like the backward years receding to the age of Elizabeth'.[1] The Great House, with its park, stands on the Avon's banks, four miles upstream from Stratford, in the level open country of the Feldon. On the west side the river's waters sweep the terrace steps; to the south a stately avenue of lime trees leads down to the old Stratford bridle road. Lucys had lived at Charlecote for generations, but not until the virus of a new malady, *la folie de bâtir*, infected the English gentry in the mid-sixteenth century did one, our Thomas (not yet knighted), rebuild his old manor house. Oaks shading the grounds furnished the open timbers for the roof of his Great Hall, from which a door opened onto the river bank. Atop the leaded cupolas crowning the octagonal turrets of the four corners of the many-gabled house, and the twin turrets of the gatehouse, gilt weather-vanes reflected the morning sun. This splendid house, completed in 1558, was the first Elizabethan mansion in Warwickshire.

Surely Shakespeare would know this part of the world: tramping across the fields from his uncle's farm in Snitterfield, two miles away, he would glimpse the weather-vanes through the surrounding foliage. Today fallow deer roam the rolling grounds of Charlecote, but they were not introduced there until the eighteenth century. Nor did the estate in Shakespeare's time boast a park to lure clandestine huntsmen. ('The word *park* indeed properly signifies any enclosure; but yet it is not every field or common, which a gentleman pleases to surround with a wall or paling, and to stock with a herd of deer, that is thereby constituted a legal park: for the king's grant, or, at least immemorial prescription, is necessary to make it so.' Thus Blackstone.[2]) What Lucy maintained was a free-warren whose dense undergrowth sheltered rabbits and hares and foxes, wood-pigeons and pheasants, and other beasts and fowls of warren. One would class fallow deer with beasts of chase. Still, the great Elizabethan judge and legal authority Sir Edward Coke included roe deer among beasts of warren, and these may have browsed in Charlecote. The provisions of the Act of 1563 apparently applied to deer in any enclosure, not just to those in legally empaled parks. Moreover Davies (as we have seen) mentions rabbits as well as venison. There was enough game in this warren to justify the employment of the several keepers whose names appear in Sir Thomas Lucy's Account Book: Antony and Humfrey, George Cox, 'keeper of my coney warren', George Scales the falconer, and others. Did one of these servants apprehend the poacher as he crouched over his quarry, and hale him, with ensanguined hand in bosom and downcast eye, before the imperious lord of the manor, as he sat horsed outside his gatehouse, with his lady, hawk, and hounds? So Joseph Nash evoked the historic scene for Victorian audiences in his survey of *The Mansions of England in the Olden Time*.

But Charlecote has had to compete with another setting for this melodramatic episode. Late in the eighteenth century, custodians of the mythos, aware that Sir Thomas kept no park at Charlecote, shifted the scene across the river to Fulbrook, two miles north, and midway between Stratford and Warwick.

Overleaf:

76 'CHARLCOTE, WARWICKSHIRE'. *From Joseph Nash,* The Mansions of England in the Olden Time *(1839–49), Third Ser., no. XV. Although persuaded that the poaching episode took place in Fulbrook park, Nash (1809–78) indulged 'a painter's licence' by setting his scene at Charlecote. He is no mere recorder of the stones of Britain. Nash shows the houses not as they then were, but as they had been, 'glowing [in the words of his editor] with the genial warmth of their fire-sides, and enlivened with the presence of their inmates and guests, enjoying the recreations and pastimes, or celebrating the festivals of our ancestors'. This item is reduced.*

1 Henry James, *English Hours* (1905), p. 201. This chapter, 'In Warwickshire', is dated 1877.
2 William Blackstone, *Commentaries on the Laws of England* (1765–9), ii. 38; cited by Edmond Malone in *The Life of William Shakspeare* (Shakespeare, *Plays and Poems*, ed. Malone (1821), ii. 147).

G*

CHARLCOTE, WARWICKSHIRE.

In his *Picturesque Views* Samuel Ireland reported,

WITHIN this park is now ftanding, on a ſpot called Daiſy Hill, a farm houſe, which was antiently the keeper's lodge. To this lodge it is reported our Shakſpeare was conveyed, and there confined at the time of the charge, which is ſuppoſed to have been brought againſt him. This ſuppoſition, how flight ſoever the foundation of it may be, I yet thought ſufficient to give an intereſt to the ſpot in which it is preſumed to have paſſed, and under that idea I have ſubjoined a ſketch of the preſent building.

77 SAMUEL IRELAND, *PICTURESQUE VIEWS ON THE UPPER, OR WARWICKSHIRE AVON, FROM ITS SOURCE AT NASEBY TO ITS JUNCTION WITH THE SEVERN AT TEWKESBURY* (1795), p. 154.

In 1828 a famous visitor to Charlecote was told by a descendant of its builder that Shakespeare had stolen his deer from Fulbrook. 'The tradition went', Sir Walter Scott noted in his journal for 8 April, 'that they hid the buck in a barn, part of which was standing a few years ago but now totally decayd.'[1] Today a few nineteenth-century dwellings near the site of Daisy Hill commemorate the tradition by still bearing the name of Deer Barn Cottages. The transfer does not, however, accomplish very satisfactorily the purpose for which it was designed. Henry VIII, it is true, had granted custody of the old royal park of Fulbrook, with its little castle built by the Duke of Bedford, to a progenitor of the Elizabethan Lucys. But subsequently the park fell into disrepair: weeds overran it, the palings tumbled down, and a new keeper, Sir William Compton, had the bricks carted off from the ruined castle to help create the glories of Compton Wynyates. Local sportsmen regarded the straggling remnants of the deer population as fair game. Before 1557 Fulbrook had been disparked. Not until 1615 did another Sir Thomas Lucy buy the lands and messuage, and enclose it with a new fence.

The setting for the story is not in any event all that crucial, for a justice of the peace could try a poacher arrested anywhere within his jurisdiction. But no officer could have ordered a whipping, because the crime (according to the operative game law) constituted a trespass, not a felony, and

1   *The Journal of Sir Walter Scott*, ed. W. E. K. Anderson (Oxford, 1972), p. 454.

was punishable by a fine amounting to three times the damages, or imprisonment not exceeding three months. If the escapade could be construed as a riot, that might bring a stiffer penalty, and if Shakespeare actually wrote a bitter ballad, that could bring into play the statutes governing criminal libels.

The legend emphasizes the severity of the magistrate, and the ballad mocks the cuckold's horns of an asinine M.P.; so it is well to consider the character of Sir Thomas. The eldest of ten children, he was only fourteen when his father arranged for him to marry Joyce Acton, aged twelve, the sole heiress of a wealthy Worcestershire landowner. Her fortune made possible the building of Charlecote. In the Great Hall in 1565 Robert Dudley, deputizing for the Queen, dubbed Thomas a knight. This straight-nosed, square-jawed man with neatly trimmed beard (so he appears in his alabaster effigy) became a power in Warwickshire. In the Parliament of 1571 he sat as Knight of the Shire, and busied himself with such godly works as laying down penalties for saying and hearing mass. He also drew up a bill, left to die in committee, for 'the better preservation of Grain and Game' by making poaching a felony. As a Justice of the Queen's Peace, this puritanical squire exercised himself mainly over recusants, one of whom he literally uncovered, starving, in a haystack; and for his inquisitorial zeal while serving on a Privy Council commission he earned the good will of that awesomely powerful body. A grateful Parliament in 1584 passed a Private Bill assuring to Sir Thomas Lucy and others certain lands confiscated from *émigré* Catholics. Stratford town wined him with sack and claret at the Bear and the Swan. In public feared and respected, Sir Thomas in his domestic affairs appears to have been not unamiable. He wrote testimonial letters for an honest gentlewoman and an ailing servant. In 1583 his good offices helped to settle a lawsuit between the son of one of his servants and Shakespeare's friend, Hamnet Sadler. Of his wife the squire declared, in the epitaph adorning their tomb in St. Leonard's, Charlecote,

When all is spoken that can be saide, a wooman so furnished & garnished with vertue as not to be bettered & hardly to be equalled by any, as shee lived most vertuously, so shee died moste Godly. Set downe by him that best did knowe what hath byn written to be true

Thomas Lucye.[1]

When Lucy died in 1600 the great Camden, Clarenceux King-of-Arms, conducted the funeral, and other heralds attended. In truth Sir Thomas does not sound very much like the tyrant of the tradition or the cuckold of the ballad, nor is he aptly caricatured as the dim-witted Shallow of *The Merry Wives of Windsor*.

Other considerations challenge faith. If the luce was Sir Thomas's heraldic device, so was it for (among others) the Gascoynes, the Earl of Northampton, and the Worshipful Company of Stockfishmongers.[2] To some students it seems alien to Shakespeare's character and art that he should nurse a grudge for some dozen years, and then vent it by lampooning his victim in a play. And, even assuming he did so, how many in a London audience — even a Court audience — would be in a position to grasp the cryptic references to a country gentleman and something that happened long since on his estate? If, moreover, the allusions were accessible to a knowledgeable few, would a professional dramatist like Shakespeare risk offending the well-placed friends of a man who had done the state some service? That would be foolhardy. Inconsistent too; for Shakespeare had, after all, treated respectfully Sir William Lucy, an ancestor of Sir Thomas, in *1 Henry IV*; and the earlier Shallow of *2 Henry IV* is depicted without malice and without, seemingly, topical allusiveness. One wonders if the legend might not have originated in Stratford long after *The Merry Wives of Windsor* was written and its author dead, among locals who read the play, recollected jests about luces and louses, and interpreted the passage in accordance with their own resentment against a powerful neighbourhood family. Time plays tricks; events merge. In 1610 another Sir Thomas Lucy, the third, did bring a Star Chamber action over the slaughter of deer by armed poachers who broke into his park at Sutton, and afterwards made an ale-house

1 Cited by Alice Fairfax-Lucy, *Charlecote and the Lucys: The Chronicle of an English Family* (1958), p. 13. This delightful and informative book has furnished me with many facts and details for the present chapter. A very great deal has been written on Lucy and the deer-poaching episode. Of the earlier authorities, Malone is most useful (Shakespeare, *Plays and Poems* (1821), ii. 118–49); the most authoritative modern account is, as so often, in EKC.
2 For other escutcheons with luces, see Leslie Hotson, *Shakespeare versus Shallow* (1931), p. 92.

boast of their depredation.[1] Maybe by devious association this later event filtered into the tradition.

Still, the opening lines of *The Merry Wives of Windsor* are clearly allusive, and, as if matters were not already complicated enough, another model for Shallow has been proposed in our own century. This candidate, yielded by the researches of a scholar rather than by the vicissitudes of legend, is William Gardiner, a Surrey justice of the peace. He boasted the same fresh fish on his coat-armour, for his first wife was the widow Frances Wayte, *née* Luce or Lucy. This Gardiner, who had some indirect connection with the Swan Theatre, belongs to Shakespeare's London years, and so will enter this narrative in a later chapter.

Meanwhile, whatever the difficulties, the Charlecote story has not entirely lost its magic. 'The deer-stealing legend has by now a hold on popular affection that no argument can weaken', argues the present-day mistress of Charlecote, the Hon. Alice Fairfax-Lucy.

If it were ever authoritatively disproved, children of the future would be deprived of something that for centuries has made the poet live for them. The portraits of Shakespeare are few and of debatable authenticity. In the shadowy throng of the Great he cuts an uninspiring figure. But set him against the background of Charlecote warren or Fulbroke park some night near dawn, with dangerous moonlight-whitening the turf, and there you have reality. Theft, capture, punishment, flight — these are all within the compass of ordinary experience.[2]

Perhaps so, and several prominent authorities in this century — Sir Edmund Chambers, G. E. Bentley, and (more recently) A. L. Rowse — believe there may be some truth to the tradition.

Even if these legends embroider, however fancifully, a genuine escapade, they describe sports and recreation, not the serious occupations of life; Shakespeare must have provisioned his growing family with more than the odd haunch of venison. Did the young husband tick off the days and weeks and months of the apprentice's statutory seven-year sentence until the fateful day of his departure from Stratford? So one late-blooming tradition, a mutation of Aubrey's butcher-boy story, holds. When a Mr. Dowdall paused before the Shakespeare monument and epitaph at Holy Trinity in 1693, the ancient parish clerk and sexton who showed him round informed his visitor 'that this *Shakespear* was formerly in this Towne bound apprentice to a butcher; but that he Run from his master to London, & there was Received Into the play house as a serviture, & by this meanes had an oppertunity to be what he afterwards prov'd'.[3] Although this story does not state that the employer was William's father, it seems to have its origin in the familiar misconception about John Shakespeare's occupation, and so has no more persuasive force than implausible gossip.

Other voices, other speculations. Impressed with the dramatist's technical knowledge of the law, Malone, a barrister turned literary scholar, conjectured that Shakespeare 'was employed, while he yet remained at Stratford, in the office of some country attorney, who was at the same time a petty conveyancer, and perhaps also the Seneschal of some manor-court'.[4] Future lawyers would take up this suggestion, and not find themselves at a loss for words in arguing it. But if Shakespeare had for some years occupied a desk in some Warwickshire solicitor's office, 'attending sessions and assizes, — keeping leets and law days, — and perhaps being sent up to the metropolis in term time to conduct suits before the Lord Chancellor or the superior courts of common law at Westminster' (as a Victorian Chief Justice imagines it),[5] surely his signature would have appeared on deeds or wills he was called upon to witness; but no such signature has ever come to light.[6] In 1859 W. J. Thoms, a peaceable antiquary, conscripted the poet for military service in the Low Countries — a William Shakespeare, he triumphantly noted, is listed in 1605 in a

1   Fairfax-Lucy, *Charlecote and the Lucys*, pp. 129–30.
2   Ibid., p. 5.
3   For the Dowdall letter, see below, item 218, p. 262.
4   'An Attempt to Ascertain the Order in which the Plays of Shakspeare Were Written', in Shakespeare, *Plays and Poems*, ed. Edmond Malone (1790), vol. i, pt. 1, p. 307; see also p. 104n.
5   John Campbell, *Shakespeare's Legal Acquirements Considered* (1859), p. 23.
6   The point was made to the Victorian popularizer Charles Knight by Robert Bell Wheler, who inspected hundreds of title-deeds and other legal documents from the decade of the eighties; see *SL*, 387.

muster roll of hired soldiers within Barlichway Hundred, in the village of Rowington.[1] But Thoms has of course confused the poet with some namesake; Rowington had its quota of Shakespeares. Other guilds — the seamen, printers, barber-surgeons, physicians, what you will — have claimed Shakespeare, but a more intriguing possibility than any of these is broached by Aubrey.

On the authority of William Beeston, he reports that 'Though as Ben: Johnson sayes of him, that he had but little Latine and lesse Greek, He understood Latine pretty well: for he had been in his younger yeares a Schoolmaster in the Countrey.'[2] Aubrey thought that Beeston knew most about Shakespeare, and certainly he was in a position to be well informed. An actor on both the Caroline and Restoration stages (he died in 1682), William was the son of Christopher Beeston. The latter rose from minor actor with Strange's men to become the manager of a succession of theatrical enterprises — Queen Anne's men, Queen Henrietta's men, Beeston's boys, among others — and the builder, in 1617, of the Phoenix playhouse. From then until his death in 1638, Christopher Beeston was the most important figure in the London theatrical scene.[3] In 1598 this Beeston belonged to Shakespeare's company, the Lord Chamberlain's men, for that year he acted with Shakespeare in Jonson's *Every Man in his Humour*.[4] So the player and the player-poet knew one another, how intimately we cannot say.

But does it follow that Aubrey's report is trustworthy? After all, Shakespeare never went up to university, and the Stratford masters (as we have seen) held Oxford or Cambridge degrees. He might, however, have filled the humbler post of usher or *abecedarius*.[5] Aubrey merely says that Shakespeare taught 'in the Countrey', that is, anywhere outside London, and elsewhere than in Stratford the civic fathers tended to set less exacting standards. As late as 1642, in *The Holy and Profane State*, Thomas Fuller — 'the great Tom Fuller', Pepys calls him — complained, of the teaching profession, that 'young scholars make this calling their refuge, yea perchance before they have taken any degree in the University, commence Schoolmasters in the countrey, as if nothing else were required to set up this profession but onely a rod and a ferula.'[6] Simon Forman, later to make his mark as physician, astrologer, and lecher, had only turned nineteen when he took up teaching — a career he shortly abandoned in order to attend Oxford, 'for to get more lerninge'.[7] The tradition of Shakespeare the rural pedagogue, thumbing the Plautus he would later draw upon for one of his earliest plays, *The Comedy of Errors*, cannot be proved, nor should it be casually dismissed. It has in any event appealed irresistibly to donnish biographers.

Whatever the young Shakespeare did — whether (in Jonson's gracious phrase) he swept his living from the posteriors of little children, or clerked it for a conveyancer, or assisted his father in the glove trade — he did not do so for long. Asked what happy gale has blown him from Padua to old Verona, Petruchio replies,

> Such wind as scatters young men through the world
> To seek their fortunes farther than at home,
> Where small experience grows.

Some time before 1592 that wind carried Shakespeare to London.

He need not have waited until his arrival in London to make his first acquaintance with acting and plays. As a boy of fifteen he could have witnessed in nearby Coventry one of the last performances of the great cycle of Mystery plays acted by the craft guilds. More than once he had an opportunity, when his father held office, to watch the professional troupes that came to town.

1 William J. Thoms, 'Was Shakespeare Ever a Soldier?', *Three Notelets on Shakespeare* (1865), p. 136. The Rowington muster roll entry was first noted by Robert Lemon of the State Paper Office, and by him communicated to J. Payne Collier, who discusses the record, without acknowledgement of Lemon, in the second edition of his *Life of William Shakespeare* (1858).

2 For the whole entry, see above, item 57, p. 58.

3 In G. E. Bentley's considered judgement; see his account of Beeston in *The Jacobean and Caroline Stage* (Oxford, 1941–68), ii. 363–70.

4 See below, item 111, p. 150.

5 So EKC suggests (i. 22).

6 Thomas Fuller, *The Holy and Profane State* (Cambridge, 1642), p. 109; cited by Joseph Quincy Adams, *A Life of William Shakespeare* (Boston and New York, 1923), p. 93.

7 *Autobiography*, cited by ME, 73–4. Forman's *Autobiography* is reprinted by A. L. Rowse, *Simon Forman* (1974), pp. 267–78.

Now and then Stratford offered a chance for some amateur acting. 'At Pentecost', the disguised Julia recalls in *The Two Gentlemen of Verona*,

> When all our pageants of delight were play'd,
> Our youth got me to play the woman's part,
> And I was trimm'd in Madam Julia's gown;
> Which served me as fit, by all men's judgments,
> As if the garment had been made for me.

On one occasion the Stratford corporation laid out money for an entertainment at Pentecost. In 1583 they paid 13s.4d. 'to Davi Jones and his companye for his pastyme at whitsontyde'. Davy Jones had been married to Elizabeth, the daughter of Adrian Quiney, and after her death in 1579 he took as his wife a Hathaway, Frances. Was Shakespeare one of the youths who trimmed themselves for this Whitsun pastime?[1]

Considered in this context, the bare records of visiting troupes in Stratford in the late eighties assume a special interest. During the dog days, when the summer sun or plague or both emptied the city, the leading London companies put fardels on their backs, and, resplendent in glaring satin suits, made their provincial circuits. In the 1583–4 season three troupes, wearing the liveries of the earls of Oxford, Essex, and Worcester, performed in the Guild Hall and presumably also in the inn-yards of Bridge Street. But the busiest year for plays in Stratford stretched from December of 1586 to December 1587. Heralded by drum and trumpets, five companies — the Queen's, Essex's, Leicester's, Lord Stafford's, and another, unnamed — passed through the town, and left their tracks in the corporation accounts. Of these Leicester's men and the Queen's especially require notice.

Players had worn Lord Robert Dudley's badge of a ragged staff since the beginning of Elizabeth's reign; led by James Burbage, they were the first company to boast a royal patent and to have a permanent playhouse, the Theatre, for their headquarters. For Shakespeare the Earl's Warwickshire connection holds a special significance. He kept his ties with the county. When in the summer of 1575 he entertained the Queen sumptuously for nineteen days at his castle in Kenilworth, twelve miles from Stratford, the local populace crowded in as spectators to watch Elizabeth as she passed in splendour, and to gape at the devices that whiled away the afternoon, or the fireworks which lit up the night sky. Some biographers have toyed with the pleasing and not implausible notion that Alderman Shakespeare pressed in among the throng with his eleven-year-old son. On the large lake in the castle grounds a water-pageant displayed Arion on the back of a dolphin carried by a boat of which the oars simulated fins. Accompanied by instrumentalists within the dolphin's belly, Arion sang (in the phrase of an eye-witness) ' a delectabl ditty of a song wel apted too a melodious noiȝ'.[2] If young William witnessed the spectacle, he found it unforgettable. 'Thou rememb'rest', Oberon reminds Puck,

> Since once I sat upon a promontory,
> And heard a mermaid on a dolphin's back
> Uttering such dulcet and harmonious breath
> That the rude sea grew civil at her song,
> And certain stars shot madly from their spheres
> To hear the sea-maid's music.

And the Captain in *Twelfth Night* says of Viola's brother, 'like Arion on the dolphin's back,/I saw him hold acquaintance with the waves/So long as I could see'.

A decade after the princely pleasures at Kenilworth, when the Earl commanded the English forces supporting the Netherlands States-General against Spain, several of his players accompanied him to the Low Countries. On 24 March 1586 Sir Philip Sidney, writing to Walsingham from Utrecht, alludes to 'Will, my Lord of Lester's jesting plaier'. Such a reference is calculated to make a bardolater's heart skip a beat; but probably Sidney had in mind Will Kempe, the celebrated clown and jigmaker whom Leicester commended a few months later to the Danish Court. The Earl died in the Armada year. For a time his company soldiered on, possibly under

---

1 ME, 83, makes the apposite reference to *The Two Gentlemen of Verona*.
2 [Robert Laneham], *A Letter: Whearin, part of the entertainment untoo the Queenȝ Majesty, at Killingwoorth Castl, in Warwik Sheer in this Soomerȝ Progress 1575. iȝ signified . . .* (n.d.), p. 43.

the patronage of the Countess; then broke up. Several of the actors joined the servants of Leicester's brother, the Earl of Warwick; others — Kempe, Bryan, Pope — took up with Strange's or the Admiral's men. Leicester's troupe may have recruited Shakespeare during the unstable period preceding their dissolution; but of course this is only guesswork.[1]

An event in the fortunes of the Queen's company opens up a more intriguing possibility. Chosen by the Master of the Revels in 1583 from among the best actors in London, and lustrous in the Queen's scarlet coats, this troupe was then in its heyday. Their stellar attraction, the peerless clown Richard Tarlton, drew throngs and laughter everywhere. In 1588 he died, and the bubble burst; but in the summer of 1587 the Queen's men were the pre-eminent troupe in the land — in Abingdon the crowd was so keen to see Tarlton and his fellows that they broke the windows in the Guild Hall. The Queen's men visited some half dozen other towns, including Stratford. On 13 June, when the company was in Thame, Oxfordshire, a melodramatic episode took place between the hours of nine and ten at night in a close called White Hound. One of the actors, William Knell — he had played Prince Hal in the anonymous *Famous Victories of Henry the Fifth* — drew his weapon and assaulted his colleague John Towne, a yeoman of Shoreditch. Cornered on a mound, and fearing for his life, Towne plunged his own sword through Knell's neck. The latter died within thirty minutes. A coroner's inquest concluded that Towne had acted in self-defence, and in due course he received a Queen's pardon. Knell's widow Rebecca remarried in less than a twelvemonth, taking as her husband the actor John Heminges, who would prove so worthy a friend to Shakespeare. Meanwhile the Queen's men went about their business. We do not know precisely when they played at Stratford in 1587: the Chamberlains' account, 'from Christmas Anno 1586, Anno xxix Elizabethe Regine for one whole yere', tells us only that the corporation rewarded the performers with the munificent sum of twenty shillings (the highest amount they ever paid) and afterwards laid out sixteen pence to repair a bench, broken, one suspects, because of the press of spectators. In whatever week these players came, they lacked one man. Before leaving Stratford, had they enlisted Shakespeare, then aged twenty-three, as their latest recruit?[2]

Pages 91-5:

78 WENCESLAUS HOLLAR, 'LONG VIEW' OF LONDON FROM BANKSIDE, 1647. *Guildhall Library; shelfmark: Large Bound Views, Box 1. When he etched his panoramic view of London as seen from the tower of St. Mary Overies in Southwark, Hollar was in exile in Antwerp, but he had access to a number of sketches made while residing in the Strand from 1636 to 1642. The view that greeted Shakespeare on his arrival in London was in some respects different: fire had not yet destroyed the houses on the six northern arches of London Bridge, nor had Inigo Jones rebuilt the south transept of St. Paul's. But Hollar's 'Long View' is the most striking, detailed, and accurate panorama of the capital prepared before the Great Fire of 1666 swept away most of medieval London. The equally famous panorama engraved by Claes Jan Visscher of Amsterdam (rear endpaper) has the merit of being contemporary with Shakespeare — it appears to be based on a drawing made around 1600 — but is unreliable and without independent authority; Visscher may never even have visited London.*

The Hollar panorama shows St. Paul's still without the steeple that lightning destroyed in 1561. The labels for the Bear Garden and Globe are reversed. The former, also known as the Hope, was built in 1613 for Philip Henslowe and his partner Jacob Meade. Modelled on the Swan, but equipped with a movable stage, it served alike for baitings and plays. The contract for its construction survives. The building with the long roof on the north side of the river, between Blackfriars and Baynard's Castle, may be Blackfriars Hall, which in 1608-9 became the winter auditorium of the King's men; see below, pp. 213ff. More detailed information about the 'Long View', as well as about other pre-Fire panoramas and maps, may be had from Arthur M. Hind, Wenceslaus Hollar and his Views of London and Windsor in the Seventeenth Century *(1922); I. A. Shapiro, 'The Bankside Theatres: Early Engravings',* Shakespeare Survey *1 (Cambridge, 1948), pp. 25-37; Irene Scouloudi,* Panoramic Views of London, 1600-1666 *(1953); Ida Darlington and James Howgego,* Printed Maps of London circa 1553-1850 *(1964); and C. Walter Hodges,* Shakespeare's Second Globe: The Missing Monument *(1973), pp. 11-43. See also below, item 184. The portion of the 'Long View' reproduced here has been reduced somewhat.*

1   EKC, i. 39-41.
2   The discovery of the slaying of William Knell we owe to ME, 82-3, whose account I follow.

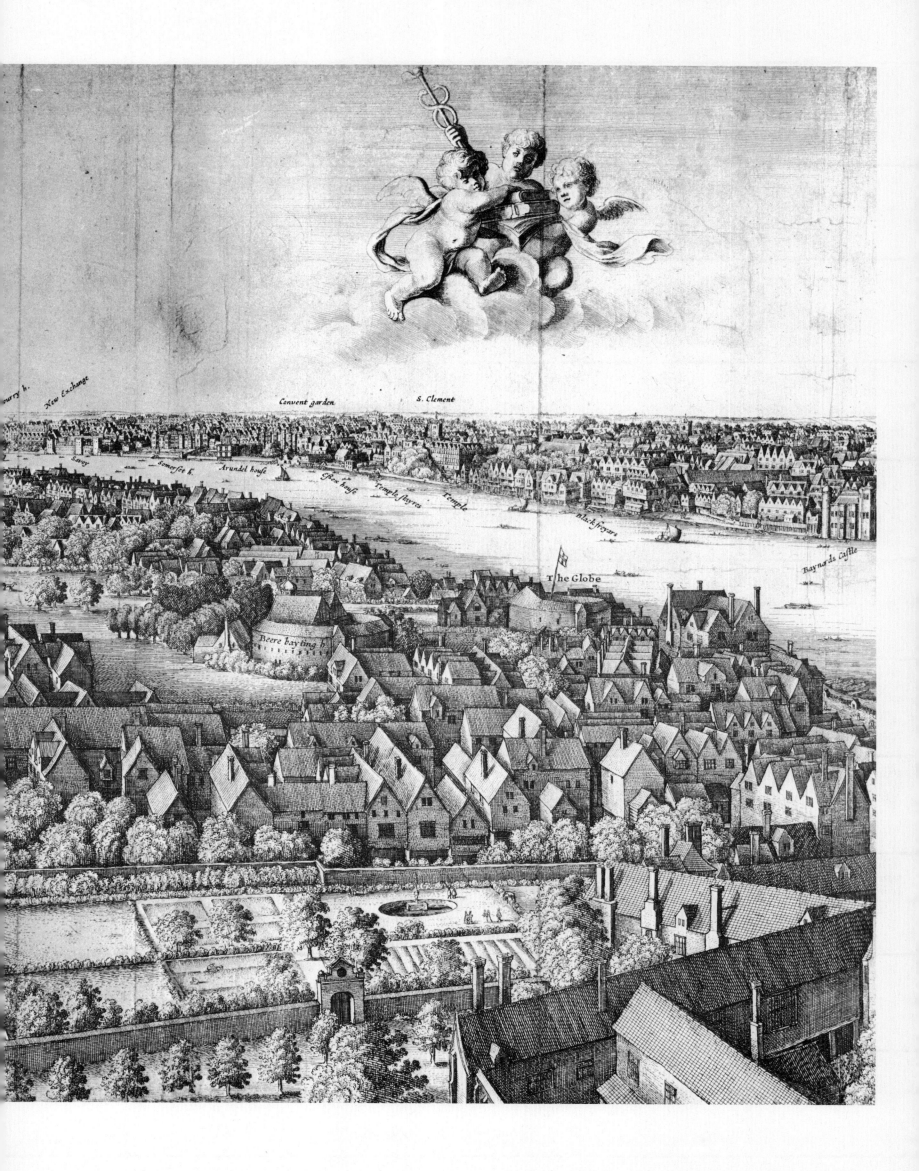

New Exchange

Convent garden　　　　　S. Clement

Savoy

Somerset E.

Arundel house

Spex house

Temple stayres

Temple

blackfryars

Baynards Castle

The Globe

Beere bayting h.

S. Pauwls Church

5. ẏ Waterhouse

S. Andre in Holborne

Heygat

Paulus wharfe

Queene hythe

The 3. Cranes

the Eel Ships

THAM

Winchester house

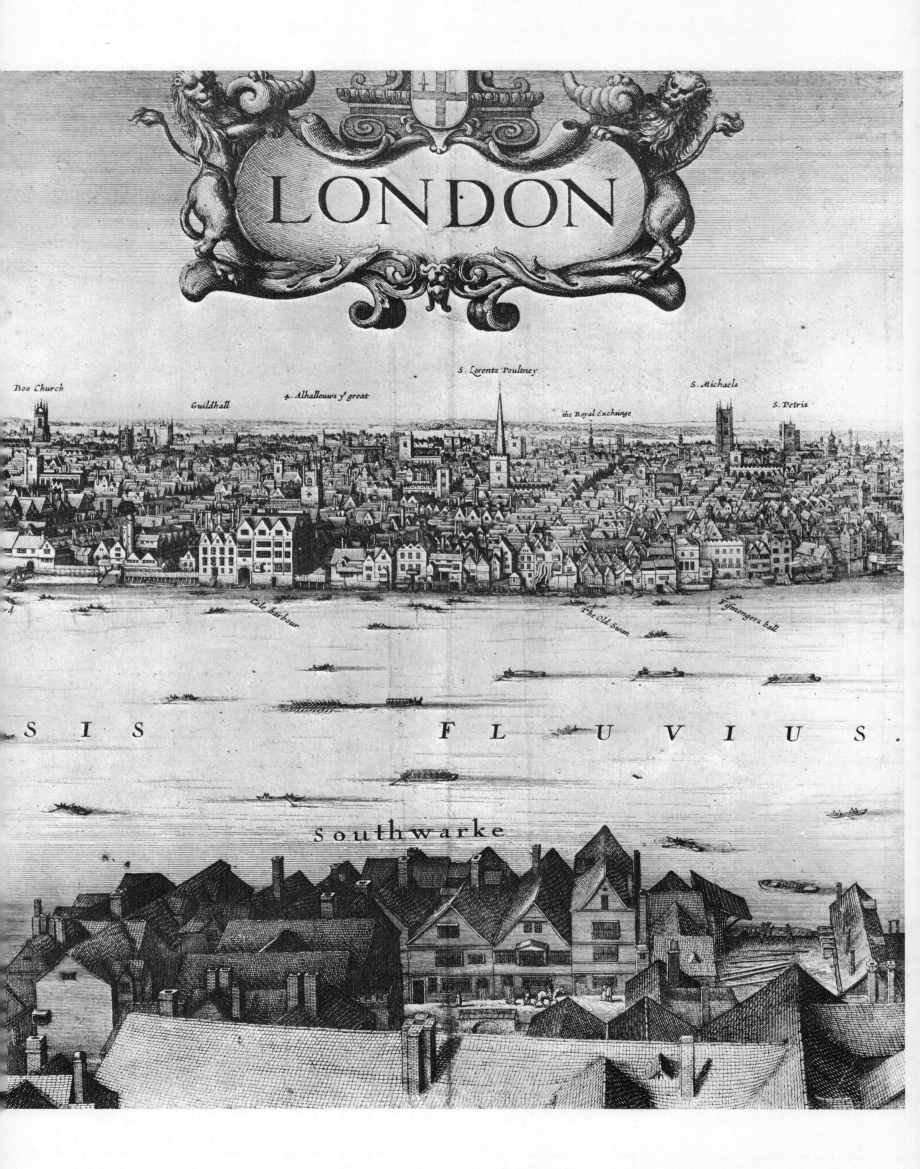

3. *S. Magnes* 2. *Gray Church* *S. Dunston in the East* 1. *Alhallows barking*

Lyon kay *Billings gate*

THE BRIDGE.

The Tower.

Tower Wharfe

S. Olafe

H

9

London and the Theatres

History unfortunately does not record when the young husband bade his long goodbye to his family — Anne, already over the threshold of thirty; Susanna and the twins; his parents, now getting on, in the family house in Henley Street — and, crossing Clopton Bridge, struck out, either on his own or with a company of players, on the high road to the capital. After he became famous and a prosperous burgher of Stratford, he would engage a horse. It is a reasonable guess that the young Shakespeare went more economically, on foot.

He had two routes to choose from, one through Oxford, and the other by way of Banbury. The former was shorter and more direct; a man could manage it in four days if he covered twenty-five miles each day; at night a penny bought clean sheets in an inn. This road led the wayfarer, *via* Shipston-on-Stour and Long Compton, over the gently rolling hills dividing Warwickshire from Oxfordshire; then past the famous stone circle called 'Roll-rich stones', through bare downs to the royal park of Woodstock, thick with ancient oaks and beeches; and on to Oxford. After that, High Wycombe and Beaconsfield. The alternative itinerary, described by Aubrey as *the* road from London to Stratford, passed by Pillerton Hercy over Edgehill; thence — through Banbury ('famous for Cakes, Cheese, and Zeale'), Buckingham, Aylesbury (approached over a little stone bridge and stone causeway), and the two Chalfonts — to Uxbridge. Here the two highways met. Shakespeare knew this latter route, if we may trust a seventeenth-century gossip's confused report that the dramatist spent a midsummer-night at Grendon, and there encountered, no doubt in a hail of malapropisms, the constable who furnished a model for Dogberry; for Grendon Underwood lay on a side road eight miles south of Buckingham.[1] From Uxbridge the single thoroughfare proceeded past Shepherd's Bush, the gallows at Tyburn, and the Lord Mayor's banqueting house in Oxford Road. Then, winding south, it reached a church (where Shaftesbury Avenue now is) in a pleasant rural village surrounded by open fields, and hence called St. Giles-in-the-fields. Next the suburb of Holborn, and having passed the churches of St. Andrew and St. Sepulchre, the traveller at last entered the great city at Newgate.[2]

This was one of the seven gates through which the principal roads led into a city encompassed, as in Chaucer's day, by 'an high and thick wall, full of Turrets and Boulwarks' (so Sir Thomas More described it). Of rough stone and tile, capped by brick and stone battlements, the wall stretched in a giant arc, over two miles long, round the city on three sides. Along Thames Street the wall defending the capital on the river side had long since yielded to the wharves, warehouses, and quays of a thriving port. The other walls have of course vanished too, and the portcullises and doors of the gates slammed ponderously shut for the last time in the eighteenth century. They survive, however, as place names — Aldgate looking eastward; Bishopsgate, Moorgate, Cripplegate, and Aldergate to the north; Newgate and Ludgate (the oldest) on the west — and in this way outline for the modern Londoner the perimeter of the old city.

If the visitor stood outside the walls on the Surrey side — say, by the imposing tower of St. Mary Overies (now Southwark Cathedral) — he could take in the breathtaking expanse of the metropolis, as captured in the marvellously detailed panoramas by Visscher and Hollar. From east to west, so far as the eye could see, stretched the mighty artery of the great tidal

1 See above, item 57, p. 58.
2 For the itinerary I mainly follow Henry B. Wheatley, 'London and the Life of the Town', *Shakespeare's England* (Oxford, 1916), ii. 153, but Charles Isaac Elton, *William Shakespeare: His Family and Friends* (1904), pp. 179–93, has furnished some details. On Elizabethan London generally, I have found most useful two older accounts, T. Fairman Ordish, *Shakespeare's London* (2nd ed., 1904) and H. T. Stephenson, *Shakespeare's London* (New York, 1905); and of course Stow has been invaluable.

river. No city in Christendom boasted such extensive river frontage.

Sweet Thames, run softly, goes the poet's refrain. More sweet were the waters of the Avon; ordure from the common sewer emptied into the Thames, and dead dogs and other carrion floated on the surface. But fish still swarmed in schools through the channel, and banks of swans glided by in such profusion as to evoke the wonderment of continental visitors. Others plied the river too. The great kept private boats moored to the steps that ran down from their palatial residences to the water's edge. Ordinary folk hired wherries at the public stairs, where the watermen shouted 'Eastward Ho!' or 'Westward Ho!'. This clientele to a large degree consisted of pleasure-seekers on their way to and from the Bankside theatres, bear gardens, and bawdy-houses. In John Taylor the watermen found their proletarian laureate, and the river its most rapturous celebrant. The Thames, he sang unmelodiously,

> beares the lame and weake, makes fat the leane,
> And keepes whole townes and countries sweet and cleane;
> Wer't not for *Thames* (as heavens high hand doth blesse it)
> We neither could have fish, or fire to dresse it,
> The very Brewers would be at a fault,
> And buy their water dearer than their mault....[1]

Shakespeare must have got to know the watermen, for whether he resided in Bishopsgate or the Clink, he would depend on them for transport when summoned with his company for a Court performance at Whitehall or Greenwich or Richmond; he could have hailed a water-taxi from the stairs at Blackfriars, or Paris Garden on the opposite bank. The costumes and properties would go separately by barge.

79   THE WATER-POET IN HIS WHERRY. *Part of the engraved title-page to* All the Workes of John Taylor the Water Poet *(1630). Copy in Cambridge University Library; shelfmark: SSS.21.13. STC 23725. The title-page is signed in the lower right-hand corner by Thomas Cockson, the most prolific Tudor engraver of small portraits.*

The river was the silver-streaming silent highway. Great three-masted merchant ships unloaded their cargoes at the crowded wharves and warehouses. At Billingsgate not only fish, but all manner of victuals — groceries (spices, dried fruit, and the like) excepted — were landed. When the Queen took to her gilt royal barge, with pennants streaming, a spirit of festival seized the Thames. One St. Mark's Day, John Machyn, Merchant Taylor and cheerful undertaker, noted in his *Diary* how after supper the Queen rowed up and down the river, with a hundred boats around

---

1   John Taylor, *Taylor on Thame Isis: or the Description of the Two Famous Rivers of Thame and Isis...* (1632), sig. B1[v].

her, and trumpets, drums, flutes, and guns, and squibs lighting up the sky, until ten at night, when her Grace decided to call it an evening, while all along the banks a thousand people stood staring at her.[1] In 1581 Elizabeth had come aboard the Golden Hind to knight Drake; now the venerable bark that had circumnavigated the globe lay rotting out Deptford way, where Christopher Marlowe would meet his violent end.

Along the length of the river the continuous row of mansions that joined London to Westminster affirmed the wealth and power of the capital. Behind the shore pressed together rows of cottages; and, rising above the gabled roofs, the steeples of more than a hundred parish churches, some of them masterpieces of the Perpendicular style. London, the poet sings,

> like a Crescent lies,
> Whose windowes seem to mock the star-befreckled skies;
> Besides her rising Spyres, so thick themselves that show,
> As doe the bristling reeds, within his Banks that growe.[2]

All this the panoramas represent.

Three imposing structures dominated the scene.

London Bridge, connecting Southwark with the city at Fish Street, was the only span crossing the Thames; 'a bridge of stone eight hundred feet in length, of wonderful work' — so wrote a German visitor in 1598.[3] The Water Poet required rhyme to express *his* enthusiasm:

> Brave *London* Bridge claimes right preheminence
> For strength, and Architects magnificence.

The heads of executed criminals stuck on iron spikes barbarically festooned the gate-house as one entered from the south. More inviting were the 'quite splendid, handsome, and well-built houses, which are occupied by merchants of consequence'.[4] These covered the length of the bridge, all twenty arches, and gave it the look of a continuous street rather than of a bridge. The tradesmen dwelt in the upper storeys, and displayed their wares in shops below, along both sides of a passage so narrow that (the Venetian ambassador sneered) two coaches meeting could not pass each other without danger. The pinmakers, a major attraction, kept their stalls here. Only three breaches in the lane afforded pedestrians a glimpse of the river, and of the lozenge-shaped timber frameworks, called 'starlings', built around the piers. At the tenth, or Great Pier, the starling formed, at low water, a platform to a winding flight of stone steps that led into the famous Chapel of St. Thomas, called St. Thomas of the Bridge. With its clustered columns and rich pointed-arch windows, this imposing Chapel (also accessible from the bridge street) had once honoured the memory of the Blessed Martyr; now, converted into a warehouse, it served Mammon.

To the west, St. Paul's, the largest and most magnificent cathedral in England, dwarfed the surrounding city-scape. The minster that Shakespeare knew had been shorn of some of its splendour, for in 1561 lightning destroyed the wooden steeple which soared up 150 feet and more. The devout had collected funds for restoration, but it never was replaced. The interior presented a mixed spectacle. In the Middle Aisle — called 'Duke Humphrey's Walk' or 'Paul's Walk' — lawyers at their pillars conferred with clients, masterless servants advertised for employers, coney-catchers cut the purses of coneys, and gallants exhibited their plumage, provoked quarrels, and arranged assignations with lewd wenches, while tailors took note of the latest fashions and displayed their cloth and lace. Delivery men used the aisle as a short-cut to Fleet Street, although they no longer (as in former days) led their horses and mules through the cathedral. Meanwhile divine services went on in the choir. In the churchyard on Sunday mornings preachers castigated

1 *The Diary of Henry Machyn*, ed. John Gough Nichols (Camden Society, 1848), p. 196; quoted (with spelling modernized) by A. L. Rowse, *The England of Elizabeth* (1950), pp. 213–14. I have found very helpful Rowse's chapter on 'London and the Towns'.
2 Michael Drayton, *Polyolbion* [1613], p. 259.
3 *Paul Hentzner's Travels in England, During the Reign of Queen Elizabeth*, transl. Richard Bentley (1797), p. 3. The title-page erroneously ascribes the translation to Horace Walpole.
4 Frederick, Duke of Württemberg, 'A True and Faithful Narrative of the Bathing Excursion. . .', *England as Seen by Foreigners in the Days of Elizabeth and James the First*, transl. and ed. William Brenchley Rye (1865), p. 9. The narrative of the Duke's travels was in fact written by his companion and private secretary, Jacob Rathgeb.

sin at Paul's Cross, which stood to the north-east. Occasionally lotteries took place in the cathedral close, but mainly this area served the book trade. Many stationers lived in the yard itself or the immediate environs and set up shop there. By the sign of the Red Lion or White Horse or Black Boy or whatever, they displayed the latest sermons or playbooks on their stalls. Most of Shakespeare's plays, those published during his lifetime, bore the imprint of stationers of St. Paul's Churchyard. The dramatist himself at one time had lodgings a short walk from St. Paul's, in Cripplegate ward. On more than one occasion he must there have thumbed books which provided him with sources for his plays, or simply have observed the daily re-enactment of the human comedy, in its own way no less diverting than the entertainments mounted at the Globe.

To the east another massive presence, this one more foreboding: the Tower, a vast complex of fortifications — a moat on three sides, drawbridge, thick walls within walls, courts, and the central keep, the White Tower, with its battlements and four onion-shaped turrets surmounting the lesser towers of the stronghold. Shakespeare in *Richard II* refers to 'Julius Caesar's ill-erected Tower',[1] but he is merely echoing folklore, for William the Conqueror began the construction of the Tower. Its functions are described by John Stow in his *Survey of London*:

This tower is a Citadell, to defend or commaund the Citie: a royall place for assemblies, and treaties. A Prison of estate, for the most daungerous offenders: the onely place of coynage for all England at this time: the armorie for war-like provision: the Treasurie of the ornaments and Jewels of the crowne, and generall conserver of the most Recordes of the kings Courts of justice at Westminster.[2]

This summary misses one or two features. Couples could have their marriages performed at the Tower. Holidaymakers visited the menagerie in the Lion Tower, which stood at the present main entrance; here Paul Hentzner, a lawyer from Brandenburg, in 1598 viewed with interest the lions, a tiger and lynx, an 'excessively old' wolf, and an eagle and porcupine.

The mortar of the Tower walls, according to FitzStephen, the twelfth-century monk of Canterbury, was tempered with the blood of beasts. Human blood too forms part of the fabric of the Tower; not without cause was one of the towers called the Bloody Tower. Guards conveyed prisoners to it *via* a covered channel that passed beneath the Tower wharf. The entrance was called Traitors' Gate. (The young Elizabeth arrived at this gate one rainy Palm Sunday, when the river waters lapped against the steps, and protested, 'Here landeth the truest subject being a prisoner, that ever landed at these stairs.'[3]) On the narrow wharf the cannon watched impassively while cranes unloaded goods. Behind the fortress, on Tower Hill, stood the wooden scaffold and gibbet. At night ghosts haunted the corridors and staircases of the Tower; some of them the same ghosts that troubled the repose of Richard III on the eve of the battle of Bosworth Field. No other edifice figures so importantly in Shakespeare's plays.

Yet the city boasted many other buildings of exceptional interest. At Baynard's Castle, on the river bank, with an entrance in Thames Street, Richard, Duke of Gloucester, 'well accompanied/ With reverend fathers and well learned bishops', waited to put by with mock humility the offer of a crown. Leicester House in the Strand, then not part of London proper but belonging to the liberty of the Duchy of Lancaster, was 'first amongst other buildings memorable for greatnes'. There resided Robert Dudley, the Queen's favourite, and after him Robert Devereux. It then became known as Essex House. To this house the Earl returned after the Irish campaign saluted by the Chorus of *Henry V*, and here he plotted the abortive rebellion which brought him to disgrace and the executioner's block. Fronting upon the Cornhill stood the Royal Exchange built by Sir Thomas Gresham on the model of the Great Bourse at Antwerp. It was in the shape of a quadrangle, with enormous arched entrances at the north and south. Within, foreign merchants and traders passed along an arched cloister lined with a double row of shops, one above the other, adorned with wax lights. They inspected armour, mouse-traps, jewelry, shoe horns, and all manner of wares. At noon and at six in the evening the great bell summoned the merchants in their hundreds to congregate for the conduct of their affairs. Although Shakespeare does not allude directly to 'the eye of London' (as Munday admiringly describes

1 Not poorly erected, but erected with ill consequences. I have profited in this paragraph from Rowse, *The Tower of London in the History of the Nation* (1972).

2 John Stow, *A Survey of London reprinted from the text of 1603*, ed. C. L. Kingsford (Oxford, 1908), i. 59.

3 The familiar episode is effectively retold by Rowse, *Tower of London*, pp. 74–5.

H*

99

the Exchange), it may have furnished him with hints for the Rialto of *The Merchant of Venice*.

As the panoramas show, to the north — beyond St. Paul's and the church steeples — stretched uncultivated fields and open country, dotted with an occasional windmill. The green belt lay closer in then, and farm produce had a shorter trip to market. London ended at Clerkenwell. St. Pancras and Charing Cross were still rural villages; Islington was a hamlet on the road leading to St. Albans; trees densely covered the hills of Hampstead. But the enclosed city could ill accommodate a population swelling to 160,000 or more, so building overflowed the walls in an untidy suburban sprawl.

To the north-east, not far from Ely Place in whose gardens grew the strawberries for which hunchbacked Richard developed his sudden longing, were situated the stews of Clerkenwell, frequented by lickerish gallants from the Inns of Court. Justice Shallow once belonged to this company, in the days when he was called 'lusty Shallow':

There was I, and little John Doit of Staffordshire, and black George Barnes, and Francis Pickbone, and Will Squele a Cotsole man — you had not four such swinge-bucklers in all the Inns o' Court again. And I may say to you we knew where the bona-robas were, and had the best of them all at commandment.

In their Christmas revels the Inns' men offered ironical homage to '*Lucy Negro*, Abbess *de Clerken-well*', and to her choir of nuns who, with burning lamps, chanted 'Placebo' to randy gentlemen of Gray's Inn. Professor Harrison believes that possibly she chanted to Shakespeare too, and found immortality as the Dark Lady of the *Sonnets*.[1] Also intrigued by the possibility, Leslie Hotson thinks that this Lucy Negro was one Luce Morgan — Black Luce, but disappointingly not a negress — who set up a bawdy house in St. John Street, Clerkenwell, and there 'traded in lust and gainful brothelry'.[2] She must, however, compete with other Dark Ladies.[3]

To the east, from St. Katherine's Hospital in the shadow of the Tower, to Wapping, the low-water mark of the Thames where executed pirates were left hanging until thrice washed by the tide, 'was never a house standing within these 40 yeares: but since the gallowes being after remooved farther off, a continuall streete, or filthy straight passage, with Alleyes of small tene-ments or cottages builded, inhabited by saylors victualers, along by the river of Thames, almost to *Radcliff*, a good mile from the Tower.'[4] Such developments made Stow, who intensely loved the city in which he lived for eighty years, long for the days described by his beloved FitzStephen:

On all sides, without the houses of the Suburbs, are the citizens gardens & orchards, planted with trees, both large, sightly, & adjoyning togither. On the north side, are pastures, & plain medows, with brooks running through them, turning water mils, with a pleasant noise. Not far off, is a great forrest, a well wooded chase, having good covert for Harts, Buckes, Does, Boores & wild Bulles. The corne fields are not of a hungry sandie mould, but as the fruitfull fields of Asia: yeelding plentifull encrease, & filling the barnes with corne. There are near London on the north side, especiall welles in the Suburbes, sweet, holesome, and cleare. Amongst which, Holywell, Clarkenwell, and saint Clemons well, are most famous, & most frequented by schollers & youthes of the City in summer evenings, when they walke forth to take the aire.[5]

The air in those parts was no longer so salubrious of a summer evening.

For life in the capital had grown unwholesome. Pestilence hung in the clouds, and at intervals struck — in 1592 and again in 1602 and 1603 — forcing the playhouses to shut down, and the inhabitants, those who could afford to do so, to flee. Population increased not so much in the normal way, through procreation, as by an influx from outside: refugees from the religious troubles in France and The Netherlands, or country folk dispossessed of their holdings by the conversion of arable land into pasture. The poor of London were numerous. They crowded into mean slum tenements of timber eked out with mud and plaster; these dwellings devoured the flowering churchyards, spread above stables, and crept into every nook and cranny of the city. Well-to-do foreign visitors were impressed by the cleanliness of the passages. 'The streets in this city are very handsome and clean', remarked Hentzner; 'but that which is named from the goldsmiths who inhabit it, surpasses all the rest: there is in it a gilt tower, with a fountain that

1　G. B. Harrison, *Shakespeare under Elizabeth* (New York, 1933), pp. 310–11.
2　Leslie Hotson, *Mr. W. H.* (1964), pp. 244–55.
3　See below, pp. 127, 134, and *SL*, 456–8, 683–8, 739–40, *et passim*.
4　Stow, *Survey*, ii. 71.
5　Ibid., ii. 70.

80 LONDON UNDER THE PLAGUE. *Title-page engraving, John Taylor,* The Feareful Summer *(1636). Copy in the British Library; shelfmark: C.30.d.31. STC 23756. The two earlier separately printed editions of* The Feareful Summer *(both 1625) lack the title-page illustration, as does the 1630* All the Workes.

plays.'[1] But he saw only the more attractive bits; not the overpopulated parishes and out-parishes like St. Giles, Cripplegate, or St. Leonard's, Shoreditch. So he made no notes about the squalor to which the Privy Council drew the attention of the Middlesex Justices in 1596: the 'multitudes of base tenements and houses of unlawfull and disorderly resort in the suburbs', and the 'great number of dissolute, loose, and insolent people harboured in such and the lyke noysom and disorderly howses, as namely poor cottages, and habitacions of beggars and people without trade, stables, ins, alehowses, tavernes, garden-houses converted to dwellings, ordinaries, dicyng-howses, bowling-allies, and brothel houses'.[2] In back alleys the lanes were too narrow to admit coaches, and the projecting upper storeys of dwellings blocked out the sunlight. Rubbish, cast from windows, lay in heaps; urine and excrement clogged the channels. In Moorfields and Finsbury Fields lay decomposing carcasses of dogs and cats and horses. The slaughter-houses of St. Nicholas-within-Newgate stood in the heart of the city; here putrified blood ran in the streets, and offal fatted the region kites and ravens, which were (like the swans) protected birds. In Scalding Alley the poulterers publicly scalded the chickens vended in the neighbouring market of the Poultry. Running round the great wall, the Town Ditch, where fish once swam, had become a noisome source of infection. Under such conditions the black rat multiplied and, infesting tenements and hovels, spread the flea that transmitted the plague bacillus. Eventually the fiercer brown rat, which preferred to breed outside dwellings, in burrows or drains, helped to eradicate the black rat. A better standard of housing helped too. But that was not to be until after Shakespeare's time, and it required a great fire which destroyed most of the London he knew.[3]

Still, despite overcrowding, filth, and infestations of rats and disease, all manner of flowers and greenery gaily decked the capital. Along the river-bank the ancient residences (as to be

1 *Hentzner's Travels*, p. 31.

2 Cited by Kingsford in Stow, *Survey*, ii. 368.

3 On the conditions that encouraged the spread of plague I have found most valuable F. P. Wilson, *The Plague in Shakespeare's London* (Oxford, 1927).

expected) had spacious gardens attached, with flower beds and fruit trees. Edmund Spenser could walk forth on a spring day in 1596,

> Along the shoare of silver streaming *Themmes*,
> Whose rutty Bancke, the which his River hemmes,
> Was paynted all with variable flowers,
> And all the meades adornd with daintie gemmes.

Wild radishes grew low in the joints of a stone wall along the Thames, by the Savoy, and could be picked when the tide receded. Under the city wall, in a garden belonging to an apothecary of London, a nettle tree flourished. Even part of the Town Ditch was filled in with gardens. There were still grassy slopes amid the ruins of dissolved priories not yet converted into tenements. In Pope Lane, in Aldergate ward, willows (some said) once grew near the parish church of St. Anne in the Willows; no longer — 'now there is no such voyde place for willowes to grow' — but some high ashes lent beauty to the churchyard. The suburb of Holborn consisted mainly of gardens; in Hackney the village women gathered small turnips to sell at the cross in Cheapside. Cinquefoil, or five-finger, grew upon the brick wall in Liver Lane; whitlow grass climbed the back wall in Chancery Lane, and in Westminster Abbey spread over the door that led from Chaucer's tomb to the old palace.

The great city of contrasts spawned stately mansions and slum tenements, gardens and midden-heaped lanes. It was the vital nerve-centre for the Court, the professions, trade and commerce, and the arts; London nourished the English Renaissance. Only in the metropolis could a playwright of genius forge a career for himself. Anyway Stratford, a hundred miles distant, had its problems too. Older townsmen remembered the plague of sixty-four, although they would never undergo a similar siege. In the summer before the Spanish Armada the Avon suddenly rose, collapsing both ends of Clopton Bridge, and carrying away all the hay in the valley. Destructive fires raged three times in Stratford during Shakespeare's lifetime. Still, by the banks of the Avon one breathed a sweeter air on summer evenings. Does and bucks still found covert in the Forest of Arden, and the cornfields yielded fruitful increase; much as they did in the environs of London in the days of FitzStephen. We need not wonder that (so tradition reports) the poet each year journeyed back to the town of his origin, or that he chose to buy most of his property there rather than in the capital, or that, at the height of his London fame, he elected to pass the twilight of his life in Stratford.

*   *   *

If a centre attracts foreign visitors, they sometimes have more to tell us than natives about principal attractions. That is certainly so with respect to the one feature of the London scene of which we have yet to speak. No guide to the stones and streets of the capital is more painstaking than John Stow, yet he is curiously uncommunicative about the playhouses that are, for us, the glory of Elizabethan England. The defunct religious drama reminds Stow that

Of late time in place of those Stage playes, hath beene used Comedies, Tragedies, Enterludes, and Histories, both true and fayned: For the acting whereof certaine publike places as the Theater, the Curtine &c. have beene erected. [*Margin:* Theater and Curten for Comedies & other shewes][1]

Elsewhere, after describing Holywell, Stow casually adds: 'And neare thereunto are builded two publique houses for the acting and shewe of Comedies, Tragedies, and Histories, for recreation. Whereof the one is called the Courtein, the other the Theatre: both standing on the Southwest side towards the field.'[2] That is all, and even these laconic references he pared for his second edition of the *Survey* in 1603. By then, to be sure, the Theatre had vanished, and the Chamberlain's men had ceased playing at the Curtain. At the Globe, however, a penny bought admission to *Julius Caesar* or *Hamlet*. Stow never mentions Shakespeare's playhouse; perhaps the mildly Puritan disposition of this 'merry old man' turned him away from such frivolities. For descriptions of Elizabethan theatres and the like we must turn to Continental travellers. As Thomas Heywood, himself a playwright, boasted, 'playing is an ornament to the Citty, which strangers of all Nations, repairing hither, report of in their Countries, beholding them here with some admiration: for

1   Stow, *Survey*, i. 93, ii. 236; E. K. Chambers, *The Elizabethan Stage* (Oxford, 1923), ii. 363.
2   Stow, *Survey*, ii. 73, 262; Chambers, *Elizabethan Stage*, ii. 363.

what variety of entertainment can there be in any Citty of Christendome, more then in London?"[1] Fortunately some of the jottings of these holiday-makers have survived.

When, in the summer of 1598, Paul Hentzner methodically did the sights, he inspected the marble tombs in St. Paul's and Westminster, as well as the armour in the Tower, and quantities of goods in the Royal Exchange. At Greenwich he gained admittance to the presence chamber (a friend made the arrangements) and caught a glimpse of the Queen, in her sixty-fifth year, with bare bosom, narrow lips, and black teeth; the English, he noted in his commonplace book, use too much sugar. For recreation Hentzner repaired to Bankside.

Without the city are some Theatres, where English actors represent almost every day tragedies and comedies to very numerous audiences; these are concluded with excellent music, variety of dances, and the excessive applause of those that are present.
Not far from one of these theatres, which are all built of wood, lies the royal barge, close to the river. . . .

But Hentzner's tastes seem to have run to less sophisticated fare than stage plays, for he dwells on a different sort of amphitheatre:

There is still another place, built in the form of a theatre, which serves for the baiting of bulls and bears; they are fastened behind, and then worried by great English bull-dogs, but not without great risque to the dogs, from the horns of the one, and the teeth of the other; and it sometimes happens they are killed upon the spot; fresh ones are immediately supplied in the places of those that are wounded, or tired. To this entertainment, there often follows that of whipping a blinded bear, which is performed by five or six men, standing circularly with whips, which they exercise upon him without any mercy, as he cannot escape from them because of his chain; he defends himself with all his force and skill, throwing down all who come within his reach, and are not active enough to get out of it, and tearing the whips out of their hands, and breaking them. At these spectacles, and every where else, the English are constantly smoking tobacco. . . . In these theatres, fruits, such as apples, pears and nuts, according to the season, are carried about to be sold, as well as ale and wine.[2]

Other visitors too, mostly German-speaking, took down notes. Samuel Kiechel, a merchant of Ulm who sojourned in England in 1585, described the playhouses — these would be the Theatre and the Curtain — as 'peculiar (*sonderbare*, i.e. *besondere*) houses, which are so constructed that they have about three galleries one above the other.'[3] It is not clear why the galleries made such an impression — perhaps he had seen no other theatres with similar seating arrangements, or maybe he had never seen any theatre. A decade later, Prince Lewis of Anhalt-Cöthen was impressed by the beautiful costumes worn by actors who impersonated kings and emperors in the four playhouses — 'vier spielhäuser' — then operating in London. A priest of St. Mary's in Utrecht, Johannes de Witt, visited London in the same year, 1596, and made, in addition to notes, a unique sketch of the interior of a theatre. These perished, but luckily De Witt's friend from his university days in Leyden took enough interest to copy them in his commonplace book, which, perfectly preserved, may be consulted today in the modest University Library in the centre of Utrecht. Before the century was out, Thomas Platter of Basle came to London, and described actual stage performances he witnessed. The notes of Platter and De Witt, along with the latter's drawing, comprise our most valuable eye-witness information about the Elizabethan theatre. We shall be returning to them.

Dramatic art thrived in London before it had expressly designed accommodation. By the sixties we begin to get reports of troupes performing at converted inns: the Bull in Bishopsgate Street, the Bel Savage on Ludgate Hill; the Bell and the Cross Keys, near one another in Grace-church Street; and the Red Lion and Boar's Head in Whitechapel. Equipped with permanent scaffolds and tiring rooms, as well as stands for spectators, these inns continued in use long after the theatres that rendered them obsolete had come into being; as late as 1594 we hear of Shakespeare's company playing 'this winter time within the citye at the Cross Keyes in Gracious Street'.

Still, the erection of the first purpose-built playhouse is an immensely significant event in the history of the English drama. James Burbage, 'the first builder of Playhowses', was by occupation a joiner but, not thriving, became a common player; by 1572 we hear of him heading the Earl of

1 Thomas Heywood, *An Apology for Actors* (1612), sig. F3.
2 *Hentzner's Travels*, pp. 29–30.
3 Quoted in *England as Seen by Foreigners*, p. 88.

Leicester's well-regarded troupe. It occurred to the itinerant actor that 'continual great profit' might be had from a building devoted solely to dramatic entertainment. He was right. In 1576, while still worth scarcely a hundred marks, he borrowed capital from his rich brother-in-law, John Brayne, who had previously financed the Red Lion Inn. The next step was to find a site.

Himself a dweller in the northern suburbs, Burbage looked in that direction, fixing on the Liberty of Holywell, which formed part of the Middlesex parish of St. Leonard's, Shoreditch, and lay just outside the Bishopsgate entrance to the city. The Liberty, which took its name from an ancient holy well, had belonged to a priory of Benedictine nuns. The convent was now dissolved, the well fed into a horsepond, and the property came within the jurisdiction of the Crown. Around the well stood undeveloped land, except for a few derelict tenements, a crumbling barn, and some gardens. Here, on a small parcel of void ground between the tenements and the old brick wall of the precinct, Burbage's workmen built the Theatre in the summer of 1576. More than half a century later his son Cuthbert memorably recalled the occasion and its aftermath:

The father of us Cutbert & Richard Burbage was the first builder of Playhowses & was himselfe in his younger yeeres a Player. The Theater hee built with many Hundred poundes taken up at interest. The Players that lived in those first times had onely the profitts arising from the dores, but now the players receave all the commings in at the dores to themselves & halfe the Galleries from the Houskepers. Hee built this house upon leased ground, by which meanes the landlord & hee had a great suite in law & by his death, the like troubles fell on us, his sonnes; wee then bethought us of altering from thence, & at like expence built the Globe with more summes of money taken up at interest.

But that event belongs to another chapter.

On the west the Theatre was bounded by a ditch dividing it from the open Finsbury Fields. As Burbage had no right of way from Holywell Lane, theatre-goers had to cross the fields, and enter by a doorway in the precinct wall. 'I would needes to the Theatre to see a play', declares

81 THE ANSWER OF CUTHBERT BURBAGE, WINIFRED ROBINSON, AND WILLIAM BURBAGE, *c.* 1 AUGUST 1635 (extract). *Public Record Office, LC/5/133, pp. 50–1. Transcript: H-P*, Outlines, *i. 317–9; EKC, ii. 65–6; BRL, ii. 519–20. The Answer is to a Petition entered by Robert Benfield and Heliard Swanston to the Lord Chamberlain, and forms part of the so-called Sharers' Papers formerly kept at St. James's Palace, along with other official manuscripts of the Lord Chamberlain of the Household. There, in the summer of 1870, H-P found the Answer in a thin manuscript folio entitled, 'Presentations and Warrants in the yeares 1631, 1632, &c.' 'Upon looking it over', he reminisced afterwards, 'I could hardly believe my eyes when coming across a list of shareholders in the Blackfriars and Globe Theatres, with information respecting their management that no amount of reading could have elicited from a million of scattered notices' (Prefatory Note, A Fragment of Mr. J. O. Halliwell's 'Illustrations of The Life of Shakespeare' (1874)). H-P published the Sharers' Papers in his Illustrations (1874), pp. 86–91. In 1885 he described the documents as 'lately' transferred to the Public Record Office.*

Tarlton's Ghost, returned from Purgatory,

where when I came, I founde such concourse of unruly people, that I thought it better solitary to walke in the fieldes, then to intermeddle my selfe amongst such a great presse. Feeding mine humour with this fancie I stept by dame Anne of Cleeres well, & went by the backside of Hogsdon: where finding the Sun to bee hot, and seeing a faire tree that had a coole shade, I sate me downe to take the aire, where after I had rested me a while I fell a sleepe....

And with that I waked, & saw such concourse of people through the fields, that I knew the play was doone....[1]

A second theatre followed on the heels of the first. This was the Curtain, which opened its doors by the autumn of 1577. Elizabethan playhouses of course had no curtains, in the theatrical sense; the house came by its name from being in the Curtain Close, some 200 yards south of the Theatre, and on the other side of Holywell Lane. The presence of two such arenas in the capital presaged the imminent triumph of Sodom, and gave a stimulus to apocalyptic rhetoric. 'Looke

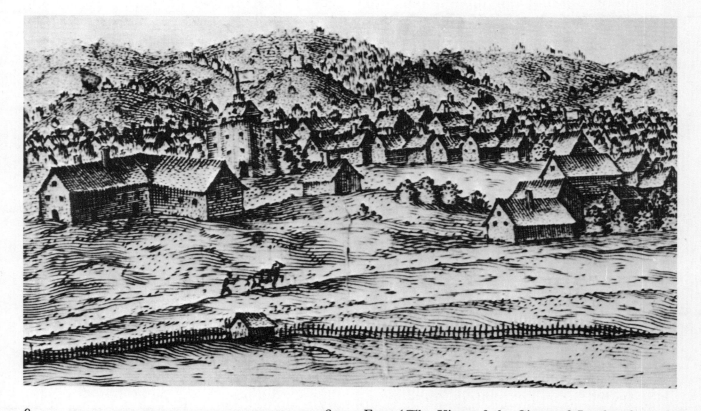

82 A SHOREDITCH PLAYHOUSE, *c.* 1597–1600. *From 'The View of the Cittye of London from the North towards the Sowth' (enlarged detail). University Library, Utrecht; shelfmark: MS. 1198, f. 83. The only known copy of this engraving survives as an insert in the manuscript journal, dated 1629–30, of Abram Booth, an agent of the Dutch East India Company, and was reproduced in an edition of Booth's journal,* Een Dienaer der Oost-Indische Companie te London in 1629, *ed. A. Merens ('s-Gravenhage, 1942). Leslie Hotson first brought the panorama to the notice of the English-speaking public in an article, '"This Wooden O": Shakespeare's Curtain Theatre Identified', in* The Times, *26 March 1954, pp. 7, 14. He identified the tall, flag-topped building in the left-hand corner of the view as the Curtain. Hotson was challenged by Sidney Fisher,* The Theatre, the Curtain & the Globe *(Montreal, 1964); he argues with some cogency for the Theatre as the playhouse represented in the panorama, and suggests that the Curtain may be seen on the right with flagpole rising above the ridge of the roof. In* The Globe Restored *(2nd ed., 1968), C. Walter Hodges accepts Hotson's identification, but he is apparently unaware of Fisher. Hodges notes that this is, Hollar excepted, the only contemporary representation of an Elizabethan theatre to show the external staircase towers and main entrance door; another feature of interest is 'a sort of battlemented tower' surmounted by the flagstaff (pp. 110–11).*

1 'Robin Goodfellow', *Tarltons Newes out of Purgatorie* (1590), pp. 1–2, 53; quoted by Chambers, *Elizabethan Stage*, ii. 386n.

but upon the common playes in London, and see the multitude that flocketh to them and followeth them', lamented Thomas White in the Sunday sermon he preached at St. Paul's Cross on 3 November 1577: 'beholde the sumptuous Theatre houses, a continuall monument of Londons prodigalitie and folly.'[1] William Harrison concurred: 'It is an evident token of a wicked time when plaiers wexe so riche that they can build suche houses.'[2] If, as seems likely, the man who built the Curtain was Henry Lanman or Laneman, he was not a player but a middle-aged Londoner who described himself as a gentleman. He was renting property in Curtain Close in 1581, and taking profits from the playhouse in 1585. He does not seem to have waxed especially rich from his wicked enterprise, for the Curtain never achieved the fame of Burbage's Theatre. Fencing exhibitions occasionally took place at the former between 1579 and 1583. Two years later it became a supplementary house — an 'easer', the records call it — to the Theatre, and Lanman and the Burbages agreed to pool their profits, an arrangement that lasted for seven years. The Chamberlain's men, Shakespeare's company, were almost certainly performing at Lanman's theatre from 1597 to 1599. It was during this period that *Romeo and Juliet* 'won Curtain plaudities'. When the Prologue to *Henry V* speaks of 'this wooden "O" ', he more likely refers to the Curtain than (as usually thought) to the Globe, and in this way immortalizes an otherwise undistinguished house.

This must have been the Bishopsgate theatre visited by Thomas Platter in 1599, for by then the Theatre was gone:

On the 21st of September, after dinner, at about two o'clock, I went with my party across the water; in the straw-thatched house we saw the tragedy of the first Emperor Julius Caesar, very pleasingly performed, with approximately fifteen characters; at the end of the play they danced together admirably and exceedingly gracefully, according to their custom, two in each group dressed in men's and two in women's apparel.

On another occasion, also after dinner, I saw a play not far from our inn, in the suburb, at Bishopsgate, as far as I remember.... At the end they danced, too, very gracefully, in the English and the Irish mode. Thus every day around two o'clock in the afternoon in the city of London two and sometimes even three plays are performed at different places, in order to make people merry [literally 'so that one make the other merry']; then those who acquit themselves best have also the largest audience. The places are built in such a way that they act on a raised scaffold, and everyone can well see everything. However, there are separate galleries and places, where one sits more pleasantly and better, therefore also pays more. For he who remains standing below pays only one English penny, but if he wants to sit he is let in at another door, where he gives a further penny; but if he desires to sit on cushions in the pleasantest place, where he not only sees everything well but can also be seen, then he pays at a further door another English penny. And during the play food and drink is carried around among the people, so that one can also refresh oneself for one's money.

The play-actors are dressed most exquisitely and elegantly, because of the custom in England that when men of rank or knights die they give and bequeath almost their finest apparel to their servants, who, since it does not befit them, do not wear such garments, but afterwards let the play-actors buy them for a few pence.

How much time they [the people] thus can spend merrily every day at plays everyone knows well who has ever seen them [the actors] act or play....[3]

The Curtain outlasted its theatrical usefulness, and was in latter days employed only for prize-fights. It still stood in 1627, when a Middlesex county record refers passingly to 'the common shoare neare the Curtain playhouse'.

These were the theatres of the northern suburbs at the time of Shakespeare's advent to the London stage. The centre of gravity for the players was, however, shifting to the Surrey side of the river, which was well equipped for amusement-seekers. A broad meadow invited picnickers, and furnished an open area for the athletically inclined to run and wrestle, to play football and bowl. (Shakespeare makes numerous references to bowling.) Archery encouraged the exercise of a traditional English manly skill; that skill which Justice Shallow, sliding into senility in bucolic Gloucestershire, recalls so nostalgically: ' 'A drew a good bow; and dead! 'A shot a fine shoot. John a Gaunt loved him well, and betted much money on his head. Dead! 'A would have clapp'd i' th' clout at twelve score, and carried you a forehand shaft a fourteen and fourteen

---

1   T[homas] W[hite], *A Sermon preached at Pawles Crosse on Sunday the thirde of November 1577. in the time of the Plague* (1578), p. 46; Chambers, *Elizabethan Stage*, iv. 197.

2   William Harrison, MS. 'Chronologie', quoted by Chambers, *Elizabethan Stage*, iv. 269.

3   Ernest Schanzer, 'Thomas Platter's Observations on the Elizabethan Stage', *Notes and Queries*, cci (1956), 466–7.

and a half, that it would have done a man's heart good to see.' Visitors could dance round the maypole. For a fee they could dance the shaking of the sheets at one of the bordellos which, licensed by authority of the Bishop of Winchester, bordered the river's edge, and made suburban garden-houses synonymous with harlotry. ('Dwell I but in the suburbs / Of your good pleasure?' Portia asks her husband. 'If it be no more, / Portia is Brutus' harlot, not his wife.') They could get drunk in taverns, or be fleeced in gaming houses. They could watch George Stone or Harry Hunks, their favourite bears, fight off ferocious mastiffs in amphitheatres which, as early as mid-century, are depicted — with stables and kennels attached — in maps of Southwark. Such pastime found its natural setting on Bankside, for the butchers dumped their offal in the Manor of Paris Garden, and thus provided ample nourishment for the beasts.

The first theatre south of the river is known to historians as Newington Butts (it does not seem to have had any usual name in its own day), after the segment of the Queen's highway where the roads from Camberwell and Clapham merged leading to Southwark. There is no evidence of ancient archery butts there, as was until recently thought. The theatre, as now seems likely, was built, or converted from an existing structure, by the enterprise of Jeremy Savage, the leading player for the Earl of Warwick's men, who secured their patron in 1575. The playhouse may have opened shortly thereafter.[1] It was reachable on foot by the road which, continuing Southwark High Street, cut across St. George's Fields. We first hear of plays being acted at Newington Butts in 1580, after the collapse of Warwick's men; but the theatre never caught on, no doubt because of the inconvenient location. In 1592 the Privy Council enjoined Strange's men to play there, then rescinded the order 'by reason of the tediousnes of the waie and that of longe tyme plaies have not there bene used on working daies'.[2] When the combined Admiral's-Chamberlain's company performed at Newington Butts for an abbreviated season in 1594, their average daily takings came to a meagre 9s., despite the fact that their repertoire included *Titus Andronicus*, *The Taming of A Shrew*, and the mysterious lost play of *Hamlet*. By 1599, we are told, the theatre was 'only a memory'.[3] People no longer had to cross the fields to see a play.

For in January 1587 Philip Henslowe and John Cholmley, a citizen and grocer of London, concluded a partnership agreement in a 'playhowse now in framinge and shortly to be erickted and sett uppe upone' a parcel of ground at the corner of Rose Alley and Maiden Lane. On this vacant lot, in former times, a rose garden flourished. This was the district of the stews; convenient to the river's edge, and to the city.[4] A theatre here could scarcely miss. On 19 February 1592 Strange's men opened at the Rose, under the leadership of Edward Alleyn — of all the tragedians of the age, the most formidable rival to Richard Burbage. The engagement led to the eventual partnership of the English Roscius and the then sole landlord of the Rose (Cholmley passes from view; probably he had died); a partnership cemented by Alleyn's marriage to Henslowe's step-daughter. They reaped a great fortune from show business, and in 1613, having retired to his country estate, Alleyn munificently endowed the College of God's Gift at Dulwich. By then the Rose had fallen into disuse — there are no records of performances there after 1603 — but it had already played its part in making Bankside the vital centre of stageland, and Henslowe the most powerful theatrical magnate of the age. There is a Shakespearian connection with the Rose. On 24 January 1594, when Sussex's men were playing there, Henslowe recorded in his *Diary* a performance of *Titus Andronicus*, which he marked as 'ne' [new],[5] a rather puzzling term that may signify that the play was newly licensed by the Master of the Revels. *Titus* is the only 'ne' work which the troupe presented during their short season at the Rose.

Hentzner refers to a theatre at the western end of Bankside, near where the royal barge had its moorings. This must have been the Swan in the Manor of Paris Garden. When Francis

1   For this reconstruction of the early history of the Newington Butts playhouse, see William Ingram, 'The Playhouse at Newington Butts: A New Proposal', *Shakespeare Quarterly*, xxi (1970), 385–98.

2   Chambers, *Elizabethan Stage*, ii. 405; iv. 313.

3   C. W. Wallace, *The First London Theatre, Materials for a History* (Nebraska *University Studies*, vol. xiii; Lincoln, Neb., 1913), p. 2. Wallace never got round to publishing his source for this assertion.

4   On prostitution in this district, see David J. Johnson, *Southwark and the City* (1969), pp. 64–7.

5   On the significance of this term, see *Henslowe's Diary*, ed. R. A. Foakes and R. T. Rickert (Cambridge, 1961), pp. xxx–xxxi.

Langley, a London draper and 'goldsmith' (in this case a euphemism for money-lender), set out to build this theatre, the Lord Mayor complained loudly, but he could do little to prevent a licence, for the land formed part of the holdings of the dissolved monastery of Bermondsey, and therefore fell within the purview of the Crown. Langley built in the north-east corner of the manor grounds, east of the manor-house, and twenty-six poles (a pole equals $5\frac{1}{2}$ yards) due south of Paris Garden stairs, where the watermen had their wherries for hire. The Swan had opened its doors to the public by the summer of 1596, for it was then (as appears likely) that Johannes de Witt made his celebrated visit. Shakespeare had some association with the proprietor of the Swan, for the names of the two men appear together in 1597 in a petition for the surety of the peace.[1]

These were the permanent public playhouses of London before the building of the Globe. As an actor and playwright, Shakespeare was acquainted with most of them; perhaps he knew them all. Theatre historians have painstakingly mulled over the antecedents for these remarkable edifices, some attaching more weight than others to the animal-baiting amphitheatres or the inn-yards or the Tudor banqueting halls with their back screens. One learned authority has even invoked the classical authority of Vitruvius, but it is doubtful whether James Burbage, joiner and player, struggled with the Latin of *De architectura* before setting his carpenters to work on the Theatre. These considerations need not detain us. The historians have also endlessly debated particulars, such as the dimensions of the various parts of the playhouse, or the means for effecting 'discoveries' (the curtained inner stage, a favourite construction of earlier authorities, now looks like being banished). Our concern is with the generic features of the theatres, familiar from innumerable stage histories or artists' impressions or scale models. We shall not go far wrong if we take for our guide a contemporary observer, De Witt.

His notes, headed 'Ex Observationibus Londonensibus Johannis de Witt', have been translated thus from the Latin:

There are four amphitheatres in London of notable beauty, which from their diverse signs bear diverse names. In each of them a different play is daily exhibited to the populace. The two more magnificent of these are situated to the southward beyond the Thames, and from the signs suspended before them are called the Rose and Swan. The two others are outside the city towards the north on the highway which issues through the Episcopal Gate, called in the vernacular Bishopsgate. There is also a fifth, but of dissimilar structure, devoted to the baiting of beasts, where are maintained in separate cages and enclosures many bears and dogs of stupendous size, which are kept for fighting, furnishing thereby a most delightful spectacle to men. Of all the theatres, however, the largest and the most magnificent is that one of which the sign is a swan, called in the vernacular the Swan Theatre; for it accommodates in its seats three thousand persons, and is built of a mass of flint stones (of which there is a prodigious supply in Britain), and supported by wooden columns painted in such excellent imitation of marble that it is able to deceive even the most cunning. Since its form resembles that of a Roman work, I have made a sketch of it above.[2]

That sketch depicts the interior of a playhouse with three tiers of galleries surrounding a circular central yard. On either side of the yard, steps (one set labelled *ingressus*) lead to the lower gallery; we cannot see the staircase that gave access to the upper tiers. A large rectangular stage (*proscænium*), improbably of greater depth than width — this is only a rough sketch — dominates the unroofed yard. The stage rests on two hefty trestles, and in turn supports, by means of a pair of Corinthian columns, the 'heavens' which provide its cover. There are three figures downstage, one of whom, a woman, sits on a bench; it might be a scene from *Twelfth Night*.[3] Is it a rehearsal or an actual performance? We cannot be sure. At the rear of the stage is a tiring-house (*mimorum ædes*), in which the players changed costume and stored their properties. They entered and exited through two massive double doors in the tiring-house façade; an open door, fitted up with curtains, would do for a discovery-space — to reveal, for example, Juliet on her bed after having swallowed Friar Lawrence's potion (the nurse 'draws the curtains'). There is no suggestion of an inner stage. Nor does De Witt's drawing show a trap door opening into the

1   On this episode see below, pp. 146–7.
2   Joseph Quincy Adams, *Shakespearean Playhouses* (Boston, 1917), pp. 167–8. For the complete Latin text of De Witt's note, see 'A Note on the Swan Theatre Drawing', *Shakespeare Survey 1* (Cambridge, 1948), pp. 23–4; also Chambers, *Elizabethan Stage*, ii. 361–2.
3   Unfortunately, however, not yet written when De Witt paid his visit.

'hell' below, although the theatre required such an aperture for ghosts and graves, as in *Hamlet*, or for the 'unhallow'd and blood-stained hole' in *Titus Andronicus*. The second storey of the façade consists of a row of six windows, apparently defining boxes in which spectators are watching the play going on below. One of these boxes would serve as a music room. They could be cleared for action aloft; this was the upper stage, used, it seems, less than earlier historians thought. Surmounting the 'heavens' is an attic loft housing the suspension-gear for flying effects, such as the descent of Jupiter in *Cymbeline*. On the roof of this hut a flagpole flies the banner of the swan,

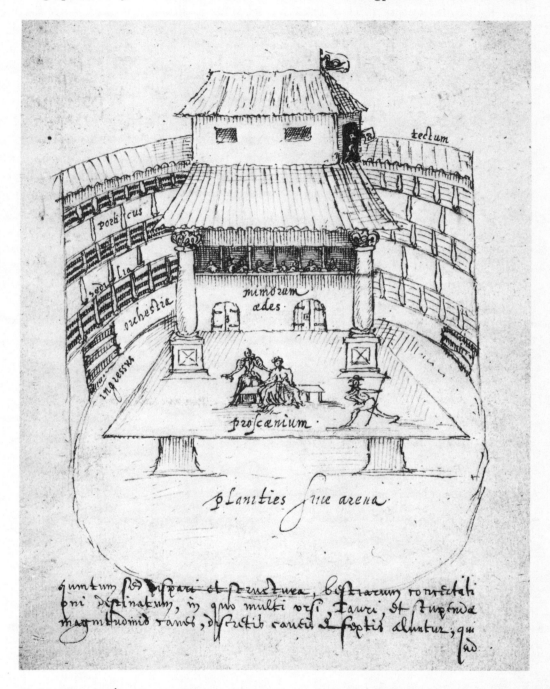

83 JOHANNES DE WITT'S SKETCH OF THE SWAN THEATRE, AS COPIED BY AREND VAN BUCH-
ELL, *c.* 1596. *University Library, Utrecht; shelfmark: MS. 842, f. 132. Transcript (of De Witt's Latin commentary, ff. 131ᵛ–2ᵛ): 'A Note on the Swan Theatre Drawing',* Shakespeare Survey 1 *(Cambridge, 1948), pp. 23–4. The drawing was discovered by Karl Theodor Gaedertz of the Royal Library, Berlin, and announced to the English-speaking world by the Berlin correspondent of* The Times *on 10 May 1888. In the same year Gaedertz published the drawing in Bremen as the frontispiece to his* Zur Kenntnis der altenglischen Bühne nebst andern Beiträgen zur Shakespeare-Litteratur. *It has been often reproduced, usually in line-block renderings. For a detailed discussion of the Swan sketch, see D. F. Rowan, 'The "Swan" Revisited',* Research Opportunities in Renaissance Drama, *x (1967), 33–48.*

hoisted to advertise a performance that day. In the doorway to the hut stands a man; he seems to be holding to his mouth a trumpet from which hangs another, smaller flag with the sign of the swan. The top gallery has a roof designated *tectum*.

The early panoramas of London provide a glimpse of the playhouses from the outside. These views show cylindrical or polygonal structures pleasantly situated among trees, meadows, and cottages; in the later panoramas the cottages crowd in upon the theatres. It is perhaps a mistake to expect cartographical precision from such guides, but the most meticulous of them, Hollar's 'Long View' of London, depicts a circular Globe and Bear Garden; we remember the 'wooden "O" '. Two exterior staircases, enclosed on the outside with lime and plaster, furnished entry to the galleries. De Witt speaks of 'a mass of flint stones' used in construction (*constructum ex coacervato lapide pyrritide*), but most of the evidence — not least that of the combustibility of the playhouses — points to timber as the chief building material, the outside being finished with the usual lime and plaster. Thatched roofing covered the galleries.

Such were the essential features of the Elizabethan theatres. To a young poet-playwright of genius, they offered the advantages of their deficiencies. The absence of scenic illusion gave a spur to the creative imagination — Arden lives the more vividly because Shakespeare's theatre furnished no woodland setting, with birds and boughs and murmuring streams, for the courtship of Rosalind and Orlando. The lack of a proscenium arch made for fluidity of dramatic movement: such a stage gave scope to the immensities of *Antony and Cleopatra*. Shakespeare might have his Chorus call for a kingdom for a stage, and lament the insufficiency of his 'unworthy scaffold to bring forth/So great an object'; but these limitations did not prevent him from triumphantly undertaking the epic historical drama of *Henry V*. All this the world knows well, although the industry of editors, with their sometimes superfluous scene divisions and literary stage directions, has sometimes obscured the exhilarating freedom of Shakespeare's art.

By the late eighties, then, London boasted an incomparable theatrical establishment and audiences ready, when the trumpet sounded, to respond to poetic drama.

10

The Upstart Crow

Shakespeare's introduction to the capital falls, frustratingly, in the void of the Lost Years, but legend has filled it with a pretty tale. The story comes under the general rubric of The Humble Origins of Great Men, and has itself a modest beginning.

The first hints emerge late in the seventeenth century, a half-century and more after Shakespeare's death. We have already encountered Mr. Dowdall, on his way back from Stratford, writing a letter filled with parish clerk's gossip about the butcher-boy who bolted and 'was Received Into the playhouse as a serviture'.[1] The first serious inquirer has nothing substantive to add: 'He was receiv'd into the Company then in being, at first in a very mean Rank; but his admirable Wit, and the natural Turn of it to the Stage, soon distinguish'd him, if not as an extraordinary Actor, yet as an excellent Writer.'[2] These statements affirm what we would anyway assume, that Shakespeare began his theatrical career as a hired man rather than a sharer. They do not tell us much else.

For the colourful elaboration that gives sustenance to the mythos we must wait until 1753 and the curious relation made in the memoir of Shakespeare in *The Lives of the Poets of Great Britain and Ireland*, published as by 'Mr Cibber', but in fact largely compiled (as Dr. Johnson informed Boswell) by Robert Shiels. Johnson knew whereof he spoke, for Shiels was his amanuensis. He precedes his contribution with a genealogy tracing it back to Sir William Davenant, the source of more than one dubious Shakespearian anecdote. Despite the pedigree, the story, trailing off into unacknowledged quotation from Rowe, probably came to Shiels *via* Johnson. Shiels presents his entry thus:

> Concerning Shakefpear's firft appearance in the playhoufe. When he came to London, he was without money and friends, and being a ftranger he knew not to whom to apply, nor by what means to fupport himfelf.——At that time coaches not being in ufe, and as gentlemen were accuftomed to ride to the playhoufe, Shakefpear, driven to the laft neceffity, went to the playhoufe door, and pick'd up a little money by taking care of the gentlemens horfes who came to the play; he became eminent even in that profeffion, and was taken notice of for his diligence and skill in it; he had foon more bufinefs than he himfelf could manage, and at laft hired boys under him, who were known by the name of Shakefpear's boys: Some of the players accidentally converfing with him, found him fo acute, and

> mafter of fo fine a converfation, that ftruck therewith, they and recommended him to the houfe, in which he was firft admitted in a very low ftation, but he did not long remain fo, for he foon diftinguifhed himfelf, if not as an extraordinary actor, at leaft as a fine writer.

84 THE SHIELS ANECDOTE. *From* The Lives of the Poets of Great Britain and Ireland, To the Time of Dean Swift. Compiled from ample Materials scattered in a Variety of Books, and especially from the MS. Notes of the late ingenious Mr. Coxeter and others, collected for this Design. *'By Mr Cibber'*, *1753. Vol. i, pp. 130–1. Reprinted in EKC, ii. 285–6.*

1 See above, p. 87; also below, item 218, p. 262.
2 Nicholas Rowe, *Some Account of the Life, &c. of Mr. William Shakespear*, in Shakespeare, *Works*, ed. Rowe (1709), i, p. vi.

To achieve marmoreal apotheosis it now required only the sonorities of the master. These Johnson in due course provided in his version for his 1765 edition of Shakespeare:

IN the time of *Elizabeth*, coaches being yet uncommon, and hired coaches not at all in ufe, thofe who were too proud, too tender, or too idle to walk, went on horfeback to any diftant bufinefs or diverfion. Many came on horfeback to the play, and when *Shakefpear* fled to *London* from the terrour of a criminal profecution, his firft expedient was to wait at the door of the play-houfe, and hold the horfes of thofe that had no fervants, that they might be ready again after the performance. In this office he became fo confpicuous for his care and readinefs, that in a fhort time every man as he alighted called for *Will. Shakefpear*, and fcarcely any other waiter was trufted with a horfe while *Will. Shakefpear* could be had. This was the firft dawn of better fortune. *Shakefpear* finding more horfes put into his hand than he could hold, hired boys to wait under his infpection, who, when *Will. Shakefpear* was fummoned, were immediately to prefent themfelves, *I am* Shakefpear's *boy, Sir.* In time *Shakefpear* found higher employment, but as long as the practice of riding to the play-houfe continued, the waiters that held the horfes retained the appellation of Shakefpear's *Boys*.

85 WILLIAM SHAKESPEARE, *PLAYS*, ED. SAMUEL JOHNSON (1765), i, p. c. *Reprinted in EKC, ii. 287–8. The passage comes after Rowe's* Account *and texts of the 1599 grant of arms and Shakespeare's will.*

The anecdote is clearly a pendant to the myth of the deer-poaching at Charlecote; early capitalist enterprise furnishes a heartening postlude to romantic pseudo-delinquency. If the story made any serious claim to authority, it would suggest that the Theatre or the Curtain was Shakespeare's first playhouse, for only these were reached by horseback.[1] But the story makes no serious claim. Rowe and Pope, cited by Johnson as his authorities, ignored it in their own editions of Shakespeare. The great Malone suspected that it owed something to exaggerated notions of the impoverishment of the Shakespeares — the young Will, friendless and unconnected, hanging loose upon society; and he rejected the story with Augustan finality: 'But, lastly, and principally, this anecdote is altogether unworthy of belief, because our author's circumstances and situation at this time, and the various extracts which I have just now given from the Records of Stratford, loudly reclaim against it.'[2]

Malone himself flirted with another tradition that has at least the merit of placing Shakespeare inside the playhouse rather than in its manured precincts: 'There is a stage tradition that his first office in the theatre was that of prompter's attendant; whose employment it is to give the performers notice to be ready to enter, as often as the business of the play requires their appearance on the stage.'[3] That was in 1780. By the time he got round to the life of Shakespeare he never lived to complete, Malone no longer attached much weight to the tradition, for he did not bother to repeat it. Instead his mind revolved upon the companies — Warwick's or Leicester's or the Queen's — which included Stratford in their provincial itineraries, and he closed his section on the horse-holding story with the kind of speculation that is more illuminating than the late efflorescences of tradition:

1 EKC, i. 60.
2 Shakespeare, *Plays and Poems*, ed. Edmond Malone (1821), ii. 164.
3 *Supplement to the Edition of Shakspeare's Plays Published in 1778 by Samuel Johnson and George Steevens*, ed. Malone (1780), i. 67. Malone added the words '*Call-boy*, or' before 'prompter's attendant' in his 1790 edition of Shakespeare (*Plays and Poems*, vol. i, pt. 1, p. 107).

It is, I think, much more probable, that his own lively disposition made him acquainted with some of the principal performers who visited Stratford, the elder Burbage, or Knell, or Bentley; and that there he first determined to engage in that profession. Lord Leicester's servants, among whom was one of the performers just mentioned, James Burbage, the father of the celebrated tragedian, had been honoured with a royal licence in 1574. With this company, therefore, or the Queen's, or Lord Warwick's comedians, it is reasonable to suppose, that he agreed to enroll himself, and that with one or the other of them he first visited the metropolis.[1]

So we find ourselves back at the resting-point for our previous chapter.

A historian following the tracks of the metropolitan companies in the eighties risks losing the scent altogether.[2] The life of the troupes was unstable. They went off on protracted tours of the hinterland; they suffered defections and absorbed new talent; they amalgamated, divided, or expired. The records for all this activity are discouragingly incomplete. It is clear, however, that throughout most of the decade the palm for popularity went to the Queen's men — the company that was, it will be recalled, lacking a man in 1587. For a time they faced only feeble competition. Derby's men fade from view altogether; other troupes — Leicester's, Sussex's, Oxford's, and Hunsdon's — kept to the provinces, with only occasional forays into the capital. The Admiral's company made a bid for London favour in 1587, but stumbled on catastrophe. During a performance in November, the players tied one of their number to a post — such a column as De Witt depicts supporting the 'Heavens' — with the intention of shooting him; but the caliver (unfortunately loaded) misfired, killing a child and a pregnant woman, and wounding another spectator. The company prudently withdrew into retirement, and for two years we do not hear of them. Meanwhile the Queen's men kept in the ascendancy. On seventeen occasions between the winters of 1583–4 and 1587–8 they performed before their monarch in plays selected by the Master of the Revels and rehearsed under his practised eye. No other troupe in those days acted so often at Court.

But the fortunes of show business are fickle. In September death took Tarlton, the clown who was so funny that the Queen had to command his removal for making her laugh excessively. With his russet coat and buttoned hat and his tabor, Tarlton was beloved of multitudes, and quite simply irreplaceable. A John Scottowe struck the appropriate elegiac note:

> The partie nowe is gone,
> and closlie clad in claye,
> Of all the Jesters in the lande,
> he bare the praise awaie.[3]

Following the usual pattern of troupes under stress, the Queen's men took to the road, picking up stray talent along the way, and wandering as far north as Lancashire, where in the early autumn of 1589 they beguiled the Earl of Nottingham with a play at his seat of New Park. For a while the company split up, one segment teaming up temporarily with Sussex's men. They diversified their offerings with tumblers, acrobatic routines, even a Turkish rope-dancer; all to no avail. The Queen's servants could not compete with the young Alleyn lending his charismatic presence to the Admiral's men at the Rose on Bankside. The Admiral's company had Marlowe, stirring theatre audiences with his high-astounding terms and a new drama of heroic dimensions. If the Queen's had Shakespeare, just beginning to make his presence in the theatre felt, we do not know definitely of any plays he wrote for them. For better or worse they certainly dealt with Robert Greene, experienced not only in letters but also in the hard school of Elizabethan low-life.[4]

He belonged to the brotherhood of University Wits: that small company of Bohemian intellectuals born in the provinces shortly after mid-century, and educated at Cambridge or Oxford. Footloose, they turned their backs on their origins, and gravitated to the capital, where they supplied the stationers with pamphlets and the players with plays. In London they led lives that were nasty, brutish, brilliant, and short. With Greene we cannot always separate fact from fiction in the fantasias he composed on autobiographical themes, or the legend made of him by

1 Shakespeare, *Plays and Poems*, ed. Malone (1821), ii. 166–7.
2 Here the most useful authority is EKC, i. 27–56.
3 British Library, MS. Harley 3885, f. 19.
4 Greene's life is recounted more fully by J. Churton Collins in his introduction to his edition of the *Plays and Poems* (Oxford, 1905), which, despite its deficiencies, has not yet been superseded.

his contemporaries. The pattern of his career — necessarily pieced together from the testimony of biased witnesses — assumes the lineaments of archetype.

He came of sound middle-class stock, the son of a Norwich saddler who educated him locally, no doubt at the Free Grammar School which, under the supervision of the mayor and aldermen, enrolled 'fourscore and four scholars'. In 1578 Greene graduated B.A. from St. John's College, Cambridge. Foreign travel provided postgraduate education; in Italy he reports learning 'all the villanies under the heavens'. Back in England, a restless libertine drowned in pride, he wandered one day into St. Andrew's Church in Norwich, where the preacher, John More — known as the Apostle of Norwich — laid before his imagination the terrors of God's Judgement. Greene repented. 'Lord have mercie upon me', he said to himself, 'and send me grace to amend and become a new man.' In 1589 he took his M.A., and married the virtuous and patient Dorothy. But the new man slipped back into the old: he got Dorothy with child, shipped her off to Lincolnshire to shift for herself as best she could, and took up again with his dissolute London companions. In his own phrase, he fell again with the dog to his old vomit.

Romances issued from Greene's facile pen; he needed to keep writing to support his prodigal life style. Having pawned sword and cloak, he shifted lodgings in stews, rioted in taverns (he was a favourite of the hostess of the Red Lattice in Tormoyle Street), and hob-nobbed with a notorious ruffian, Ball — called Cutting Ball — who would eventually meet his end on the gibbet at Tyburn. For his mistress, Greene took Ball's sister. She bore him a son, ironically named Fortunatus; he would die young. His experiences Greene exploited for his own brand of superior, if sensational, journalism. In a series of pamphlets Greene made his notable discoveries of cosenage, laying bare the practices by which cross-biters, priggars, gripes, nips, foists, and lifts preyed upon conies — young gentlemen, country folk, apprentices. Meanwhile he somehow managed to turn out plays also: *Alphonsus King of Aragon*, *The Scottish History of James IV*, *A Looking Glass for London and England* (with his fellow-wit, Thomas Lodge), and a minor masterpiece, *Friar Bacon and Friar Bungay*, in the vein of wonder and romance he could still intermittently command. One episode involving the Queen's men shows him capable of the double-dealing he exposed in others. 'Aske the Queens Players', demanded the pseudonymous Cuthbert Cunny-Catcher in 1592, 'if you sold them not *Orlando Furioso* for twenty Nobles, and when they were in the country, sold the same Play to the Lord Admirals men for as much more. Was not this plaine *Conny-Catching* Maister R.G.?'[1]

The charge, even if true, no longer really mattered much. In August 1592, flaunting finery his means could ill sustain, he ate a last meal with Nashe and other cronies. That evening he overindulged in Rhenish wine and pickled herrings, and this excess brought on his last illness. He was then lodging with his mistress, 'a sorry ragged queane', and their bastard in the house of a shoemaker of Dowgate, one Isam, and his wife. For a month Greene lingered in squalor, deserted by friends but attended by troops of lice. Mrs. Isam gave him the penny-pot of malmsey he pitifully begged, while Gabriel Harvey exulted in the downfall of the wicked.

> A rakehell: A makeshift: A scribling foole:
> A famous bayard in Citty, and Schoole.
> Now sicke, as a Dog: and ever brainesick:
> Where such a raving, and desperate Dick?[2]

Between prayers Greene scribbled his last confessions, and near the end wrote piteously to his abandoned Dorothy, asking her to forgive him and pay the ten pounds he owed his host. When he died, Mrs. Isam crowned him with a garland of bays, in accordance with his last wish. Before the year was out the bookstalls of St. Paul's Churchyard displayed *The Repentance of Robert Greene, Maister of Artes* and *Greenes Groats-worth of witte, bought with a million of Repentance. Describing the follie of youth, the falshood of make-shifte flatterers, the miserie of the negligent, and mischiefes of deceiving Courtezans. Written before his death and published at his dyeing request.*

Thus lived and died Robert Greene, the saddler's son who would not willingly let the world forget that he was a Master of Arts. His progress furnishes a direct antithesis to that of the glover's son from Stratford who never proceeded beyond grammar school. But Greene's career holds more

1 'Cuthbert Cunny-Catcher', *The Defence of Conny Catching* (1592), sig. C3^{r-v}.
2 [Gabriel Harvey], *Foure Letters, and certaine Sonnets* (1592), p. 4.

than an exemplary interest. In the *Groats-worth of Witte* he makes the first unmistakable reference to Shakespeare in London.

'The Swan sings melodiously before death, that in all his life time useth but a jarring sound,' the author reminds his Gentlemen Readers in the preface.

Greene though able inough to write, yet deeplyer serched with sicknes then ever heeretofore, sendes you his Swanne like songe, for that he feares he shall never againe carroll to you woonted love layes, never againe discover to you youths pleasures. How ever yet sicknesse, riot, Incontinence, have at once shown their extremitie yet if I recover, you shall all see, more fresh sprigs, then ever sprang from me, directing you how to live, yet not diswading ye from love.[1]

Self-pity and self-reproach here strike a comfortable alliance sustained in the thinly disguised autobiographical fiction which follows. This recounts the adventures of Roberto, an impoverished graduate who, fleeced by a whore, goes off to curse his destiny. Being a poet, he inveighs in numbers, and, while sighing sadly in Latin, is approached by a gorgeously apparelled stranger, who has eavesdropped from the other side of the hedge. The stranger, it turns out, is a player keen to book new writing talent for his company. In the old days, when the world was hard, he carried fardels on his back; now he commands a wardrobe worth over £200, and gives the appearance of a gentleman of substance. He has thundered terribly on the stage (Roberto finds his voice 'nothing gratious'), and can still at a pinch indite a pretty speech; for he was 'a countrey Author, passing at a Morrall, . . . and for seven yærs space was absolute Interpreter to the puppets'. Seeing no alternative, Roberto joins forces with the player, and becomes 'an Arch-plaiemaking-poet', his purse now full, now empty; the darling of lewd swearing companions, the observer and unmasker of 'all the rabble of that uncleane generation of vipers'.

One authority has suggested that the unnamed player with gentlemanly airs is Shakespeare: he must have spoken with a broad provincial accent; hence the ungracious voice. He was a country author, and his seven years' apprenticeship at acting covers neatly the period between the birth of the twins in 1585 and the composition of the *Groats-worth* in 1592.[2] But the hedge encounter, which must be at least partly fanciful, takes place not in 1592 but in Roberto's past; the Morals that the player boasts of having written (he mentions *Man's Wit* and the *Dialogue of Dives*) belong to the pre-Shakespearian drama; and Greene, clearly represented as junior, was actually six years older than Shakespeare.

Yet the *Groats-worth of Witte* contains — no question — a desperate shaft directed at Shakespeare. The author hurls it later, after having abandoned any pretence at fiction; he speaks as Greene, offering, while life still beats, the bitter wisdom of experience. He sets down a set of religious wholesome rules for good conduct, and then, in a letter, addresses some special advice to three of his 'fellow Schollers about this Cittie': Marlowe and (probably) Nashe and Peele. There follows the celebrated denunciation of 'an upstart Crow, beautified with our feathers'.

> Bafe minded men all three of you, if by my miferie you be not warnd: for vnto none of you (like mee) fought thofe burres to cleaue : thofe Puppets (I meane) that fpake from our mouths, thofe Anticks garnifht in our colours. Is it not ftrange, that I, to whom they all haue beene beholding: is it not like that you, to whome they all haue beene beholding, fhall (were yee in that cafe as I am now) bee both at once of them forfaken? Yes truft them not : for there is an vp-ftart Crow, beautified with our feathers, that with his Tygers hart wrapt in a Players hyde, fuppofes he is as well able to bombaft out a blanke verfe as the beft of you : and beeing an abfolute Iohannes fac totum, is in his owne conceit the onely Shake-fcene in a countrey. O that I might intreat your rare wits to be imploied in more profitable courfes : & let thofe Apes imitate your

1   Robert Greene, *Groats-worth of witte, bought with a million of Repentance* (1592), sig. A3ᵛ.
2   A. L. Rowse, *Shakespeare the Man* (1973), p. 60.

I*

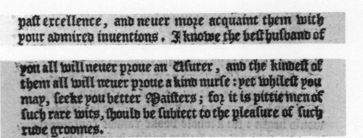

past excellence, and neuer moze acquaint them with
your admired inuentions . I knowe the best husband of

you all will neuer proue an Usurer, and the kindest of
them all will neuer proue a kind nurse : yet whilest you
may, seeke you better Maisters ; for it is pittie men of
such rare wits, should be subiect to the pleasure of such
rude groomes.

86 ROBERT GREENE, *GREENES GROATS-WORTH OF WITTE, BOUGHT WITH A MILLION OF REPENTANCE* (1592), sigs. F1ᵛ–2. *Copy in the British Library; shelfmark: C.57.b.42.* STC *12245. Thomas Tyrwhitt (1730–86), best remembered as the editor of Chaucer and of Aristotle's* Poetics, *first noticed the passage, and provided George Steevens with a note about it which the latter included in the second edition of the Johnson–Steevens* Plays of William Shakspeare *(1778), vi. 565–6. Tyrwhitt reasonably sees the* Henry VI *plays as having 'at the time of their appearance, a sufficient degree of excellence to alarm the jealousy of the older playwrights'.*

That Greene has singled out Shakespeare for attack is evident from the punning reference to a Shake-scene, and confirmed by a parodic allusion to one of Shakespeare's earliest plays. In *3 Henry VI* Queen Margaret has taken the Duke of York prisoner at the battle of Wakefield; she will kill him, but first she taunts him with a handkerchief dipped in his slain son's blood, and in a long tirade he responds with the only weapon left him, the rhetoric of invective. York's speech contains the line, 'O tiger's heart wrapp'd in a woman's hide!' (I. iv. 137). By changing one word Greene has accused Shakespeare of cruelty.

It is not his only charge. The rest, being obscure in the best Elizabethan tradition, has inspired debate without end. The thrust of the passage as a whole is against the actors ('Puppets . . . that spake from our mouths') who batten on the dramatists. A contempt for mean players came naturally to a Cambridge M.A. dependent upon these affluent inferiors for his penny-pot and lice-infested bed, and such contempt would mingle with other, equally disagreeable emotions engendered by the accusation that he had fobbed off the same playbook on two companies. These feelings find a focus in the fable of the crow.

From antiquity the bird gifted with powers of mimicry but not of invention had been likened to the actor. In Macrobius, Greene found the stories of Roscius and the cobbler's crow he used in *Francescos Fortunes*: 'why *Roscius*, art thou proud with *Esops* crow, being pranct with the glorie of others feathers? of thy selfe thou canst say nothing, and if the Cobler hath taught thee to say *Ave Caesar*, disdain not thy tutor, because thou pratest in a Kings chamber.'[1] Roscius here stands for Alleyn. Shakespeare too was an actor, and is attacked as such; the phrase about the 'upstart Crow, beautified with our feathers' continues the idea expressed in 'Anticks garnisht in our colours'. Moreover, the mere actor has the audacity to set himself up as a universal genius (*Johannes Factotum*) who can, by turning out stilted and bombastic blank verse, rival his superiors and deprive them of employment. Many have interpreted the passage in this way.

But does it harbour a more sinister charge? Perhaps the crow is not the bird taught to imitate its betters that derives ultimately from Aesop, Martial, and Macrobius; instead Greene may allude to Horace's third *Epistle*, in which the poet uses the image of a crow (*cornicula*) divested of its plundered lustre (*furtivis nudata coloribus*) in connection with the idea of plagiarism. These lines were well known in the Renaissance. In *A Strappado for the Divell* Richard Brathwait sneers at thieving crows that steal 'selected flowres from others wit'.[2] Is Greene then maliciously suggesting that Shakespeare has appropriated the flowers of *his* wit? This is the second interpretation, and is of long standing. As far back as the eighteenth century it gave rise to the view that Shakespeare began his literary career as a Johannes Factotum in the sense of a Jack-of-all-trades who — in addition to acting — revised and adapted the plays of others, including Greene.

However, few today accept this theory. It is inherently improbable that a company would entrust to a novice the task of improving the work of experienced professional dramatists. Most of the more reliable authorities now think that Greene was complaining because Shakespeare, a mere uneducated player, had the effrontery to compete as a dramatist with his betters; not because the same base fellow pilfered his wares from others. But of course it is not impossible that

1   Greene, *Francescos Fortunes : Or the second part of Greenes Never too Late* . . . (1590), sigs. B4ᵛ–C1.
2   Arthur Freeman draws attention to the Brathwait passage in 'Notes on the Text of "2 Henry VI", and the "Upstart Crow" ', *Notes and Queries*, ccxiii (1968), 129–30.

Greene was making a double accusation, thus conflating Aesop's crow with Horace's, which were anyway closely associated in the minds of his audience.[1]

Whatever the drift of this notorious passage, the pamphlet gave ample cause for offence; for Greene's notorious letter libelled not only Shake-scene but also two old comrades. He rebukes the 'famous gracer of Tragedians' — Marlowe — for atheism and for discipleship of Machiavelli; with false delicacy he reproves 'yong Juvenal, that byting Satyrist' — presumably Nashe — for indulging in 'too much liberty of reproofe'. When the *Groats-worth* appeared the improbable rumour circulated in London that Nashe, not Greene, had written it. In his *Pierce Penilesse*, printed only a month after Greene's death, Nashe recoiled in horror from the suggestion: 'Other news I am advertised of, that a scald trivial lying pamphlet, cald *Greens groats-worth of wit*, is given out to be of my doing. God never have care of my soule, but utterly renounce me, if the least word or sillable in it proceeded from my pen, or if I were any way privie to the writing or printing of it.'[2] The publisher of the *Groats-worth*, William Wright, evidently anticipated a storm, for he took the unusual precaution of disassociating himself from the pamphlet; when he entered it on the Stationers' Register on 20 September 1592, he added to the licence the exculpatory clause, 'uppon the perill of Henrye Chettle'.

Attention now focuses on Chettle. Of about Shakespeare's age, he was a Londoner; an easygoing sort, puffing and sweating because of his overweight. By trade a printer who had served his seven years' apprenticeship, Chettle nourished literary aspirations. For Henslowe at the Rose he would write wholly or in part forty-eight plays over a period of five years, but his furious scribbling would not spare him the embarrassment of poverty and debt. Although a contemporary praised Chettle for his comedies, as a playwright he is remembered, if at all, for his revenge tragedy of *Hoffman*. In 1592 these activities lay ahead. He was then a master printer whose partnership with William Hoskins and John Danter, two fairly disreputable members of the Stationers' Company, had lately come unstuck; Danter would go on to print the first quartos of *Titus Andronicus* and *Romeo and Juliet*. To Chettle, at loose ends, fell the task of preparing copy of the *Groats-worth* for the printers. His share in this venture brought interesting repercussions.

In 'To the Gentlemen Readers' prefacing his own *Kind-Harts Dreame*, printed by the same William Wright before the year was out, Chettle makes his famous apology to Shakespeare:

> *About three moneths since died M. Robert Greene, leauing many papers in sundry Booke sellers hands, among other his Groatsworth of wit, in which a letter written to diuers play-makers, is offensiuely by one or two of them taken, and because on the dead they cannot be auenged, they wilfully forge in their conceites a liuing Author: and after tossing it two and fro, no remedy, but it must light on me. How I haue all the time of my conuersing in printing hindred the bitter inueying against schollers, it hath been very well knowne, and how in that I dealt I can sufficiently prooue. With neither of them that take offence was I acquainted, and with one of them I care not if I neuer be: The other, whome at that time I did not so much spare, as since I wish I had, for that as I haue moderated the heate of liuing writers, and might haue vsde my owne discretion (especially in such a case) the Author beeing dead, that I did not, I am as sory, as if the originall fault had beene my fault, because my selfe haue seene his demeanor no lesse ciuill than he exelent in the qualitie he professes: Besides, diuers of worship haue reported, his vprightnes of dealing, which argues his honesty, and his fatious grace in writing, which aprooues his Art.*

87   HENRY CHETTLE, *KIND-HARTS DREAME* [1592], sigs. A3ᵛ-4. *Copy in the Bodleian Library; shelfmark: Malone 670(2). STC 5123. Malone is the first to draw attention to the allusion to Shakespeare in what he describes as 'a very scarce pamphlet'* (Shakespeare, Plays and Poems, *1790 ed., vol. i, pt. 1, pp. 274-6). He quotes the relevant extract from Chettle's prefatory epistle.*

1   J. Dover Wilson, 'Malone and the Upstart Crow', *Shakespeare Survey 4* (Cambridge, 1951), p. 65. I have profited from Wilson's valuable close analysis of the passage.

2   Thomas Nashe, *Pierce Penilesse his Supplication to the Divell*, in *Works*, ed. Ronald B. McKerrow (rev. F. P. Wilson; Oxford, 1958), i. 154.

It is a carefully worded passage. 'Facetious [i.e. polished] grace' gracefully echoes Cicero's praise of Plautus in *De Officiis*. Chettle's allusions are circumspect. The complainant whose acquaintance Chettle disdains while at the same time revering his learning appears to have offered threats ('him I would wish to use me no worse than I deserve'). This must have been Marlowe. Chettle reveals that he struck out from Greene's letter an aspersion which 'had it beene true, yet to publish it, was intollerable' — could this have been an accusation against Marlowe of homosexuality? And who were the 'divers of worship' who sprang to Shakespeare's defence? Some enthusiasts, eager to supply their idol with the glamour of patrician connections, have suggested the intervention of noble lords. Shakespeare had not yet made the acquaintance of the Earl of Southampton — that would come the next year — but the biographer can always round up a stray aristocrat or two: perhaps the worshipful benefactor was Ferdinando, Lord Strange, patron of poets and players, and friend of the Queen's favourite, the Earl of Essex; perhaps it was the mercurial Essex himself. Dover Wilson indulges in a pleasing fancy: 'Possibly the emissary was no other than Shakespeare himself, bearing a sharply worded letter from his patron, and smoothing matters over for Chettle by his own charming manners.'[1] Should the epistle, whether carried by Shakespeare himself or delivered to Chettle afterwards, one day come to light, it is unlikely to bear a nobleman's seal. The Elizabethans made careful distinctions in their forms of address. Noblemen they would refer to as divers of honour; *worship* applied to gentlemen.[2] Anyway Shakespeare did not yet have a patron, and there is no evidence that he ever enjoyed the favour of Strange or Essex. Who his influential supporters were we can hardly begin to guess.

The *Groats-worth* episode presents still another tantalising problem. Chettle in his preface complains about Greene's villainous scrawl, which no licenser or printer could be expected to read; and he says that he copied it over as best he could, suppressing the scandalous tenor of the letter but not, he swears, adding a word of his own — 'for I protest it was all Greenes, not mine nor Maister Nashes, as some unjustly have affirmed'. Now, almost 400 years after Chettle wrote, the spectre that he sought — successfully it seemed — to lay has been raised once again by Professor Warren Austin.[3] What if the *Groats-worth of Witte* is a fabrication after all? What if Chettle, a journeyman of letters, always needy, impersonated Greene's style and, in collusion with his colleagues in the printing trade, foisted the hoax on a public intrigued by the sensational circumstances surrounding the demise of a University Wit? The motive for the attack on Shakespeare would be a crass journalistic desire to give the pamphlet the spice of added topical interest; to stir up that tempest which in fact took place. Self-defence always arouses suspicions of culpability. Others before Austin have worried about the authorship of the *Groats-worth*, but he is the first to enlist the electronic computers in his cause.[4] The resultant formidable array of data — 'Lexical Choice Variables', 'Morphological Variables', and 'Syntactical Variables' — is calculated to disarm the scruples of orthodox sceptics. It is an intriguing thesis, elaborately set forth.

Still, doubts present themselves. Greene wrote voluminously; the surviving Chettle corpus is meagre. For his inquiry, Austin has quarried five selections from Greene, and three from Chettle; a statistically unimpressive sampling. Some of the 'Chettle' characteristics appear in Greene pieces not included in the survey. There are other problems as well.[5] This does not mean that the hypothesis is invalid, only that Austin has not proved his case. It is unlikely that such a case can be proved. In the absence of conclusive proof to the contrary, Greene must continue to bear responsibility for his mean death-bed diatribe, and we may accept, with some traces of unease,

1 Dover Wilson, *The Essential Shakespeare* (Cambridge, 1932), p. 62.

2 See William A. Ringler, Jr., 'Spenser, Shakespeare, Honor, and Worship', *Renaissance News*, xiv (1961), 159–61.

3 Warren B. Austin, *A Computer-Aided Technique for Stylistic Discrimination. The Authorship of* Greene's Groatsworth of Wit (U. S. Department of Health, Education and Welfare, 1969).

4 J. Payne Collier first suggested that Chettle 'possibly' wrote the *Groats-worth of Witte* in his 1844 *Life of William Shakespeare*, and H-P picked up the suggestion in his *Life*, p. 143. The Folger Shakespeare Library has a copy of the *Life* (shelfmark: PR2894.H28.1848) with a marginal comment by C. M. Ingleby alongside the passage: 'An absurd conjecture. Greene's work is full of genius, whereas Chettle was a poor stick, & could hardly write English.' At the least Austin has shown that the conjecture is not so absurd as Ingleby thought.

5 For the several strictures, see the reviews of Austin by R. L. Widmann, *Shakespeare Quarterly*, xxiii (1972), 214–5, and by T. R. Waldo, *Computers and the Humanities*, vii (1972), 109–10.

Chettle's apologia. A substitution of authors does not, in any event, resolve the interpretative problems, which are after all paramount.

Chettle's defence of Shakespeare's 'uprightnes of dealing' would seem to imply that he took Greene's innuendoes as impugning the poet's honesty. Were they not so taken by R. B., Gent. (conceivably Richard Barnfield) in one of the poems comprising the curious little collection entitled *Greenes Funeralls*?

> *Greene*, is the pleasing Object of an eie:
> *Greene*, pleasde the eies of all that lookt uppon him.
> *Greene*, is the ground of everie Painters die:
> *Greene*, gave the ground, to all that wrote upon him.
> Nay more the men, that so Eclipst his fame:
> Purloynde his Plumes, can they deny the same?[1]

This last contemporary reference shows, it would seem, that some of Greene's mud still clung to Shakespeare, here again recalled as an upstart crow decked in University Wit feathers. So, at any rate, almost everybody has thought since *Greenes Funeralls* came to light almost a century and a half ago, and the passage has served to bolster the view that Greene's audience understood him to be charging Shakespeare with plagiarism. But Professor Austin has argued, this time more conclusively, that the object of R. B.'s vitriolic reproaches is not Shakespeare but Greene's enemy, Gabriel Harvey, who eclipsed Greene's fame (i.e. blackened his reputation) by traducing him, within days of his death, in the *Foure Letters*.[2] Even the borrowed-feathers reference, which seems so clearly to echo the *Groats-worth*, has a more likely inspiration in Harvey's pamphlet: 'Thanke other', he rebukes Greene, 'for thy borrowed & filched plumes of some little Italianated bravery. . . .'

So many ambiguities and perplexities attach to Greene's attack on Shakespeare and the sequel in Chettle's apology that one can sympathize with the exasperation voiced by one distinguished commentator in this century. 'This passage from Greene has had such a devastating effect on Shakespearian study', Smart complains, 'that we cannot but wish it had never been written or never discovered.'[3] Still, if the episode had not taken place, we should have been deprived of the handsome early tribute to Shakespeare in *Kind-Harts Dreame*, the first glimpse we get of him as a man, and all the more effective for being offset by the evocation, however brief and glancing, of the turbulent Marlowe, to whom no apology is forthcoming. And what of the rancorous passage, so offensive to bardolaters, that prompted the amends? It too pays its own unpremeditated compliment to Shakespeare, for this is the tribute which envy renders to achievement. Greene's *Groats-worth of Witte* is, as the author says but not in the sense that he intended, a swansong; the dying outcry of a generation of university-trained playwrights who were passing from the scene.[4]

1   *Greenes Funeralls*, ed. McKerrow (1911), p. 81.
2   Austin, 'A Supposed Contemporary Allusion to Shakespeare as a Plagiarist', *Shakespeare Quarterly*, vi (1955), 373–80.
3   John Semple Smart, *Shakespeare: Truth and Tradition* (1928), p. 196.
4   The point is made by EKC, i. 58.

11

Plays, Plague, and a Patron

If by 1592 Shakespeare had made his mark as a playwright, with what plays, we may ask. He had nothing yet in print, but this need hardly cause surprise. In that time an author retained little control over his literary creations once they left his hands. The profession of letters as we know it did not yet exist; authors were unprotected by a law of copyright — the regulations formulated and enforced at Stationers' Hall catered for the interests of the printers. Of all writers a dramatist had least to say about the publication of his works. He strove, after all, to please audiences in the theatre, not a reading public. The artefacts he sold to his theatrical company became their property, and so long as they remained viable on the stage, the actors would jealously guard them from print; for once a playbook appeared on the stalls, anybody could buy a copy, and have it produced. In Richard Brome's contract with the Salisbury Court company in Caroline times (the only such agreement of which we have knowledge, although there must have been others) the dramatist formally consented to abstain from publishing his plays without the express licence of the troupe.[1] Sometimes plays reached print anyway because of the misfortunes of the company — plague, financial stress, bankruptcy, or disbanding — or because pirated texts, inevitably corrupt, found their way into the printing-house. For one or other of these reasons, about half of Shakespeare's plays appeared in quarto editions during his lifetime; but all this came about after 1592. Clues to his earliest play-writing achievements must be sought in contemporary allusions. Fortunately the ill-will of Robert Greene in this respect renders an unintended benefaction.

The 'tiger's heart' reference in *Groats-worth* shows that *3 Henry VI* was then on the boards, and hence, most likely, the first two instalments of the trilogy as well. This plausible inference receives confirmation in the famous tribute paid by Nashe to the popularity of *1 Henry VI*. 'How would it have joyed brave *Talbot* (the terror of the French)', he exclaims, 'to thinke that after he had lyne two hundred yeares in his Tombe, hee should triumphe againe on the Stage, and have his bones newe embalmed with the teares of ten thousand spectators at least (at severall times), who, in the Tragedian that represents his person, imagine they behold him fresh bleeding.'[2] This passage, which occurs in *Pierce Penilesse* (entered on the Stationers' Register on 8 August 1592), recalls Act IV, scene vii, in which old Talbot dies with his young son — his Icarus, his blossom — dead in his arms, and, frozen emblematically in the posture of a funerary sculpture, receives from Sir William Lucy his elaborate epitaph:

> . . . the great Alcides of the field,
> Valiant Lord Talbot, Earl of Shrewsbury,
> Created for his rare success in arms
> Great Earl of Washford, Waterford, and Valence,
> Lord Talbot of Goodrig and Urchinfield,
> Lord Strange of Blackmere, Lord Verdun of Alton,
> Lord Cromwell of Wingfield, Lord Furnival of Sheffield,
> The thrice victorious Lord of Falconbridge,
> Knight of the noble order of Saint George,

1 The details of Brome's 1635 contract, revised and renewed in 1638, are known from *Heton* v. *Brome*, a suit in the Court of Requests in 1640. Anne Haaker published transcripts of the documents in 'The Plague, the Theater, and the Poet', *Renaissance Drama*, N.S., i (1968), 283–306. See also G. E. Bentley, *The Profession of Dramatist in Shakespeare's Time 1590–1642* (Princeton, N.J., 1971), pp. 113–44, 264–8.

2 Thomas Nashe, *Pierce Penilesse his Supplication to the Divell*, in Nashe, *Works*, ed. R. B. McKerrow (rev. F. P. Wilson; Oxford, 1958), i. 212.

Worthy Saint Michael, and the Golden Fleece,
Great Marshal to Henry the Sixth
Of all his wars within the realm of France.

The enthusiasm of Elizabethan theatregoers for the *Henry VI* plays — an enthusiasm evident not only from Nashe but also from their subsequent publishing history — has moved some latter-day biographers to puzzlement and condescension. 'The series is unplayable today', writes Miss Marchette Chute, 'if only for its lack of characterization and its jingoistic view of English history, but in its own day it ranked as one of the best series of productions that the London theatre had to offer.'[1] Miss Chute, having no critical pretensions of her own, merely reflected the consensus when she wrote, in 1951; and so her remark illustrates the ephemeral validity of such pronouncements. Shakespeare's first English history plays have since triumphantly returned to the stage in Stratford, as *The Wars of the Roses* (heavily adapted, to be sure), and elsewhere. Strictly speaking, the documentary biographer should stand aloof from criticism, whether interpretative or judgemental, but it seems permissible to savour the fact that Shakespeare, while still in his twenties, had conceived and executed a sequence of historical dramas of a scale and complexity entirely novel to the London stage. If, as is certainly possible, he also wrote *Richard III* before 1593, he had extended trilogy into tetralogy, and epically transformed the amorphous materials of his narrative chronicle sources. Only the Mystery plays of the cathedral towns, which he had perhaps himself witnessed as a boy in Coventry, afforded a precedent for drama on the Shakespearian scale.

What else had he written? In the absence of a firm chronology one must speculate, and some guesses are better than others. There are critics who regard *Love's Labour's Lost* as very early work, but the problem of dating is complicated by evidences of revision, and on grounds of style a date around 1595 seems more likely. *The Taming of the Shrew*, in every way ruder, has a more convincing claim to precedence. So too *The Comedy of Errors* and *Titus Andronicus* convey an impression of youth, and may be taken, despite startling surface dissimilarity, as opposite sides of the same coin: academic comedy and academic tragedy, both transfused with the life-giving blood of the popular stage (*Titus* literally thus transfused). For *The Comedy of Errors* Shakespeare adapted two plays of Plautus, the *Menaechmi* — the principal source — and *Amphitruo*. In *Titus* he pays homage to his beloved *Metamorphoses*; but Seneca's *Thyestes* also provided fare to banquet on. If there is merit to the tradition that Shakespeare spent some of his Lost Years teaching in the country, he would have a pedagogue's familiarity with these classics. The Latinity of *The Comedy of Errors* and *Titus Andronicus* would moreover come naturally enough to a grammar-school man competing, at the outset of his career, with university trained playwrights.[2]

We have one external clue to the date of *Titus*. In his Induction to *Bartholomew Fair*, performed at the Hope in 1614, Jonson has the Scrivener propose, as one of several articles of agreement with the spectators, that 'Hee that will sweare, *Jeronimo*, or *Andronicus* are the best playes, yet, shall passe unexcepted at, heere, as a man whose Judgement shewes it is constant, and hath stood still, these five and twentie, or thirtie yeeres.'[3] *Jeronimo* is an alternative title for Kyd's *Spanish Tragedy*, to the resounding popular success of which Shakespeare is responding. Twenty-five or thirty years carries us back to 1584–9. Of course Jonson is not writing with the needs of future theatrical historians in mind; he rounds off his numbers, and perhaps overstates the antiquity of plays to underscore his point about the backwardness of audience taste. But the reference supports a very early date for *Titus Andronicus*.

It is fair to allow that, from almost the first days of Shakespeare scholarship, connoisseurs have questioned his sole responsibility for *Titus*, and also (somewhat later) for the *Henry VI* trilogy. In *1 Henry VI*, the irreverent treatment of Joan of Arc, depicted not as a christian martyr but as a sorceress and virago, gave offence. The same authorities thought that Shakespeare, setting out in the theatre as a play-botcher, lightly revised two anonymous plays which were the originals

---

1   Marchette Chute, *Shakespeare of London* (1951), p. 85.
2   This reasonable suggestion is made by Peter Alexander, *Shakespeare's Henry VI and Richard III* (Cambridge, 1929), p. 8.
3   *Ben Jonson*, ed. C. H. Herford and Percy and Evelyn Simpson (Oxford, 1925–52), vi. 16.

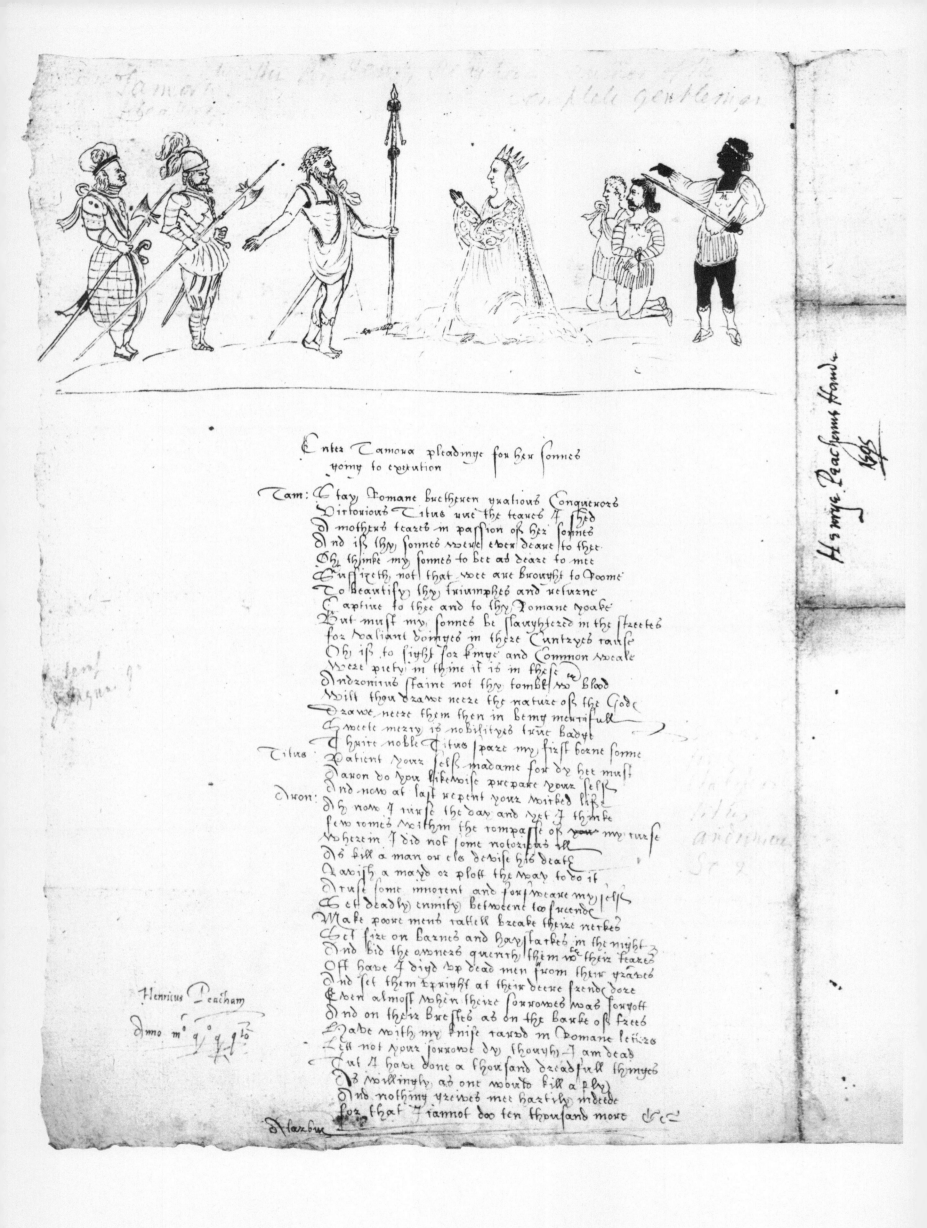

Henrye Peachams Hande

1595

Enter Tamora pleadinge for her sonnes
going to execution

Tam: Stay, Romane bretheren gratious Conquerors
Victorious Titus rue the teares I shed
A mothers teares in passion of her sonnes
And if thy sonnes were ever deare to thee
Oh, thinke my sonnes to bee as deare to mee
Sufficeth not that wee are brought to Roome
To beautify thy triumphes and returne
Captive to thee and to thy Romane yoake
But must my sonnes be slaughtered in the streetes
For valiant doinges in there Cuntryes cause
Oh if to fight for kinge and Common weale
Were pietye in thine it is in these
Andronicus staine not thy tombe with blood
Wilt thou drawe neere the nature of the Gods
Drawe neere them then in beinge mercifull
Sweete mercy is nobilityes true badge
Thrice noble Titus spare my first borne sonne
Titus   Patient your self madame for dy hee must
Axon do you likewise prepare your self
Axon: Ah now I curse the day and yet I thinke
Fewe comes within the compasse of my curse
Wherein I did not some notorious ill
As kill a man or els devise his deate
Ravish a mayd or plott the way to do it
Accuse some innocent and forsweare my selfe
Set deadly enmity betweene too freende
Make poore mens cattell breake theire necks
Set fire on barnes and haystackes in the night
And bid the owners quench them with their teares
Oft have I digd up dead men from their graves
And set them upright at their deere frends dore
Even almost when theire sorrowes was forgott
And on their Brestes as on the barke of trees
Have with my knife carved in Romane letters
Lett not your sorrowe dy though I am dead
Tut I have done a thousand dreadfull thinges
As willingly as one would kill a fly
And nothing greives mee hartily indeede
For that I cannot do ten thousand more &c

Henricus Peacham
Anno m° q° q° q°

Martius

of *2* and *3 Henry VI*, the former supposedly being based on *The First part of the Contention betwixt the two famous Houses of Yorke and Lancaster*, printed in 1594, and the latter on *The True Tragedie of Richard Duke of Yorke*, published the next year. From as far back as 1687, readers have sought to relieve Shakespeare of the burden of *Titus* — 'the most incorrect and indigested piece in all his Workes', Ravenscroft sneered; 'It seems rather a heap of Rubbish then a Structure.'[1] Such commentators allow Shakespeare a 'master-touch' or two, the occasional blossom on the dung-heap, while shifting the play as a whole onto some lesser breed of playwright — a George Peele, perhaps — outside the laws of dramatic decorum; anyone but the incomparable Bard. Behind the dismissal lurks, one suspects, a fastidious distaste for cannibalism, rape, and mutilation.

Yet the 'heap of Rubbish' drew multitudes to the playhouse. How it appeared to a contemporary is uniquely recorded in the Longleat manuscript, with its drawing of Tamora on her knees, pleading with Titus to spare her two sons. Behind her the sons also kneel, and behind them stands, with sword drawn, the isolated figure of Aaron the Moor. Did whoever sketched the scene — the name Henry Peacham appears in the margin — remember 'the actual action and grouping of Shakespeare's fellows in Shakespeare's theatre', as Dover Wilson has suggested?[2] Or does the drawing capture a particular moment in a private performance of the play? These questions elude solution, but the Longleat drawing makes clear that *Titus Andronicus* left a vivid impression.

In modern times revival, beginning with the celebrated Brook/Olivier production in 1955, has once again demonstrated the stage vitality of a formerly contemned play, and revealed also how the author distances the barbarities by stylized dramaturgy and formal rhetoric. Anyway, literary connoisseurship provides no reliable instrument for resolving questions of authenticity. In 1929 Peter Alexander demonstrated that the *Contention* and *True Tragedie* are in fact corrupt texts — bad quartos — of Shakespearian originals. The fact that the playwright's friends and fellows from the King's men, Heminges and Condell, included *Titus Andronicus* and all three parts of *Henry VI* in the First Folio carries powerful presumptive evidence of Shakespeare's authorship of these works. If he completed these plays by 1592, and *The Comedy of Errors* as well (not to mention *Richard III* and *The Taming of the Shrew*), he had experimented, with extraordinary success, in the three dramatic genres — comedy, tragedy, and history — recognized by his first editors.

It remains an *if*. We do not have a record of the performance of *The Comedy of Errors* until

Opposite:

88   TITUS ANDRONICUS IN PERFORMANCE, 1595 (?). *MS. in the library of the Marquess of Bath at Longleat (Harley Papers, vol. i, f. 159ᵛ). Transcript: E. K. Chambers, 'The First Illustration to "Shakespeare"', The Library, 4th Ser., v (1925), 327–9; J. Dover Wilson, 'Titus Andronicus on the Stage in 1595', Shakespeare Survey 1 (Cambridge, 1948), pp. 17–18. The signature in the lower left-hand margin suggests that a Henry Peacham transcribed the forty lines of verse and perhaps made the drawing too. The purport of the date underneath the signature, 'Anno mᵒ qᵒ g qᵗᵒ', is less clear, but is probably to be interpreted as 1594 or 1595. Henry Peacham, the schoolmaster and miscellanist best known as the author of* The Compleat Gentleman, *left a number of pen-and-ink drawings which the* Dictionary of National Biography *describes as 'very neat'. He commenced B.A. at Trinity College, Cambridge, in 1595; his father Henry, a classical scholar, was then still alive, and so might also conceivably be the Peacham of the Longleat drawing. The document, consisting of a single folded sheet, bears the endorsement, 'Henry Peachams Hande 1595', in an Elizabethan script; this may, however, be a forgery by J. Payne Collier, who perpetrated much mischief with similar fabrications. In any event, the signature alongside the text is authentic enough.*

Mrs. S. C. Lomas calendared the document in 1907 (H. M. C., Longleat Papers, ii. 43), and Chambers brought it to public notice in the article cited above.

---

1   Edward Ravenscroft, Address 'To the Reader', *Titus Andronicus, or The Rape of Lavinia* (1687), sig. A2; in EKC, ii. 254–5.

2   William Shakespeare, *Titus Andronicus*, ed. J. Dover Wilson (The New Shakespeare; Cambridge, 1948), p. 99; see also Wilson, '*Titus Andronicus* on the Stage in 1595', *Shakespeare Survey 1* (Cambridge, 1948), pp. 17–22.

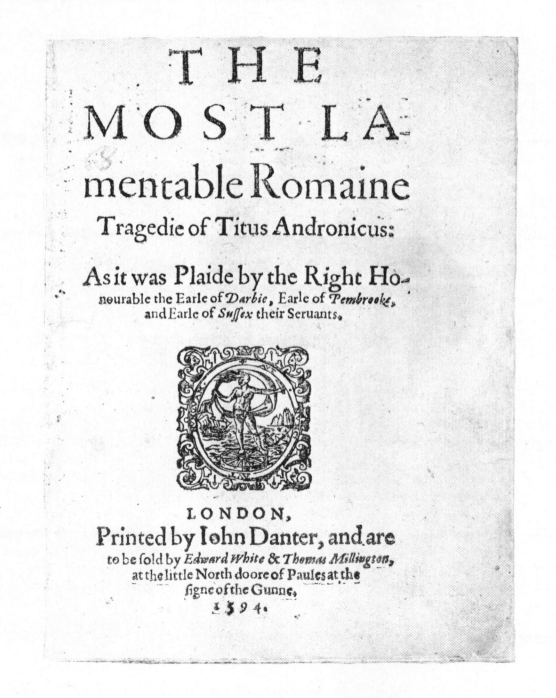

89   *TITUS ANDRONICUS* ENTERED ON THE STATIONERS' REGISTER, 6 FEBRUARY 1594. *Stationers' Hall, Register B, f. 304ᵛ. Transcript: Arber, ii. 644; EKC, i. 312; Greg, i. 10. The deletions were made at the time of the entry. George Steevens first brought together 'Extracts of Entries on the Books of the Stationers' Company' in the 1778* Plays of William Shakspeare, *i. 252–62.*

THE MOST LA-
mentable Romaine
Tragedie of Titus Andronicus:

As it was Plaide by the Right Ho-
nourable the Earle of *Darbie*, Earle of *Pembrooke*,
and Earle of *Suffex* their Seruants.

LONDON,
Printed by Iohn Danter, and are
to be fold by *Edward White* & *Thomas Millington,*
at the little North doore of Paules at the
figne of the Gunne,
1594.

90   TITLE-PAGE OF THE FIRST QUARTO OF *TITUS ANDRONICUS,* 1594. *From the unique copy in the Folger Shakespeare Library; shelfmark: STC 22328. STC 22328. Greg 117.*

124

28 December 1594. The first references to *Titus Andronicus* belong to that year too. The printer John Danter entered the latter in the Stationers' books on 6 February 1594, and before the year was out Edward White and Thomas Millington were hawking it on their stalls at the sign of the Gun at the little north door of St. Paul's. In *A Knack to Know a Knave*, registered the previous month, occurs the allusion,

> As Titus was unto the Roman Senators,
> When he had made a conquest on the Goths . . . .

Lastly, when Sussex's men produced *Titus Andronicus* at the Rose on 24 January 1594, Henslowe entered the performance as 'ne' in his *Diary*. The evidence would seem to point rather conclusively to 1594 as the year of composition; that is, until one examines that evidence more closely. Although licensed by the stationers in 1594, *A Knack to Know a Knave* was acted by Strange's men two years before, on 10 June 1592; so we learn from Henslowe's *Diary*. And (as we have seen) 'ne' may mean newly licensed or produced rather than newly written; a possibility supported by the title-page statement that this 'Most Lamentable Romaine Tragedie' was acted by 'the Right Honourable the Earle of *Darbie*, Earle of *Pembrooke*, and Earl of *Sussex* their Servants'. As the 'servants' of the Earls of Derby and Pembroke receive mention before those of Sussex, *Titus Andronicus* may have been new only to the last-mentioned in 1594. In any event, with such a production history, the play could scarcely have issued new-minted from the author's brain the same year.

One must proceed just as circumspectly in tracing Shakespeare's relations with the acting companies. If he began as a player with the Queen's men, he may have decided early to improve his prospects by moving on. Although not a single one of his pieces is known to have been produced by the Queen's, it is an intriguing fact that eventually Shakespeare got round to using three old plays from their repertoire as plot-sources: *The Troublesome Reign of King John*, *The Famous Victories of Henry the Fifth*, and *The True Chronicle History of King Leir, and his three daughters*. When he came to write his own versions, did Shakespeare draw upon memory of their antecedents on the stage, years past, during the Queen's men days? This is mere speculation. Some Queen's plays, however, passed over into the repertoire of Alleyn's company, Strange's men; and Henslowe's *Diary* — that unique store-house of information — reveals that this troupe performed 'Harey the vi' fourteen times, with large takings, at the Rose on Bankside between 3 March and 20 June 1592. To be sure, other playwrights than Shakespeare may have felt compelled to dramatize the unedifying reign of Henry VI, just as they turned (along with Shakespeare) to Julius Caesar and to Troilus and Cressida.[1] If the Rose piece was his, it must have been, as we shall see, *1 Henry VI*. Henslowe's dry book-keeping therefore accords with Nashe's emotive portrayal of thronged houses. But no evidence connects the dramatist himself with Strange's troupe: Alleyn is silent about Shakespeare in his correspondence, nor is the latter named in the warrant of 6 May 1593, which lists members (probably sharers only) of the company. From the title-pages of the debased versions printed as the *Contention* and *True Tragedie*, we know that the Earl of Pembroke's men — the company that for a time performed *Titus Andronicus* — had *2* and *3 Henry VI* in their repertoire. *The Taming of A Shrew*, possibly but not certainly a corrupt rendering of *The Taming of the Shrew*, saw print in 1594 'As it was sundry times acted by the Right honorable the Earle of Pembroke his servants'. Shakespeare may have written one or more of these plays for Pembroke's men. It is also possible that they passed to Pembroke's from another company; certainly *Titus Andronicus* made the rounds. Conceivably Shakespeare for a while freelanced as a dramatist. It is more romantically appealing, however, to imagine him as one of Pembroke's players at around the same time that Marlowe was giving that company his last play, *Edward II*. The two men may have been acquainted; certainly Shakespeare knew Marlowe's work, and responded to it in his own first efforts: Tamburlaine stalks in *Henry VI*. Shakespeare would allusively mourn Marlowe as the dead shepherd in *As You Like It*.

Dover Wilson has given us an intriguing, admittedly conjectural, reconstruction of the origin

---

1 Alexander cites several such duplications (*Shakespeare's Henry VI and Richard III*, pp. 191-2); see also the New Arden *1 Henry VI*, ed. Andrew S. Cairncross (1962), p. xxxiii.

of Pembroke's men.[1] In 1590 Strange's servants and the Admiral's company had merged under Alleyn, the combined company using the two Shoreditch playhouses, Burbage's Theatre and its 'easer', the Curtain. But the amalgamation broke down. In May 1591 Alleyn quarrelled with the elder Burbage, and stormed off with his fellows to the opposition playhouse on the Surrey bank, Henslowe's Rose. So much we know; the rest is hypothesis. Wilson suggests that not everybody elected to cross the river with Alleyn. Burbage's son Richard, then about twenty-four and already envisaging himself as a rival to the laurels of 'famous *Ned Allen*', induced a number of actors to stay on with him in Shoreditch and form a new company. They then persuaded the Earl of Pembroke to take them under his protection. Hence began the association between Burbage the player and the theatre-loving Pembrokes; an association terminated only by the tragedian's death, which in 1619 left the third Earl of Pembroke so grieved that he tender-heartedly refrained from visiting the playhouse where his 'old acquaintance' had trod the boards. A Shakespearian connection with the Pembrokes re-emerges late, in 1623, when Heminges and Condell dedicated the First Folio of their worthy friend and fellow's plays 'To the most noble and incomparable, paire of brethren', William, Earl of Pembroke, and Philip, Earl of Montgomery. The mythos adds its morsel of corroboration. In 1865 William Cory, then a master at Eton, was received at Wilton House by Lady Herbert, who told him, 'we have a letter, never printed, from Lady Pembroke to her son, telling him to bring James I from Salisbury to see *As You Like It*; "we have the man Shakespeare with us". She wanted to cajole the king in Raleigh's behalf — he came.' James did visit Salisbury, and on at least one occasion kept his court at Wilton; but unfortunately no such letter has ever been produced.[2] Some scholars have believed that this Pembroke is the Fair Youth celebrated by Shakespeare in the *Sonnets*.

Wilson's imaginative reconstruction is pleasing, and seems plausible; but a newly discovered will by a previously unknown actor suggests that Pembroke's men more likely began life as a touring company without Burbage or Shakespeare, and not in 1591 but in the wake of the catastrophe that overtook London the next year.[3] For that summer the plague struck. Some years previously, in a sermon preached at Paul's Cross, the Revd. T. Wilcocks had syllogistically demonstrated that 'the cause of plagues is sinne, if you looke to it well: and the cause of sinne are playes: therefore the cause of plagues are playes'.[4] Whether plays caused plagues or no, the authorities were concerned, legitimately enough, with the dangers posed by theatres in a time of pestilence. They reasoned that public congregations including idlers, whores, and other riff-raff, not to mention many 'infected with sores running on them', were 'perilous for contagion'. When the deaths returned in the bills of mortality reached alarming proportions, the Privy Council intervened to prohibit the acting of stage plays. 'We thinke yt fytt', they informed the Lord Mayor and Aldermen of London, as well as the Surrey and Middlesex Justices of the Peace,

that all manner of concourse and publique meetinges of the people at playes, beare-baitinges, bowlinges and other like assemblyes for sportes be forbidden, and therefore doe hereby requier you and in her Majesty's name straightlie charge and commande you forthwith to inhibite within your jurisdiction all plaies, baiting of beares, bulls, bowling and any other like occasions to assemble any nombers of people together (preacheing and Devyne service at churches excepted), wherby no occasions be offred to increase the infection within the cittie, which you shall doe both by proclamacion to be published to that ende and by spetiall watche and observacion to be had at the places where the . . . like pastimes are usually frequented.[5]

That was on 28 January. The restraint applied to assemblies within a seven-mile radius of London. Throughout most of 1593 the plague raged with special ferocity. According to Stow it claimed 10,675 lives between 29 December 1592 and 20 December 1593; others give higher estimates. But mere statistics fail to convey the human dimensions of the calamity; it is what happened to individual families that brings home the meaning of the plague. Robert Browne, formerly an actor with Worcester's men, was playing at Frankfurt fair during the long hot summer of 1593.

1 Shakespeare, *2 Henry VI*, ed. J. Dover Wilson (The New Shakespeare; Cambridge, 1952), pp. xii–xiv.
2 See *Extracts from the Letters and Journals of William Cory*, ed. Francis Warre Cornish (1897), p. 168; EKC, ii. 329.
3 Mary Edmond, 'Pembroke's Men', *Review of English Studies*, N.S., xxv (1974), 129–36.
4 Quoted by F. P. Wilson, *The Plague in Shakespeare's London* (Oxford, 1927), p. 52.
5 E. K. Chambers, *The Elizabethan Stage* (Oxford, 1923), iv. 313.

His family remained in Shoreditch. Plague wiped them out — wife, children, the whole household.

The following winter the visitation abated sufficiently for the playhouses to reopen for a short season, but on 3 February 1594 the Privy Council saw fit to give order 'that thear bee no more publique playes or enterludes exercised by any Compaine whatsoever within the compas of five miles distance from London, till upon better lykelyhood and assurance of health farther direction may bee given from us to the contrary'.[1] In the spring of 1594 the theatres opened their doors again, but the next summer the authorities were worried lest infected persons, eager for recreation after long confinement at home, should 'resort to suche assemblies' and spread contagion 'throughe heate and thronge'. This protracted closing, the longest in the brief history of the London theatrical industry, wrought havoc on the companies. The Privy Council might grant warrants to Sussex's servants or Strange's to play outside the seven-mile limit, but the troupes could hardly maintain themselves intact through a seemingly endless banishment to the hand-to-mouth existence of the provincial circuit. When the great plague of 1592–4 at last abated, the actors were faced with the task of picking up the pieces of their lives, and reconstituting themselves as companies.

What did Shakespeare do with himself during this extended season of enforced inactivity? One pleasant hypothesis has him wandering on the Continent. Perhaps (it is suggested) he explored the inland waterways of Northern Italy, finding his way from Ferrara on the River Po to the marshy territories of the Venetian Republic. Such experience would furnish him with his knowledge of Italian customs, ceremonials, and characteristics, and of the topography of the northern towns, as well as with his smattering of the language. Then, back in London after the plague had lifted, he conjured up the atmosphere and fragrance of Italy — of Venice and Verona, of fair Padua in 'fruitful Lombardy/The pleasant garden of great Italy' — in a series of plays rich in local colour. In *The Merchant of Venice* Shakespeare even mentions the 'traject', or *traghetto*, 'the common ferry', as Portia describes it, 'Which trades to Venice'.[2]

But he could as well have stored his imagination with these materials of his art from books or the reports of returned travellers, or from conversing with Italians in London. The Oliphant, a Bankside inn, catered for an Italian clientele. Shakespeare must have passed it on his way to or from the playhouse; in *Twelfth Night* (admittedly set in Illyria, but no matter) The Elephant is recommended as 'best to lodge'. A Paolo Marco Lucchese, born in Lucca, ran a restaurant in the parish of St. Olave's, Hart Street, and lodged Italian visitors in his house. (Did Shakespeare know Lucchese? When, in *Othello*, the reverend signiors gather in the council-chamber, the Duke asks, 'Marcus Lucchese, is he not in town?') John Florio, compiler of the first Italian-English dictionary, was well known in aristocratic and intellectual circles; some commentators think that Shakespeare gently mocked him as the pedant Holofernes in *Love's Labour's Lost*. The numerous Bassanos, natives of Venice, were attached to the Court as musicians in the service of the Queen. Shakespeare calls a character in *The Merchant of Venice* Bassanio, although his counterpart in the source *novella* is named Gianneto. Dr. Rowse believes that Emilia Bassano, the natural daughter of Baptist, was the dark seductress of the *Sonnets*. Possibly — but the key word in the manuscript describing her was not, as first reported, brown, but brave.[3] It is useful for a Dark Lady to be demonstrably dark.

A harmless fantasy to imagine Shakespeare enjoying an Italian holiday while in London the bell tolled for the dead. But most likely he stayed on in England. There he tried his hand at non-dramatic composition, and found himself a patron.

He was Henry Wriothesley, third Earl of Southampton, and Baron of Titchfield. His grandfather Thomas, the first Earl, was Lord Chancellor in the days of Henry VIII, and celebrated his own importance by building at Titchfield the 'right stately house' so admired by the King's

1   Ibid., iv. 314–5.
2   See Mario Praz's article, 'Italy', in *The Reader's Encyclopaedia of Shakespeare*, ed. Oscar James Campbell and Edward G. Quinn (1966), pp. 388–93; also John S. Smart, 'Shakespeare's Italian Names', *Modern Language Review*, xi (1916), 339. The *traghetto* plied between Venice and the mainland.
3   See A. L. Rowse, *Shakespeare the Man* (1973), p. 106. He silently revises his account of Emilia in *Simon Forman* (1974), pp. 99–117. Stanley Wells corrected 'brown' (*TLS*, 11 May 1973).

K

antiquary Leland. The second Earl, an impenitent Catholic, found himself out of his depth in political conspiracy on behalf of Mary of Scotland. He managed not to sink, but died before his son Henry — Shakespeare's patron — had turned eight. The boy's elder brother was already dead, and so, in October 1581, Henry Wriothesley succeeded to the peerage. Through most of his minority his mother remained a widow, the young peer therefore finding himself the royal ward of Lord Burghley, the Lord Treasurer. At Cecil House, along with other wards, young Southampton received the education of a courtier in the select academy maintained for the sons of the nobility. There followed four years at Burghley's college, St. John's, Cambridge, from which Southampton took his M.A. at sixteen in 1589. At Court the accomplished youth attracted the favourable notice of the Queen, and formed an attachment to her brilliant but doomed favourite, the Earl of Essex, several years his senior. In the autumn of 1592 Southampton joined the troop of noblemen who accompanied the Queen to Oxford. No one there was more comely, according to the panegyrical pen of John Sanford, 'no young man more outstanding in learning, although his mouth scarcely yet blooms with tender down'.[1] Burghley endeavoured to marry him off to his granddaughter, Lady Elizabeth Vere, but Southampton resisted matrimony, not without vacillation.

He encouraged scholars and poets. John Florio joined his entourage as Italian tutor. One of Burghley's secretaries dedicated a Latin poem of *Narcissus* to Southampton in 1591. In offering his *Unfortunate Traveller* to this 'ingenuous honorable Lord' two years later, Nashe complimented 'a dere lover and cherisher . . . as well of the lovers of Poets, as of Poets themselves'. As a boy of thirteen Southampton had favoured his guardian with a precocious essay in Ciceronian Latin on the topic, 'All men are spurred to the pursuit of virtue by hope of reward'. A worldly theme for one so young; but Wriothesley gave it an idealistic turn by identifying the reward as 'praise and reputation'. Such gifts the noble lord could receive from poet-suppliants. They in turn looked for something more tangible, which was not always forthcoming. 'Of your gracious favor I despaire not, for I am not altogether Fames out-cast,' Nashe wrote in his dedication. 'Your Lordship is the large spreading branch of renown, from whence these my idle leaves seeke to derive their whole nourishing: it resteth you either scornfully shake them off, as worm-eaten & worthles, or in pity preserve them and cherish them, for some litle summer frute you hope to finde amongst them.'[2] Apparently the Earl did not fancy the fruit, for the epistle drops out from subsequent editions of *The Unfortunate Traveller*, and the unfortunate author had to seek his nourishment elsewhere. In 1593 or '94 Nicholas Hilliard painted a miniature of the lovely boy with languid golden tresses. The face — with its soft features, delicately arched eyebrows, and

91 SOUTHAMPTON AT TWENTY. *Portrait by Nicholas Hilliard in the Fitzwilliam Museum, Cambridge. In later portraits the Earl is no longer beardless, and by* c. *1605 he is wearing his hair shorter.*

1   John Sanford, *Apollinis et Musarum Euktika Eidyllia* (Oxford, 1592), cited and transl. G. P. V. Akrigg, *Shakespeare and the Earl of Southampton* (1968), p. 36. Akrigg and Rowse (*Shakespeare's Southampton* (1965)) furnish compendious modern biographies.
2   Thomas Nashe, *The Unfortunate Traveller*, in *Works*, ed. McKerrow, ii. 202.

lips curving ever so slightly upward at the corner in complacent superiority — clearly belongs to an aristocrat, and one who might fittingly receive the tribute of a poem entitled *Narcissus*. Around the time that the Earl sat for Hilliard, Shakespeare dedicated his first poem to Southampton. The poet was then twenty-eight, the dedicatee not yet quite twenty.

Venus and Adonis belongs, with *The Comedy of Errors* and *Titus Andronicus*, to Shakespeare's early classical phase. (The Adonis myth appealed to him. 'Dost thou love pictures?', the tinker Sly is asked in *The Taming of the Shrew*. 'We will fetch thee straight/Adonis painted by a running brook . . . .') Once more Shakespeare draws upon the *Metamorphoses*, his myth-making imagination finding scope in an elaborate narrative on an erotic theme. It was a fashionable genre that produced, almost exactly contemporaneously, its supreme exemplar in Marlowe's fragmentary *Hero and Leander*. Shakespeare might well have expected his poem to please its high-born recipient, for what youth of nineteen, cultivated in his tastes, would not find his palate gratified by the story of Adonis repudiating with adolescent masculine disdain the frenzied importunities of the goddess of love? At the same time Shakespeare was making a bid for a new audience: sophisticated, pleasure-loving, impressed by intellect without necessarily being intellectual; such an audience as Thomas Lodge, himself a gentleman of Lincoln's Inn, envisaged for his erotic epyllion, *Scillaes Metamorphosis* — 'Verie fit for young Courtiers to peruse, and coy Dames to remember'.

No author's name appears on the title-page of *Venus and Adonis*, but the dedication is signed:

TO THE RIGHT HONORABLE
Henrie VVriothesley, Earle of Southampton,
and Baron of Titchfield.

Right Honourable, I know not how I shall offend in dedicating my vnpolisht lines to your Lordship, nor how the worlde vvill censure mee for choosing so strong a proppe to support so vveake a burthen, onelye if your Honour seeme but pleased, I account my selfe highly praised, and vowe to take aduantage of all idle houres, till I haue honoured you vvith some grauer labour. But if the first heire of my inuention proue deformed, I shall be sorie it had so noble a god-father : and neuer after eare so barren a land, for feare it yeeld me still so bad a haruest, I leaue it to your Honourable suruey, and your Honor to your hearts content, vvhich I wish may alvvaies ansvvere your ovvne vvish, and the vvorlds hopefull expectation.

Your Honors in all dutie,

William Shakespeare.

92 DEDICATION, *VENUS AND ADONIS* (1593), sig. A2. *Copy in the Bodleian Library; shelfmark: Malone 325.* STC *22354.*

The tone here — elaborately courteous but not servile, self-deprecatory but with an undertow of confidence — argues no great intimacy between poet and patron. The title-page motto, also from Ovid, qualifies the self-effacement of the dedication: 'Vilia miretur vulgus: mihi flavus Apollo/Pocula Castalia plena ministret aqua.' 'Let base conceited witts admire vilde things,/Fair *Phoebus* lead me to the Muses springs'; so Marlowe translated the passage from the fifteenth book of the *Amores*.

The phrase 'first heire of my invention' has given pause to the commentators. Did Shakespeare compose, or at least draft, *Venus and Adonis* as a young man in Warwickshire, and come up to London with an epyllion in his pocket, then circulate the manuscript until Southampton agreed to accept it? That kind of history would account for the vivid evocation of rural nature — the dive-dapper, the milch-doe with swollen dugs, the courser coping the breeding jennet, above all poor Wat the terrified hare fleeing his pursuers — which seems to owe more to the environs of his Uncle Henry's farm than to the Arcadia of the Roman poets. It is perilous, though, to make compositional inferences from such data; as Alexander Dyce drily observed more than a century ago, 'I have yet to learn that the fancy of Shakespeare could not luxuriate in rural images even amid the fogs of Southwark and the Blackfriars.'[1] The 'idle hours' of the dedication more likely glance at the poet's involuntary retirement from the London stage during the plague season than at Stratford lassitude. Shakespeare may have described *Venus and Adonis* as the first heir of his invention simply because it marked his début as a published author. Or perhaps he was distinguishing between a serious literary venture, properly launched in a printed book with a dedication, and those ephemeral entertainments which the masses admired in Shoreditch and on Bankside. As an aspiring man of letters he may have accepted, as a fact of life, his age's condescending valuation of plays and playwrights. He would go to his grave not knowing, and possibly not caring, whether *Macbeth* or *The Tempest* or *Antony and Cleopatra* ever achieved the permanence of print.

Venus and Adonis was another matter. Shakespeare took pains with the first offspring of his dedicating muse. The 1593 quarto is exceptionally free from misprints and like misdemeanours; it seems clear that, whether or not the author himself corrected proof, he supplied the printer with a fair copy of his manuscript. And he picked an excellent printer.

He was Richard Field, a fellow townsman who operated a shop in the Blackfriars.[2] Three years Shakespeare's senior — the Stratford register lists his baptism on 16 November 1561 — he was the son of Henry Field, a tanner in Bridge Street. The elder Field figures in the early town records: in 1560 he was fined, with fifteen others, 'for heavynge and sufferynge ther dogges & bytchys goynge at lardge in the streets'. When Henry died in 1592, John Shakespeare helped to appraise the old bedsteads and other household stuff comprising Field's modest estate. Though unprosperous himself, Field had given his son a good start by apprenticing him to the printing trade in London. George Bishop, to whom Richard was originally bound, handed him over for a six-year term to Thomas Vautrollier, a Huguenot with a shop in the Blackfriars. An accomplished masterprinter, Vautrollier did justice to such demanding assignments as De Beau Chesne and Baildon's *Booke Containing Divers Sortes of Hands*. The Huguenot's energetic wife, Jacqueline, was capable of looking after the shop when her husband was in Edinburgh managing another printing business. In 1587 the master died, and the following year his widow married their only apprentice. He was then twenty-seven, and had only lately been made free of the Stationers' Company. In Jacqueline Field, Mrs. Charlotte Stopes thinks she has found Shakespeare's Dark Lady: '. . . she was a Frenchwoman, therefore likely to have dark eyes, a sallow complexion, and that indefinable *charm* so much alluded to.'[3] For *charm*, read loose morals. Mrs. Stopes's reasoning is not impeccable.

Richard Field entered *Venus and Adonis* on the Register at Stationers' Hall on 18 April 1593. Less than two months later, an elderly gentleman, Richard Stonley, Esq., saw the poem on the stalls of John Harrison's shop at the sign of the White Greyhound in St. Paul's Churchyard, and bought a copy for sixpence. One of the four tellers of the Exchequer, Stonley had a London house in Aldersgate, but spent his weekends on his Doddingshurst estate in Essex; at the advanced age of seventy-seven this civil servant who had spent his whole career dealing with Crown finances found himself imprisoned in the Fleet because of massive personal debt. A figure of some consequence in his own day, but later forgotten, Stonley has the minor distinction of being the first recorded purchaser of Shakespeare's first publication.

1   Shakespeare, *Works*, ed. Alexander Dyce (1857), i, p. xlv; cited by Hyder Edward Rollins in the New Variorum edition of *The Poems* (Philadelphia and London, 1938), p. 385.
2   For an excellent, full account of Field, see A. E. M. Kirwood, 'Richard Field, Printer, 1589–1624', *The Library*, 4th Ser., xii (1931), 1–39.
3   C. C. Stopes, *Shakespeare's Environment* (2nd ed., 1918), p. 155. Mrs. Stopes gives Mrs. Field's christian name as Jacquinetta, thus conflating the printer's wife with the country wench of *Love's Labour's Lost*.

93   STONLEY DIARY ACCOUNT BOOK (1593), f. 9. *Folger Shakespeare Library, MS. V.a.460. The other book bought by Stonley that day, Eliot's* The Survey, or Topographical Description of France: with a new Mappe, *was first printed in 1592, and went into a second edition the next year.*

   Stonley's Diary and the Venus and Adonis *entry were known in the eighteenth century. On 7 May 1794 the antiquary Francis Douce wrote to George Steevens about the item (Folger Shakespeare Library, MS. C.b.10). Douce must be the acquaintance referred to in the note included by Malone in his* Inquiry into the Authenticity of Certain Miscellaneous Papers and Legal Instruments *(1796): 'the following entry [has] been found in an ancient MS. Diary, which some time since was in the hands of an acquaintance of Mr. Steevens, by whom it was communicated to me: "12th of June, 1593. For the Survay of Fraunce, with the Venus and Athonay p[r] Shakspere, xii.d." ' (p. 67n). The reference is also cited in Isaac Reed's 1803 Variorum edition of* Shakespeare *(ii. 152). Thereafter the diary disappeared from view until it resurfaced in San Francisco and was acquired by the Folger in 1972. While routinely reading through the three volumes, Mrs. Laetitia Yeandle, the Library's Curator of Manuscripts, discovered the entry, which the Folger announced on 23 April 1973. It is* Survey *and* Adhonay *(not, as in Malone,* Survay *and* Athonay*) in the entry.*

   Multitudes bought *Venus and Adonis*, the poem going through sixteen editions before 1640. No other work by Shakespeare achieved so many printings during this period. Readers thumbed it until it fell to pieces; so we may infer from the fact that for most of the editions only a single copy has survived.

   At the turn of the seventeenth century the students of St. John's College, Cambridge, mounted an amateur play, *The Return from Parnassus*, in the course of which one of the characters expresses his enthusiasm for Shakespeare. 'Let this duncified worlde esteeme of Spencer and Chaucer', Gullio rhapsodizes: 'Ile worshipp sweet M[r] Shakspeare, and to honoure him will lay his *Venus and Adonis* under my pillowe, as wee reade of one (I do not well remember his name, but I am sure he was a kinge) slept with Homer under his beds head.' 'O sweet M[r] Shakspeare', he sighs elsewhere, 'Ile have his picture in my study at the courte.'[1] Biographers have interpreted Gullio's testimonial as recognition from the university,[2] but, if so, it is backhanded recognition. The applause after all comes from a fool, as signified by his name, his philistine dismissal of Chaucer and Spenser, and his inability to recall that the king who admired Homer was Alexander the Great. Still, this allusion and others testify to the continuing popularity of *Venus and Adonis* with a certain class of readers: university students, courtiers, Inns of Court men, witlings, and gallants about town. Field must have viewed the commercial success of the poem with some chagrin, for he had parted early with it. After printing two editions, he relinquished his rights in the work to John Harrison, who had been selling the book without owning the copyright. Perhaps Field would have mistrusted the potential of any poet who hailed from his own market town, more celebrated for malting than the arts.

   The 'graver labour' promised by the author in his first dedicatory epistle found fruition the following spring in another elaborate Ovidian narrative, a companion piece to *Venus and Adonis*. If the latter explores the theme of Eros denied through the failed seduction of a coy youth, *The Rape of Lucrece* treats the subject of Eros gratified through the successful violation of a sober matron.

---

1   *The First Part of the Return from Parnassus*, in *The Three Parnassus Plays (1598–1601)*, ed. J. B. Leishman (1949), pp. 185, 192–3.
2   See, for example, Joseph Quincy Adams, *A Life of William Shakespeare* (1923), p. 238; also Rowse, *Shakespeare the Man*, p. 75.

K*

The complaining females make an oddly contrasting pair. Once again Field did the printing, and in accordance with his usual high standard. This time, however, 'Mᣴ Harrison' held the copyright from the first, as is shown by the entry to him, in the Stationers' Register on 9 May 1594, of a book 'intituled the Ravyshement of Lucrece'.

94   *THE RAPE OF LUCRECE* ENTERED ON THE STATIONERS' REGISTER, 9 MAY 1594. *Stationers' Hall, Register B, f. 306ᵛ. Transcript: Arber, ii. 648; EKC, i. 545.*

There is again a dedication to Southampton:

TO THE RIGHT
HONOVRABLE, HENRY
VVriothesley, Earle of Southhampton,
and Baron of Titchfield.

THE loue I dedicate to your Lordship is without end: wherof this Pamphlet without beginning is but a superfluous Moity. The warrant I haue of your Honourable disposition, not the worth of my vntutord Lines makes it assured of acceptance. VVhat I haue done is yours, what I haue to doe is yours, being part in all I haue, deuoted yours. VVere my worth greater, my duety would shew greater, meane time, as it is, it is bound to your Lordship; To whom I wish long life still lengthned with all happinesse.

Your Lordships in all duety.

William Shakespeare.

95   DEDICATION, *THE RAPE OF LUCRECE* (1594), sig. A2. *Copy in the Bodleian Library; shelfmark: Malone 34(1).* STC *22345.*

As is to be expected, Shakespeare's two dedications have been minutely compared. Interpretations differ. 'A super-subtle criticism', writes Sir Edmund Chambers, 'detects a great advance in the poet's intimacy with his patron between the two addresses, which I am bound to say is not apparent to me.'[1] But Chambers belongs to a minority; most students (including this one) do discern a progression of warmth. This is a matter that each reader, with the text of the dedications before him, may decide for himself.

The Rape of Lucrece enjoyed a less spectacular success than its predecessor, but nevertheless went through a respectable eight editions before 1640. The two poems, embellished with all the flowers of Renaissance rhetoric, established Shakespeare as a poet of love. In the last of the *Parnassus* plays, the *Second Return*, acted in the same Cambridge hall during the Christmas revels of 1602–3, Judicio expresses the verdict of the judicious:

> Who loves not *Adons* love, or *Lucrece* rape?
> His sweeter verse contaynes hart robbing lines,
> Could but a graver subject him content,
> Without loves foolish lazy languishment.[2]

Evidently word of *Julius Caesar* and *Henry V* had not yet found its way to cloistered Cambridge. Or, being plays, perhaps they did not count.

As to how the young Earl responded to the two dedications, contemporary report is silent. Tradition, however, first coming to light in Rowe's memoir, fills the gap:

> There is one Inftance fo fingular in the Magnificence of this Patron of *Shakefpear*'s, that if I had not been affur'd that the Story was handed down by Sir *William D'Avenant*, who was probably very well acquainted with his Affairs, I fhould not have ventur'd to have inferted, that my Lord *Southampton*, at one time, gave him a thoufand Pounds, to enable him to go through with a Purchafe which he heard he had a mind to. A Bounty very great, and very rare at any time, and almoft equal to that profufe Generofity the prefent Age has fhewn to *French* Dancers and *Italian* Eunuchs.

96 NICHOLAS ROWE, *SOME ACCOUNT OF THE LIFE, &C. OF MR. WILLIAM SHAKESPEAR*, IN SHAKESPEARE, *WORKS*, ED. ROWE (1709), i, p. x. *Unaware of the existence of* The Rape of Lucrece, *Rowe describes* Venus and Adonis *as 'the only Piece of his Poetry which he [Shakespeare] ever publish'd himself'.*

Although any intelligence transmitted on the authority of Davenant must awaken suspicions in the wary, a recent biographer of both Shakespeare and Southampton inclines to acceptance.[3] The sum mentioned, described by Dr. Rowse as 'goodly', would have done justice to an Elizabethan Maecenas, but it is unlikely that Shakespeare had the luck of Horace or Vergil. In the nineties Southampton was under financial pressure. Rumour had it that the Earl was obliged to part with £5,000 for going back on an ill-advised promise to marry the Lord Treasurer's granddaughter; it is a fact that pecuniary embarrassment forced him, in November 1594, to lease out the porter's lodge, as well as other buildings and rooms, of his London residence,

1 EKC, i. 61–2.
2 *The Second Part of the Return from Parnassus*, in *Three Parnassus Plays*, ed. Leishman, p. 244.
3 Rowse, *Shakespeare the Man*, p. 125; see also the same author's *Shakespeare's Southampton*, p. 85, where the Earl's munificence to the poet is described as an authentic tradition.

Southampton House.[1] So far as we know, Shakespeare's investments over a lifetime did not in their aggregate come to £1,000. It has been suggested that he used the money to buy an interest in the Chamberlain's company in 1596; but this is no more than an attempt to rationalize an outlandish figure. Shakespeare did not again dedicate one of his writings to a noble lord. Southampton now departs from the biographical record.

He does not, however, drop out of speculation. Many commentators, perhaps a majority, believe that the Earl is the Fair Youth urged to marry and propagate in the *Sonnets*, and there immortalized by the poet who addresses him in the extravagant terms of Renaissance male friendship. The object of this devotion, the Master-Mistress of the sonneteer's passion, has 'a woman's face' but (worse luck for his heterosexual celebrant) a man's phallus. Nature, Shakespeare ruefully declares in Sonnet 20,

> as she wrought thee, fell a-doting,
> And by addition me of thee defeated
> By adding one thing to my purpose nothing.
>   But since she prick'd thee out for women's pleasure,
>   Mine be thy love, and thy love's use their treasure.

The portrait here does not accord ill with Hilliard's miniature of the feminine youth. A dating of the *Sonnets* during the Southampton period, say 1592–5, would help with the identification. Several topically allusive poems — the so-called 'dating sonnets' — support (according to some enthusiasts) this putative chronology; but the ambiguous language of poetry resists the fragile certitude of interpreters. And even if we might confidently date individual sonnets, we could not therefore rule out the possibility that the sequence as a whole occupied its creator over an extended period; sporadic entries, as it were, in a poet's rhyming diary. Some of the impassioned later sonnets manifest a psychological and metaphorical — not to say metaphysical — complexity unparalleled in what we know Shakespeare was writing in the early nineties. To the greatest authority on the *Sonnets* in this century, Hyder Rollins, writing in 1944, the solution to the question of chronology, on which depend solutions to the other questions, 'has been and remains an idle dream'.[2] So it still remains, despite the best and brightest efforts. Nor can we rest secure that the printed order of the *Sonnets* is correct. It is not clear to what extent the personages of these poems — Fair Youth, Dark Lady, Rival Poet — represent real individuals: the imperatives of Art, no less than the circumstances of Nature, dictate their roles. And what of the role of the speaker himself, the naked 'I' which we here encounter for the first and only time in the entire Shakespeare corpus? 'With this key', Wordsworth said of the cycle, 'Shakespeare unlocked his heart.' But the doubt haunts us that the speaker may be, at least in part, another dramatic characterization. If the persona of the *Sonnets* addresses us with the resonance of authenticity, so do Shylock and Hamlet. Here as elsewhere, the biographer, in his eagerness for answers to the unanswerable, runs the risk of confusing the dancer with the dance.

The mystery is not lightened by the cryptic poem entered in the Stationers' books on 3 September 1594, and printed the same year with the title *Willobie his Avisa. Or The true Picture of a modest Maid, and of a chast and constant wife*. This curious work seems to have something to do with the *Sonnets*. In a prefatory epistle one Hadrian Dorrell reveals how the *Avisa* came to be printed. Dorrell shared a chamber, presumably at the university, with a promising young scholar, Henrie Willobie, who entrusted his friend with the key to his study before going abroad in the Queen's service. Among Willobie's papers Dorrell found the *Avisa*, which he so fancied that he had it published without his room-mate's knowledge. A Henry Willobie of West Knoyle, Wiltshire, matriculated from St. John's College, Oxford, in 1591, but transferred to Exeter College, where he took his degree in 1595. This must be the Willobie of the *Avisa*. There was no Hadrian Dorrell at Oxford during those years, although a Thomas Darell was enrolled in Brasenose College; perhaps Hadrian is a Willobie pseudonym — it is one of many puzzles.

The poem describes how Avisa — '*This* Brytan Bird' that '*out-flies them all*' — repels assaults upon her chastity by a motley succession of suitors. While yet of 'tender age' she fends off an

1 See Akrigg, *Shakespeare and the Earl of Southampton*, pp. 38–9, 47.
2 Shakespeare, *The Sonnets*, ed. Rollins (New Variorum; Philadelphia and London, 1944), ii. 53.

aged Nobleman; after matrimony she resists, in turn, a 'Cavaleiro' (afflicted by piles or pox), 'D.B. a French man', 'Dydimus Harco. Anglo-Germanus', and 'Henrico Willobego. Italo–Hispalensis'. This last, referred to as 'H.W.', has a 'familiar frend W.S. who not long before had tryed the curtesy of the like passion, and was now newly recovered of the like infection . . . & in vewing a far off the course of this loving Comedy, he determined to see whether it would sort to a happier end for this new actor, then it did for the old player.' *H.W.*, *W.S.*, *new actor, old player* — the veiled references tease; and the situation vaguely resembles that of the *Sonnets*. Moreover, one can trace a tenuous Shakespearian connection with Willobie. The latter's elder brother William in 1590 married Eleanor Bampfield; her sister Katherine in the same month married Thomas Russell. There is evidence that Henry Willobie was on amiable terms with his sister-in-law's husband. Russell was a friend of Shakespeare, although we do not know how long they knew one another; the dramatist named him an overseer of his will, and left him £5. If (as tradition holds) Shakespeare stopped over in Oxford when he took the road that led from London to Stratford, he might possibly have there met Willobie through Russell. This is all speculative, no doubt; but one can appreciate the temptation to identify 'W. S.' with William Shakespeare, and 'H. W.' with Henry Wriothesley, the proposed Fair Youth of the *Sonnets*.

There is the lady too, dwelling in a house 'where hanges the badge/Of Englands Saint'. Shall we then knock on the door of any inn called the George or the St. George in the West Country (for the poem offers geographical clues as well), and there inquire after the Dark Lady in the guise of the landlord's beautiful daughter? So several, most notably Arthur Acheson, have done.[1] But these possibilities, at first so tantalizing, dissolve upon closer acquaintance. H. W. are also of course the initials of Henry Willobie, a candidate closer to home than the Baron of Titchfield. The invincible chastity of Avisa doubtfully qualifies her for the part of the promiscuous temptress of the *Sonnets*. In 1970 Professor B. N. De Luna made an interesting case for identifying Avisa with the Virgin Queen, and her house with Elizabeth's palaces, flying (during her residence) banners bearing the Cross of St. George.[2] With so much doubtful in this obscure allegory, all that emerges clearly is that *Willobie his Avisa* does not help us much with the *Sonnets*.

The poem has nevertheless an indisputable Shakespearian interest, for the commendatory verses prefacing it include this stanza, containing our first reference by name to Shakespeare as a poet:

Though Collatine *haue deerely bought,*
To high renowne, a lasting life,
And found, that most in vaine haue sought,
To haue a Faire, and Constant *wife,*
    Yet Tarquyne *pluckt his glistering grape,*
    And Shake-speare, *paints poore* Lucrece *rape.*

97   HENRY WILLOBIE, WILLOBIE HIS AVISA (1594), sig. A4. Copy in the British Library; shelfmark: 239.i.16. STC 25755. In his second edition of Shakespeare's Comedies, Histories, Tragedies, and Poems *(1858), J. Payne Collier was the first to reprint the stanza (vi. 526), and apparently also the first to suggest that Willobie's 'W. S.' may stand for William Shakespeare (i. 115n).*

By the autumn of 1594, when *Willobie his Avisa* appeared on the stalls, the plague had relaxed its grip on the capital, and normal patterns of life reasserted themselves. On 8 October 1594, 'the time beinge such as, thankes be to god, there is nowe no danger of the sicknes', Henry Carey, first Baron Hunsdon, requested the Lord Mayor of London to suffer Hunsdon's 'nowe companie of Players' to exercise their quality that winter at the Cross Keys inn in Gracious Street. Now an old man, Hunsdon was the Lord Chancellor who had championed the players in their skirmishes with the municipal authorities. According to the widely acquainted astrologer Simon

---

1   See Arthur Acheson, *Mistress Davenant* (1913) and *Shakespeare's Sonnet Story* (1922).
2   B. N. De Luna, *The Queen Declined : An Interpretation of Willobie his Avisa* (Oxford, 1970), pp. 5–43.

Forman, he had formerly kept as his mistress Emilia Lanier — Dr. Rowse's Dark Lady — and she had borne his child. He had now less than two years to live. Hunsdon's new troupe had performed for a brief season in June 1594 for Henslowe at Newington Butts: our first record of the Chamberlain's men. During the Christmas festivities the following December the company played twice at Court. On 15 March 1595 the Accounts of the Treasurer of the Queen's Chamber list William Shakespeare as joint payee, with William Kempe and Richard Burbage — all three 'servauntes to the Lord Chamberleyne' — for plays performed before her Majesty the previous St. Stephen's Day (26 December) and Innocents' Day (28 December) at the royal palace at Greenwich. The Innocents' Day citation is probably a mistake; a payment to the Admiral's men for the 28th appears in the same Accounts, and the Chamberlain's players seem to have had another date that day.[1] But that is a trifling detail. This record is the first to connect Shakespeare with an acting company, and the only official notice of his name with respect to a theatrical performance. The entry shows that Shakespeare had become a leading member of the Lord Chamberlain's men. He would stay with that company, which eventually passed under royal patronage, until he retired from the stage altogether.

98 SHAKESPEARE A PAYEE OF THE CHAMBERLAIN'S MEN, 15 MARCH 1595. *Public Record Office, Exchequer, Pipe Office, Declared Accounts, E. 351/542, f. 107ᵛ. Transcript: TB, 14; EKC, ii. 319; BRL, i. 206. H-P discovered this record in the accounts of the Treasurer of the Chamber, and printed it (with accompanying line facsimile) in his* Illustrations of the Life of Shakespeare (1874), *p. 31. This item is slightly reduced.*

1   See below, pp. 137–38.

12

The Lord Chamberlain's Man

The record of payment for the two royal performances at Greenwich in 1594 shows Shakespeare as now set on his professional course. The lineaments of his career at last emerge from the shadows; debate and speculation, never entirely absent, recede; events fall into place. In his entry the Treasurer of the Queen's Chamber brackets Shakespeare with the Chamberlain's foremost clown — 'Monsieur du Kempe', Nashe eulogized him, 'Jest-monger and Vice-gerent generall to the Ghost of Dicke Tarlton' — and with the great tragedian who would create the title roles of *Hamlet*, *Othello*, and *King Lear*. Although Shakespeare achieved no comparable thespian pre-eminence, it is as a player that the Treasurer by implication classes him, and certainly he served his troupe in this capacity. Shakespeare moreover became a shareholder (or 'housekeeper') in his company, unlike most Elizabethan dramatists who eked out their precarious livelihood — *vide* Greene — as employees of the players. Probably he helped stage his own plays and also those of others. Above all, he was his troupe's regular dramatist, in the sense that he wrote exclusively for them; their 'ordinary poet', in Elizabethan theatrical parlance. The entire period produced only a handful of like professional writers, among them Heywood, Fletcher, and Dekker, who were even more prolific than the poet who, according to his awe-struck fellows, never blotted a line. *Professional* is in this context a key term. Shakespeare's combined achievements as actor, sharer, and playwright made him, as our greatest living authority on the Elizabethan and Jacobean stage observes, 'the most complete man of the theater of his time'.[1] Few in any age have served the stage so variously. Not Racine or Ibsen or Shaw; only Molière, besides Shakespeare, among playwrights of world stature.[2]

Posterity, understandably enough, reserves veneration for the dramatist — not the player or manager whose triumphs, however applauded, were transitory — and accords to the book of his plays that immortality which the author, if he dreamed of it at all, envisaged as forthcoming in recognition of the poems he dedicated to a noble lord. Yet, despite the ephemerality of performance, a special interest attaches to an evening in the mid-nineties when a Shakespearian play was acted under unusual circumstances. An eyewitness recorded the event.

On 28 December 1594 professional players hired for the occasion — no doubt these were the Chamberlain's men — performed *The Comedy of Errors* as part of the Christmas 'law-revels' at Gray's Inn. This was the largest of the four Inns of Court where young gentry studied for the bar and disported themselves in their leisure hours with literature, theatricals, and the ladies. The first Yuletide festivities after the great plague, when too many invitations were issued and accepted, produced the pandemonium on Innocents' Day described in *Gesta Grayorum*:

> When the Ambassador was placed, as aforesaid, and that there was something to be performed for the Delight of the Beholders, there arose such a disordered Tumult and Crowd upon the Stage, that there was no Opportunity to effect that which was intended: There came so great a number of worshipful Personages upon the Stage, that might not be displaced; and Gentlewomen, whose Sex did privilege them from Violence, that when the Prince and his Officers had in vain, a good while, expected and endeavoured a Reformation, at length there was no hope of Redress for that present. The Lord Ambassador

---

1   G. E. Bentley, *Shakespeare: A Biographical Handbook* (New Haven, 1961), p. 119. The 'director' as a theatrical functionary did not then exist.

2   Kenneth Muir makes this point in *Shakespeare the Professional* (1973), pp. 3–4.

> and his Train thought that they were not fo kindly entertained, as was before expected, and thereupon would not ftay any longer at that time, but, in a fort, difcontented and difpleafed. After their Departure the Throngs and Tumults did fomewhat ceafe, although fo much of them continued, as was able to diforder and confound any good Inventions whatfoever. In regard whereof, as alfo for that the Sports intended were efpecially for the gracing of the *Templarians*, it was thought good not to offer any thing of Account, faving Dancing and Revelling with Gentlewomen ; and after fuch Sports, a Comedy of Errors (like to *Plautus* his *Menechmus*) was played by the Players. So that Night was begun, and continued to the end, in nothing but Confufion and Errors ; whereupon, it was ever afterwards called, *The Night of Errors.*

99 *GESTA GRAYORUM: OR, THE HISTORY OF THE HIGH AND MIGHTY PRINCE, HENRY PRINCE OF PURPOOLE . . .* (1688), p. 22. *The elected 'Prince' was Henry Helmes. Although the revels described belong to 1594–5, the tract was not printed until almost a century later. John Nichols included* Gesta Grayorum *in* The Progresses, and Public Processions, of Queen Elizabeth *(1788), ii (separately paginated). Donald Bland has edited it for the English Reprints Series (Liverpool, 1968).*

'The next Night . . .', the narration continues, in the pompously facetious style affected for the occasion, 'we preferred Judgments thick and threefold, which were read publickly by the Clerk of the Crown, being all against a Sorcerer or Conjurer that was supposed to be the Cause of that confused Inconvenience.' The arraignment charges that this sorcerer had (among other misdemeanours) 'foisted a Company of base and common Fellows, to make up our Disorders with a Play of Errors and Confusions; and that that Night had gained to us Discredit, and it self a Nickname of Errors'.

Another early comedy by Shakespeare has also been associated with a particular festive occasion. By virtue of its brevity, special casting requirements, and (in Sir Edmund Chambers's quaint phrase) 'the hymeneal character of the theme', *A Midsummer-Night's Dream* would appear to be well suited to grace a wedding celebration. The many female and fairy parts required boy actors — would the Chamberlain's men have the resources to fill them without special recruitment for the nonce? The text seemingly provides alternative endings for public presentation in a theatre, and private performance at a great house. 'Lovers to bed', Duke Theseus decrees after the fifth-act dance;

> 'tis almost fairy time.
> I fear we shall out-sleep the coming morn,
> As much as we this night have overwatch'd.
> This palpable-gross play hath well beguil'd
> The heavy gait of night. Sweet friends, to bed.

The comedy might well thus end in the playhouse. But with midnight struck and the stage cleared, Puck enters broom in hand, and the fairies steal through the house to bless the bridal bed with fortunate increase, and hallow each chamber with 'sweet peace'. How appropriate to a hymeneal occasion!

Biographers and editors have suggested a number of aristocratic weddings as the setting for the first night of *A Midsummer-Night's Dream*. These range over a decade, from the marriage of Robert Earl of Essex and Frances Lady Sidney in the spring of 1590, to that of Henry Lord Herbert and Anne Russell in June 1600; but most now prefer, by reason of date and circumstance, the wedding of Sir Thomas Heneage, the elderly Treasurer of the Chamber, to the mother of Shakespeare's patron, Mary Countess of Southampton — although the bride would perhaps have found doubtfully flattering the allusion to ' . . . a dowager, / Long withering out a young man's revenue'. One recent biographer goes so far as to state as a fact that Shakespeare composed his fantasy for the festivities at Southampton House on 2 May 1594.

But the suggestion, at first so beguiling, becomes less appealing under rigorous scrutiny. Dr. Stanley Wells puts the negative case most cogently:

There is no outside evidence with any bearing on the matter. The theory has arisen from various features of the play itself. It is, certainly, much concerned with marriage; but so are many comedies. It ends with the fairies' blessing upon the married couples; but this is perfectly appropriate to Shakespeare's artistic scheme, and requires no other explanation. . . . *A Midsummer Night's Dream* (like *Love's Labour's Lost*) appears to require an unusually large number of boy actors. Hippolyta, Hermia, Helena, Titania, Peaseblossom, Cobweb, Moth, and Mustardseed would all have been boys' parts. Puck and Oberon too may have been played by boys or young men. But the title page of the first edition, printed in 1600, tells us that the play was 'sundry times publicly acted by the Right Honourable the Lord Chamberlain his servants'. If Shakespeare's company could at any time muster enough boys for public performances, we have no reason to doubt that it could have done so from the start. Thus the suggestion that the roles of the fairies were intended to be taken by children of the hypothetical noble house seems purely whimsical. The stage directions of the first edition, which was probably printed from Shakespeare's manuscript, show no essential differences from those in his other plays; a direction such as '*Enter a* Fairie *at one doore, and* Robin goodfellow *at another*' (II.i.0) suggests that he had in mind the structure of the public theatres. Furthermore, although noble weddings in Shakespeare's time were sometimes graced with formal entertainments, usually of the nature of a masque, the first play certainly known to have been written for such an occasion is Samuel Daniel's *Hymen's Triumph*. This was performed in 1614, some twenty years after the composition of *A Midsummer Night's Dream*. By this time the tradition of courtly entertainments had developed greatly; and *Hymen's Triumph* does not appear to have been played in a public theatre.[1]

Although Shakespeare did not seek the publication of his plays (for reasons noted earlier), publication came anyway. In this respect 1594 is again a landmark year. Two of his pieces, and perhaps a third, reached print. *Titus Andronicus*, entered on the Stationers' Register on 6 February, was the first to be published, followed quickly by *The First Part of the Contention betwixt the two famous Houses of Yorke and Lancaster* (Stationers' Register: 12 March), the debased text, assembled from actors' recollections, of *2 Henry VI*. If *The Taming of A Shrew* indeed represents a corrupt redaction of *The Taming of the Shrew*, which differs from it radically, then that play too was initially printed in 1594; the authentic version, familiar to all readers and playgoers, did not appear until seven years after the dramatist's death. In none of these four quartos of 1594 is Shakespeare mentioned by name. Nor does he receive billing on the title-pages of plays printed, evidently without his consent, during the next three years. These pieces are *The True Tragedie of Richard Duke of Yorke* (the Bad Quarto of *3 Henry VI*) in 1595, and *Romeo and Juliet* (another Bad Quarto), *Richard II*, and *Richard III* in 1597. The last three had immense popularity. In 1599 appeared a second edition of *Romeo and Juliet* which, despite the title-page boast that it was 'Newly corrected, augmented, and amended', contains numerous errors. This edition too was anonymous. But the second quartos of *Richard II* and *Richard III*, both of 1598, bore Shakespeare's name. In 1598 too *Love's Labour's Lost* was published as 'By W. Shakespere'; this is the earliest extant impression, although the title-page describes it as 'Newly corrected and augmented'. The year 1598 also saw the publication of *1 Henry IV* without the author's name, the oversight being remedied on the title-page of the third edition ('Newly corrected by W. Shake-speare') in 1599. Thus, by 1598 at least eight, and possibly nine, of Shakespeare's plays had made their appearance on the booksellers' stalls. He had written more than that, as the informative Francis Meres makes clear.

A scion of the Lincolnshire Mereses, famous in the Fens, Francis was born one year after Shakespeare. The title-page of Meres's first publication, a sermon entitled *Gods Arithmeticke*, describes him succinctly as 'Maister of Arte of both Universities, and Student in Divinity'. In London, where he dwelt in Botolph Lane and enthusiastically familiarized himself with the literary and theatrical scene, Meres undertook to contribute to a series of volumes initiated in 1597 by Bodenham's *Politeuphuia: Wits Commonwealth*. These consisted of collected apophthegms, or pithy precepts, on morals, religion, and the arts — printed counterparts to the commonplace books in which thoughtful Elizabethans jotted down observations of life and tit-bits of wisdom from authors ancient or modern, mostly the former, to be hauled out when a public or literary occasion called for the seasoning of discourse with authority. Meres's *Palladis Tamia. Wits Treasury. Being the Second Part of Wits Commonwealth* follows his own dictum that 'all the source of wit . . . may flowe within three chanels, and be contrived into three heads; into a Sentence [i.e. maxim], a Similitude, & an Example'.[2] Nourished by euphuism, Meres revelled above all in similitudes, and packed thousands into his squat little octavo volume of almost seven hundred pages. 'As

1 William Shakespeare, *A Midsummer Night's Dream*, ed. Stanley Wells (New Penguin Shakespeare; 1967), introd., pp. 13–14.
2 Francis Meres, *Palladis Tamia* . . . (1598), sig. A2.

A . . ., so B . . .,' runs his endlessly repeated formula, applied to a range of subjects that begins with God and ends with Death. Thus, 'As a Cocke croweth in the darkenesse of the night: so a preacher croweth in the darkenesse of this world.' Meres is no women's liberationist: 'As Pigeons are taken with beanes, and children intised with Balles; so women are wonne with toyes.' Nor is he especially enterprising; despite his lengthy list of acknowledgements to sacred and profane writers, his similitudes are mostly Erasmus's *Parabolae sive Similia* Englished, and for his historical examples he cheerfully ransacked Ravisius Textor's popular and encyclopaedic *Officina*.[1] Along the way, however, Meres finds space for a sixteen-page 'Comparative discourse of our English Poets, with the *Greeke, Latine, and Italian Poets*'. On this section, and to a lesser degree on the brief chapters that follow on painting and music, his fame rests. For by comparing the best among his contemporaries with the ancients and with the masters of Renaissance Italy, he provides a unique indication of how a patriotic Elizabethan, not himself artistic, evaluated the cultural life of his day. There is nothing in the age comparable to Meres's comparative discourse in the *Palladis Tamia*. This work behind him, he retired into provincial obscurity, and passed the remainder of his long life (he died in 1647) as rector and schoolmaster of Wing in Rutland.

It is Meres's commendations of Shakespeare that principally engage interest. He lauds the poet for 'mightily' enriching the English language, and gorgeously investing it 'in rare ornaments and

100 FRANCIS MERES, *PALLADIS TAMIA. WITS TREASURY* (1598), ff. 281ᵛ–2. *Copy in the Bodleian Library; shelfmark: Malone 389. STC 17834. Meres's list of Shakespeare's plays was first noticed by Bishop Percy and Thomas Tyrwhitt almost simultaneously. In* Reliques of Ancient English Poetry *(1765), i. 191, Percy refers to* The Merchant of Venice *as 'being mentioned together with eleven other of his [Shakespeare's] plays in Meres's WITS TREASURY &c. 1598'. Tyrwhitt remarks on the passages in* Observations and Conjectures upon Some Passages of Shakespeare, *published anonymously in 1766 (pp. 15–16). He leaves a blank space for Meres's name. Of* Love's Labour's Won *Tyrwhitt writes: 'If there should be a Play in being, with that title, though without* Shakespeare's *name, I should be glad to see it; and I think the Editor would be sure of the publick thanks, even if it should prove no better than the* Love's labour lost.*'*

1 Don Cameron Allen succinctly analyses Meres's sources in his introduction to the Scholars' Facsimile edition of *Palladis Tamia*, pp. vii–viii. See also Allen's *Francis Meres's Treatise 'Poetrie': A Critical Edition* (Urbana, Ill., 1933).

resplendent abiliments'. Shakespeare is one of the best for lyric poetry, comedy, and tragedy, as well as one of 'the most passionate among us to bewaile and bemoane the perplexities of Love'. Sandwiched between praise of Shakespeare as the 'mellifluous & hony-tongued' Ovidian poet and deviser of 'fine filed' phrases comes the celebrated passage enumerating Shakespeare's writings.

Meres's remarks show that the *Sonnets*, at least some of them, were in existence before 1598. *The Comedy of Errors* had entered the record earlier, in the account of the boisterous revels at Gray's Inn, but for five of the plays — *The Two Gentlemen of Verona*, *Love's Labour's Won*, *A Midsummer-Night's Dream*, *The Merchant of Venice*, and *King John* — Meres furnishes our earliest external evidence of date. For the investigator faced with the daunting task of charting the sequence of Shakespeare's works, his testimony can scarcely be overvalued.

Surely the most intriguing entry concerns *Love's Labour's Won*. Has Meres simply made a mistake? Or does he refer to a lost play of Shakespeare's? Or is *Love's Labour's Won* an alternative title for an extant piece? The first possibility — that of error — was ruled out by the discovery, as recently as 1953, of a manuscript scrap which bookbinders used more than three centuries ago to make the back hinge of a volume of sermons. The paper contains a stationer's notations of books he had in stock in August 1603. Among the items listed is 'loves labor won', which follows (logically enough) 'loves labor lost'. Most likely *Love's Labour's Won* is an alternative title for a known play. If so, it is unlikely to be one of the other comedies cited by Meres. Some authorities have favoured *The Taming of the Shrew*, in which love's labour is unmistakably won; although early, the play is omitted from *Palladis Tamia*. But the stationer includes 'taming of a shrew' as a separate entry in his inventory. The fact that most comedies have a love interest and end in prosperity does not facilitate the task of identification. *Much Ado About Nothing*, straining against the outer time-limit of Meres's range, is a possibility. Professor T. W. Baldwin, who with a whole book on the subject is our leading authority on a non-existent play, leans to *All's Well that Ends Well*, in which Helena 'wins' her obnoxious husband by the bed trick; but such reasoning presupposes, without adequate evidence, a lost early draft of the Jacobean problem comedy.[1] A more adventurous authority interprets 'love's labour's won' to mean 'love's pains earned', and opts for *Troilus and Cressida*;[2] but nobody seems to have seconded this unlikely nomination. *Love's Labour's Won* remains a minor Shakespearian enigma.

Because of the accident of chronology that made him the earliest recorded enthusiast of Shakespeare, Francis Meres begins the story of the poet's reputation. According to one historian of Shakespearian criticism, the encomiums in *Palladis Tamia* show 'how early the conception of Shakespeare as a universal genius had dawned'.[3] Meres occupies his niche of honour in biographies bearing such chapter headings as 'Rise in Fame and Social Dignity'. But this pretender to, and admirer of, wit is himself a writer of disarming witlessness. Sometimes the strain in finding an apt simile shows. Thus, 'As *Anacreon* died by the pot: so *George Peele* by the pox', where the sound, not sense, yokes the comparison. Meres is a remarkably undiscriminating panegyrist. He lavishes praise on Sidney ('our rarest Poet') and on *The Faerie Queene* ('I knowe not what more excellent or exquisite Poem may be written'), but Shakespeare must share praise for comedy with such decidedly lesser talents as 'Maister *Rowley* once a rare Scholler of learned Pembrooke Hall in Cambridge' and '*Anthony Mundye* our best plotter', not to mention a quartet of Henslowe's impecunious journeymen: Porter, Wilson, Hathaway, and Chettle. As a tragedian Shakespeare competes with his Warwickshire neighbour Michael Drayton. If the former is 'hony-tongued', Drayton is '*Golden-mouth'd*', and there does not seem to be much to choose between the two epithets. Drayton is, with Shakespeare, a bewailer of the perplexities of love. The former also wins praise for his moral virtue, an attribute that Meres overlooks mentioning for Shakespeare, who was not in this respect deficient. Drayton is clearly the compiler's favourite, being cited a record thirteen times, although Meres lists more titles for Shakespeare than for anyone else. In all, Meres commends 125 Englishmen. C. S. Lewis best sums up his status as a critic. 'Meres's

---

1   T. W. Baldwin, *Shakspere's* Love's Labor's Won: *New Evidence from the Account Books of an Elizabethan Bookseller* (Carbondale, Ill., 1957), p. 15. *All's Well that Ends Well*, as we have it, is tentatively dated 1603–4 by G. K. Hunter, who surveys the evidence disinterestedly in his introduction to the New Arden edition (1959), pp. xviii–xxv.

2   Leslie Hotson, 'Love's Labour's Won', *Shakespeare's Sonnets Dated and Other Essays* (1949), pp. 37–56.

3   Augustus Ralli, *A History of Shakespearian Criticism* (1932), i. 1.

patterned equivalences', Lewis writes, 'bear about the same relation to real criticism as Fluellen's comparison of Macedon and Monmouth bears to real geography.'[1]

One of the plays listed by Meres, *Henry IV* — he does not distinguish between parts — was newly composed in 1598. This drama created a fortuitous stir that would not entirely subside for half a century and more. In his *Church-History of Britain* Thomas Fuller writes:

Stage-Poets have themselves been very *bold* with, and others very *merry* at, the Memory of Sʳ *John Oldcastle*, whom they have fancied a *boon Companion*, a *jovial Royster*, and yet a *Coward* to boot, contrary to the credit of all Chronicles, owning him a *Martial man* of merit. The best is, Sʳ *John Falstaffe*, hath relieved the Memory of Sʳ *John Oldcastle*, and of late is substituted *Buffoone* in his place, but it matters as little what *petulant Poets*, as what *malicious Papists* have written against him.[2]

'Of late is substituted *Buffoone*': a curious phrase, in view of the fifty-seven years separating *Henry IV* and the *Church-History*. In 1662 Bishop Fuller was still vexed enough to grumble. 'Now as I am glad that Sir *John Oldcastle* is *put out*', he declares in his *Worthies of England*, 'so I am sorry that Sir *John Fastolfe* is *put in* . . . .'[3] Originally, as these remarks indicate, Shakespeare had called his fat knight Oldcastle. The choice of a name was a blunder, as the repercussions quickly proved.

The historical Oldcastle, styled Lord Cobham, was a distinguished and tragic figure. A Wycliffite who denounced the Pope as anti-Christ, he was hanged and burnt for his heretical faith on the Lollard gallows in St. Giles's Fields, and afterwards enrolled by John Foxe in his *Book of Martyrs*. Needless to say, Catholics viewed Oldcastle somewhat differently. In his *Examen of the Calendar or Catalogue of Protestant Saints*, the Jesuit Parsons wrote, 'The second Moneth of *February* is more fertile of rubricate Martyrs, then *January*, for that yt hath 8. in number, two Wickliffians, *Syr John Oldcastle*, a Ruffian-knight as all England knoweth, & commonly brought in by comediants on their stages: he was put to death for robberyes and rebellion under the foresaid K. *Henry* the fifth.'[4] Complaint about the slur on a name revered by Protestants was most likely lodged by William Brooke, seventh Lord Cobham, or by his successor — after his death in 1597 — Henry, eighth Lord Cobham; they were lineally descended, on the mother's side, from Oldcastle. It has been suggested that Shakespeare's original choice of a name was deliberately provocative, an act of retaliation against a dynasty hostile to the stage; but there is no evidence of the Cobhams' puritanical leanings, and more likely the dramatist took the name, without a second thought, from his source play, *The Famous Victories of Henry the Fifth*. A second thought would have been advisable.

The Brookes wielded power at Court. William, a Privy Councillor and Lord Chamberlain, could have ordered the change directly or used his influence with the Master of the Revels. His son Henry — the brother-in-law of Sir Robert Cecil and intimate of Raleigh — was an adversary of Essex and of Shakespeare's patron Southampton. No matter that the Essex faction mocked Brooke as 'my lord Fool'; he had successfully weathered the opposition to his appointment, in 1596, as Lord Warden of the Cinque Ports. Identification of the Cobham who remonstrated (assuming one did remonstrate) depends on the precise dating of *1 Henry IV*, which may have reached the boards before or after William's death.

The protest, whatever its source, carried weight. Shakespeare changed Oldcastle to Falstaff, a name suggested by the cowardly bit-player in *1 Henry VI* who takes to his heels from the battlefield without 'having struck one stroke'. For good measure the playwright also altered the names of Oldcastle-Falstaff's tavern mates, Harvey and Russell, to Bardolph and Peto — best not to offend the Earls of Bedford, who bore the name Russell, or Sir William Harvey, shortly to marry the dowager Countess of Southampton, who had already survived two husbands. (Harvey is thought by some to be the mysterious 'Mr. W. H.' of the *Sonnets* dedication.[5]) Shakespeare

1   C. S. Lewis, *English Literature in the Sixteenth Century Excluding Drama* (Oxford History of English Literature; Oxford, 1954), p. 430; see also Bentley, *Shakespeare*, pp. 199–203.
2   Thomas Fuller, *The Church-History of Britain; from the Birth of Jesus Christ, until the year 1648* (1655), bk. iv, cent. xv, p. 168.
3   Fuller, *The Worthies of England* (1662), ii. 253.
4   'N.D.' [Nicholas Dolman, pseudonym of Robert Parsons], *The Third Part of a Treatise, Intituled: of three Conversions of England: An Examen of the Calendar or Catalogue of Protestant Saints . . . by John Fox* (1604). *The Last Six Monethes* (1604), p. 31; quoted in EKC, ii. 213.
5   See below, p. 219.

To my Noble friend Sr henrye
Bourchier.

*

Sir Harrie Bourchier, you are descended of Noble Auncestrie, and
in the dutie of a good man loue to heart and see fair reputation
preserued from slandr and oblivion. whearfore to you I dedicate
this edition of Ocleve where Sr Jhon Oldcastlee appeares to haue
binne a man of valour and vertue, and onely lost in his
owne times because he would not bowe vnder the foule superstition of papistrie from whence in so great light of Gospel and
learning that there is not yet a most Vniuersall deperture
is to — the greatest scorne of men. But of this more in another
place, and in preface will you please to heart mee that which
followes. A young Gentle Ladie of your acquaintance having
read yt works of Shakespeare made me this question. How
Sir Jhon Falstaffe, or Fastolf as it is written in ye statute book of Maudlin Colledge in Oxford where everye daye
could be dead in ye time of Harrie ye fift & againe liue in ye time of Harrie ye sixt to be banisht
for cowardize. Whereto I made answeare that this was
one of those humours and mistakes for which plato banisht all poets out of his commonwealth. that Sir Jhon
Falstaffe was in those times a Noble valiant souldier as
appeares by a book in the heralds office dedicated vnto him
by a herald whoe had binne with him if I will remember
for ye space of 25 yeeres in ye French wars. that he seemes
allso to haue binne a man of learning because in a libra-
rie of Oxford I finde a book of dedicating churches sent
from him for a present vnto Bisshop Waimflete and
inscribed with his owne hand. That in Shakespeares first
playe of Harrie ye fift, ye person with which he vndertook to
playe a buffone was not Falstaffe, but Sr Jhon Oldcastle,
and that offence beinge worthily taken by personages descended from his title as Perardventure by manie others allso whoe
ought to haue him in honourable memorie, the poet was
putt to make an ignorant shifte of abusing Sr Jhon Fa—
Fastolphe, a man not inferior of vertue though not
so famous in pietie as the other whoe gaue witnesse vnto
the truth of our reformation with a constant and reso-
lute martyrdom, vnto which he was pursued by the
priests, Bishops, Moncks, and Friers of those dayes.
Noble Sir this is all my preface. God keepe you, and mi and
all Christian people from the bloodie designes of that cruell
religion.

yours in all observance

Rich. James.

101 RICHARD JAMES, EPISTLE-DEDICATORY TO SIR HENRY BOURCHIER, c. 1625. *Bodleian Library, MS. James 34. The epistle is prefixed to a copy of Occleve's* Legend and Defence of Sir John Oldcastle. *Transcript:* The Poems etc., of Richard James B.D. (1592–1638), *ed. Alexander B. Grosart (1880), pp. 137–8; EKC, ii. 241–2. The Revd. Philip Bliss drew James's letter to the attention of H-P, who printed it for the first time in* On the Character of Sir John Falstaff, as originally exhibited by Shakespeare in the Two Parts of King Henry IV (1841), *pp. 18–20.*

covered, as best he could, the traces of references that would grate on proud sensibilities, but Harvey and 'Rossil' surface in a stage direction, and Oldcastle lingers in a metrically deficient line, a botched pun ('my old lad of the castle', i.e. roisterer), and a surviving speech prefix, 'Old'. But most telling of all is the author's humble Epilogue disclaimer: '. . . Falstaff shall die of a sweat, unless already 'a be kill'd with your hard opinions; for Oldcastle died a martyr and this is not the man.'

In 1599 a team of dramatists from the rival Admiral's men — Drayton, Munday, Wilson, and Hathaway — produced *The true and honourable historie, of the life of Sir John Old-castle, the good Lord Cobham*.

> It is no pamperd glutton we present,
> Nor aged Councellor to youthfull sinne,
> But one, whose vertue shone above the rest,
> A valiant Martyr and a vertuous peere.

Thus speaks the Prologue, not without smugness; and concludes: 'Let faire Truth be grac'te,/ Since forg'de invention former time defac'te.' By a nice irony *Sir John Oldcastle* in time came to be associated with Shakespeare's name, and found a place in the Third Folio of his plays in 1664. Such are the vagaries of show business.

The earliest mention of the behind-the-scenes brouhaha comes in a letter written, around 1625, by Dr. Richard James. 'A short, red-bearded, high-coloured fellow' (so an enemy described him), James was a divine whose appetite for travel took him as far as Russia; he was also a small poet who trailed in the tribe of Ben, and — not least — the antiquary in charge of Sir Robert Cotton's great library. In his letter, addressed to Sir Harry Bourchier, James considers the question put to him by a young gentlewoman of Bourchier's acquaintance: how could Sir John Falstaff die in the reign of Henry VI, and live again to be banished for cowardice in Henry V's time? To which James replies:

That in Shakespeares first shewe of Harrie ye fift, ye person with which he undertook to playe a buffone was not Falstaffe, but Sr Jhon Oldcastle, and that offence beinge worthily taken by personages descended from his title, as peradventure by manie others allso whoe ought to have him in honourable memorie, the poet was putt to make an ignorant shifte of abusing Sr Jhon Fastolphe, a man not inferior of vertue though not so famous in pietie as the other. . . .

A late embellishment of the episode draws no less a personage than the sovereign herself into the intrigue: '. . . this Part of *Falstaff*', according to Rowe, 'is said to have been written originally under the Name of *Oldcastle*; some of that Family being then remaining, the Queen was pleas'd to command him to alter it; upon which he made use of *Falstaff*.'[1]

A royal command also figures in the sequel story of how Shakespeare came to write the last of his Falstaff plays. This famous tradition first reaches print in the defensive apologia prefixed in 1702 by John Dennis to his *Comical Gallant*. An adaptation of *The Merry Wives of Windsor*, Dennis's play had just failed on the stage, there being no way the hapless author could placate his two camps of detractors, one of which (he lamented in his dedicatory epistle) believed the original play 'to be so admirable, that nothing ought to be added to it; the others fancied it to be so despicable, that any ones time would be lost upon it'. Thus caught between Scylla and Charybdis, Dennis defends his own meddling pen by invoking a more glorious past:

> *That this Comedy was not despicable, I guess'd for several Reasons: First, I knew very well, that it had pleas'd one of the greatest Queens that ever was in the World, great not only for her Wisdom in the Arts of Government, but for her knowledge of Polite Learning, and her nice taste of the Drama, for such a taste we may be sure she had, by the relish which she had of the Ancients. This Comedy was written at her Command, and by her direction, and she was so eager to see it Acted, that she commanded it to be finished in fourteen days; and was afterwards, as Tradition tells us, very well pleas'd at the Representation.*

102 JOHN DENNIS, EPISTLE DEDICATORY 'TO THE HONOURABLE GEORGE GRANVILLE, ESQ.', IN *THE COMICAL GALLANT: OR THE AMOURS OF SIR JOHN FALSTAFFE* (1702), sig. A2. *Reprinted in EKC, ii. 263.*

1 Nicholas Rowe, *Some Account of the Life, &c. of Mr. William Shakespear*, in Shakespeare, *Works*, ed. Rowe (1709), i, p. ix.

In his prologue the adaptor again alludes to the fourteen days of composition time. Two years later, however, in replying with heavy sarcasm to Jeremy Collier's *Dissuasion from the Play-Houses*, Dennis improved upon the anecdote by contracting the fortnight into ten days: 'Nay the poor mistaken Queen her self, encouraged Play-Houses to that degree, that she not only commanded *Shakespear* to write the Comedy of the *Merry Wives*, and to write it in Ten Days time; so eager was she for the wicked Diversion . . . .'[1] Rowe next adds an appealing circumstantial detail. He is speaking of the 'many gracious Marks of her Favour' that Queen Elizabeth gave Shakespeare.

> She was so well pleas'd with that admirable Character of *Falstaff*, in the two Parts of *Henry* the Fourth, that she com-

> manded him to continue it for one Play more, and to shew him in Love. This is said to be the Occasion of his Writing *The Merry Wives of* Windsor.

103 NICHOLAS ROWE, *SOME ACCOUNT OF THE LIFE, &C. OF MR. WILLIAM SHAKESPEAR*, IN SHAKESPEARE, *WORKS*, ED. ROWE (1709), i, pp. viii–ix.

Finally, just a year later, the publisher's hack Gildon (doubtfully immortalized by Pope in *The Dunciad*) retells the tradition in the *Remarks on the Plays of Shakespear* which, without benefit of an invitation from the editor, he published as a supplement to Rowe:

> The *Fairys* in the fifth Act makes a Handsome Complement to the Queen, in her Palace of *Windsor*, who had oblig'd him to write a Play of Sir *John Falstaff* in Love, and which I am very well assured he perform'd in a Fortnight; a prodigious Thing, when all is so well contriv'd, and carry'd on without the least Confusion.

104 CHARLES GILDON, *REMARKS ON THE PLAYS OF SHAKESPEAR*, IN SHAKESPEARE, *WORKS* (1710), vii. 291. *On Gildon's* Remarks, *see EKC, ii. 262, where this passage is reprinted.*

The assurances of which Gildon boasts probably have as their source the printed remarks of Dennis and Rowe, but the citation of the Fairies is (as we shall see) pertinent.

A report unremarked for over a century, and then exhumed for special pleading, must arouse sceptical misgivings. How Dennis came upon the story we do not know; possibly, as Malone supposed, from Dryden who may have had it from Davenant. The tradition, however, receives some confirmation from the fact that *The Merry Wives of Windsor* is described on the title-page of the 1602 Quarto as having been acted 'before her Majesty'. Apparently none of these early authorities — Dennis, Rowe, or Gildon — had seen the Quarto.[2]

A royal occasion conceivably inspired the original production. Shakespeare sets the scene for *The Merry Wives* at Windsor, where the installation of the Knights of the Garter took place each year in the chapel of St. George, the patron saint of the order. In Act V the Fairy Queen's speech — with its gracious allusions to the stalls in the choir chapel, the crests, blazons, and coat-armour of the Garter knights, and the motto of the order, *Honi soit qui mal y pense* — underscores the Garter connection of the play. Some hold that *The Merry Wives of Windsor* had its first performance in 1597, not at the formal installation (unattended by the Queen) in St. George's chapel, but at the Garter Feast in the royal Whitehall Palace a month earlier, on St. George's day, 23 April. That

---

1 Dennis, *The Person of Quality's Answer to Mr. Collier's Letter* (1704), p. 4; quoted by EKC, ii. 263.
2 Shakespeare, *The Merry Wives of Windsor*, ed. H. J. Oliver (New Arden Shakespeare; 1971), introd., p. xlv.

year George Carey, Lord Hunsdon, was one of the five newly elected Knights. Upon his father's death in 1596 Hunsdon had taken over the sponsorship of Shakespeare's company, and the next year, in mid-April, his Queen, who had a dear regard for him, appointed him Lord Chamberlain. Thus for Hunsdon April was a kind month, bringing him a double recognition. What more natural than that the Lord Chamberlain, who lavished large sums on the Garter celebration, should commission his leading dramatist to produce, on the spur, a play on the theme of Falstaff in love, for presentation by the Chamberlain's servants at the magnificent Feast honouring the new Knights? It is an appealing enough hypothetical reconstruction of the events leading up to the first night of *The Merry Wives of Windsor*, and not implausible as such hypotheses go.

The year before the Garter Feast there took place on Bankside a puzzling episode which its modern discoverer would connect with the composition of *The Merry Wives of Windsor*. In the autumn of 1596 William Wayte petitioned for sureties of the peace against William Shakspere, Francis Langley, Dorothy Soer wife of John Soer, and Anne Lee, *'ob metum mortis'* — 'for fear of death', a conventional legal phrase in such documents. The writ of attachment, issued to the sheriff of Surrey, was returnable on the last day of Michaelmas Term, 29 November. To obtain such a writ, the complainant swore before the Judge of Queen's Bench that he stood in danger of death, or bodily hurt, from a certain party. The magistrate then commanded the sheriff of the appropriate county to produce the accused person or persons, who had to post bond to keep the peace, on pain of forfeiting the security.

105 THE LANGLEY WRIT, 1596. *Public Record Office, Court of King's Bench, Controlment Roll, Michaelmas Term 1596, K.B. 29/234. Transcript: BRL, i. 218 (text and translation). Leslie Hotson discovered the document, which he published and discussed in 'A Great Shakespeare Discovery',* The Atlantic Monthly, cxlviii *(1931), 419–36, and in* Shakespeare versus Shallow *(1931).*

Of the *dramatis personae* in this minor legal drama, we have already encountered Langley. A money-broker fifteen years Shakespeare's senior, he had built the Swan playhouse in Paris Garden. (It has been suggested by Leslie Hotson that the Chamberlain's men were at the Swan in 1596, but there is no evidence to show that they were.) Dorothy Soer and Anne Lee are otherwise unknown; it is a minor solace that nobody has yet cast either for the part of Dark Lady. About Wayte we have more information. These writs of attachment were often retaliatory, and in fact Langley had earlier in the same term sworn the peace against Wayte and Wayte's stepfather William Gardiner, a Surrey justice of the peace with jurisdiction in Paris Garden and Southwark. A deposition in another case sneeringly describes Wayte as 'a certain loose person of no reckoning or value, being wholly under the rule and commandment of the said Gardiner'.[1] This Gardiner was known and detested by many in the district. Through money-lending and sharp practices (he married a prosperous widow, and proceeded to defraud her son and brothers and sisters), the Justice had risen to wealth and civic dignity. He made numerous enemies, including his own son-in-law John Stepkin. On his death-bed Stepkin darkly suspected that Gardiner was responsible for his fatal illness; was he not, after all, a sorcerer who kept two toads? In the spring of 1596 Gardiner quarrelled with Langley, who denounced him as 'a false perjured knave'. The Justice in turn sought to put the Swan out of business.

Somehow Shakespeare was drawn into this feud. Dr. Hotson believes that Gardiner, not Sir Thomas Lucy, was satirized as Justice Shallow in *The Merry Wives of Windsor*, and also in *2 Henry IV*; and that the dramatist lampooned Wayte in the figure of Slender. The Surrey Justice owned an enclosed deer park in Godstone. By virtue of his marriage he was entitled to impale upon his

---

1 Hotson, *Shakespeare versus Shallow* (1931), p. 24. He fully describes the personages and legal procedures.

coat of arms — a golden griffin — three white luces; hence the allusion to louses in Act 1, scene i, of *The Merry Wives of Windsor*. Gardiner arranged an advantageous match for his kinsman Wayte; in the play Shallow tries to mate his simpleton cousin Slender with Anne Page, who possesses (in addition to brown hair and a small womanly voice) £700 and possibilities. These parallels between life and art are intriguing, but the edifice of argument rests on a fragile foundation. Shallow — foolish, senile, essentially harmless — will hardly pass muster as a caricature of the overbearing Justice Gardiner. There is no evidence that Shakespeare ever set eyes upon Gardiner. For all we know the poet may have been an innocent bystander (he lived in the neighbourhood),[1] although Langley's theatrical associations suggest a more direct involvement. But all that has come to light is the single laconic record. The rest is speculation.

One can readily imagine Shakespeare present, as a leading member of his troupe, in Whitehall Palace at the Garter Feast which coincided (if we may accept the traditional anniversary) with his thirty-third birthday, and anxiously watching the première of his play. It is a harmless fancy to toy with. Perhaps he acted in *The Merry Wives of Windsor*; he must have done a good deal of acting, especially in the earlier years.

The Names of the Principall Actors
in all these Playes.

William Shakespeare.	Samuel Gilburne.
Richard Burbadge.	Robert Armin.
John Hemmings.	William Ostler.
Augustine Phillips.	Nathan Field.
William Kempt.	John Underwood.
Thomas Poope.	Nicholas Tooley.
George Bryan.	William Ecclestone.
Henry Condell.	Joseph Taylor.
William Slye.	Robert Benfield.
Richard Cowly.	Robert Goughe.
John Lowine.	Richard Robinson.
Samuell Crosse.	John Shancke.
Alexander Cooke.	John Rice.

106 WILLIAM SHAKESPEARE, *COMEDIES, HISTORIES, & TRAGEDIES* (1623), sig. B2. *Copy in the British Library; shelfmark: C.39.k.15.* STC *22273.*

1 On Shakespeare's London residences, see below, pp. 161–4.

About his life as a mime Shakespeare seems to have entertained ambivalent feelings. The *Sonnets* reveal that he chafed at the social inferiority of actors; he confesses having made himself 'a motley to the view', and arraigns Fortune

> That did not better for my life provide
> Than public means which public manners breeds.
> Thence comes it that my name receives a brand,
> And almost thence my nature is subdu'd
> To what it works in, like the dyer's hand.

But such passing moods must have yielded to a dominant professionalism. The First Folio that gathers together Shakespeare's plays also pays tribute to the player. His old fellows, Heminges and Condell, place him — appropriately enough, given the occasion — at the head of their catalogue of 'the Principall Actors in all these Playes' on the ninth preliminary leaf to the Folio. *All* is a big number; we should welcome more precise information.

The epigram included by John Davies of Hereford in his *Scourge of Folly*, if cryptic, has at least the merit of being contemporary.

107 JOHN DAVIES OF HEREFORD, *THE SCOURGE OF FOLLY* (N.D.; STATIONERS' REGISTER: 8 OCTOBER 1610), Epig. 159, pp. 76–7. *Copy in the Bodleian Library; shelfmark: Malone 406. STC 6341. Alexander B. Grosart collected and edited Davies's* Complete Works *for the Chertsey Worthies' Library, 1878, 2 vols. The next year it found a place in* The Shakspere Allusion-Book *when C. M. Ingleby included Epig. 159 in his compilation,* Shakespeare's Centurie of Prayse (*as the second edition of the* Allusion-Book *was called*), *for the New Shakspere Society.*

In what sense was Shakespeare a king 'among the meaner sort'? How was he fitted to be 'a companion for a *King*'? And which kingly parts did he play? Some biographers believe that Shakespeare donned the sceptre and crown of Duncan, Henry IV, and Henry VI. These are guesses. He is not thought to have taken the stellar roles of Lear and Macbeth, which Burbage made famous.

In 1699 an anonymous enthusiast of the stage, perhaps the antiquary and play-collector James Wright, remarked in a vague but not unreasonable parenthesis that '*Shakespear* . . . was a much better Poet, than Player'.[1] Rowe, gathering material for his memoir of Shakespeare, tried to find out more, with little success:

His Name is Printed, as the Custom was in those Times, amongst those of the other Players, before some old Plays, but without any particular Account of what sort of Parts he us'd to play; and tho' I have inquir'd, I could never meet with any further Account of him this way, than that the top of his Performance was the Ghost in his own *Hamlet*.

108 NICHOLAS ROWE, *SOME ACCOUNT OF THE LIFE, &C. OF MR. WILLIAM SHAKESPEAR*, IN SHAKESPEARE, *WORKS*, ED. ROWE (1709), i, p. vi.

1   *Historia Histrionica: an Historical Account of the English Stage . . . In a Dialogue, of Plays and Players* (1699), p. 4.

The Ghost in *Hamlet*; that at least tells us something. To this traditional intelligence the disorderly antiquary Oldys adds another morsel a half-century later. This item appears in the ragbag of notes which the great Shakespearian scholar Steevens rescued from oblivion:

" One of Shakefpeare's younger brothers, who lived to a good old age, even fome years, as I compute, after the reftoration of *K. Charles II.* would in his younger days come to London to vifit his brother *Will,* as he called him, and be a fpectator of him as an actor in fome of his own plays. This cuftom, as his brother's fame enlarged, and his dramatic entertainments grew the greateft fupport of our principal, if not of all our theatres, he continued it feems fo long after his brother's death, as even to the latter end of his own life. The curiofity at this time of the moft noted actors to learn fomething from him of his brother, &c. they juftly held him in the higheft veneration. And it may be well believed, as there was befides a kinfman and defcendant of the family, who was then a celebrated actor among them, [*Charles Harte.* See Shakefpeare's Will] this opportunity made them greedily inquifitive into every little circumftance, more efpecially in his dramatick character, which his brother could relate of him. But he, it feems, was fo ftricken in years, and poffibly his memory fo weakened with infirmities (which might make him the eafier pafs for a man of weak intellects) that he could give them but little light into their enquiries; and all that could be recollected from him of his brother *Will,* in that ftation was, the faint, general, and almoft loft ideas he had of having once feen him act a part in one of his own comedies, wherein being to perfonate a decrepit old man, he wore a long beard, and appeared fo weak and drooping and unable to walk, that he was forced to be fupported and carried by another perfon to a table, at which he was feated among fome company, who were eating, and one of them fung a fong." See the character of *Adam* in *As you like it.* Act. II. Sc. ult.

109 WILLIAM SHAKESPEARE, *PLAYS*, ED. SAMUEL JOHNSON AND GEORGE STEEVENS (1778), i. 204. *Reprinted by EKC, ii. 278.*

So, if this report is true, Shakespeare played Adam in *As You Like It*, as well as Hamlet's Ghost; characters with either one or both feet in the grave. Dignified parts. Oldys's authority is not very reassuring, however, for none of Shakespeare's three brothers lived into the Restoration.

A little later in the eighteenth century Edward Capell, justly celebrated for his editorial labours on Shakespeare, retailed the same anecdote, but the source has now become a senile ancient of Stratford.

A traditional ftory was current fome years ago about Stratford, — that a very old man of that place, — of weak intellects, but yet related to Shakefpeare, — being afk'd by fome of his neighbours, what he remember'd about him; anfwer'd, — that he faw him once brought on the ftage upon another man's back; which anfwer was apply'd by the hearers, to his having feen him perform in this fcene the part of Adam: That he fhould have done fo, is made not unlikely by another conftant tradition, — that he was no extraordinary actor, and therefore took no parts upon him but fuch as this: for which he might alfo be peculiarly fitted by an accidental lamenefs, which, — as he himfelf tells us twice in his "*Sonnets,*" v. 37, and 89, — befell him in fome part of life; without faying how, or when, of what fort, or in what degree; but his expreffions feem to indicate — latterly.

110 EDWARD CAPELL, *NOTES AND VARIOUS READINGS TO SHAKESPEARE* [1779], vol. i, pt. i, p. 60. *The* Notes *are separately paginated following the Glossary.*

In Sonnet 37 the poet complains of being 'made lame by Fortune's dearest spite', and in 89 he threatens, 'Speak of my lameness, and I straight will halt'. Metaphor, it seems, is not Capell's strong suit, but in his descent into literalism he has good company. The idea of a hobbling Bard appealed to Sir Walter Scott, himself lame. 'He is a stout man at quarterstaff, and single falchion', Sussex describes Shakespeare (a 'gamesome mad fellow') in *Kenilworth*, 'though, as I am told, a halting fellow; and he stood, they say, a tough fight with the rangers of old Sir Thomas Lucy of Charlecote, when he broke his deer-park and kissed his keeper's daughter.'[1] Here Sussex stands at the crossroads where legends meet.

Despite the imaginary afflictions he owes to the unimaginativeness of his critics, Shakespeare managed to act in the plays of fellow dramatists for the Chamberlain's men, as well as in his own. When Ben Jonson brought his plays together in 1616 for the first of the great dramatic folios of the age, he gave Shakespeare pride of place in the list of 'principall Comœdians' in *Every Man in his Humour*, acted in 1598.

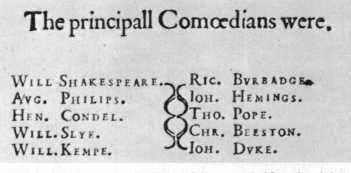

The principall Comœdians were.

WILL SHAKESPEARE. RIC. BVRBADGE.
AVG. PHILIPS.   IOH. HEMINGS.
HEN. CONDEL.   THO. POPE.
WILL. SLYE.   CHR. BEESTON.
WILL. KEMPE.   IOH. DVKE.

111   BEN JONSON, *WORKES* (1616), p. 72. *Bodleian Library; shelfmark: AA.83.Art.* STC *14751*.

Did Shakespeare take the part of elder Knowell? He presumably did not act in the sequel *Every Man out of his Humour*, for his name fails to appear in the cast-list. He is, however, numbered among the tragedians who enacted the same dramatist's *Sejanus* in 1603.

The principall Tragœdians were,

RIC. BVRBADGE.   WILL. SHAKE-SPEARE.
AVG. PHILIPS.   IOH. HEMINGS.
WILL. SLY.   HEN. CONDEL.
IOH. LOWIN.   ALEX. COOKE.

112   BEN JONSON, *WORKES* (1616), p. 438. *Bodleian Library; shelfmark: AA.83.Art.* STC *14751*.

According to a late tradition, Shakespeare gave Jonson, eight or nine years his junior, his start with the Chamberlain's men. Rowe tells the story.

> His Acquaintance with *Ben Johnson* began with a remarkable piece of Humanity and good Nature; Mr. *Johnson*, who was at that Time altogether unknown to the World, had offer'd one of his Plays to the Players, in order to have it Acted; and the Persons into whose Hands it was put, after having turn'd it carelesly and superciliously over, were juſt upon returning it to him with an ill-natur'd Anſwer,

---

1   Sir Walter Scott, *Kenilworth*, ch. xvii.

that it would be of no service to their Company, when *Shakespear* luckily cast his Eye upon it, and found something so well in it as to engage him first to read it through, and afterwards to recommend Mr. *Johnson* and his Writings to the Publick. After this they were profess'd Friends; tho' I don't know whether the other ever made him an equal return of Gentleness and Sincerity.

113 NICHOLAS ROWE, *SOME ACCOUNT OF THE LIFE, &C. OF MR. WILLIAM SHAKESPEAR*, IN SHAKESPEARE, *WORKS*, ED. ROWE (1709), i, pp. xii–xiii.

The dark connotations of the last sentence evoke the familiar picture of Shakespeare and Jonson as mighty opposites, with Gentle Will inspiring envious passions in rare and rivalrous Ben. Such images, belonging to the mythos, will in due course occupy us, as will Jonson's comments on Shakespeare.

The mythos, to which we owe so many small pleasures, outdoes itself in the legendary playhouse encounter of the actor and the Queen. Much repeated, the story achieves definitive statement in a bookseller's compilation, the *Dramatic Table Talk* of Richard Ryan, published in 1825.

SHAKSPEARE AND QUEEN ELIZABETH.

IT is well known that Queen Elizabeth was a great admirer of the immortal Shakspeare, and used frequently (as was the custom with persons of great rank in those days) to appear upon the stage before the audience, or to sit delighted behind the scenes, when the plays of our bard were performed. One evening, when Shakspeare himself was personating the part of a King, the audience knew of her Majesty being in the house. She crossed the stage when he was performing, and, on receiving the accustomed greeting from the audience, moved politely to the poet, but he did not notice it! When behind the scenes, she caught his eye, and moved again, but still he would not throw off his character, to notice her : this made her Majesty think of some means by which she might know, whether he would depart, or not, from the dignity of his character, while on the stage.—Accordingly, as he was about to make his exit, she stepped before him, dropped her glove, and re-crossed the stage, which Shakspeare noticing, took up, with these words, immediately after finishing his speech, and so aptly were they delivered, that they seemed to belong to it :

" And though now bent on this high embassy,
Yet *stoop* we to take up our *Cousin's* glove !"

He then walked off the stage, and presented the glove to the Queen, who was greatly pleased with his behaviour, and complimented him upon the propriety of it.

114 RICHARD RYAN, *DRAMATIC TABLE TALK; OR SCENES, SITUATIONS, & ADVENTURES, SERIOUS & COMIC, IN THEATRICAL HISTORY & BIOGRAPHY* (1825), ii. 156–7. *Reprinted by EKC, ii. 300–1.*

So agreeable is it to have this glimpse of the courtly Warwickshire provincial exercising his extempore wit with his sovereign that one is almost tempted to overlook a few considerations hostile to romance.[1] In Elizabethan theatres performances took place in the afternoon, not at night; the stage afforded no scenery for eavesdroppers to conceal themselves behind; the Queen is not known to have professed admiration for Shakespeare; she was disinclined to expose herself to the multitude by visiting the playhouse; and she restrained herself publicly (as in private) from flirtations with subjects of inferior station. These details unfortunately impair faith in a story which, in its naïve way, shows Shakespeare in a kingly part and as a fit companion for a monarch.

Burbage had his female admirers too, if we may trust the scurrilous anecdote that Edward Curle, a student at the Middle Temple, related to his room-mate John Manningham, and which the latter jotted down in his manuscript *Diary* on 13 March 1602. When (according to Manningham) Burbage was playing Richard III, a citizeness became infatuated with him, and they arranged an assignation; but Shakespeare overheard the conversation, arrived first, and 'was intertained, and at his game ere Burbidge came'. When the message arrived that Richard III was at the door, the triumphant lover, with some relish, returned word that William the Conqueror preceded Richard III. 'Shakespeares name William', Manningham helpfully adds.

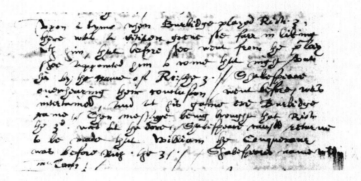

115 JOHN MANNINGHAM'S ANECDOTE ABOUT SHAKESPEARE AND BURBAGE, 1602. *British Library, MS. Harley 5353, f. 29ᵛ. Transcript: TB, 39; EKC, ii. 212; BRL, i. 317. The Manningham Diary was first brought to the public notice by J. Payne Collier in his* History of English Dramatic Poetry to the Time of Shakespeare: and Annals of the Stage to the Restoration *(1831), i. 320–38, although the story itself had circulated, unattributed, for some time (see SL, 335n). Collier prints the anecdote on pp. 331–2. John Bruce edited Manningham's Diary for the Camden Society in 1868; his transcript of the present item appears on p. 39. Manningham's informant, whose name follows the anecdote, is given as Tooly by Collier, and Touse (?) by Bruce, but later authorities (among them Greg) have identified him as 'mᵃ Curle'. Manningham had as his 'chamberfellow' an Edward Curle whose sister Anne he later married; a 'Mᵣ Mᵃ. Curle' is cited on f.117ᵛ. Anything passing through Collier's hands must engender suspicion, and Sidney Race has suggested that the two Shakespeare entries in Manningham's Diary — especially the present item — may be forgeries ('Manningham's Diary: The Case for Re-examination', Notes and Queries, cxcix (1954), 380–3). But the evidence, including recent microscopic and ultra-violet examination, strongly argues its genuineness. See also below, item 117.*

If this anecdote, which carries more weight than legendary accretions, is true, and the leading player and the leading playwright of the Chamberlain's men competed for the favours of stage-struck ladies of the town, they also (and this admits of no question) co-operated wholeheartedly to maintain the pre-eminence of their company. In 1597 the company faced its most dangerous crisis, for on 13 April James Burbage's lease on the Theatre, their regular house, expired.

Negotiations for a new agreement had got under way between Burbage and the ground land-lord, Giles Allen. For a while it looked as though they might be able to come to terms. Burbage agreed to a higher rent — £24 a year instead of £14 — and even, reluctantly, to allowing the landlord to take eventual possession of the building. But when Allen demanded permission to convert the playhouse to his own uses after a period of only five years, Burbage drew the line. He

---

1   These are not overlooked by Bentley (*Shakespeare*, p. 9), whose analysis covers the same points as my own.

now prudently cast about for an alternative theatrical site, and thought he had found it in the old Frater, or refectory, of the dissolved Blackfriars monastery which, although within the city walls, was subject to the Crown, not the Lord Mayor and aldermen of London. Burbage laid out £600 for the Frater, and at the cost of several hundred pounds more refurbished the structure for theatrical use. But the aristocratic residents of the fashionable district, alarmed at the prospect of a common playhouse in their midst, protested to the Privy Council. They had their way, although in the fullness of time Shakespeare's company would put their Blackfriars property to good use.

Meanwhile troubles crowded in on the Chamberlain's men. In February 1597 James Burbage died. April came and went without a new lease. In July, reacting to the scandal caused by the seditious *Isle of Dogs* at the Swan, the Privy Council ordered the 'fynall suppressinge of . . . Stage playes' and the destruction of all theatres in and about the capital. Fortunately the final solution was not final, and the acting companies were soon back in business. The Chamberlain's servants played for a while longer at the Theatre, at the landlord's sufferance, but by the end of the year they had moved to the Curtain. Their old playhouse now stood empty, and provided a minor satirist of the day with an image of desolation:

> But see yonder,
> One like the unfrequented Theater
> Walkes in darke silence, and vast solitude.[1]

Shakespeare's company found itself without a permanent home.

It was now the task of Burbage's son Cuthbert to resume discussions with a landlord at once avaricious and puritanical. When Allen came to town and put up at the George Inn in Shoreditch, as he did four times a year to receive his rents, Cuthbert pleaded with him to grant a new lease, and in the autumn of 1598 capitulated to terms he viewed as extortionate — only to have Allen refuse to accept Richard Burbage as security. Sanguine that 'the right and Interest of the sayd Theatre was both in lawe and Conscience absolutely vested' in him, Allen made plans 'to pull downe the same, and to convert the wood and timber thereof to some better use . . . .' *To some better use*; the phrase sufficiently indicates his prejudice. But he never had a chance to visit his righteous wrath on the playhouse; for report of what was afoot reached the Burbages.

On 28 December 1597, with Allen away in the country, a determined party gathered at the Theatre under the cover of night. While Widow Burbage looked on approvingly, her sons Cuthbert and Richard, along with their friend and financial backer William Smith of Waltham Cross, their chief carpenter Peter Street, and ten or twelve workmen, proceeded to dismantle the Theatre: an action specifically permitted them by a covenant of the expired lease. The episode is described by Giles Allen, still impotently furious four years after the event. Cuthbert Burbage and his crew, he deposed, did

ryotouslye assemble themselves together and then and there armed themselves with divers and manye unlawfull and offensive weapons, as namelye, swordes daggers billes axes and such like And soe armed did then repayre unto the sayd Theater And then and there armed as aforesayd in verye ryotous outragious and forcyble manner and contrarye to the lawes of your highnes Realme attempted to pull downe the sayd Theater wheruppon divers of your Subjectes servauntes and farmers then goinge aboute in peacable manner to procure them to desist from that their unlawfull enterpryse, They the sayd ryotous persons aforesayd notwithstanding procured then therein with greate vyolence not onlye then and there forcyblye and ryotouslye resisting your subjectes servauntes and farmers but allso then and there pulling breaking and throwing downe the sayd Theater in verye outragious violent and riotous sort to the great disturbance and terrefyeing not onlye of your subjectes sayd servauntes and farmers but of divers others of your majesties loving subjectes there neere inhabitinge.[2]

The timber from the dismantled Theatre — there is no mention of the ironwork known to have been used in its construction — these riotous men then ferried across the river to Bankside, where they erected a new playhouse more splendid than any London had yet seen. This they called the Globe.

---

1 [Edward Guilpin], *Skialetheia, or, a shadowe of Truth, in certaine Epigrams and Satyres* (1598), sig. D6.
2 C. W. Wallace, *The First London Theatre: Materials for a History*, in Nebraska *University Studies*, xiii (1913), 278–9.

They built on garden plots and grounds in St. Saviour's parish, in the environs of the Rose and the Bear Garden, and the handsome big church of St. Mary Overies;[1] near to Maiden Lane — 'a long straggling Place', Stow's eighteenth-century editor describes it, 'with Ditches on each side the Passage to the Houses being over little Bridges, with little Garden Plotts before them, especially on the North side which is best both for Houses and Inhabitants'.[2] Shakespeare and his fellows must have watched the work progress. Allen did not stand by; instead he brought suit against carpenter Street, Burbage's agent, in the Queen's Bench, claiming £800 damages, a sum that included 40s. for trampling on the grass. Among other charges, Allen accused the Burbages of not having spent £200 (as the old lease required) in improvements of tenements on the property; but James Burbage had years earlier anticipated this tactic by commissioning an expert craftsman to take before-and-after 'views' giving proof of repairs and of the erection of new tenements. The court decided in favour of the Burbages. Allen brought other actions before other tribunals. Finally, the Court of Requests ordered him to desist from bringing any further suits respecting the demolition of the Theatre. He sued anyway, but got nowhere. Meanwhile the Chamberlain's men were playing at the Globe. On the afternoon of 21 September 1599 Thomas Platter of Basle crossed the Thames with his companions and in the straw-thatched house saw a play on Julius Caesar very ably acted by a company of about fifteen ('mitt ohnegefahr 15 personen sehen gar artlich agieren'). If, as is most likely, this was Shakespeare's *Julius Caesar*, it is the first recorded performance at the Globe.

The competitive presence of a new theatre on Bankside was most acutely felt by the Admiral's men, under Alleyn and Henslowe, at the Rose a few hundred yards away. Although not quite fifteen years old, the house was dangerously decayed, and, because of its position on swampy ground, uninviting in bad weather. Sensibly, the Admiral's company decided to decamp. Alleyn leased a plot of ground on the other side of the Thames, near the fields of St. Giles without Cripplegate, in the liberty of Finsbury; an up-and-coming district that met the essential condition of being outside City jurisdiction. Alleyn and Henslowe then contracted with Peter Smith — the principal carpenter of the Globe — to build a playhouse between Whitecross Street and Golding (or Golden) Lane. The agreement, which survives among the Henslowe papers at Dulwich College, calls for a structure generally modelled on the Globe, but square: 80 feet by 80 on the outside, and 55 feet each way within. The stage projecting into the yard was 43 feet wide. The Fortune (as the house was called) is the only Elizabethan theatre for which we have authenticated specifications, and these help us to visualize the dimensions of the Globe. Henslowe and Alleyn supplied their carpenter with a 'plot', or drawing, of the stage and staircases, but this has disappeared. The playhouse, flying the flag of Dame Fortune, opened in the autumn of 1600, and remained a fixture of Finsbury for two decades.

The men who built the Globe had formed a syndicate. Jointly they bore the expense of leasing the site, and of putting up and operating the playhouse. Together they shared in the profits that accrued to them from their investment. The original agreement drawn up by the solicitors and formally signed on 21 February 1599 was a 'tripartite lease', the three parties being Sir Nicholas Brend (who owned the grounds), the Burbage brothers, and five members of the Chamberlain's troupe: William Shakespeare, John Heminges, Augustine Phillips, Thomas Pope, and William Kempe. Of these players only Shakespeare was a playwright as well. His four partners all excelled in their quality. Most famous was Kempe, who inherited Tarlton's mantle; he played Peter in *Romeo and Juliet* and Dogberry in *Much Ado About Nothing*, and enthralled London by his exuberant feat of dancing the morris to Norwich. These five Chamberlain's men held half of Brend's lease, the other half belonging to the Burbages. The actors now converted their joint tenancy into a tenancy in common, which made separate estates of their shares; otherwise their rights would pass in survivorship. Shakespeare thus held one fifth of a moiety, or half interest, in the Globe enterprise; ten per cent of the whole. The value of a share fluctuated as the original housekeepers decreased or augmented their number. Kempe soon dropped out, making Shake-

---

1 This was the old name for what is now St. Saviour's parish.
2 John Stow, *A Survey of the cities of London and Westminster . . . Corrected, Improved, and very much Enlarged . . . by John Strype* (1720), vol. ii, bk. iv, p. 28; quoted by Joseph Quincy Adams, *Shakespearean Playhouses* (Boston, 1917), p. 243.

speare's holding one eighth of the total. But his share fell to a twelfth when Condell and Sly came in during 1605–8; one fourteenth after the incorporation of Ostler in 1611. When Shakespeare's company began, around 1609, to use the Blackfriars as their winter playhouse, he had (as we shall see) a stake in that operation too. These facts are known because Heminges and Condell set them forth when they testified as defendants in a suit brought in the Court of Requests three years after Shakespeare's death.[1]

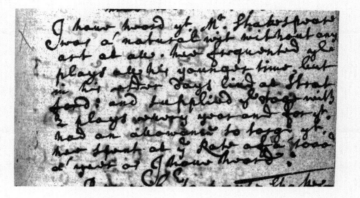

116 JOHN WARD ON SHAKESPEARE'S SPENDING, 1661–3. *Folger Shakespeare Library, MS. V.a.292 (formerly MS. 2073.5), f. 140. Transcript: EKC, ii. 249. Seventeen volumes of John Ward's Note-books were acquired by the Medical Society of London late in the eighteenth century. Charles Severn, M.D., newly appointed as Registrar to the Society, first examined the Note-books, and published extracts, including all but one of the Shakespeare entries, in the* Diary of the Rev. John Ward, A.M., Vicar of Stratford-upon-Avon *in 1839. The Shakespeare items appear on pp. 183–4. When the Society sold the Note-books to A.S.W. Rosenbach in 1928, they numbered sixteen volumes. All these are now in the Folger Library (shelfmark: V.a. 284–99). For another Ward item, see below, item 201.*

Attempts to calculate the poet's earnings have produced widely divergent figures. The earliest report derives from the mythos: a diary entry made sometime between 1661 and 1663 by the Revd. John Ward, who was vicar of Stratford in the days when Shakespeare's daughter Judith still lived. For supplying the stage with two plays a year, Ward notes, the dramatist had 'an allowance so large' that 'hee spent att ye Rate of a 1000l. a year as I have heard'. The amount is extraordinary, and Ward does not claim for it more than the status of rumour: 'as I have heard'.

But how much *did* Shakespeare earn? Malone estimated about £200 a year from the theatre. In our own century Sir Sidney Lee concluded, on the basis of elaborate computations, that 'Shakespeare, during fourteen or fifteen years of the later period of his life, must have been earning at the theatre a sum well exceeding 700l. a year in money of the time'.[2] Sir Edmund Chambers disagrees; Shakespeare's professional income, he estimates, came to roughly a third as much. That would seem closer to the mark. Of course a sharer's proceeds fluctuated, depending upon the size of his holding, and the house's takings. A plague season would be ruinous. An average annual return of £200 was excellent by Elizabethan standards — ten times what a well-paid schoolmaster could hope for. In his excellent *Shakespeare: His World and his Work*, M. M. Reese assumes that at some time, presumably during retirement, Shakespeare sold his theatrical interests for 'a substantial capital sum'.[3] Quite possibly; but we do not actually know whether

---

1 The action, *Witter v. Heminges and Condell*, was discovered in the Public Record Office by Charles William Wallace, who announced his findings in 'Shakespeare's Money Interest in the Globe Theatre', *The Century Magazine*, lxxx (1910), 500–12. Wallace printed the texts of the ten documents comprising the action the same year in the Nebraska *University Studies*, x ('Shakespeare and his London Associates as Revealed in Recently Discovered Documents'). The most authoritative discussion of Shakespeare's financial interests in the Globe and Blackfriars is in EKC, ii. 52–71; Chambers gives, in abridged form, the Answer of Heminges and Condell in the suit. The same material is discussed, with transcripts, in BRL, ii. 508–20.

2 Sidney Lee, *A Life of William Shakespeare* (4th ed. of revised version, 1925), p. 315.

3 M. M. Reese, *Shakespeare: His World and his Work* (1953), p. 365. He is more cautious earlier when he describes the fate of the dramatist's holdings in the Globe and the Blackfriars as 'one of the unsolved mysteries of Shakespeare's life' (p. 214).

he disposed of his shares or held on to them until the end. Eventually they passed to the families of Heminges and Condell. These shares commanded substantial sums on the open market. In 1634, when the Blackfriars was the principal house of Shakespeare's company, one Blackfriars and two Globe shares went for £350.

The profits made by the Chamberlain's men after they settled in at the Globe were the rewards for golden achievement; the company dominated the theatrical scene. Ward was right in putting Shakespeare's production at two pieces a year. That was, of course, on average. Chronology blurs at the edges, but between 1598 and 1601 he seems to have composed *Henry V*, *Much Ado About Nothing*, *Julius Caesar*, *As You Like It*, *Twelfth Night*, and *Hamlet*. The Chamberlain's servants twice played at Court during the Christmas season in 1598–9; three times in 1599–1600. Which plays the records fail to show — the troupe acted favourites from their repertoire as well as new pieces. Sometimes their patron laid on a special performance at Hunsdon House in the Black-friars as part of the entertainment for a visiting dignitary. 'All this Weeke the Lords have bene in London, and past away the Tyme in Feasting and Plaies', Rowland Whyte reported in a letter to Sir Robert Sidney on 8 March 1600, 'for *Vereiken* dined upon *Wednesday*, with my Lord Trea-surer, who made hym a Roiall Dinner; upon *Thursday* my Lord Chamberlain feasted hym, and made hym very great, and a delicate Dinner, and there in the After Noone his Plaiers acted, before *Vereiken*, Sir *John Old Castell*, to his great Contentment.'[1] Two years later, on 2 February, John Manningham attended a feast in the Middle Temple. The comedy mounted by the Cham-berlain's men that night took his fancy; he made a note in his *Diary*. Much like the *Menaechmi* of Plautus, Manningham observed, and even more like the Italian play called *Inganni*. To make the steward believe, by means of a counterfeit letter, that 'his Lady widdowe' was in love with him, and to tell him how to smile and dress, 'And then when he came to practise making him beleeve they tooke him to be mad' — that was a 'good practise'. There was laughter in the Middle Temple that night of *Twelfth Night*.

Most dramatists for the popular stage at some time or other wrote in collaboration. The amiable Dekker, who (in Lamb's phrase) had poetry enough for anything, shared his poetry with Middleton and Webster, and later with Ford; Heywood boasted that he had had 'either an entire hand, or at the least a maine finger' in 220 plays. Even the imperious Jonson joined forces with Chapman and Marston on *Eastward Ho*, which caused an uproar and almost cost him his ears. Shakespeare was unusual in holding aloof from joint authorship, at least until towards the

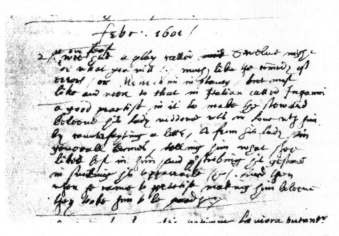

117 JOHN MANNINGHAM SEES *TWELFTH NIGHT*, 2 FEBRUARY 1602. *British Library, MS. Harley 5353, f. 12ᵛ. Transcript: TB, 108; EKC, ii. 327–8. J. Payne Collier is the first to discuss the Manningham Diary, in his* History of English Dramatic Poetry to the Time of Shakespeare: and Annals of the Stage to the Restoration *(1831), i. 320–38; he prints this anecdote on pp. 327–8. John Bruce edited Manningham's* Diary *for the Camden Society in 1868; his transcript of the present item appears on p. 18. See also above, item 115.*

---

1   Arthur Collins, *Letters and Memorials of State . . . written and collected by Sir Henry Sydney, Sir Philip Sydney, Sir Robert Sydney, &c.* (1746), ii. 175; quoted by EKC, ii. 322.

end of his play-writing career, when he seems to have worked together with the young dramatist who would succeed him as the 'ordinary poet' of the company. Being a shareholder helped him to keep his independence. On one occasion, however — so the evidence indicates — he was called upon to doctor a play written by other hands, for which company is uncertain.

That play survives, in damaged and chaotic shape, in a manuscript with the title 'The Booke of Sir Thomas Moore'. In its original form a fair copy prepared by a scribe, the playbook had been submitted by the company to Sir Edmund Tilney, the Master of the Revels, who exercised the prerogatives of censorship. Subsequently the manuscript underwent extensive revision, with passages marked for deletion, and scenes removed or inserted. The text contains additions in no fewer than five hands. If Shakespeare made any of these revisions, they would hold extraordinary interest as the only extant specimen of dramatic manuscript in his hand. A number of authorities in fact believe that he wrote the three pages of the Ill May-Day scene of 'Sir Thomas More', the pages of British Library MS. Harley 7368 occupying folios 8 and 9, and labelled as in hand D.

A play on the life of More required extraordinary tact, for, although a great man, and recognized as such, he was a steadfast Catholic who brought on his own martyrdom by refusing to bow to the Tudor monarch who demanded acknowledgement of his supremacy. This, the signal act of More's career, does not even come in for mention in the play that goes by his name. Originally this evasive historical drama had been put together by Chettle and the Munday admired by Meres as 'our best plotter'; Dekker had a hand in it too, but whether from the first is not clear. Something went awry. Either the script ran foul of the censor or dissatisfied the company, maybe both. A directive at the beginning of one deleted scene reads, 'This must be newe written', but the injunction is not in Tilney's hand, and may reflect playhouse rather than Revels Office intervention. Anyway much of the play was new written. Dekker supplied additions; very likely Heywood too. Finally (if this conjectural reconstruction has merit) the company turned to Shakespeare. He contributed the scene in which More, as Sheriff of London, deploys his homely eloquence to pacify the apprentices in their May-Day rebellion against the foreigners in their midst. This attempt by three poets to rescue a sinking play failed. Not until the present century did 'Sir Thomas More' achieve performance.

The Ill May-Day scene parallels a memorable episode in a later play: Menenius Agrippa using his eloquence and cajolery to calm the plebs in Coriolanus's Rome. Actually a broad spectrum of evidence supports the Shakespearian attribution. Palaeographers, most notably Sir Edward Maunde Thompson, have minutely compared the three pages in hand D with the six authenticated Shakespeare signatures, and concluded that in every instance the same penman wielded the quill. Thompson's most striking exhibit is the extremely rare spurred *a* found in one of the signatures, and most closely approximated in the word *that* at line 105. In both *a*'s 'the pen, descending in a deep curve from the overhead arch, is carried to the left into the horizontal spur and then to the right *horizontally* till it ascends to form the second minim'.[1] Palaeographical confidence is qualified, however, by the fact that the sampling of Shakespeare's hand is so small, and most of what we have abnormal because of illness (a dying man signed the will) or the cramping confines of conveyancing seals. Spelling affords another kind of evidence. At line 50 *scilens*, for *silence*, is most unusual, but also appears eighteen times in the speech prefixes for Justice Silence in the Quarto of *2 Henry IV*. For the comfort of modern readers, editors have regularized away such orthographic idiosyncrasies, behind which almost certainly lies the author's original draft or foul papers.

Most striking, though, are the likenesses of style and thought. The dark forebodings of chaos, the commitment to the values of an ordered, hierarchic society, the complexly ambivalent attitudes towards the mob — these strike a familiar note. More's metaphorical identification of the rioters with a surging flood recalls the 'bounded waters' lifting 'their bosoms higher than the shores' in *Troilus and Cressida*; his apocalyptic vision of the consequences of rebellious insolence — his prophecy of a time when 'men lyke ravenous fishes/would feed on on [i.e. one] another' — brings to mind the universal wolf devouring himself in Ulysses's touchstone speech on degree.

---

1 Sir Edward Maunde Thompson, quoted by R. C. Bald, '*The Booke of Sir Thomas More* and its Problems', *Shakespeare Survey 2* (Cambridge, 1949), p. 55. This essay is a masterly survey of the problems.

The specific image comparing devouring men to the devouring fishes is, to be sure, a commonplace traceable back to the Church Fathers; but the concatenation of parallel figures and ideas is nevertheless impressive.[1] The cumulative evidence for Shakespeare's hand in the 'More' fragment may not be sufficient to sweep away all doubts — but who else in this period formed an *a* with a horizontal spur, spelt *silence* as *scilens*, and had identical associative patterns of thought and image? All roads converge on Shakespeare.[2]

When he turned to 'Sir Thomas More', if he did turn, presents another problem. Munday, Chettle, and Dekker were not Chamberlain's men, but in fee to Henslowe. Some think the revision took place in 1593, when the Lord Strange's men, with Shakespeare possibly one of them, temporarily amalgamated with the Admiral's company. But, in the view of others, stylistic considerations point to a later date for the Ill May-Day scene, 1600 or early 1601. In the summer of 1600 the Admiral's men, biding their time until their new playhouse the Fortune opened, went on tour, and Henslowe for a while made few diary entries of payments to his chronically indigent playwrights. What more natural than that they should, for the nonce, offer their wares to the rival Chamberlain's men? If 'Sir Thomas More' was written then — and this is only speculation — its theme of rebellion and execution would assume an ominous topical significance.

For on 8 February 1601 the charismatic but unstable Earl of Essex, once the Queen's darling, made his bid for supreme power. With his fellow conspirators he marched on the Court, but finding the way barred, marched back through the city in a desperate bid to enlist the support of the populace. But the people held prudently aloof, and the Earl barricaded himself in Essex House, then surrendered. The prime movers of the insurrection were executed in February and March of 1601. 'God for his pittie help these troublous times', beseeches a sheriff of London in 'Sir Thomas More' after the collapse of the May-Day insurrection,

> The streetes stopte up with gazing multitudes,
> commaund our armed Officers with Halberds,
> make way for entraunce of the prisoners.
> Let proclamation once againe be made,

Opposite:

118 'ILL MAY-DAY': ADDITION IIc, 'SIR THOMAS MORE', 1601 (?). British Library, MS. Harley 7368, f. 9. Transcript: The Book of Sir Thomas More, *ed. W. W. Greg (Malone Society Reprints, 1911) (entire manuscript); Edward Maunde Thompson,* Shakespeare's Handwriting *(Oxford, 1916), pp. 32–7 (Addition IIc); William Shakespeare,* Complete Works, *ed. C. J. Sisson (1954), pp. 1238–66 (modern-spelling text of entire manuscript, ed. Harold Jenkins); Thomas Clayton,* The 'Shakespearean' Addition in The Booke of Sir Thomas Moore *(Shakespeare Studies Monograph Series, i; Dubuque, 1969), pp. 14–21 (Addition IIc; old spelling), pp. 78–82 (modern spelling).*

'Sir Thomas More' was first edited, for the Shakespeare Society, by Alexander Dyce in 1844. In an article in Notes and Queries, *4th Ser., viii (1871), 1–3, 'Are There Any Extant MSS. in Shakespeare's Handwriting?', Richard Simpson argued 'that portions of the MS. Harleian 7368 in the British Museum are in his writing'. Around the middle of the nineteenth century, after the appearance of Dyce's edition, thick yellow tracing paper was pasted over a number of the leaves, including two of Addition IIc. The thickening of the paste over the years has served to obscure the writing so badly that there seemed little point in reproducing these leaves in the present volume. Excellent collotype facsimiles of all three leaves are, however, to be had in Maunde Thompson's* Shakespeare's Handwriting, *and the whole play was made available in 1910 in J. S. Farmer's* Tudor Facsimile Series.

The leaf included in this volume is on permanent display in the Manuscript Saloon of the British Museum. The catchword 'all' on the verso is here reproduced for the first time.

1   See R. W. Chambers, 'The Expression of Ideas — Particularly Political Ideas — in the Three Pages and in Shakespeare', in Alfred Pollard et al., *Shakespeare's Hand in the Play of Sir Thomas More* (Cambridge, 1923), pp. 142–87, esp. 158–60. For the commonplace, see F. P. Wilson, 'Shakespeare's Reading', *Shakespeare Survey 3* (Cambridge, 1950), pp. 19–20.
2   Scholarly opinion now also favours ascription to Shakespeare of a shorter addition, a twenty-one line speech by More, which is, however, in the hand of a professional playhouse scribe.

9

nay certainly you ar

for to the king god hath his office lent
of dread of Iustyce, power and Comaund
hath bid him rule, and willd you to obay
and to add ampler matie to this
he hath not only lent the king his figure
his throne and sword, but gyven him his owne name
calls him a god on earth, what do you then
rysing gainst him that god himsealf enstalls
but ryse gainst god, what do you to yor sowles
in doing this o desperat as you are.
wash your foule mynds wt teares and those same hands
that you lyke rebells lyft against the peace
lift up for peace, and your vnreverent knees
make them your feet to kneele to be forgyven

~~...~~

tell me but this lawfull as you
are a nomber
that still the rout ... will obay to trayterus
or how can well that proclamation sounde
whe their is no addition but a rebell
to qualify a rebell, youle put downe straingers
kill them cutt their throts possesse their howses
and leade the matie of law in lyon
to slipp him lyke a hound, alas alas ... now the king
as he is clement, yf thoffendor moorne
should so much com to short of your great trespas
as but to banysh you, whether wold you go.
what Country by the nature of your errors
should gyve you harber go you to ffraunc or flanders
to any Jarman province to spane or portu[g]all
nay any where that not adheres to england
why you must needs be straingers, wold you be pleasd
to find a nation of such barbarous temper
that breaking out in hiddious violence
wold not afford you, an abode on earth
whett their detested knyves against your throtes
spurne you lyke doggs, and lyke as yf that god
owed not nor made not you, nor that the elaments
wer not all appropriat to ther Comforts,
but Chartered vnto them, what wold you thinck
to be vsd thus, this is the straingers case
and this your momtanish inhumanyty

farewell all

all
al Linco   fayth a saies trewe letts vs do as we may be don by
woold be ruld by your masters moor yf youle stand our

moo   Submyt you to theise noble gentlemen
       entreate their mediation to the kinge
       gyve vp yor self to forme obay the maiestrat
       and theres no doubt, but mercy may be found yf you so seek

> that every housholder, on paine of deathe
> keep in his Prentises, and every man,
> stand with a weapon readie at his doore,
> as he will answere to the contrary.[1]

These lines would have special reverberations in the winter of 1601. Somebody in the censor's office or the playhouse marked them for deletion.

Shakespeare's patron and Shakespeare's company played their parts in the February adventure, and both fared better than they might reasonably have hoped. Southampton, still under the Essex spell, had joined in the conspiracy and was tried and condemned to death with his idol. But Southampton moved compassion by virtue of his demeanour and (although no stripling, having turned twenty-seven) his youth. The dowager Countess pleaded piteously with Secretary Cecil for mercy to her miserable son, led astray by bad company. She prevailed, the sentence was commuted, and Southampton spent the remaining years of Elizabeth's reign incarcerated in the Tower, where he had his books, a room with a view, and a black and white cat which (legend holds) joined him by climbing down the chimney. As for the Chamberlain's men, money — not allegiance — enticed them into the web. One of the plotters, Sir Gilly Meyrick, paid them forty pieces of silver to put on, against their better judgements, a stale play depicting the deposition and murder of a king. *Richard II*, Shakespeare's friend and fellow Augustine Phillips testified, was 'so old and so long out of use' that the players felt 'that they shold have small or no Company at yt'. But Meyrick had his way — 'So earnest hee was to satisfie his eyes with the sight of that tragedie which hee thought soone after his lord should bring from the stage to the state, but that God turned it upon their owne heads.' Thus spoke the Crown's chief prosecutor, Sir Francis Bacon. At Tyburn Meyrick suffered the hangman's noose 'with a most undaunted resolution'. On the eve of Essex's execution, 24 February, the Chamberlain's men amused the Queen with a play — the title is not recorded — at Court. So they suffered not at all. 'How this happened history does not tell us', Dover Wilson speculates, 'but if the Lord Chamberlain was a sensible man, a few words of explanation from the author of the play [i.e. *Richard II*] as to its exact tenour and purport should have placed matters in a proper light.'[2] This is perhaps to overestimate the importance of playwrights in the Elizabethan scheme of things.

Forgiveness did not erase bitter memories. Summer came. In her Privy Chamber at East Greenwich 'her Majestie fell upon the reign of King Richard II. saying, "I am Richard II. know ye not that? . . . He that will forget God, will also forget his benefactors; this tragedy was played 40^{tie} times in open streets and houses." ' Some believe that the fall of Essex, the meteor Shakespeare had saluted in *Henry V*, left an enduring imprint on the poet's imagination. Did he, in the enigmatic Prince of Denmark, set up for spectators in the Globe Theatre a mirror of the inmost part of the enigmatic Earl who was 'th'observ'd of all observers' and (to his followers) 'th'expectancy and rose of the fair state'?[3] However that may be, and it is probably no more than romance, few will doubt that with *Hamlet*, written while the old Queen still ruled, we have intimations of a new mood. The Jacobean Shakespeare is in the wings.

1   *The Book of Sir Thomas More*, ed. W. W. Greg (Malone Society Reprints, 1911), ll. 584–92; cited by Bald, p. 53.
2   John Dover Wilson, *The Essential Shakespeare: A Biographical Adventure* (Cambridge, 1932), p. 103.
3   Ibid., pp. 104–7.

13

A Gentleman of Means

If Shakespeare was indifferent to the ultimate fate of the plays that immortalized him, he showed no similar nonchalance about assembling and passing down intact his estate. As early as 1737 Alexander Pope made the point in the elegant couplets of *The First Epistle of the Second Book of Horace*:

> Shakespear, (whom you and ev'ry Play-house bill
> Style the divine, the matchless, what you will)
> For gain, not glory, wing'd his roving flight,
> And grew Immortal in his own despight.[1]

'Habits of business are not incompatible with the possession of the highest genius', observed the most indefatigable nineteenth-century student of the Shakespeare records, J. O. Halliwell (later Halliwell-Phillipps), and he concluded: 'No doubt . . . can exist in the mind of any impartial critic, that the great dramatist most carefully attended to his worldly interests; and confirmations of this opinion may be produced from numerous early sources.'[2] What Halliwell says with the complacent assurance of Victorian philistinism is in fact true, and Shakespeare's non-theatrical activities — more especially his pursuit of wealth and dignities — supply the principal burden of this chapter.

By the mid-nineties Shakespeare was a householder in London; so the Subsidy Rolls and other accounts in the Exchequer office reveal. From time to time Parliament granted subsidies to the Crown, in fixed amounts, on land and personal property. The last of three such subsidies voted in 1593 was at the rate of 2s.8d. in the pound on the value of goods, and collectable in two instalments; the first at 1s.8d. in the pound, the second at 1s. The modesty of the assessment failed to discourage evasion. Local commissioners, served by Petty Collectors, had the responsibility for rounding up the taxes. They reported defaulters to the Exchequer, which in turn instructed the sheriffs of the counties to recover the arrears and answer for them at the annual inspection of their accounts. On 15 November 1597 the Petty Collectors for Bishopsgate ward swore that certain persons, whose names followed, had either died, vacated the parish, or avoided payment. The list for St. Helen's parish, which had seventy-three rateable residents, includes the name of William Shackspere, assessed 5s. on goods valued at £5 (the property of the most prosperous inhabitant of the parish was valued at £300). The assessment, made in October 1596, had fallen due the following February.

Shakespeare's ward straddled Bishopsgate Street, the main thoroughfare leading from London Bridge, past Moor Fields and Finsbury Fields, to the Theatre and Curtain in windswept Holywell. A cosmopolitan, mostly upper-middle-class neighbourhood, Bishopsgate boasted 'diverse fayre Innes, large for receipt of travellers' (the Bull, the Angel, and, outside the gate, the Dolphin were especially notable), as well as some fine houses. On the right-hand side of the newly constructed conduit, which supplied the district with fresh water, stood Crosby Place, handsomely built of stone and timber. There, where Richard Crookback had once lodged, the Lord Mayor held court. Another mansion celebrated the worldly achievement of Sir Thomas Gresham; this house would shortly become a school for London merchants. Bishopsgate had pockets of squalor too. In Petty France, on the bank of the town ditch, the French community crowded into tenements, and polluted the ditch, here running into a narrow channel, 'with unsavourie things'. Bethlehem Hospital, popularly known as Bedlam, housed the lunatics who provided Sunday

---

1   Alexander Pope, *Imitations of Horace*, ed. John Butt (2nd ed., 1953), p. 199 (The Twickenham Pope, vol. iv).
2   *A Life of William Shakespeare*, in Shakespeare, *Works*, ed. H-P (1853–65), i. 151.

diversion for amusement seekers. Within the parish church of St. Helen's, its Gothic spire dominating the scene, Gresham and other distinguished parishioners had their tombs and monuments. Shakespeare presumably worshipped in St. Helen's on Sundays. During the week he could easily get to the playhouse on foot.[1]

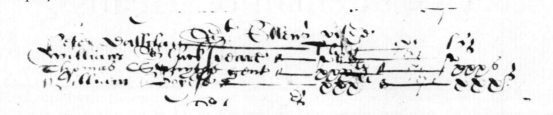

119 SHAKESPEARE A TAX DEFAULTER IN BISHOPSGATE WARD, 15 NOVEMBER 1597. *Public Record Office, Exchequer, King's Remembrancer, Subsidy Roll, E. 179/146/354. Transcript: TB, 18 (extracts); EKC, ii. 87 (extracts); BRL, i. 264–5 (extracts). Although one of the records of Shakespeare as a tax-eligible householder in St. Helen's parish was known as far back as 1845 (see item 120), the sequence of Exchequer documents in the Lord Treasurer's Remembrancer's Department was first traced by R. E. G. Kirk at the beginning of the present century, and reported by J. W. Hales on 11 October 1902 at a meeting of the Surrey Archaeological Society held in St. Saviour's Church (now Southwark Cathedral). Hales followed up his announcement with a communication, 'London Residences of Shakespeare', in* The Athenæum, *26 March 1904, pp. 401–2. M.S. Giuseppi, who furnished Hales with his information, analysed all five documents in greater detail in 'The Exchequer Documents Relative to Shakespeare's Residence in Southwark',* Transactions of the London and Middlesex Archaeological Society, N.S., v (1929), 281–8. *This remains the standard treatment, although EKC (ii. 88–90) is helpful, as is N. E. Evans,* Shakespeare in the Public Records *(1964), pp. 9–12. On the history of subsidies, and the system of grants of fifteenths and tenths to which they are related, Stephen Dowell,* A History of Taxation and Taxes in England *(2nd ed., 1888), ii. 67–71, although in some respects outdated, is still concisely informative.*

Whether he ever paid his 5*s.* tax is not known. When the Parliament of 1597 voted a new subsidy, Shakespeare was again assessed, this time 13*s.*4*d.* on goods valued at £5; so the rate had gone up. Once more the due date, 1 October 1598, passed, and the Petty Collectors — Thomas Symons, skinner, and the engagingly named Ferdinando Clutterbook, a draper — reported the delinquent on 6 October. The abbreviation *Affid*, for *Affidavit*, in the left-hand margin alongside Shakespeare's name, means that the collectors certified he had not paid his tax.

120 SHAKESPEARE AGAIN DEFAULTS FOR TAXES, 1 OCTOBER 1598. *Public Record Office, Exchequer, King's Remembrancer, Subsidy Roll, E. 179/146/369. Transcript: TB, 19 (extract); EKC, ii. 87 (extract); BRL, i. 266–8. This document was discovered by Joseph Hunter, who printed it complete in* New Illustrations of the Life, Studies, and Writings of Shakespeare *(1845), i. 77–9. H-P included the list of defaulters, with some corrections of Hunter, in* Life, *pp. 180–2.*

They next list him, in copies of accounts prepared for the Exchequer, with persons who do not answer because they have no goods, chattels, lands, or tenements in the district.

121 SHAKESPEARE CITED IN THE ENROLLED SUBSIDY ACCOUNT, 1598–9. *Public Record Office, Exchequer, Lord Treasurer's Remembrancer, Accounts of Subsidies, E. 359/56. Transcript: EKC, ii. 88 (extract); BRL, i. 269 (extract). For the discovery and announcement of this document, see above, item 119. The extract reproduced has been reduced slightly.*

1   Stow supplies most of these details; see also A. L. Rowse, *William Shakespeare* (1963), pp. 280–1.

These delinquents, Shakespeare among them, were entered by the Exchequer in the residuum, or back-tax, accounts for London. The marginal note *Surrey*, and the reference to 'Residuum Sussex', added later, signify that Shakespeare had migrated across the river to the Surrey Bankside. (At that time Surrey and Sussex managed with one sheriff between them.)

122 SHAKESPEARE INCLUDED IN THE *RESIDUUM LONDON* ACCOUNTS, 6 OCTOBER 1599. *Public Record Office, Exchequer, Lord Treasurer's Remembrancer, Pipe Rolls, E. 372/444, m. 'Residuum London'. Transcript: EKC, ii. 88 (extract); BRL, i. 269 (extract, with translation). TB gives a translation only (19). For the discovery and announcement of this document, which is here reduced, see above, item 119.*

In the last Exchequer notice of Shakespeare, dated 6 October 1600, the tax bill of 13*s*.4*d*. is still outstanding. The notation *Episcopo Wintonensi* in the left-hand margin indicates that the Court of Exchequer had referred the dramatist's arrears to the Bishop of Winchester, whose liberty of the Clink in Surrey lay outside the sheriff's jurisdiction. The natural inference is that Shakespeare now lived in the Clink, although it is a curious fact that his name has not been traced in any of the annual lists of residents of the Clink parish (St. Saviour's) compiled by the officers who made the rounds to collect tokens purchased by churchgoers for Easter Communion, which was compulsory.[1] In his accounts for 1600–1 the Bishop reported, without naming names, a sum collected from the rate-payers referred to him. It has been assumed that the amount includes Shakespeare's 13*s*.4*d*.

123 SHAKESPEARE INCLUDED IN THE *RESIDUUM SUSSEX* ACCOUNTS, 6 OCTOBER 1600. *Public Record Office, Exchequer, Lord Treasurer's Remembrancer, Pipe Rolls, E. 372/445, m. 'Residuum Sussex'. Transcript: EKC, ii. 88; BRL, i. 270 (includes translation). TB gives a translation only (19–20). For the discovery and announcement of this document, see above, item 119.*

If he found his way onto any other subsidy rolls, these have not come to light. In 1796, however, Edmond Malone mentioned documents with information about Shakespeare's London residences. Malone never alludes to these curious papers anywhere else, and they have since vanished without trace; but it is (as we shall see) unlikely that Shakespeare was still in Southwark as late as 1608.[2]

> From a paper now before me, which formerly belonged to Edward Alleyn, the player, our poet appears to have lived in Southwark, near the Bear-Garden, in 1596. Another curious document in my possession, which will be produced in the History of his Life, affords the strongest pre-
>
> sumptive evidence that he continued to reside in Southwark to the year 1608

124 EDMOND MALONE, *AN INQUIRY INTO THE AUTHENTICITY OF CERTAIN MISCELLANEOUS PAPERS AND LEGAL INSTRUMENTS* (1796), pp. 215–6.

---

1 This information I owe to Professor William Ingram.
2 See below, pp. 208ff.

M*

To sum up: Shakespeare was living in St. Helen's parish, Bishopsgate, at some date before 1596; perhaps as early as the winter of 1596–7, but certainly no later than 1598, he had taken up residence in the liberty of the Clink in Southwark. In other words Shakespeare crossed the river when his company did. So we would have guessed had we no records at all; but the documents, so laboriously sought and studied, do provide certainty in place of plausible assumption, and yield more precise addresses for Shakespeare in the nineties.

London addresses. In the great metropolis, which catered for every taste and aspiration, he ordered his life according to his professional needs, with first the Theatre and afterwards the Globe as the fixed foot of his compass; but he maintained and over the years strengthened his ties with his native Stratford, where he had left behind a wife and three children. If they ever visited him in St. Helen's parish or the Clink, no record shows it. In Stratford his daughters married and bore offspring, and in Stratford they were laid to rest, as were their parents, in Holy Trinity Church or the churchyard divided by the avenue of lime trees. 'He was wont to goe to his native Country once a yeare,' Aubrey noted for his Brief Life. It is reasonable to suppose that Shakespeare was there on 11 August 1596, when the parish register records the burial of his son Hamnet, aged eleven and a half. His death doomed the male line of the Shakespeares to extinction.

125 HAMNET SHAKESPEARE BURIED, 11 AUGUST 1596. *Stratford parish register, burials, f. 29. Shakespeare Birthplace Trust Records Office; shelfmark: DR 243/1.*

On occasion, according to the mythos, Shakespeare found solace at the sign of the bush in Oxford, where he would break the journey between London and Stratford. This wine-house was called the Taverne, rechristened the Crown half a century after the poet's death; an unpretentious two-storey house with twin gables, fronting on the Cornmarket, just a few yards from the High Street, and convenient to the main highway running to Warwickshire and the north. The landlord, John Davenant, was a melancholy sort, never seen to laugh; yet his fellow townsmen so well esteemed him that in 1622 they made him the mayor of Oxford. He had a wife and seven children, of whom one, Robert, remembered years later (when he had become a parson) being showered with a hundred kisses by the acclaimed playwright from London. The vintner's wife was reputedly very beautiful, '& of a very good witt and of conversation extremely agreable'. She had less discretion than her husband, though, if there is truth to the salacious gossip that began making the rounds late in the seventeenth century. This held that Mistress Davenant shared her bed with the poet who had extricated himself from the meshes of the Dark Lady.

Ordinarily a wine-shop offered neither lodging nor stabling, but these amenities were available at the Cross Inn bounding the Taverne on the north, with which it shared a common courtyard. Of course an overnight guest could at a pinch sleep upstairs at the Taverne. There a fire roared in winter in the huge brick hearth; an interlacing pattern of vines and flowers adorned the walls, and along the top a painted frieze exhorted the pious to 'Feare god above althynge'. When these decorations came to light in 1927, a newspaper described the Painted Chamber as 'the room in which Shakespeare slept'.[1] Did he indeed here take his leave of the landlord's beautiful and witty wife, and proceed refreshed, if not edified, on the road to Stratford, where Anne, eight years his senior, awaited him?

The legend of Shakespeare's liaison with Mistress Davenant originates with her poet son. When merry over his wine with Samuel Butler, the celebrated author of *Hudibras*, and other cronies, Sir William would own to being the literal — as well as the poetical — son of Shakespeare. Perhaps Davenant was jesting, not very tastefully, in his cups; possibly he wished merely to claim membership in the tribe of Will, as others belonged to the tribe of Ben. Aubrey, however, who first

1   Arthur H. Nethercot, *Sir William D'Avenant* (Chicago, 1938), p. 20. Nethercot describes the Taverne in detail (pp. 16–20).

reports the story, took it as a profession of bastardy, and that is how the age took it. 'That notion of Sir William's being more than a poetical child only of Shakespeare, was common in town', Alexander Pope observed to Joseph Spence; 'and Sir William himself seemed fond of having it taken for truth.'[1] In his diary Thomas Hearne, a keeper of the Bodleian Library and knowledgeable local antiquary, recorded the episode as an Oxford tradition.

126 THOMAS HEARNE ON SHAKESPEARE AND DAVENANT, 1709. *Bodleian Library, MS. Hearne, Diaries 20, ff. 126ᵛ–7. Transcript: EKC, ii. 269–70. Printed in* Remarks and Collections of Thomas Hearne, *ed. C. E. Dobel et al., for the Oxford Historical Society (1885–1921), ii (1886), 228.*

That was in 1709. More than thirty years later, at a dinner party given by the Earl of Oxford, Pope — who would not have known Hearne's diary — regaled the guests with the same anecdote. William Oldys, present that night, made a note of the conversation.

> " If tradition may be trufted, Shakespeare often baited at the Crown Inn or Tavern in Oxford, in his journey to and from London. The landlady was a woman of great beauty and fprightly wit; and her hufband, Mr. John Davenant, (afterwards mayor of that city) a grave melancholy man, who as well as his wife ufed much to delight in Shakefpeare's pleafant company. Their fon young Will Davenant (afterwards Sir William) was then a little fchool-boy in the town, of about feven or eight years old, and fo fond alfo of Shakefpeare, that whenever he heard of his arrival, he would fly from fchool to fee him. One day an old townf-man obferving the boy running homeward almoft out of breath, afked him whither he was pofting in that heat and hurry. He anfwered, to fee his *god*-father Shakefpeare.

[1] Joseph Spence, *Observations, Anecdotes, and Characters of Books and Men, Collected from Conversation*, ed. James M. Osborn (Oxford, 1966), i. 184.

> There's a good boy, said the other, but have a care that you
> don't take *God's* name in vain. This story Mr. Pope told
> me at the Earl of Oxford's table, upon occasion of some dis-
> course which arose about Shakespeare's monument then
> newly erected in Westminster Abbey; and he quoted Mr.
> Betterton the player for his authority. I answered that I
> thought such a story might have enriched the variety of those
> choice fruits of observation he has presented us in his pre-
> face to the edition he had published of our poet's works.
> He replied—" There might be in the garden of mankind
> such plants as would seem to pride themselves more in a
> regular production of their own native fruits, than in hav-
>
> **ing the repute of bearing a richer kind by grafting; and this
> was the reason he omitted it."**

127   WILLIAM SHAKESPEARE, *PLAYS*, ED. SAMUEL JOHNSON AND GEORGE STEEVENS (1778), i. 203–4. *Reprinted by EKC, ii. 277–8.*

When Pope repeated the story to Spence a year or so later, the schoolboy's interlocutor had become 'a head of one of the colleges (who was pretty well acquainted with the affairs of the family)'.[1] A pleasant jest, and one that evidently could bear repetition; but it does not originate in the Davenant–Shakespeare context. As the learned Oldys recalled, John Taylor the Water Poet had included the anecdote in his *Wit and Mirth* in 1629.[2] In that version the godfather is not Will Shakespeare but goodman Digland the Gardener. For what it is worth, an Oxford connection remains, for (Oldys reports) Taylor picked up other jests for his collection there.

The story filtered into print. In 1698 Gildon coyly intimated, in *The Lives and Characters of the English Dramatick Poets*, that Shakespeare on his numerous journeys into Warwickshire had much frequented the Davenant tavern, 'whither for the Beautiful Mistress of the House, or the good Wine, I shall not determine'.[3] A half century later the former prompter of Drury Lane, William Rufus Chetwood, of whom Chambers observed, not unjustly, that 'his ignorance is certain and his *bona fides* improbable', was more direct. Chetwood devotes a single terse sentence to the rumour in his *General History of the Stage*: 'Sir *William Davenant* was, by many, supposed the natural Son of *Shakespear*.'[4] He scrutinized the frontispiece portrait of Davenant in the 1673 folio of his *Works* for resemblances to Shakespeare, but found himself handicapped by the fact that Davenant had lost his nose as the result of mercury treatment for syphilis. 'The Features', Chetwood concluded, 'seem to resemble the open Countenance of *Shakespear*, but' — and with this part of the verdict it is difficult to quarrel — 'the want of a Nose gives an odd Cast to the Face.'[5]

Once broadcast, the piquant tale was endlessly repeated. Sir Walter Scott found a place for it in *Woodstock*. 'Out upon the hound!' Colonel Everard explodes when told of Davenant's boast; 'would he purchase the reputation of descending from poet, or from prince, at the expense of his mother's good fame? — his nose ought to be slit.' The colonel is reminded that such an operation would prove difficult.

A wise child knows his own father, but Davenant showed small wisdom in his eager efforts to legitimatize the offspring of his muse by proclaiming his own illegitimacy. Still, even if his revelation bears all the earmarks of dubiously self-serving invention, it seems likely enough that Shakespeare knew the Taverne and the Cross Inn in Oxford, and that he was there (in Aubrey's phrase) 'exceedingly respected'. Not only as an admired writer. After 1596 Shakespeare could command the respect due to a gentleman.

It will be recalled that his father had made a preliminary approach to the Heralds' office at some time after he became bailiff of Stratford in 1568, but then, as troubles closed in on him, let the matter drop. The heralds commanded heavy fees when the Shakespeares, beset by creditors, could ill afford them. Then, in 1596, John Shakespeare renewed his application — or, more

1   Ibid., i. 185.
2   Reprinted in *All the Workes of John Taylor the Water-Poet* (1630), p. 184 (sig. Qq4ᵛ).
3   Gerard Langbaine, *The Lives and Characters of the English Dramatick Poets . . .*, ed. Charles Gildon [1699], p. 32.
4   William Chetwood, *A General History of the Stage . . .* (1749), p. 21n.
5   Ibid.

likely, his son did so in his father's name. John was in his sixties, an old man for those days, and he would think twice before making the long and tiring journey by horse to London. On the other hand, William was there on the spot. If he started from scratch with a new application in his own name while his father still lived, the College of Arms would have regarded such a course as irregular; but there was nothing to prevent the eldest son from setting into motion the machinery for a grant in which the entire family would take pride.

Preserved at the College are two rough drafts of a document, dated 20 October 1596 and prepared by Sir William Dethick, Garter King-of-Arms, granting the request of John Shakespeare for a coat of arms. A note at the foot of one of these drafts describes 'This John' as having presented a 'patierne' on paper 'under Clarent Cooks hand . . . xx years past'. That is how we know of the earlier application. The twenty years alluded to, carrying us back to 1576, may be taken as approximate. A 'patierne', or pattern, was a suggested design for a trick of arms. Robert Cook, the Clarenceux King-of-Arms, would for a fee have sketched it on paper, reserving parchment for the approved drawing. That stage was never reached when John first applied.

These heraldic documents often yield interesting genealogical details, but the 1596 draft grant is not in this respect especially communicative. Garter states that he has been 'by credible report informed' — this is sufficiently vague — that the petitioner's 'parentes & late antecessors' had been rewarded for valiant service by King Henry VII of famous memory, and that 'the said John hathe maryed the daughter & one of the heyres of Robert Arden of Wilmcoote in the said Counte esquire'.[1] (In this second draft Dethick has inserted 'Grandfather' above 'antecessors', and 'esquire' replaces 'gent'.) That is all; a reference to John's service and his marriage. Four soldiers surnamed Shakespeare are known to have held the rank of archers a half-century after the battle of Bosworth Field, but Garter's haziness has led some to wonder whether he is not implying, with heraldic courtesy, that the earlier Shakespeares were socially acceptable but undistinguished as the College of Arms measured distinction. However, the note appended to the document furnishes a few supporting facts about the applicant himself — that 'xv or xvi years past' (a mistake for xxvi?) he was a justice of the peace and bailiff, and a Queen's officer; that he had 'Landes & tenementes of good wealth. & Substance', worth £500; and that he had taken for his wife the daughter of a gentleman of worship. John Shakespeare was indeed the Queen's officer, for as bailiff he held the fortnightly Court of Record — a Crown court — and as coroner, almoner, and the like, also represented the Crown.

In consideration of these claims of honour, the Garter King-of-Arms declares that he has assigned and confirmed this shield: 'Gould. on A Bend Sables. a Speare of the first steeled argent. And for his Creast or Cognizance a falcon. his winges displayed Argent. standing on a wrethe of his Coullors. supporting a Speare Gould. steeled as aforesaid sett upon a helmett with mantelles & tasselles as hathe ben accustomed and dothe more playnely appeare depicted on this margent.' In the upper left-hand corner of both drafts appears, as Garter indicates, a rough sketch of the trick of arms. At a time when heraldry tended towards fussiness and over-elaboration, the Shakespeare arms have a classic simplicity.[2]

Above the shield and crest the clerk has written 'non, sanz droict'. The phrase gave him trouble. He scored it through, then repeated it, above, with initial capitals: 'Non, Sanz Droict'. At the head of the document he had a third go, this time putting the words in capitals and omitting the comma: 'NON SANZ DROICT'. Could the phrase conceivably signify an endorsement of heraldic correctness? Probably not — more likely it represents a motto, 'the Invention or Conceit of the Bearer' (as one contemporary remarks), which required no *imprimatur* from the heralds. 'Non sanz droict' — *Not without right* — makes better sense than 'Non, Sanz Droict' — *No, without right*. In his *Poetaster* Jonson sneers at common players who aspire to heraldic distinctions — 'They forget they are i' the *statute*, the Rascals, they are *blazond* there, there they are trickt, they and their Pedigrees: they neede no other *Heralds* I wisse' — and some have seen mockery of Shakespeare's motto in *Every Man out of his Humour*, in which the rustic clown Sogliardo, fresh from

---

1   The second draft, with missing words supplied from the first, as in EKC (ii. 19).
2   The point is made by C. W. Scott-Giles in *Shakespeare's Heraldry* (1950), p. 33. In these paragraphs I am especially indebted to Mr. Scott-Giles's modestly authoritative account.

128   THE GRANT OF ARMS, 1596. *College of Arms, MS. Vincent. 157, art. 23. Transcript: Stephen Tucker*, The Assignment of Arms to Shakespere and Arden, 1596–1599 *(1884), pp. 5–6; H-P, Outlines, ii. 56; TB, 15–17; BRL, i. 210. George Steevens drew attention to this document, and also to item 129, in a note to his second edition of the Johnson–Steevens* Plays of William Shakspeare *(1778), i. 191. H-P first printed the complete text of this, the earlier of two rough drafts, in* Life, *pp. 76–7. The document is here slightly reduced. See also next item.*

129　THE GRANT OF ARMS, 1596. *College of Arms, MS. Vincent. 157, art. 24. Transcript: Stephen Tucker,* The Assignment of Arms to Shakespere and Arden, 1596–1599 *(1884), pp. 7–8; TB, 17 (note at end only); EKC, ii. 18–20; BRL, i. 211–2. EKC furnishes lacunae in angular brackets from item 128. George Steevens drew attention to this document, and also to item 128, in a note to his second edition of the* Johnson–Steevens *Plays of William Shakspeare (1778), i. 191. Malone first discussed the grant of arms in detail in his posthumous* Life of William Shakspeare *in the 1821 Variorum (ii. 28–41, 88–96). He gives the full text of art. 24 (ii. 541–2), printing separately the note at the end (ii. 89). By the time H-P brought out his 1848 biography, the last 10½ words of the note were 'decayed and lost from the MS' (Life, p. 77n). He supplies the deficiency from Malone, as does Chambers.*

130 THE COAT OF ARMS, 1599. College of Arms, MS. R. 21 (formerly G. 13), p. 347. Transcript: Stephen Tucker, The Assignment of Arms to Shakespere and Arden, 1596–1599 (1884), pp. 9–10; H-P, Outlines, ii. 60–1; TB, 32–4; EKC, ii. 20–2; BRL, i. 301. The words from the missing lower right-hand corner are provided by H-P from 'an old transcript'; EKC follows H-P.

Alexander Pope first printed the 1599 draft, which was transmitted to him by John Anstis, Garter King-of-Arms, in vol. i of his edition of The Works of Shakespear (1725), following Rowe's Account.

having laid out £30 for his arms, is mocked with the 'word', *Not without mustard*. The parallel is suggestive, but Sogliardo is not an actor, and his coat-armour, which flaunts a boar's head, is unlike Shakespeare's. If the latter did choose 'Non sanz droict' as his motto, neither he nor his descendants seem ever to have used it. No motto appears above the arms displayed in relief on the Shakespeare monument in Stratford church, nor did his daughter Susanna include the phrase on her gravestone.

A fair copy of the draft of 1596 has never come to light, and John Shakespeare was still described as a yeoman in January 1597, when he sold a strip of land to George Badger; but there is no reason to doubt (with Sir Sidney Lee) that the grant was executed. Three years later John again applied to the heralds. This time they are a little more specific about the petitioner: they speak of John as a Queen's officer and bailiff of Stratford, and describe his ancestor as having been 'advaunced & Rewarded with Landes & Tenementes geven to him in those partes of Warwike-shere where they have continewed bie some descentes in good reputacon & credit'. The document confirms and exemplifies the Shakespeare arms — hence Lee's misgivings — but the applicant's real purpose was to obtain allowance to combine his arms with those of his wife's family. The grant authorizes the Shakespeares to divide their shield vertically, with the Shakespeare bearings on the dexter half, and the Arden on the sinister. But the heralds worried about the Ardens of Wilmcote (misspelt *Wellingcote* by the clerk). Did they trace their descent from the prestigious Ardens of Park Hall in Warwickshire? That would entitle them to 'Ermine, a fess checky gold and azure', a coat derived from the Beauchamps, Earls of Warwick.[1] At first the heralds opted for this device, and sketched it impaled with the Shakespeare arms, then changed their minds, scratched it out, and alongside drew a differenced form of the ancient Arden coat, 'Gules, three cross-crosslets fitchées gold, and on a gold chief a martlet gules.'[2] Evidently they felt, on second thought, that the Wilmcote Ardens rated only the less illustrious old coat. In the end the Shakespeares decided not to impale their arms.

A few years later their honours contributed to a heraldic tempest in a teacup. In the restricted and self-contained society of the College of Arms quarrels and rivalries flourished. These the personality of Sir William Dethick abetted. The greedy and despotic Garter King-of-Arms was easily vexed. Once he had struck his own father with his fist; he stabbed his brother with a dagger, and raised eyebrows at the funeral of Sir Henry Sidney by assaulting the minister in the church. In the Heralds' office he berated, reviled, and sometimes beat his colleagues. Such a man makes enemies, and in the person of the less violent but no less contentious York Herald, Peter Brooke, *alias* Brokesmouth, he found almost — but not quite — his match. In 1602 Brooke accused Dethick of elevating base persons, and assigning devices already in use. (Earlier in his career Sir William had aroused criticism for granting the royal arms of England, slightly differenced, to a plasterer named Daukins.) Brooke drew up a list of twenty-three cases where, he alleged, Dethick and his associate Camden, Clarenceux King-of-Arms, had abused their authority.

131 THE YORK HERALD'S COMPLAINT, 1602. *Folger Shakespeare Library, MS. V.a.156 (formerly MS. 423.1). Transcript: BRL, ii. 342. Sidney Lee examined the document when it was at Messrs. Pearson and Company, Pall Mall, and remarked on it in the 1915 recension of his* Life of William Shakespeare *(pp. 286–7). BRL is the first to discuss the manuscript in some detail.*

1   *Fess:* in heraldry, a broad horizontal band drawn across the centre of a shield.
2   *Fitchées:* in heraldry, pointed at the lower extremity; applied to crosses.

Shakespeare's name appears fourth on the list. Elsewhere in the manuscript, beneath a rough sketch of the familiar arms, Brooke has written, 'Shakespear y^e Player by Garter'. The appellation *player* is no doubt pejoratively intended.

132 THE YORK HERALD'S COMPLAINT, 1602. *Folger Shakespeare Library, MS. V.a.350, p. 28 (formerly MS. 423.3). This volume, consisting of two manuscripts bound together, was in the William Constable collection; in January 1907 Henry Clay Folger purchased it from Bernard Dobell. BRL first analysed the document, and reproduced it in facsimile (ii. 342–4).*

133 GARTER AND CLARENCEUX'S REPLY TO THE YORK HERALD, 1602. *Bodleian Library, MS. Ashmole 846, f. 50 (no. ix, originally a separate leaf). The College of Arms possesses another draft (MS. W.Z., p. 276^v) in which the relevant passage, although differing in details of phraseology, is essentially the same. Transcript: Stephen Tucker, The Assignment of Arms to Shakespere and Arden, 1596–1599 (1884), p. 11 (College of Arms, MS. W.Z., p. 276^v); EKC, ii. 22 (MS. Ashmole 846); BRL, ii. 345 (College of Arms, MS. W.Z., p. 276^v; MS. Ashmole 846).*

Edward Bernard lists the Bodleian draft as item 7245 in Catalogi Librorum Manuscriptorum Angliae et Hiberniae in Unum Collecti *(1697), where it is described as 'The Answers of Garter and Clarencieux Kings of Armes, to the scrole of Armes exhibited by Raffe Brokesmouth, called York Herald'. Pope, in his 1725 edition of Shakespeare's* Works, *included the following headnote to the text of the 1599 grant of arms:* 'There is also a Manuscript in the Herald's Office, marked *W.2. p. 276*; where Notice is taken of this Coat, and that the Person to whom it was granted, had born Magistracy at *Stratford* upon *Avon*' *(i, p. xlii). This is the first printed mention of the item in a Shakespearian context.*

Apparently the York Herald compiled these notes in preparation for a formal hearing by the commissioners for the Office of Earl Marshal. The particulars of Brooke's complaint are not recorded, but may be inferred from the joint reply of Garter and Clarenceux. They defended the eligibility of John Shakespeare — a magistrate 'of good substance and habelite' who had married an heir of Arden — and insisted that the device prepared for him did not infringe upon the arms of Lord Mauley, *Gold, a bend sable*: 'the Speare on the Bend', after all, was 'a patible [i.e. acceptable] difference'. Other families displayed a black bend with gold on their shields, for example (as Dethick and Camden pointed out), the Harleys and Ferrers. So too did Shakespeare's Stratford neighbours the Quineys, whose arms sealed the only surviving letter to the poet. Anyway some devices were bound to resemble one another, so many had been conferred. Dethick, for all his faults, knew his business. The charges came to nothing.

In 1597 Shakespeare bought a fine house for himself and his family. This was New Place, built by Stratford's greatest benefactor, Sir Hugh Clopton, at the corner of Chapel Street and Chapel Lane (otherwise known as Walker's Street or Dead Lane). It had a chequered history. Across the road stood the chapel re-edified by Sir Hugh, where priests chanted prayers for the repose of his soul, but, despite these spiritually satisfying environs, the Cloptons do not seem to have used New Place much. Sir Hugh died in London, and his heirs preferred to live at Clopton Manor, two miles distant from Stratford, and on the edge of the Welcombe Hills. In 1540 (it will be recalled) New Place sufficiently impressed the King's antiquary for him to make a note of the 'praty house of brike and tymbar'. A Quiney had been dwelling there. Towards mid-century the mansion found a distinguished tenant when Dr. Thomas Bentley, formerly physician to Henry VIII and president of the College of Physicians, leased it from a Clopton. But when Bentley died in 1549, his landlord complained in Chancery that the doctor had 'lefte the said manour place in great ruyne and decay and unrepayryd'.[1] In 1563 another Clopton, pressed for cash, gave up the title of New Place to William Bott, whom the next year he accused of defrauding him of rents, and forging a deed related to Clopton lands. Others, including his own son-in-law, regarded Bott as unsavoury — a false harlot and a false villain, as Roland Wheler told him to his face at the Swan. In 1565 the corporation expelled Alderman Bott for indiscreetly allowing 'that ther was never a honest man of the Councell or the body of the corporacyon of Stratford'. Two years later Bott sold New Place to an Inner Temple Lawyer, William Underhill, who was clerk of assizes at Warwick and a substantial property holder in the county. New Place passed to his son and heir William — described as 'a subtle, covetous, and crafty man' — who sold the house to Shakespeare. The foot of fine, or essential part, of the deed transferring the dwelling to William Shakespeare is dated 4 May 1597, and records the payment to Underhill of £60 in silver (*sexaginta libras sterlingorum*). For Sir Hugh Clopton's Great House, however decayed, the figure may well seem absurdly low; but in fines of this period the consideration mentioned is customarily a legal fiction. We do not know how much Shakespeare actually laid out.

Two months later Underhill died at Fillongley under circumstances suggesting foul play. Suspicion pointed to his first-born Fulke. In 1599 Fulke, still a minor, was executed at Warwick for poisoning his father. The law took the forfeit of the Underhill estate for felony, but it was regranted to Fulke's younger brother Hercules when he came of age in 1602. In Michaelmas term of that year, Hercules Underhill confirmed the sale of New Place to Shakespeare, who paid the prescribed fee, equal to one quarter of the yearly value of the property, to clear the title.

The house that he bought was the second largest in Stratford.[2] It had a frontage of over sixty feet in Chapel Street, a depth (along Chapel Lane) of at least seventy feet in some parts, and a height of over twenty-eight feet at the northern end, which abutted the houses of Shakespeare's friends the Nashes. No fewer than ten fireplaces warmed New Place in winter, and there were probably more rooms than fireplaces, the latter being a taxable luxury.[3] In the eighteenth century George Vertue made two pen-and-ink sketches of Shakespeare's house, as someone, perhaps a descendant of the poet's sister Joan Hart, remembered it. One drawing depicts a handsome

---

1 H-P, *An Historical Account of the New Place, the Last Residence of Shakespeare* (1864), p. 10; ME, 87.
2 The most imposing house was the old College, Crown property leased in 1596 to Thomas Combe.
3 A hearth-tax return for 1663 establishes the number of fireplaces; see H-P, *Historical Account*, p. 162.

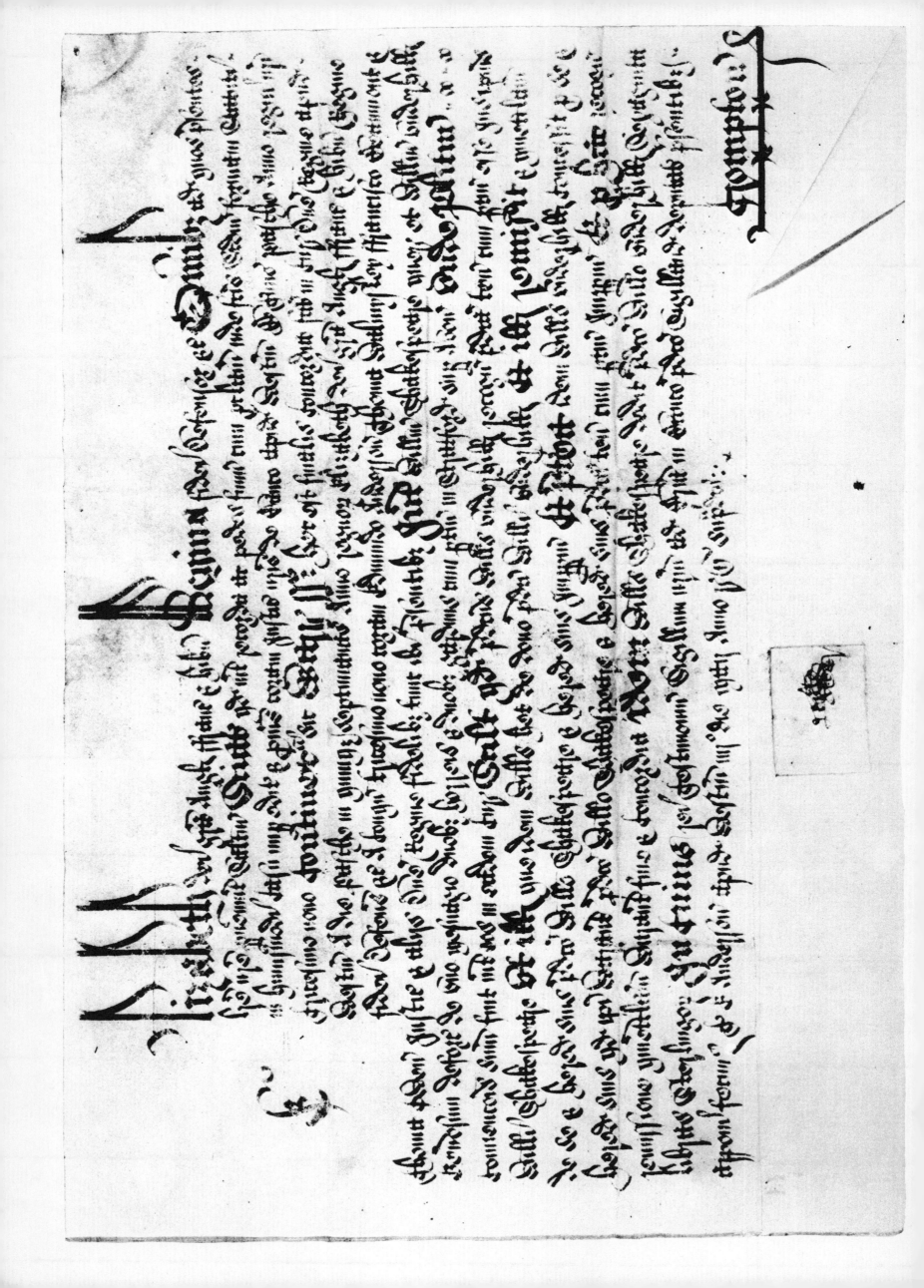

Opposite:

134 SHAKESPEARE BUYS NEW PLACE FROM WILLIAM UNDERHILL, 4 MAY 1597. *Shakespeare Birthplace Trust MS., item 1, case 8, in New Place Museum, Nash House. Transcript: EKC, ii. 95–6 (extract); BRL, i. 238–9 (text and translation).*

Several documents record Shakespeare's purchase of New Place. The exemplification of fine, here reproduced, was the legally attested copy of the foot of fine that the buyer would keep among his title-deeds. Also preserved, among the records of the Court of Common Pleas in the Public Record Office, are the concord of fine — the concord, or agreement, between the parties, made in open court or before commissioners of the court — and the indentures, which were engrossed in triplicate (see item 135). The press-mark for the concord is C.P. 24 (1)/15; for the third copy (or foot) of the indenture, filed by the court: C.P. 25 (2)/237, Easter 39 Eliz. I. H-P gives a transcript of the foot of fine (Outlines, ii. 104–5); also TB (20–1; with translation) and BRL (i. 237). There is a good facsimile (Plate II) in N. E. Evans, Shakespeare in the Public Records (1964).

135 HERCULES UNDERHILL RECONVEYS NEW PLACE TO SHAKESPEARE, 1602. *Public Record Office, Court of Common Pleas, Feet of Fines, C.P. 25 (2)/237, Michaelmas 44 & 45 Eliz. I, no. 15. Transcript: TB, 42 (extract); EKC, ii. 96 (extract); BRL, ii. 355–6 (text and translation). The chirographer — the officer of the Common Pleas who engrossed fines, or chirographs — made three copies of the indenture on a single piece of parchment, which was then divided, along indented lines, into individual copies for the vendor, the purchaser, and the court files; hence the wavy edge at the top of the last copy, here reproduced.*

In a letter to Jordan, dated 3 July 1790, Malone refers to coming upon a record showing the transfer from Hercules Underhill to Shakespeare, in 1602, of 'one messuage, two barns, two gardens, and two orchards, with the appurtenants in Stratford upon Avon' (Original Letters from Edmund Malone, the Editor of Shakespeare, to John Jordan, the Poet, ed. H-P (1864), p. 26). J. Payne Collier first printed the document, which he misdated 1603, in New Facts Regarding the Life of Shakespeare (1835), pp. 29–30. It was then among 'Fines preserved at the Chapter House, Westminster'. H-P, Life, p. 203, reprinted the record, correcting date and text. In 1886 Richard Sims found the purchaser's and vendor's exemplifications in the manuscript collections of J. E. Severne of Wallop; Sims announced his discovery in The Athenæum, 13 February 1886, p. 241. Acquired by H-P (they are item 140 in his Calendar of the Shakespearean Rarities . . . preserved at Hollingbury Copse . . . (1887)), the exemplifications eventually came into the possession of the Folger Shakespeare Library, where they bear the shelfmarks MS. Z.c.36 (110) and MS. Z.c.36 (111) (both formerly MS. 2068.2).

This Something by memory and y description of Shakespears House which was in Stratford on Avon. where he livd and dyed. and his wife after him 1623.

chappel +

This the outward appearance towards the Street. the gate and entrance, (at the Corner of chappel lane) the chappel. X founded by S.r Hu. Clopton. who built it and the Bridge over Avon.

besides this front or outward gate there was before the House it self (that Shakespeer livd in.) within a little court yard. grass growing there — before the real dwelling house. this out side being only a long gallery &c. and for servants.

the House

Lane

the chappel

the gate.

This House of Shakespears was pulld down about 40 years ago and then was built a handsome brick house. by. and now in posession of the Cloptons.

136   GEORGE VERTUE, SKETCHES OF THE FRONTAGE AND PLAN OF NEW PLACE, 1737. *British Library, MS. Portland Loan 29/246, p. 18. An engraver and antiquary, Vertue in October 1737 accompanied the Earl of Oxford on a tour to Oxford, returning to London via Stratford-upon-Avon, where he made his sketches of New Place. See Frank Simpson, 'New Place: The Only Representation of Shakespeare's House, from an Unpublished Manuscript', Shakespeare Survey 5 (Cambridge, 1952), pp. 55–7; also item 206, below.*

NEW PLACE.

137 NEW PLACE IN MALONE'S *SHAKSPEARE*, 1790. *From the* Plays and Poems, *vol. i, pt. 1, facing p. 116. Executed by A. Birrell from a sketch supplied by John Jordan, the engraving bears the caption, 'From a Drawing in the Margin of an Ancient SURVEY, made by Order of SIR GEORGE CAREW, (afterwards BARON CAREW of Clopton, and EARL of TOTNESS) and found at Clopton near Stratford upon Avon, in 1786'. By 1790 this survey, which Jordan claimed to have come upon accidentally at Clopton House, was not to be found — it perhaps had never existed — and Malone perforce relied on Jordan, not without misgivings. 'Before Shakspeare's house', Malone wrote to him on 25 March 1790, 'there were certainly no iron rails, that not being the mode of his time. I suppose what you have represented are intended for wooden pales, and perhaps, on a larger scale, were more distinct.' While regretting the loss of the survey, Malone found Jordan's account of the drawing of New Place on the whole 'very satisfactory', and proceeded to publish it; not, however, without first judiciously removing the railings. The 1790 engraving, although incompatible with Vertue's representation of the house, is still sometimes reproduced without question of its authority.*

138 RICHARD GRIMMITT REMEMBERS NEW PLACE, 1767. *Folger Shakespeare Library, MS. S.a.115 (formerly MS. 452). Transcript: EKC, ii. 99; BRL, i. 241; ME, 90. Richard Grimmitt's reminiscence was set down by the Revd. Joseph Greene, the headmaster of the Stratford grammar school. H-P acquired the note (item 5 in his* Calendar of the Shakespearean Rarities . . . preserved at Hollingbury Copse . . . (1887)), *and printed it in* An Historical Account of the New Place, Stratford-upon-Avon, the Last Residence of Shakespeare (1864), *pp. 181–2.*

big house of three storeys and five gables, with ornamental beams (the timber Leland mentions). The other shows the gate and entrance at the corner of Chapel Lane, the courtyard before New Place, and, on either side of the court, buildings, one being the servants' quarters. In 1767 Richard Grimmitt, then in his eighties, recalled having played as a child with a Clopton lad in the Great House called New Place — there was a brick wall, 'with a kind of porch', at the end next to the chapel, and the boys would cross 'a small kind of Green Court before they enter'd yᵉ House which was bearing to yᵉ left, & fronted with brick, with plain windows, Consisting of common panes of Glass set in lead, as at this time'. This testimony confirms Vertue.

Shakespeare's house stood in ample grounds. In 1563 Bott sued a neighbour for removing twelve pieces of sawed timber from 'le barne yarde' near 'le newe place gardyn' in 'Dede Lane'. This is the first mention of the gardens of New Place. The fine of 1597 speaks of a messuage (a dwelling house with adjacent lands) with two barns and two gardens (*uno messuagio cum duobus horreis et duobus gardinis*); the second fine adds two orchards (*duobus pomariis*). The garden must have been fairly small at first, but Shakespeare added to it land to the east, in Chapel Lane. This had formerly belonged to the dissolved priory of Pinley, and was now part of the estate of a John Gilbert. To extend his garden Shakespeare had to knock down a cottage that stood between New Place and the Gilbert property. The combined gardens, stretching over three-quarters of an acre, came to be known as the Great Garden. A tradition, better than most, holds that Shakespeare planted the mulberry tree that grew in the Great Garden until 1758, when it was cut down and fashioned into more authentic relics than a single mulberry tree — even one with a stock six inches in diameter — might be thought capable of yielding. New Place was also famous for its vines. Fifteen years after the poet's death, Sir Thomas Temple, Baronet, commissioned one of his men, Harry Rose, to ride to Stratford at his first opportunity and gather from the vines of New Place '2 or 3 of the fairest of those budes on some few shutes of the last yeares vines'.[1] Sir Thomas's sister-in-law had much commended the vines — they were probably grape-vines. She lived across the road from Shakespeare's house, at the corner of Chapel Street and Scholar's Lane. Her house, with numerous modern improvements and extensions, now welcomes visitors to Stratford as the Falcon Hotel.

Shakespeare moved into New Place before the year was out or, at the latest, early in the new year. We know because, in a survey of corn and malt made on 4 February 1598, he is listed as a resident of Chapel Street ward, in which New Place was situated. The inventory gives his holding as ten quarters (equivalent to eighty bushels), presumably of malt, because elsewhere in the survey corn is specified as such. Three successive wet summers had resulted in shortage of grain, inflated prices, and (inevitably) hoarding. The municipal authorities responded by limiting the quantity of malt a household could store for their own brewing. (Malting, as previously noted, was Stratford's principal industry). The Shakespeares' ten quarters represented an average holding. Of their thirteen neighbours in Chapel Street ward, two stored more: Thomas Dyxon and schoolmaster Aspinall. Sir Thomas Lucy of Charlecote, listed as a 'strainger', hoarded the most, sixteen quarters in Richard Dixon's barn, and twelve and a half quarters with Abraham Sturley, of whom we shall be hearing more.

The house described as run down a half century earlier underwent restoration by its new owner. In his 1733 edition of Shakespeare, Lewis Theobald reports being told by John Clopton, a scion of the family that built New Place, that Shakespeare had 'repair'd and modell'd it to his own mind'. The corporation in 1598 paid 'mʳ Shaxspere' ten pence for a load of stone, which it used (fittingly enough) to mend Clopton Bridge. The import of the record is not certain — it might, in the absence of a christian name, conceivably refer to the dramatist's father — but most likely the stone was left over from the repairs executed at New Place.

What did fellow townsmen make of the distinguished playwright of the Chamberlain's company and admired poet of love's languishment who sojourned each year in their midst? They probably troubled their heads little enough about the plays and poems. Business was another matter; they saw Shakespeare as a man shrewd in practical affairs, and approachable (if need be)

---

1 Stowe MSS. in the Huntington Library; 'A Document Concerning Shakespeare's Garden', *The Huntington Library Bulletin*, i (1931), 199–201; ME, 91. The text in ME is the more accurate.

139 SHAKESPEARE A HOLDER OF CORN AND MALT, 4 FEBRUARY 1598. *Shakespeare Birthplace Trust Records Office, Misc. Doc. I, 106. Transcript: TB, 24 (extract); EKC, ii. 99 (extract); BRL, i. 281–4. The document, brought to the attention of the Shakespeare Society, was quoted and analysed by its director, J. Payne Collier, in* The Life of William Shakespeare *(1844), in Shakespeare,* Works, *ed. Collier (1842–53), i, pp. clxiii–clxv.*

140 SHAKESPEARE SELLS A LOAD OF STONE, 1598. *Shakespeare Birthplace Trust Records Office, Corp. Rec., Chamberlain's Accounts, 1585–1619, p. 44. Transcript: TB, 30; EKC, ii. 96. H-P cites and discusses this record, and furnishes a line-block facsimile (Outlines, ii. 373–4).*

for a substantial loan on good security. Anyway the Quineys so regarded him. Just after William Shakespeare bought his own house in Stratford, Adrian Quiney, John Shakespeare's old neighbour and fellow tradesman, told Abraham Sturley that the master of New Place might have a mind to make some investments. This Sturley hailed from Worcester; he had studied at Queens' College, Cambridge, and after a spell in the service of Sir Thomas Lucy had come to Stratford, where he thrived — in 1596 he was bailiff. His sister married Adrian's son Richard. On 24 January 1598 Sturley wrote to his brother-in-law, who was then in London. 'It semeth bi him [Adrian Quiney]', Sturley informed Richard, 'that our countriman m^r Shaksper is willing to disburse some monei upon some od yardeland or other att Shottrei or neare about us; he thinketh it a very fitt patterne to move him to deale in the matter of our Tithes.' A purchase of tithes would bring perquisites as well as income. Did his Stratford neighbours guess that Shakespeare, who now signed himself gentleman, was keen to improve his status in other respects? In any event, if they dangled land and tithes before him, he was not ready to bite. Not yet.

October came, and Richard Quiney was again in London, this time to petition the Privy Council for a corporation charter on better terms and for relief from the latest subsidy voted by Parliament. With the bad weather and two devastating fires, Stratford had fallen on hard times;

N*

141 RICHARD QUINEY'S LETTER TO SHAKESPEARE, 25 OCTOBER 1598. *Shakespeare Birthplace Trust Records Office, MS. ER 27/4. Transcript: TB, 28; EKC, ii. 102; BRL, i. 229; ME, 93. Malone discovered the letter in a bundle of Quiney correspondence while finding his way through 3,000 documents in the Stratford archives in 1793. In a letter to Bishop Percy, dated 15 November, he describes the 'very pretty little relick,* about *three inches long by two broad'. These are its approximate dimensions folded. Malone never published his discovery, but James Boswell, the biographer's son, found Malone's transcript among papers left in a 'scattered state', and printed it in the posthumous* Life of William Shakspeare *included in the 1821 Variorum (ii. 485). Chambers interprets the H above the direction as H[aste]; but see BRL, i. 229.*

so Quiney had a good case. But he was forced to wait in London for four months. He looked for support from the lord of the manor, Sir Edward Greville, who had promised money 'for prosecuting the cause' (as Sturley put it). Meanwhile, on 25 October, Quiney thought it prudent to get off a letter from his inn, the Bell in Carter Lane, to his 'Loveinge good ffrend & contreymann m^r w^m Shackespere'. In his small, rapid hand, Quiney asked his loving countryman's help with a loan of £30 upon his own security and that of Master Bushell or Master Mytton. 'Mr Rosswell', on whom he had counted, 'is nott come to London as yeate & I have especiall cawse.' Richard Mytton and Peter Roswell were gentlemen in Greville's service. 'Yo^w shall ffrende me muche', the letter continues, 'in helpeing me out of all the debettes I owe in London I thancke god & muche quiet my mynde which wolde nott be indebeted. I am nowe towardes the Cowrte' — the watermen would ferry him to Richmond — 'in hope of answer for the dispatche of my Buysenes.' Shakespeare never received this anxious communication, for Quiney took it back with him to Stratford, and when he died in office as bailiff after a tavern brawl with Greville's men in 1602, the letter found a place among the Quiney papers in the corporation archives.

Why did he not dispatch it? Perhaps Quiney decided to get together personally with Shakespeare; maybe the playwright called on his countryman at the Bell, near St. Paul's. A distinguished biographer of Shakespeare, Joseph Quincy Adams, has concluded: 'By whatever means they met, Shakespeare good-naturedly agreed to secure the money for Quiney, for before the day was over Quiney had written the news to his brother-in-law.'[1] This is to make facts of possibilities. Quiney did indeed write that day; on 4 November Sturley speaks of this communication, importing 'that our countriman m^r Wm Shak. would procure us monei' — but he comments, 'which I will like of as I shall heare when wheare & howe: and I prai let not go that occasion if it mai sort to ani indifferent condicions.'[2] The phrasing does not suggest a mission accomplished. Around the same time, Adrian Quiney advised his son and partner Richard that, if he bargained with Shakespeare or received money from him, he would do well to buy some knit stockings at Evesham for their mercer's shop. This seems to refer to a business deal rather than to the loan. In fact we do not know whether Shakespeare came to Richard Quiney's aid, although he likely enough did. The sequel is happy. Eventually the Queen agreed to relieve 'this towne twise afflicted and almost wasted by fire', and the Exchequer reimbursed Quiney for his expenses in London. The Quineys and the Shakespeares continued on cordial terms, Richard's son Thomas marrying Shakespeare's younger daughter, although it was not (as things turned out) a fortunate union.[3]

There were deaths as well as marriages. In March 1601 Thomas Whittington, the Hathaway shepherd, died after drawing up a will in which he remembered the 40s. owed him by the Shakespeares.[4] Sentimental biographers have envisaged Whittington as an archetype of the noble shepherd, rather like the loyal Adam of *As You Like It*, who had helped Anne out with a loan while her husband was preoccupied with playwriting in the indifferent metropolis; but the sum might equally well have represented Whittington's uncollected wages or savings held for safekeeping. On 8 September 1601 John Shakespeare was buried in the churchyard of Holy Trinity. In the absence of a will the double house in Henley Street would pass to his eldest son William. According to English common law, the widow retained the right of residence, as well as a life interest of a third. No doubt Mary Shakespeare stayed on at the family house she had known for half a century. Some of her children kept her company, grandchildren too — her daughter Joan, married to the hatter Hart, lived there with her growing family. The widow survived another seven years. On 9 September 1608 the Stratford register records the burial of 'Mayry Shaxspere wydowe'.

142 MARY SHAKESPEARE BURIED, 9 SEPTEMBER 1608. *Stratford parish register, burials, f. 39^v. Shakespeare Birthplace Trust Records Office, DR 243/1.*

1   Joseph Quincy Adams, *A Life of William Shakespeare* (1923), p. 259.
2   Sturley's letter (Shakespeare Birthplace Trust Records Office, Misc. Doc. I, 136) was badly damaged by water leakage during the Second World War. Ultra-violet light failed to render the writing legible, nor was I able to track down a photograph. H-P, however, printed a line-block facsimile of an extract (*Shakespearian Facsimiles . . .* (1863), Plate IX, item 1); in *Outlines*, ii. 59–60, he gives the complete text. The letter was first published in the appendix to Malone's posthumous *Life of William Shakspeare* in the 1821 Variorum (ii. 569–72). There is a transcript in EKC, ii. 103; ME, 95, gives an extract. Another Sturley letter to Quiney (Misc. Doc. I, 135; EKC, ii. 101–2) was similarly affected.
3   See below, pp. 238–41.
4   See above, pp. 66–9, and item 61, p. 68.

143 SHAKESPEARE SUES PHILIP ROGERS, *c.* 1604. *Shakespeare Birthplace Trust Records Office, MS. ER 27/5. Transcript: EKC, ii. 113; BRL, ii. 369–71 (text and translation). H-P first printed the declaration, which he describes as 'one of the most curious documents connected with Shakespeare's personal history known to exist' (Life, pp. 208–9).*

144 SHAKESPEARE SUES JOHN ADDENBROOKE, 17 AUGUST 1608–7 JUNE 1609. *The document here reproduced (Shakespeare Birthplace Trust Records Office, Misc. Doc. V, 116) lists the jurors, and records their verdict (with costs and damages) for the plaintiff. The other documents in the case, all in the same archive, comprise (a) the order to arrest Addenbrooke, 17 August 1608 (Misc. Doc. V, 139); (b) the order to empanel a jury, 21 December 1608 (Misc. Doc. V, 127a); (c) the panel of twenty-four jurors (Misc. Doc. V, 127b); (d) the order binding jurors to appear at the next court sitting, 15 February 1609 (Misc. Doc. V, 115); (e) the order to produce Addenbrooke at the next court sitting, 15 March 1609 (MS. ER 27/6); and (f) the order against Thomas Horneby, 7 June 1609 (MS. ER 27/7). Transcript: H-P, Outlines, ii. 78–80; BRL, ii. 393–400 (text and translations). TB gives a synopsis with a few extracts (57–9); EKC summarizes, with extracts, all the items except (f), which he gives in full (ii. 114–16). EKC, ii. 114, misdates (a) December 1608. The suit was discovered by R. B. Wheler, who published items (a) and (f) in his* History and Antiquities of Stratford-upon-Avon *(Stratford-upon-Avon, [1806]), pp. 144–5. Reproduced here are the recto and the relevant portion of the verso.*

Of how Shakespeare spent his days away from London the records reveal little. They merely chronicle, in dry legalistic fashion, petty disputes over money matters that found their way into court. A man with more than sufficient malt for his domestic brewing sometimes parted with a few bushels on credit, and, when the bill went unpaid, he would resort to litigation. Shakespeare was in this respect no different from others. In the spring of 1604 he sold his neighbour Philip Rogers twenty bushels of malt, and on 25 June lent him 2s. Rogers was an apothecary who (by licence) sold ale as well as drugs and tobacco; we hear of him dispensing his potables in Chapel Street and the High Street, not far from New Place. His whole obligation to Shakespeare came to a little over £2, of which Rogers had returned 6s., leaving a balance of 35s.10d. With William Tetherington as his lawyer, Shakespeare brought Rogers to the Court of Record, which sat fortnightly, the bailiff presiding, and heard cases representing debts not in excess of £30. The plaintiff demanded his 35s.10d., plus 10s. damages. How the court ruled is not known.

It was not the only time the poet sued. A few years later he was back in the same court seeking the recovery of £6, plus 24s. damages, from John Addenbrooke. He may have been the Addenbrooke who sold licences for starch in Warwickshire around 1600. The action dragged on for almost a year, from 17 August 1608 until 7 June 1609, leaving a trail of records more numerous than interesting. The court issued a summons which the serjeant served, a jury was empanelled, the defendant was cited to appear, the jury reached a verdict favourable to the plaintiff, the court ordered John Addenbrooke to appear and this time to satisfy William Shackspeare for both debt and damages, and finally, when he failed to come, asked Addenbrooke's surety, Thomas Horneby, to show cause why he should not pay the £6 and the 24s. damages. Horneby was a blacksmith who kept an alehouse in Henley Street. Whether Shakespeare ever collected is not recorded. His persistence may strike moderns as heartless, but the course Shakespeare followed was normal in an age without credit cards, overdrafts, or collection agencies.

Such vexations were infrequent. Shakespeare must have passed his time mainly with his family or cultivating the gardens of New Place, with their mulberry tree and flourishing vines. Formal records neglect the unsensational events of quotidian life, although the mythos does now and then gratify curiosity with an informal glimpse of the playwright in his provincial setting. George Steevens preserves a tradition, plausible enough, that Shakespeare enjoyed his weekly cup at his local.

> The late Mr. James West, of the Treasury, assured me, that at his house in Warwickshire he had a wooden bench, once the favourite accommodation of Shakspeare, together with an earthen half-pint
>
> mug, out of which he was accustomed to take his draughts of ale at a certain publick house in the neighbourhood of Stratford, every Saturday afternoon.

145 EDMOND MALONE, *SUPPLEMENT TO THE EDITION OF SHAKSPEARE'S PLAYS PUBLISHED IN 1778 BY SAMUEL JOHNSON AND GEORGE STEEVENS* (1780), ii. 369–70. *George Steevens's note to* Sir John Oldcastle. *Reprinted in EKC, ii. 295–6.*

When crossed, he availed himself (so Oldys reports) of the exquisite revenges of art.

> " Old Mr. Bowman the player reported from Sir William Bishop, that some part of Sir John Falstaff's character was drawn from a townsman of Stratford, who either faithlessly broke a contract, or spitefully refused to part with some land, for a valuable consideration, adjoining to Shakespeare's, in or near that town."

146 WILLIAM SHAKESPEARE, *PLAYS*, ED. SAMUEL JOHNSON AND GEORGE STEEVENS (1778), i. 205.

The mythos is crueller to John Combe, the wealthiest bachelor — indeed the wealthiest citizen — in Stratford, who reputedly amassed his fortune by exacting his usury at the legally acceptable rate of ten in the hundred. This Combe, the tale went round, served as a butt for Shakespeare's extempore wit. Amongst 'the gentlemen of the Neighbourhood',

> it is a Story almoſt ſtill re-
> member'd in that Country, that he had a par-
> ticular Intimacy with Mr. *Combe*, an old Gen-
> tleman noted thereabouts for his Wealth and
> Uſury : It happen'd, that in a pleaſant Con-
> verſation amongſt their common Friends,
> Mr. *Combe* told *Shakeſpear* in a laughing man-
> ner, that he fancy'd, he intended to write his
> Epitaph, if he happen'd to out-live him; and
> ſince he could not know what might be ſaid
> of him when he was dead, he deſir'd it might
> be done immediately: Upon which *Shakeſpear*
> gave him theſe four Verſes.
>
> *Ten in the Hundred lies here ingrav'd,*
> *'Tis a Hundred to Ten, his Soul is not ſav'd.*
> *If any Man ask, Who lies in this Tomb?*
> *Oh! ho! quoth the Devil, 'tis my* John-a-Combe.
>
> But the Sharpneſs of the Satyr is ſaid to have
> ſtung the Man ſo ſeverely, that he never for-
> gave it.

147 NICHOLAS ROWE, *SOME ACCOUNT OF THE LIFE, &C. OF MR. WILLIAM SHAKESPEAR,* IN
SHAKESPEARE, *WORKS*, ED. ROWE (1709), i, p. xxxvi.

This version by Nicholas Rowe climaxes a long development. In 1634, while touring in Warwickshire, a Lieutenant Hammond 'of the Military Company in Norwich' examined the monuments in Stratford Church, and after pausing, suitably impressed, over the 'neat Monument of
that famous English Poet, Mr Wm Shakespeere', turned to another — 'one of an old Gentleman a Batchelor, Mr Combe, upon whose name, the sayd Poet, did merrily fann up some witty,
& facetious verses, which time would nott give us leave to sacke up'.[1] Hammond did not trouble
to set down the verses, but the oversight was remedied (with an unanticipated bonus) by Nicholas
Burgh, a Poor Knight of Windsor, who around mid-century included in his commonplace book
not only the poet's epitaph on 'John A Combe', the Devil's son, but also Shakespeare's handsome
verse amends to the bachelor who made 'the poore his Issue'. Aubrey too found a place for anecdote and epitaph in his jottings.

A tradition so variously reported might, at first glance, seem worthy of credit, but the doggerel
rhyme itself, so un-Shakespearian in flavour, invites scepticism. Doubts are reinforced by the fact
that similar epitaphs, but on an unnamed usurer, had appeared earlier in *The More the Merrier*
(1608) by 'H. P.', and also in Camden's *Remaines, Concerning Britaine* (1614 ed.), among a group of
'conceited, merry, and laughing Epitaphes, the most of them composed by Master *John Hoskines*
when he was young'. Later in the century other renderings substituted names — Stanhope,
Spencer, or Pearse — for Combe. Among the 'divers select Epitaphs and Hearce-attending
Epods' annexed to his *Remains after Death*, printed in 1618, Richard Brathwait included the
familiar verses 'upon one John Combe of Stratford upon Aven, a notable Usurer, fastened upon
a Tombe that he had caused to be built in his life time'. No matter that Combe built no tomb in

---

1 *A Relation of a short Survey of 26. Counties . . . By a Captaine, a Lieutennant, and an Ancient. All three of the Military
Company in Norwich,* British Library, MS. Lansdowne 213, f. 332^v; EKC, ii. 243.

148 SHAKESPEARE'S SUPPOSED EPITAPH ON JOHN COMBE, *c.* 1650. *Bodleian Library, MS. Ashmole 38, p. 180. Transcript: EKC, ii. 246. The MS. is a Caroline commonplace book in the hand of Nicholas Burgh, a Poor Knight of Windsor, who was still living in 1661. H-P*, Life, *p. 241, first printed the anecdote. For another item from the same source, see below, no. 168.*

his lifetime; Brathwait has the right usurer. But he neglects to mention Shakespeare. Only later did the oft-repeated epitaph become attached, through the machinery of myth, to a celebrated Stratford name.

The episode had an aftermath much later, in 1740, when Francis Peck, a Leicestershire parson and dilettante antiquary, reported another Shakespearian epitaph on a different Combe.

Explanatory & Critical Notes on divers passages of SHAKESPEARE'S *plays.*
I Cannot, I think, better introduce these remarks on *Shakespeare,* than with Mr. *Thomas Combe's* epitaph. Every body knows *Shakespeare's* epitaph for *John a Combe.* And I am told he afterwards wrote another for *Tom a Combe,* alias *Thin-Beard,* brother of the said *John ;* & that it was never yet printed. It is as follows.

' *Thin* in *beard,* & thick in purse ;
' Never man beloved worse:
' He went to th' grave with many a curse;
' The Devil & He had both one nurse.'

This is very sour

149 FRANCIS PECK, 'EXPLANATORY & CRITICAL NOTES ON DIVERS PASSAGES OF SHAKE-SPEARE'S PLAYS', IN *NEW MEMOIRS OF THE LIFE AND POETICAL WORKS OF MR. JOHN MILTON* (1740), pp. 222–3. *Reprinted in EKC, ii. 273.*

All that now remained was for the inimitable Jordan to join together the epitaphs for the Combe brothers in a single immensely unreliable anecdote. The episode now shelters under the roof of the Bear (see item 150 opposite).

But Shakespeare did not nurse a hatred for the Combes, nor did the latter go to the grave with bitterness in their hearts towards their witty tavern companion. John Combe remembered Shakespeare in his will by leaving him £5, and in his own will the poet bequeathed his sword as a keepsake to Combe's nephew and heir Thomas.[1] Shakespeare (as we shall see) amicably did business with John Combe, and the two men remained friends until the end.

1   In fairness to Jordan it should be noted that he was aware of this bequest.

were intimately aquainted, the former one day in a tavern
[said to be the sign of the Bear in the Bridge Street in
Stratford] said to the other, 'I suppose you will write my Epitaph
when I am dead you may as well do it now that I may know
what you will say of me when I am gone immediately he replied
it shall be this:

" Ten in the hundred lies here ingrav'd,
" 'Tis a hundred to ten his soul is not sav'd,
" If any man ask, who lies in this tomb?
" Oh! Oh! quoth the devil, 'tis my John a Combe.

The company instantly burst into a loud laugh perhaps from
the justness of the idea, and the hatred that all men have to the
character of a miser and usurer, the violence of the mirth somewhat
subsiding they desired to hear what he had to say of Mr Thomas
Combe brother of the former gentleman, when he instantly said

" But thin in beard, tho' thick in purse,
" He's gone to hell, with many a curse,
" The Devil and he, suck'd both one nurse,
" For never man was loved worse,

This brother was remarkable for the thinness of his Beard
and no doubt also for his covetuous disposition, therfore the
poignancy of the sarcasm afforded no small diversion among
the convivial meeting; but it is said the severity of the satire
made so deep an impression upon the two brothers that they
never forgave the Author of their Epitaphs; whether this
is true is not now to be known, tho' it is by no means
improbable

150   JORDAN ON SHAKESPEARE AND THE COMBES, 1790. *MS. in the Shakespeare Library, Birmingham Public Library; shelfmark: S977, pp. 25–6. Jordan set down the story more than once; see EKC, ii. 293–4.*

And to the poore of Stretford five poundes Item I give vnto william whit fortie shillinges to be
he oweth me by bonde yf he be Lyvinge at my decease and the same bonde to be cancelled to mr
william Shakspere five poundes and to my Lord Lord John Davies xls, Item I give and bequeath
vnto ffrauncis Collins thelder of the borrough of ward tenne poundes of Lawfull Englishe

151   JOHN COMBE'S BEQUEST TO SHAKESPEARE, 28 JANUARY 1613. *Public Record Office, Prob. 11/126 (formerly P.C.C. 118 Wood). Transcript: H-P, Life, pp. 234–40; TB, 75 (extract); EKC, ii. 127 (extract). The will was first printed by H-P as 'a late act of justice to a man who does not appear to have in any way deserved the popular slander that has descended on his name' (Life, p. 234). This item is reduced slightly.*

'He hath much land, and fertile . . .', Hamlet says of the contemptible Osric. ''Tis a chough; but, as I say, spacious in the possession of dirt.' Earlier the Prince had pondered the fate of another landholder. 'This fellow', he muses, contemplating the skull in his hand, 'might be in's time a great buyer of land, with his statutes, his recognizances, his fines, his double vouchers, his recoveries. Is this the fine of his fines, and the recovery of his recoveries, to have his fine pate full of fine dirt?'[1] The author of these lines himself became, shortly after writing them, spacious in the possession of dirt. On 1 May 1602 William Shakespere, gentleman, turned over £320 in cash to William Combe and his nephew John for four yardlands of arable land in Old Stratford, with rights of common for livestock in the outlying fields. A yardland varied in size, according to locality, but usually came to about thirty acres.[2] Old Stratford was farming country to the north of the borough, of which it originally formed part. William Combe gave his address as Warwick, which he had represented in Parliament. In 1593 he had bought the Old Stratford freehold to the west of Welcombe, where his nephew lived. Now, almost a decade later, the parties present interchangeably set their hands and seals to the conveyance. The purchaser did not attend the formalities, but left his younger brother Gilbert to take possession in front of the witnesses: Anthony Nash, Humphrey Mainwaring, and others. The prolix document speaks of the premises as being 'nowe or late in the severall tenures or occupacions of Thomas Hiccoxe and Lewes Hiccoxe'. These were the tenants of the freehold; whether they stayed on after the ownership changed hands is not known. The name Hiccoxe is ordinary enough. After 1603 a Lewis Hiccox with his wife Alice — 'old goody hicox' — kept an inn in Henley Street: probably the eastern house of the Birthplace, which (as later records show) was converted into the Maidenhead Inn.[3] Did Hiccox exchange the plough for the tap?

(In 1610, as provided by the original contract, a fine was entered in the Court of Common Pleas to confirm Shakespeare's title.[4] It describes the freehold as consisting of 107 acres of land, and 20 of pasture. Some biographers have thought that the pasturage represents an addition to the original purchase, but these twenty acres formed part of the parcel bought by Combe in 1593.)

Five months after he bought his land in Old Stratford, on 28 September 1602, Shakespeare acquired the copyhold title to a quarter-acre of land, comprising a garden with cottage, on the south side of Chapel Lane, facing the garden of New Place. This property, plus one or two other parcels in Stratford, belonged to the manor of Rowington, held by the dowager Countess of Warwick, the lady of the manor. In accordance with the feudal custom still in force, Walter Getley, deputy seneschal in the court baron of the Countess, surrendered the cottage with its appurtenances to Shakespeare and his heirs forever.

Opposite:

152 THE COMBES SELL SHAKESPEARE ARABLE LAND IN OLD STRATFORD, 1 MAY 1602. *Shakespeare Birthplace Trust Records Office, MS. ER 27/1. Transcript: H-P, Outlines, ii. 17–19; TB, 39–42 (extract); EKC, ii. 107–8 (extract); BRL, ii. 330–3. R. B. Wheler printed the unexecuted counterpart, then in his possession, in his History and Antiquities of Stratford-upon-Avon [1806], pp. 139–44. The original indenture, here reproduced, was first published by H-P, Life, pp. 198–200. He describes both purchase deed and counterpart as being 'in the possession of Mr. Wheler' (p. 197). The counterpart, deposited on loan in the Shakespeare Birthplace Trust Records Office by Lord Brooke of Warwick Castle in 1970, bears the shelfmark: DR 232/1. The deed is here reduced by about one third, and the verso, with the endorsement recording delivery to Gilbert Shakespeare, is also reproduced.*

1   Edward Dowden is apparently the first to treat Hamlet's reflections in relation to his creator's real-estate interests (*Shakspere: A Critical Study of his Mind and Art* (1875)); see also *SL*, 492ff.
2   The deed describes the parcel as 'Conteyninge by estimacion One hundred and Seaven acres be they more or lesse' of arable.
3   ME, 103.
4   Public Record Office, Court of Common Pleas, Feet of Fines, C.P. 25(2)/365, Trinity 8 James I, *no.* 15. H-P found this foot of fine in the Chapter House, and published a transcript in his *Life*, p. 231. Transcripts are also to be found in H-P, *Outlines*, ii. 25; EKC, ii. 109; and BRL, ii. 413 (text and translation). Also in the Public Record Office is the concord of fine (Court of Common Pleas, C.P. 24 (2)/7).

153 SHAKESPEARE ACQUIRES THE CHAPEL LANE COTTAGE, 28 SEPTEMBER 1602. *Shakespeare Birthplace Trust Records Office, MS. ER 28/1. Transcript: TB, 43–4 (text and translation); EKC, ii. 111–12; BRL, i. 348–9 (text and translation). The document was first printed by H-P, Life, pp. 201–2.*

154 SHAKESPEARE A PROPERTY-OWNER IN ROWINGTON MANOR, 24 OCTOBER 1604. *Public Record Office, Exchequer, Special Commission, E.178/461. Transcript (extract): TB, 44–5; EKC, ii. 112; BRL, ii. 352; N. E. Evans, Shakespeare in the Public Records (1964), p. 21. This entry, which refers to the Chapel Lane copyhold, was apparently first printed in H-P, Outlines (1886 ed., ii. 355–6).*

Shakespeare is also listed as a customary tenant in Rowington Manor on 1 August 1606 in the books of the Auditors of the Land Revenue (Public Record Office, Exchequer, Land Revenue, L.R. 2/228, f. 199). There are transcripts in EKC (ii. 112) and BRL (ii. 352).

No doubt the cottage came in handy as quarters for a servant or gardener. A survey of Rowington manor on 24 October 1604 recorded that William Shakespere held 'there one cottage and one garden by estimation a quarter of one acre', and paid a nominal annual rent of 2s.6d. The year after his decease his daughter Susanna and her husband were admitted as tenants of the cottage.

On 24 July 1605 Shakespeare made his most ambitious investment. For £440 he procured a half-interest in a lease of 'Tythes of Corne grayne blade & heye' in three nearby hamlets — Old Stratford, Welcombe, and Bishopton — along with the small tithes of the whole of Stratford parish, with certain exceptions honouring former rights: the minister of Luddington chapel, for example, continued to farm the tithes of his village.[1] As drawn up in 1544 between the warden of the College of Stratford and William Barker, the lease had a duration of ninety-two years. But after the Dissolution the property of the College, as of other religious foundations, passed to the Crown, which in turn reassigned a parcel of the tithes to the corporation of Stratford. Barker's lease remained valid, however, although it would eventually revert to the corporation. In 1580 he sold the lease to Ralph Hubaud[2] of Ipsley, formerly a sheriff of Warwickshire, at the same time reserving a rental income for himself and his heirs. It was from Hubaud that Shakespeare bought his moiety in a lease that now had thirty-one years left to run. Shakespeare's friend Anthony Nash of Welcombe served as a witness, as he had three years before on the occasion of the Old Stratford freehold transaction. Shakespeare's lawyer Francis Collins, who drew up the indenture, witnessed it too. A member of the town council from 1602 to 1608, Collins was a personal friend, and some years later would be named an overseer of the poet's will. When Hubaud died in 1606 the inventory of his lands and goods included a debt of £20 'Owinge by Mr. Shakespre'.

The latter agreed to pay yearly rents of £5 to John Barker, a lifelong gentleman usher to the Queen (his monument is in Hurst in Berkshire), and another £17 to the bailiffs and burgesses of Stratford. A Chancery bill in 1617 reveals that Shakespeare's interest in the tithes brought him £60 per annum net. When his heirs sold most of their share back to the corporation in 1625, they valued it at £90, or £68 clear, for £22 still went into rents. Shakespeare did not farm his own tithes, but entrusted collection to Anthony Nash. A respected gentleman of substance, Nash had a son Thomas, who would marry Shakespeare's granddaughter.

Other townsmen had larger tithe interests than Shakespeare, and were richer. But by 1605 he had more than restored his family's decayed fortunes. In addition to his tithe income he owned arable and pasture lands, the Birthplace in Henley Street, and the Great House of New Place with its extensive gardens and cottage. All this in addition to his theatrical earnings. The applause of multitudes no doubt gratified the creator of *Hamlet*; but after four captains had borne the Prince from the stage, accompanied by the peal of ordinance, the applause died away and the audience streamed into the Bankside dusk. Such rewards were transient. An entailed estate, passed down successively from generation to generation, represented permanence. So perhaps he thought. But his direct line was extinguished before the century was out, the corporation repossessed the tithes, a later owner razed New Place, the fields of Old Stratford are now traceable only in long-expired conveyances.[3] Only the art, as he prophesied in his *Sonnets* when the eternizing mood was on him, endures. A somewhat later poet makes the point with lyrical grace:

> Trust to good Verses then;
>   They onely will aspire,
> When Pyramids, as men,
>   Are lost, i' th' funerall fire.

---

1   EKC, ii. 125.
2   *Huband* in earlier biographies. On the spelling, see ME, who assembles the facts about Hubaud (105).
3   Dr. Levi Fox, Director of the Shakespeare Birthplace Trust, informs me that the Trust acquired the 107 acres in 1930.

14

His Majesty's Servant

While folk in Stratford went about the ordinary affairs of life, great events were taking place on the national stage. Slowly but inexorably, the Queen declined. She had ruled for almost half a century; most of her subjects had never known another sovereign. Towards the end a heavy dullness and irritability, the infirmities of advanced age, overtook her. She had the wedding ring, symbolizing her marriage to England, filed from her fingers: her attendants could not twist it off, so deeply embedded was it in her flesh. The Chamberlain's men played before her for the last time on 2 February 1603; they cannot have given her much amusement. As Elizabeth sat dying — she refused to lie down, for fear she would never rise — her ministers crowded round to hear a successor named. She procrastinated, as she always had, but finally whispered to Cecil, 'I will that a king succeed me, and who but my kinsman the King of Scots.' On 24 March she died, the Privy Council at once proclaimed the accession of James VI of Scotland as James I of England, and Sir Robert Carey took horse to bear the tidings to Edinburgh. In London bonfires blazed in the streets. Thus ended the Tudor dynasty, and thus began the reign of the house of Stuart, amidst popular rejoicing over the peaceful change of crowns.

The new monarch began his leisurely month's progress from Scotland to London. At Newark-upon-Trent, on 21 April, he made a great impression when a cutpurse in the throng was apprehended 'doing the deed'. The King immediately ordered 'this silken base theefe' hanged, but before leaving Newark he also set free all the wretched prisoners held in the castle. By these acts he demonstrated both his justice and his gracious mercy, in accordance with the theories 'Of a Kings Duetie in his Office' he had set forth in his *Basilicon Doron*. The following Christmas season, on St. Stephen's night (26 December), Shakespeare's company entertained the Court in the Banqueting House at Whitehall with a new comedy probably first acted during the previous summer season. 'A play Caled Mesur for Mesur' dealt with themes of justice and mercy in a way calculated to strike a responsive chord in the new sovereign; the character of Duke Vincentio, who like James abhors crowds, offered an idealized authority figure with whom he could easily sympathize. To suggest that *Measure for Measure* was a royal play planned and written expressly for Court performance is to strain interpretation.[1] Still, the universalities of Shakespeare's art have their topical aspect, and it is a fact that a special relation was established early on between his company and the new monarch. They became his players.

Only ten days after his arrival in the capital, James had through his secretary instructed the Keeper of the Privy Seal, 'our right trusty and welbeloved Counselor' Lord Cecil, to prepare for Shakespeare's company letters patent under the Great Seal of England. The royal warrant, dated 17 May 1603, furnished the Keeper of the Privy Seal with the form and also the actual wording of the formal Patent enrolled two days later. In Polonius's vein, the latter licenses and authorizes

theise our servauntes lawrence ffletcher William Shakespeare Richard Burbage Augustyne Phillippes John heninges henrie Condell William Sly Robert Armyn Richard Cowly and the rest of theire Assosiates freely to use and exercise the Arte and faculty of playinge Comedies Tragedies histories Enterludes moralls pastoralls Stageplaies and suche others like as theie have alreadie studied or hereafter shall use or studie aswell for the recreation of our lovinge Subjectes as for our Solace and pleasure when wee shall thincke good to see them duringe our pleasure. . . .

1 Some have gone so far; they are forcefully rebutted by Richard Levin, 'The King James Version of *Measure for Measure*', *Clio*, iii (1974), 129–63. The topical allusiveness of the play is argued by, among others, David Lloyd Stevenson, in 'The Historical Dimension in *Measure for Measure*: The Role of James I in the Play', an appendix to *The Achievement of Shakespeare's* Measure for Measure (Ithaca, 1966), pp. 134–66.

o

And whether these servants are publicly exercising their quality 'within theire nowe usuall howse called the Globe', or in any city, university town, or borough of the realm, the Patent instructs all justices, mayors, other officers, and loving subjects 'to allowe them such former Curtesies as hath bene given to men of theire place and quallitie and alsoe what further favour you shall shewe to theise our Servauntes for our sake', for such favour 'wee shall take kindlie at your handes'.

Lawrence Fletcher, mentioned for the first time as Shakespeare's associate, was a newcomer to the company, but he had twice acted before James in Scotland. The royal Patent (renewed in 1619 and again, after the king's death, in 1625) testifies to the pre-eminence of the company now known as the King's men. The other regular London troupes — the Admiral's company and Worcester's — passed under the patronage of less illustrious members of the royal family, and were henceforth called Queen Anne's men and Prince Henry's men.

None of the troupes was playing when James entered the metropolis. Once again the plague gripped London, and such was the virulence of the epidemic that he had to postpone his coronation for almost a year. When at last it took place on 15 March 1604, each of the King's men named in the Patent was entitled to receive, as a Groom of the Chamber and hence a member of the royal household, four and a half yards of scarlet-red cloth for his livery. This issue of cloth Sir George Home, Master of the Great Wardrobe, recorded in his account. Shakespeare's name, second in the Patent, this time heads the list.

On such occasions the Crown lavishly distributed red cloth. Not all the recipients, however, joined in the solemn coronation procession which, commencing at the Tower, wended its way — to the accompaniment of music, song, and orations — past symbolic pageants and through triumphal arches to Whitehall. Mainly the marchers consisted of noblemen and courtiers and government functionaries arranged in appropriate order by the Heralds. No players receive mention in the elaborate accounts, some written by theatre men, of the Magnificent Entertainment of King James.[1]

The players were, however, in attendance on a sensitive diplomatic occasion the next summer. For eighteen days in August they waited upon the new Spanish ambassador and his train at the Queen's palace, Somerset House, which James had placed at the ambassador's disposal. The payment of £21.12s. recorded in the Declared Accounts of the Treasurer of the King's Chamber specifically cites only Augustine Phillips and John Heminges, but Shakespeare, as a senior member of the company, must have been one of the 'tenne of theire ffellowes' who were also rewarded. England had not enjoyed diplomatic relations with Spain since the defeat of the Armada in 1588. Now, with a peace treaty in the air, the distinguished emissary from Madrid, Don Juan Fernandez de Velasco, no doubt received courtesies befitting his titles: Constable of Castile and Legion, Duke of the City of Fryas, Earl of Haro, Lord of the Towns of Villapano and Pedraca de la Syerra, Lord of the House of Velasco, and of the Seven Infants of Lara, Great Chamberlain unto Philip III King of Spain, Counsellor of State, and War, and President of Italy.[2]

No troupe acted more often before James than the King's men. They played at least 107 times between the issuance of the Patent and the year of Shakespeare's death. For the year commencing 1 November 1604 and ending 31 October 1605, the account of the Master of the Revels, Sir Edmund Tilney, lists eleven performances by his Majesty's players. There would have been a twelfth, but the play laid on for that night was cancelled.

Of the eleven pieces shown, seven were by Shakespeare, most of them past favourites from the repertoire — *The Comedy of Errors*, *Love's Labour's Lost*, *The Merry Wives of Windsor*, etc. — but the king also watched the newish *Othello* and (as mentioned) *Measure for Measure*. *The Merchant of Venice*, almost a decade old, he saw twice. The trial scene especially must have arrested his attention; justice and mercy again. In the Revels account the scribe considerately lists in the margin the poets who made the plays, but his spelling of Shakespeare — *Shaxberd* — is odd. Perhaps he was a newly arrived Scot who indulged his burr orthographically. The then Clerk of the Revels was William Honyng, but diligent investigation has not yet succeeded in determining whether he was a native of Scotland, or even whether he drew up this particular account.

1 BRL, ii. 368.
2 The inventory of the envoy's titles is given by Joseph Quincy Adams, *A Life of William Shakespeare* (1923), p. 364, and the occasion is described in detail by Ernest Law, *Shakespeare as a Groom of the Chamber* (1910).

‹ 1604 ›

The pla: Hallamas Day being the first of The poets
iers names Nouembar A play in the Banketinge hous wh mayd the
By the Kings Ma^tis Hous after hit maull Called the Moor of plaies &c:
plaiers: teins:

By his Ma^tis The Sunday ffollowinge A play
plaiers &. of the Merry wiues of winsor:.

By his Ma^tis On S^t stiuens night in the Shaxberd:
plaiers:. hall A play Caled Mesur for Mesur:

On St Iones night A maske &c
musike presented by the Erl of penbrok
the Lord willowbie: 6: Knightes more &c &c

By his Ma^tis On Inosents night The plaie of Shaxberd:
plaiers:. Errors

By the Queens On Sunday ffollowinge A plaie Hewood
Ma^tis plaiers: Caled How to Larne of a woman to wooe

The Boyes of On Newers Night A playe By Georg
the Chapell: Cauled All Foolles: Chapman

By his Ma^tis Betwin Newers Day And
plaiers:. Twelfe day A play of Loues Labours Lost:

13/2

160 THE REVELS ACCOUNT, 1604–5. *Public Record Office, Audit Office, Accounts, Various, A.O.
3/908/13. Transcript: TB, 50–1 (extracts); EKC, ii. 331–2. An abstract of the 1604–5 Revels Account was
found, about 1885, by H-P among the Malone papers in the Bodleian Library, where it is classified as Malone
MS. 29. This, the so-called 'Malone Scrap', is evidently in the hand of Sir William Musgrave, First Commis-
sioner of the Board of Audit. On 2 December 1799 he wrote to Malone, 'I enclose a memorandum about a MS.
which you have probably met with already — if not it may furnish matter for some of your illustrations of
Shakespear.' His reference, while sufficiently vague, may be to the Revels Account. In the next century Peter
Cunningham, chief clerk in the Audit Office, discovered — or rediscovered — Tilney's original account, and*

158 SHAKESPEARE AND HIS FELLOWS GRANTED SCARLET CLOTH FOR THE KING'S ENTRY INTO LONDON, 15 MAY 1604. *Public Record Office, Lord Chamberlain's Department, Special Events, L.C.2/4(5), f. 78. Transcript (extracts): TB, 48–9; EKC, ii. 73; BRL, ii. 368. H-P announced the record, and printed the relevant entries, in a communication to The Athenaeum for 30 April 1864 ('A Shakespearian Discovery', pp. 612–13). The list of players is continued on the next page of the accounts.*

159 THE KING'S MEN ATTEND UPON THE SPANISH AMBASSADOR, AUGUST 1604. *Public Record Office, Audit Office, Declared Accounts, Treasurer of the Chamber, A.O. 1/388/41. Transcript: TB, 49; BRL, ii. 372; G. E. Bentley, Shakespeare: A Biographical Handbook (New Haven, 1961), pp. 113–14. The document was first mentioned by H-P in The Athenaeum, 8 July 1871, p. 51, and printed in the same paper by Charlotte Carmichael Stopes on 12 March 1910 ('Shakespeare of the Court', pp. 319–20). That year Ernest Law, who had come upon the record independently, made it the basis for his monograph, Shakespeare as a Groom of the Chamber.*

The plaiers | On Twelfe Night | The poete

By his Ma^tis plaiers: — On the 7. of January was played the play of Henry the fift:

By his Ma^tis plaiers: — The 8. of January: A play Cauled Every on out of his Umor

By his Ma^tis plaiers: — On Candelmas night A playe Every one In his Umor

The Sunday ffollowing A playe proued And discharged

By his Ma^tis plaiers: — On Shroufunday A play of the Marthant of venis — Shaxberd

By his Ma^tis plaiers: — On Shroumonday A Tragidye of the Spanishe Maz:

By his ma^tis players: — On Shroutusday A play Cauled The Marchant of venis Againe Comanded By the Kings Matie — Shaxberd:

published it, under Shakespeare Society auspices, in Extracts from the Accounts of the Revels at Court, in the reigns of Queen Elizabeth and King James I *(1842), pp. 203–5. The authenticity of the document has been challenged, by H-P among others (*Outlines, *ii. 161–7), and more recently by Samuel A. Tannenbaum (*Shakespeare Forgeries in the Revels Account *(1928)). Such conservative authorities as Greg and Chambers have, however, defended it as genuine, and in* The Disputed Revels Account *(1930) their verdict has received corroboration from A. E. Stamp on the basis of a range of evidence, including chemical and microscopic examination. The controversy now appears to have been settled. The document is on permanent display in the Record Office Museum (case W, item 2). Two pages (f. 2^{r-v}) are here reproduced, with slight reduction.*

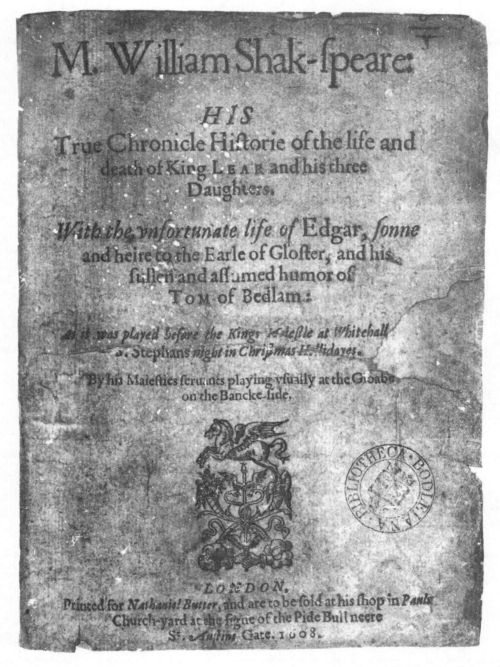

161 *KING LEAR* ENTERED ON THE STATIONERS' REGISTER, 26 NOVEMBER 1607. *Stationers' Hall, Register C, f. 161ᵛ. Transcript: Arber, iii. 366; EKC, i. 463; Greg, i. 24.*

162 *KING LEAR*: THE FIRST QUARTO, 1608, TITLE-PAGE. *Copy in the Bodleian Library; shelf-mark: Arch. G. d. 42. STC 22292. Greg 265.*

The first decade of the seventeenth century represents the high tide in the artistic fortunes of the King's men. These years saw the first production by them of (among others) *Othello*, *King Lear*, *Macbeth*, and *Antony and Cleopatra*. Shakespeare's foremost rival gave the same company *Volpone* and *The Alchemist*. *King Lear*, perhaps for our time the quintessential Shakespearian tragedy, was first acted (as seems likely) in early 1605 at the Globe, with Burbage in the title role and Armin as the Fool. On 26 December 1606 it was played before King James at Whitehall: thus much we learn from the Stationers' Register entry and the title-page of the first Quarto, both of which give the author deferential prominence. Such acknowledgement was unusual in an age in which dramatic publication was as often as not anonymous.

Shakespeare also received the more equivocal compliment of having foisted upon him plays for whose paternity the tests of evidence absolve him. Earlier editions of apocryphal plays — *Locrine* in 1595, *Thomas Lord Cromwell* in 1602 — had borne the initials 'W.S.', but *The London Prodigal* (1605) and *A Yorkshire Tragedy* (1608) broadcast Shakespeare's name unabashedly. The King's servant now stood at the height of his celebrity as well as of his powers.

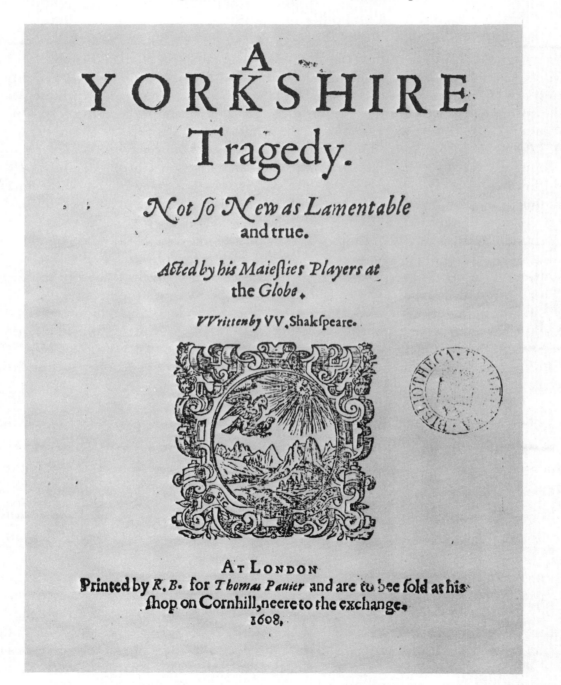

163   *A YORKSHIRE TRAGEDY*: 1608 QUARTO, TITLE-PAGE. *Copy in the Bodleian Library; shelfmark: Arch. G. d. 41. STC 22340. Greg 272.*

The mythos ratifies fame after its own fashion. Once again Davenant is the ultimate source. An advertisement to an anonymously edited *Collection of Poems . . . By Mr. William Shakespeare*, printed for the stationer Bernard Lintot about 1709, offers this information:

> That moſt learn'd Prince, and great Patron of Learning, King *James* the Firſt, was pleas'd with his own Hand to write an amicable Letter to Mr. *Shakeſpeare*; which Letter, tho now loſt, remain'd long in the Hands of Sir *William D'avenant*, as a credible Perſon now living can teſtify.

164 ADVERTISEMENT TO LINTOT'S EDITION OF SHAKESPEARE'S *POEMS* (*c.* 1709), sig. A2ᵛ. *Printed in EKC, ii. 270.*

In his marginalia Oldys identified the 'credible person' as John Sheffield, Duke of Buckingham (1648–1721), and reported that Buckingham had it from Davenant himself.[1] It is a pity that the latter never published the 'amicable Letter', for nobody has since managed to produce it.

In the spring of 1604 Augustine Phillips died. He and Shakespeare had worked together for over a decade, ever since the formation of the Chamberlain's troupe after the great plague of 1592–3. Like Shakespeare and a handful of other players, Phillips was one of the original sharers in the company. He and Shakespeare acted together in Jonson's *Every Man in his Humour* and *Sejanus*. Phillips also performed in Shakespeare's plays; which parts we do not know, but his name appears fourth in the First Folio in the list of 'the Principall Actors in all these Playes'. During these active years Phillips and his family — his wife Anne and their four daughters — lived close to the Bankside theatre district in Bullhead Alley in St. Saviour's, Southwark, but shortly before he drew up his will in May 1604 they had moved into a newly purchased house in Mortlake, Surrey. In his testament, proved 16 May, the player remembered his fellows in the King's company. To the hired men he left £5 to be distributed equally amongst them. His apprentice Samuel Gilborne inherited (along with other bequests) Phillips's purple cloak and mouse-coloured velvet hose. Shakespeare heads the list of sharers in the will: 'Item I geve and bequeathe to my ffellowe william Shakespeare a Thirty shillings peece in gould.' Only one other housekeeper (Condell) received as large an individual bequest. It testifies to Shakespeare's warm personal relations with a valued colleague.

165 AUGUSTINE PHILLIPS BEQUEATHS SHAKESPEARE A THIRTY-SHILLING GOLD PIECE, 4 MAY 1605. *Public Record Office, Prob. 10/Box 232. Transcript (extract): TB, 52; EKC, ii. 73–4. George Chalmers first brought the will to public notice; he prints it complete in* An Apology for the Believers in the Shakspeare-Papers, which were exhibited in Norfolk-Street *(1797), pp. 431–5n. J. Payne Collier also gives the full text in* The History of English Dramatic Poetry to the Time of Shakespeare *(1879 ed.), iii. 327–9. EKC cites the registered copy, P.C.C. 31 Hayes (now Public Record Office, Prob. 11/105), but his transcript seems to derive from the copy reproduced (with slight reduction) here.*

1 EKC, ii. 280.

Literary geniuses are not, on the whole, celebrated for their amiable dispositions — 'Nice people are two a penny', George Mikes consoles himself; 'great writers are few and far between' — yet, in an age of sharp-toothed satire, almost everyone seems to have thought well of Shakespeare. Only Greene, dying without room for magnanimity in his heart, speaks harshly of him, to be followed immediately by Chettle's report that divers of worship commended Shakespeare's uprightness of dealing. The obscure Anthony Scoloker, in his epistle to *Diaphantus, or The Passions of Love*, remarks on 'Friendly Shakespeare's Tragedies'. Did the two men know one another, as the phrase suggests? This reference excepted, Scoloker is utterly unknown. John Davies of Hereford calls Shakespeare 'good *Will*' in *The Scourge of Folly*; in *Microcosmus* Davies owns to loving players, and sees 'W.S.' as one transcending, by his qualities of character, the baseness of the quality:

> And though the *stage* doth staine pure gentle *bloud*,
> Yet generous yee are in *minde* and *moode*.[1]

A minor playwright for a rival company describes Shakespeare as 'so deere lov'd a neighbor'.[2] In this period the impressions of contemporaries sometimes find their distillation in a single apt epithet that clings to a name. Jonson, who aspired to be remembered as Honest Ben, is instead known as Rare Ben Jonson, *honest* falling to the unassuming Tom Heywood. Man proposeth, but posterity disposeth. Shakespeare is enshrined in consciousness as Gentle Will Shakespeare. One cannot imagine a more fitting designation for the innate gentleman who was not gently born.

These miscellaneous testimonials of the minnows who swam in the Elizabethan literary and theatrical stream receive confirmation from the mythos. Aubrey, in touch with a living tradition through the actor Beeston, admired Shakespeare the more because 'he was not a company keeper' in Shoreditch — he 'wouldnt be debauched', excusing himself when approached ('& if invited to, writ: he was in paine'). So Aubrey jotted down, helter-skelter, on a miscellaneous scrap. In his comparatively polished Brief Life of Shakespeare, he makes the point more affirmatively: 'He was a handsome well shap't man: very good company, and of a very readie and pleasant smooth Witt.'[3] In the next century Rowe once more summed up a tradition: 'Besides the advantages of his Wit, he was in himself a good-natur'd Man, of great sweetness in his Manners, and a most agreeable Companion; so that it is no wonder if with so many good Qualities he made himself acquainted with the best Conversations of those Times.' That was in London. In Stratford,

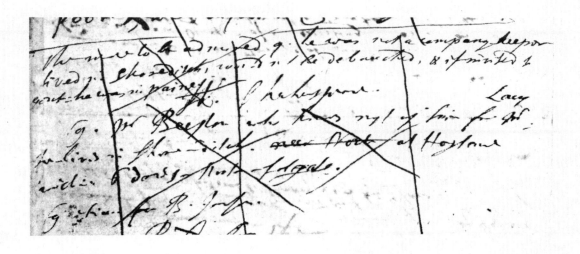

166 THE AUBREY SCRAP, 1681. *Bodleian Library, Aubrey MS. 8, f. 45ᵛ. Transcript: EKC, ii. 252; BRL, i. 318. Aubrey's note appears on a leaf inserted in the third part* (Auctarium Vitarum) *of the* Brief Lives. *In his edition (1898) Andrew Clark incorporated the memorandum in the life of William Beeston, but later authorities have shown that Shakespeare is the subject; see EKC, ii. 252. For Aubrey's Brief Life of Shakespeare, see above, item 57.*

1   John Davies, *Microcosmus* (1603), p. 215; quoted by EKC, ii. 213.
2   William Barksted, *Myrrha, the Mother of Adonis: or, Lustes Prodegies* (1607), sig. E1; quoted by EKC, ii. 216.
3   See item 57, p. 58, above.

Shake=speare was godfather
to one of Ben: Johnsons children,
and after the christning being in a
deepe study, Johnson came to cheere himp,
and askt him why he was so Melancholy? no
faith Ben: (sayes he) not I, but I haue beene
considering a great while what should bethe fittest
gift for me to bestow vpon my god=child, and I
haue resolud at last; I prythe what, sayes he? I
faith Ben: He e'en giue him a douzen good Lattin
Spoones, and thou shalt translate them.

167 L'ESTRANGE'S ANECDOTE OF SHAKESPEARE AND JONSON, 1629–55. *British Library, MS. Harley 6395, f. 2. Transcript:* The Shakspere Allusion-Book, *ed. John Munro (Oxford, 1909), ii. 8; Ben Jonson,* Works, *ed. C. H. Herford and Percy and Evelyn Simpson (Oxford, 1925–52), i. 186; EKC, ii. 243. The manuscript, bearing the title* Merry Passages and Jeasts, *is anonymous, but almost certainly compiled by L'Estrange. The initials 'S[ir] N. L.' following many items suggest that these were set down after 1629, when L'Estrange became a baronet; he died in 1655. From the index ascription to 'Mr Dun:' some students have inferred that John Donne was the source. Elsewhere in the index, however, the poet's name is spelt 'Donne'; 'Dun:' is most probably, as Munro suggests, an abbreviation for Duncomb, a Capt. Duncomb receiving credit for several of the anecdotes. The entry was first printed by Edward Capell in* Notes and Various Readings to Shakespeare *[1779–80], pt. 2, pp. 93–4, from a transcript by the historian and biographer Thomas Birch. In* Anecdotes and Traditions, Illustrative of Early English History and Literature *(Camden Society, 1839), William J. Thoms edited a selection from L'Estrange's 'upwards of six hundred articles, of which the greater portion are unfit for publication'.*

168 BURGH'S ANECDOTE OF SHAKESPEARE AND JONSON, *c.* 1650. *Bodleian Library, MS. Ashmole 38, p. 181. Transcript: EKC, ii. 246. H-P first printed the anecdote (Life, p. 186). 'It is not particularly easy to appreciate the exact force of the wit here exhibited', he remarks, 'but the anecdote comes to us in a "questionable shape", and is most probably corrupted.' For another Burgh item, see 148 above.*

169 PLUME'S ANECDOTES OF SHAKESPEARE AND JONSON, *c.* 1657. *MS. 25, ff. 77, 161, in the Plume Library at Maldon, Essex. The first item is repeated, with minor variants, on f. 51 (bis). Transcript:* The Shakspere Allusion-Book, *ed. John Munro (Oxford, 1909), ii. 68; Jonson,* Works, *ed. C. H. Herford and Percy and Evelyn Simpson (Oxford, 1925–52), i. 184; EKC, ii. 247. For another Plume anecdote, and details of first publication, see item 33, above.*

'His pleasurable Wit, and good Nature, engag'd him in the Acquaintance, and entitled him to the Friendship of the Gentlemen of the Neighbourhood.'[1]

Nowhere, one suspects, was Shakespeare's good nature more severely tested than in his complexly ambivalent relationship with Jonson; ambivalent at least on the latter's side.[2] The mythos fastens upon the rivalry between the two masters. In the seventeenth century, hearsay anecdotes found a place in the notations of Sir Nicholas L'Estrange, Nicholas Burgh, and Thomas Plume. These anecdotes show agile Will overcoming ponderous Ben. Shakespeare, standing godfather to one of Jonson's children, and faced with the necessity of thinking of an appropriate christening gift, comes out of 'a deepe study' inspired. 'I'le e'en give him a douzen good Lattin Spoones', he tells Ben, 'and thou shalt translate them.' (For modern readers this feeble jest requires a gloss: *latten* was a brass or brass-like alloy.) In a merry tavern meeting Jonson begins his own epitaph ('Here lies Ben Johnson that was once one'), then passes the pen to Shakespeare, who completes it:

> Who while hee liv'de was a sloe things [*sic*]
> And now being dead is Nothinge.

This tradition finds most memorable expression in the famous passage in Bishop Fuller's brief memoir of Shakespeare for his *History of the Worthies of England*.

> Many were the *wit-combates* betwixt him and *Ben Johnson*, which two I behold like a *spanish great Gallion*, and an *English man of War*; Master *Johnson* (like the former) was built far higher in Learning; *Solid*, but *Slow* in his performances. *Shake-spear* with the *English-man of War*, lesser in *bulk*, but lighter in *sailing*, could turn with all tides, tack about and take advantage of all winds, by the quicknes of his Wit and Invention. He died *Anno Domini* 16... and was buried at *Stratford* upon *Avon*, the Town of his Nativity.

170 THOMAS FULLER ON SHAKESPEARE AND JONSON. *From* The History of the Worthies of England (*1662*), '*Warwickshire*', *p. 126*.

'Which two I behold', writes Fuller. The picture he had formed exists only in the mind's eye; this is a literary evocation, not a reminiscence derived from report. The rest of Fuller's short biography, starkly devoid of concrete data, confirms the impression. Although he perambulated the countryside in quest of matter for his *Worthies*, he failed to dig up the year of Shakespeare's death, for which he leaves a pathetic blank in his text ('He died *Anno Domini* 16 . . .'). Yet the date is plain to see on the monument in Stratford Church.

The anecdotes, however dubious, suggest a good-natured competition between these antithetical giants — the handsome, well-shaped Shakespeare; corpulent Jonson with his mountain belly — who conceived and fashioned their art on mutually exclusive principles. The tradition of Jonson's malevolence derives from the scattered aspersions in his writings. In his Prologue to the revised version of *Every Man in his Humour* he glances scathingly at a contemporary playwright so indifferent to the neo-classical unities as to have a swaddled child metamorphose into a bearded sexagenarian, or a few rusty swords enact the Wars of the Roses, or a Chorus waft audiences over the seas. The Induction to *Bartholomew Fair* sneers at 'those that beget *Tales*, *Tempests*, and such like *Drolleries*'. It is not difficult to guess the object of these shafts. Still Shakespeare's closest friends in the King's men invited Jonson to contribute the principal eulogy to the First Folio, and he responded with one of the most admired commendatory poems in the language. When not under encomiastic obligations, in notebooks that lay unpublished until after his death, Jonson recalls affectionately — but not uncritically — his friend already dead a decade and more. Ben's tribute gains rather than loses force from the stubborn reservations, dictated by artistic conscience, about Shakespeare's fluency. These after all pertain to the craft, not the craftsman. 'Hee was (indeed) honest. . . .' From Jonson there can be no higher praise.

1 Nicholas Rowe, *Some Account of the Life, &c. of Mr. William Shakespear*, in Shakespeare, *Works*, ed. Rowe (1709), i, pp. viii, xxxv–xxxvi.
2 I have dealt more largely with this subject in 'Shakespeare and Jonson: Fact and Myth', *Elizabethan Theatre II*, ed. David Galloway (Toronto, 1970), pp. 1–19. See also below, pp. 258–60.

I remember, the Players have often mentioned it as an honour to *Shake-* De *Shake-*
speare, that in his writing, (whatsoever he penn'd) hee never blotted out *speare*
line. My answer hath beene, would he had blotted a thousand. Which *nostrat.*
they thought a malevolent speech. I had not told posterity this, but for
their ignorance, who choose that circumstance to commend their friend

by, wherein he most faulted. And to justifie mine owne candor, (for I
lov'd the man, and doe honour his memory (on this side Idolatry) as
much as any.) Hee was (indeed) honest, and of an open, and free nature: had an excellent *Phantsie*; brave notions, and gentle expressions:
wherein hee flow'd with that facility, that sometime it was necessary he
should be stop'd: *Sufflaminandus erat*; as *Augustus* said of *Haterius*. His
wit was in his owne power; would the rule of it had beene so too. Many
times hee fell into those things, could not escape laughter: As when hee
said in the person of *Cæsar*, one speaking to him; *Cæsar thou dost me wrong*.
Hee replyed: *Cæsar did never wrong, but with just cause*: and such like;
which were ridiculous. But hee redeemed his vices, with his vertues.
There was ever more in him to be pray<sup>sed, then to be pardoned.

Augustus in Hat.

171 JONSON ON 'OUR FELLOW COUNTRYMAN SHAKESPEARE', 1626–37. *From* Timber: or, Discoveries; Made upon Men and Matter *(1641), in Ben Jonson,* Workes *(1640 title-page), pp. 97–8. Copy in the Bodleian Library; shelfmark: Douce. I. 303. STC 14753.*

A romantic legend brings Jonson and Shakespeare together, along with Donne, Beaumont, and other men of talent and genius, at the Mermaid Tavern in Bread Street, where flowed rich canary wine and words nimble and full of subtle wit. A tradition so firmly entrenched in literary folklore no doubt renders analysis impotent, but the unconvivial biographer must nevertheless observe that the Mermaid sessions did not get under way until after Shakespeare had retired permanently from the London theatrical scene.[1] He did, however, know the tavern and its genial host, William Johnson, a vintner who more than once got into trouble with the law by letting his customers have a morsel of meat on fish days. Johnson was a party to Shakespeare's last property transaction.[2] For a while the poet had lodgings not far from Bread Street, to the east of St. Paul's.

In 1604, and perhaps for a time before and after, 'one mr Shakespeare . . . laye in the house' of Christopher Mountjoy, a French Huguenot tire-maker (i.e. manufacturer of ladies' ornamental headgear) in Cripplegate ward, an enclave within the north-west corner of the city walls. Perhaps Shakespeare heard of the Mountjoys from his friends the Fields. Jacqueline Field would know Mme Mountjoy from the French church in London; besides, from 1600 the Fields lived in Wood Street, close to the Mountjoy house. The latter, a substantial dwelling with shop on the ground floor and lodgings above, was situated at the north-east corner of Monkswell (Muggle) and Silver Streets. A map drawn a half-century earlier depicts the twin-gabled house with its eaves extending over the shop front.

On the opposite corner stood the 'great house built of stone and timber, now called the Lord Windsors house, of old time belonging to the Nevels'.[3] Silver Street, so named from the silver-smiths dwelling there, had 'divers fayre houses'. Just down the road was the parish church of St. Olave's, 'a small thing, and without any noteworthy monuments'. Several of the city companies had their halls in the area — the Barber-Surgeons, the Haberdashers, and (a little farther off) the Wax-chandlers — and maintained almshouses providing a roof and pittance for decayed

1   I. A. Shapiro analyses this legend in 'The "Mermaid Club"', *Modern Language Review*, xlv (1950), 6–17.
2   See below, p. 223. Leslie Hotson has investigated Johnson's career ('Shakespeare and Mine Host of the Mermaid', *Shakespeare's Sonnets Dated and Other Essays* (1949), pp. 76–88).
3   The references in this paragraph to Silver Street and environs are from John Stow, *A Survey of London*, ed. C. L. Kingsford (Oxford, 1908), i. 291ff. The quoted phrases about Paul's Walk are from John Earl, *Microcosmographie* (1628), sig. I11ᵛ. A. L. Rowse, *Shakespeare the Man* (1973), p. 197, has also furnished a few details.

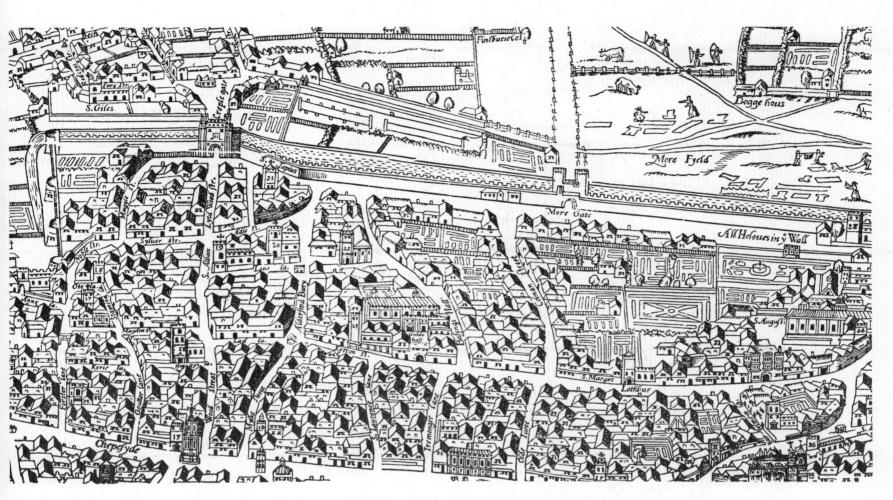

172 THE 'AGAS' MAP, 'CIVITAS LONDINUM', 1553–9 (detail). *From the copy in the Guildhall Library. The engraver and antiquary George Vertue first attributed this woodcut map to Agas, but the evidence for the ascription is very fragile. Although the extant copies were printed* c. *1633, the map depicts the capital as it appeared in the period 1553–9. Agas was born around 1540. Houses are represented in conventionalized fashion. For a fuller account, see Ida Darlington and James Howgego,* Printed Maps of London circa 1553–1850 *(1964), pp. 12–16, 54–5. The portion here reproduced is slightly reduced.*

members. Shakespeare could handily stroll over to his friends Heminges and Condell in the adjoining parish of St. Mary's, Aldermanbury, where the actor-sharers lived as pillars of the community: Condell a churchwarden, and Heminges a sidesman. If the middle-class respectability of Silver Street became oppressive, Shakespeare could escape, down Wood Street or Foster Lane, to Paul's Churchyard, with its displays of the latest books, or listen in the Middle Aisle of St. Paul's to the 'strange humming or buzze, mixt of walking, tongues and feet' — the 'still roare or loud whisper' of humanity.

Christopher Mountjoy did a flourishing business creating his tires of gold and silver and precious stones for high-born ladies (the Queen herself once patronized him). Silver Street was the centre of the wig trade — 'All her teeth were made i' the Blacke-*Friers*', Jonson's Captain Otter remarks in *Epicoene*: 'both her eyebrowes i' the *Strand*, and her hair in *Silver-street*'. Meanwhile Mme Mountjoy, like the wives in Elizabethan city comedies, carried on an amour with a tradesman. He was Henry Wood, a mercer and cloth trader in Swan Alley, a short distance (along Coleman Street) from Silver Street. We know about the affair because Mme Mountjoy consulted the physician-magus Simon Forman when she became pregnant. A note in a Forman case-book reads, rather mysteriously, 'Mary Mountjoy alained [i.e. concealed]'; matter here for a sequel to *The Merry Wives of Windsor*. The pregnancy proved a false alarm, Mme Mountjoy and Mrs. Wood did not (as they for a time considered doing) keep a shop together, the Mountjoys' union remained intact.[1]

1   A. L. Rowse has brought these facts to light ('Secrets of Shakespeare's Landlady', *The Times*, 23 April 1973, p. 6). See also Rowse's *Simon Forman: Sex and Society in Shakespeare's Age* (1974), pp. 98–9.

173 THE BELOTT–MOUNTJOY SUIT: DANIELL NICHOLAS'S DEPOSITION, 19 JUNE 1612 (extract). *Public Record Office, Court of Requests, Documents of Shakespearian Interest, Req. 4/1. Transcript: EKC, ii. 92–3; BRL, ii. 432. In 1909 Charles William Wallace, working with his wife Hulda in the Public Record Office, found twenty-six documents pertaining to the suit; he announced and summarized them in an article, 'New Shakespeare Discoveries: Shakespeare as a Man among Men', in* Harper's Monthly Magazine, *cxx (1910), 489–510. Later that year Wallace published transcripts of all twenty-six in the Nebraska University Studies, vol. x, no. 4 ('Shakespeare and his London Associates as Revealed in Recently Discovered Documents', pp. 261–360). The deposition here is reduced somewhat.*

They had an only child, a daughter Mary, who helped in the shop along with the three apprentices, Stephen Belott, Gui Asture, and Ufranke de la Coles (we know the names of the last two only from Forman's fractured French). Belott was the son of a French widow whose second husband, Humphrey Fludd, described as 'one of the King's trumpetors', had bound him to Mountjoy. After completing his apprentice term in 1604, Stephen went off to see the world, but he soon returned to Silver Street, this time on a fixed salary. Shakespeare, then living in the house, was drawn into a domestic drama involving the Mountjoys and their former apprentice. We know because eight years afterwards, in the late spring of 1612, the poet came up to London from Stratford to testify in a Court of Requests suit, *Belott* v. *Mountjoy*.

The depositions unravel the history of a courtship and its aftermath. Belott was an eligible bachelor who, everybody agreed, conducted himself irreproachably in the Mountjoy ménage. Shakespeare testified that Stephen 'did well and honestly behave himselfe' and was 'A very good and industrious servant in the said service' — although he did not (in Shakespeare's hearing) avouch 'that he had gott any great profitt and comodytye by the service'. Mountjoy, however, did 'beare and shew great good will and affeccion' to the young man. The tire-maker and his wife fancied their industrious former apprentice for a son-in-law, and encouraged the 'shewe of goodwill' — the words are those of Joan Johnson, then a servant in the house — 'betweene the plaintiff and defendantes daughter Marye'. She goes on: 'And as she Remembreth the defendant did send and perswade one m^r Shakespeare that laye in the house to perswade the plaintiff to the same marriadge.' The services of a match-maker were needed because Belott, a practical sort, was holding out for a more advantageous marriage settlement. Daniell Nicholas, a friend of the family, furnishes some details:

Shakespeare tould this deponent that the defendant tould him that yf the plaintiff would Marrye the said Marye his daughter he would geve him the plaintiff A some of monney with her for A porcion in Marriadge with her. And that yf he the plaintiff did not marry with her the said Marye and shee with the plaintiff shee should never coste him the defendant her ffather A groat, Whereuppon And in Regard Mr Shakespeare hadd tould them that they should have A some of monney for A porcion from the father they Weare made suer by m^r Shakespeare by gevinge there Consent, and agreed to marrye.

The wedding took place on 4 November 1604, in the parish church of St. Olave. The records do not show whether Shakespeare attended.

Complications followed upon conjugality. Instead of staying on in the Silver Street shop, as Mountjoy expected, the couple set up a rival establishment with an apprentice of their own. Belott had looked forward to a portion of £60 with Mary, and, after her father's death, an inheritance of £200. Instead the old man fobbed them off with £10 for their purse, and some paltry household stuff: old furniture and an old feather bolster, worn blankets, coarse napkins, a bobbin box and two pairs of scissors — small scissors at that. When Mme Mountjoy, who had urged her husband to be more generous, died in 1606, the Belotts moved back to Silver Street to keep house for the widower and become partners in the business. But arguments over money followed, Stephen and Mary packed up and left, Mountjoy sank into dissipation. These vicissitudes took place over a space of years. Finally rumours circulated that Mountjoy intended to cut off his daughter and her husband penniless. Hence the suit.

174 THE BELOTT–MOUNTJOY SUIT: SHAKESPEARE CITED TO APPEAR AS A WITNESS, 1612. *Public Record Office, Court of Requests, Documents of Shakespearian Interest, Req. 4/1. Transcript: BRL, ii. 428. For the announcement and first publication of the documents relating to this action, see preceding item.*

175 THE BELOTT–MOUNTJOY SUIT: SHAKESPEARE'S DEPOSITION, 11 MAY 1612. *Public Record Office, Court of Requests, Documents of Shakespearian Interest, Req. 4/1. Transcript: TB, 68–9; EKC, ii. 91–2; BRL, ii. 429–30. For the announcement and first publication of the documents relating to this action, see item 173, above. The deposition, now permanently displayed in the Record Office Museum (case W, item 3), is reduced by one third in the present reproduction.*

The court had the task of determining what financial settlement had been agreed upon at the time of the marriage. Belott persuaded Nicholas to go with his wife to Shakespeare to ascertain the truth about 'how muche and what' Mountjoy had promised. 'And askinge Shakespeare therof, he [Shakespeare] Answered that he promissed yf the plaintiff would marrye with Marye his the defendantes onlye daughter, he the defendant would by his promise as he Remembered geve the plaintiff with her in marriadge about the some of ffyftye poundes in money and Certayne houshould stuffe.' Such evidence was of course hearsay; vague hearsay, at that. Only Shakespeare himself could resolve the question, and the two sides must have looked forward, with hope or apprehension, to his testimony. But Shakespeare's memory of the precise details of events long since past failed him. Why should he have recalled? He had no personal stake in the matter. Mountjoy had promised Belott a dowry of some sort, and there had been many conferences, but what the portion was, or when it was to be paid, Shakespeare could not say, nor could he vouch that 'the defendant promissed the plaintiff twoe hundered poundes with his daughter Marye at the tyme of his decease'. The witness likewise professed ignorance of 'what implementes and necessaries of houshold stuff' Mountjoy gave with Mary.

That was on 11 May 1612. The court appointed a second hearing for 19 June, and Shakespeare's name appears in the margin for a set of interrogatories; but he did not testify again. Others did — Nicholas, William Eaton (then an apprentice in Silver Street), Mountjoy's tire-maker brother Nowell — and although they all agreed that Shakespeare had acted as honest broker in the match, nobody could remember the sums discussed. The court in the end referred the case for arbitration to 'the Reverend & grave overseers and Elders of the french Church in London', who decided that both father and son-in-law were a bad lot — 'tous 2 pere & gendre desbauchez' — but awarded Belott twenty nobles (£6.13s.4d.). A year later Mountjoy had still not paid the sum, but (according to later church registers) he was able to afford to keep up his licentious life: 'sa vie desreglée & desbordé'.

Of all the Shakespeare records, only the Belott–Mountjoy suit shows him living amidst the raw materials for domestic comedy. The proceedings, for all their mercenary or sordid overtones, reveal the poet-dramatist of superhuman powers as a somewhat baffled mortal, or (in the discoverer's words) as 'a man among men'.[1] One biographer has even envisaged Shakespeare buying a beginner's conversational manual in Paul's Churchyard, and with Mary alongside to help him in his halting efforts, learning the elements of spoken French he would put to such good use in the scene of Princess Katherine's English lesson.[2] 'Comment appelez-vous la main en Anglais?' 'La main? Elle est appelée de hand.' A pretty thought; but Shakespeare seems to have written *Henry V* before lodging with the Mountjoys.

Meanwhile important events were taking place in the fortunes of his company. In August 1608 the King's men assumed the lease of the Blackfriars theatre. As a principal sharer, Shakespeare would have a voice in this crucial decision. The Blackfriars, it will be recalled, was the disused monastery that James Burbage a decade earlier had selected for a projected playhouse, only to abandon the scheme after investing heavily in renovations. His sons extended the property, and leased it to Henry Evans, a Welsh scrivener turned entrepreneur of the children's troupes. Evans used Blackfriars as a private showcase for the boy actors — the 'little eyases' to whom Hamlet refers. They had a tumultuous history. More than once Blackfriars children incurred the displeasure of the authorities, and finally, with their production in 1608 of Chapman's *Conspiracy and Tragedy of Charles, Duke of Byron*, they so scandalized the French ambassador that the king ordered their suppression. Evans now surrendered his lease to Richard Burbage. The playhouses were anyway closed because of the plague. By the late autumn of 1609, however, the King's men had begun operations in their new house in the heart of London, only some hundred yards south-west of St. Paul's.

It was, compared with the Globe, an intimate theatre. The rectangular auditorium into which James Burbage had converted the upper-storey Parliament Chamber of the Upper Frater

1   C. W. Wallace, 'New Shakespeare Discoveries: Shakespeare as a Man among Men', *Harper's Monthly Magazine*, cxx (1910), 489–510.
2   Adams, *Life of William Shakespeare*, pp. 380–1.

P

measured 46 feet by 66 feet. At one end the tiring-house extended across the full breadth of the hall; on the second storey of the façade three boxes served for music room, Lords' room, and (when required) action above. Candles suspended in branches illuminated the stage. The house accommodated around 700 spectators, only a fraction of the 3,000 on Bankside. The whole audience — whether in pit, galleries, or boxes — sat, and for this privilege they paid a minimum admission of sixpence: six times the price of the cheapest entry to the Globe. At Blackfriars, in a glittering and hushed atmosphere, the King's men catered for a sophisticated clientele of courtiers, hangers-on, professional types, and intelligentsia, rather than the heterogeneous masses who frequented the Globe, and who (it may be said for them) did not find *Hamlet* or *King Lear* over their heads.[1]

Theatre historians have seen the transfer as profoundly influencing the stagecraft of Shakespeare's last plays: henceforth, Professor Bentley suggests, Shakespeare wrote 'with the Blackfriars in mind and not the Globe'.[2] An intimate theatre, without unruly groundlings, invited intimate scenes; sentiment rather than passion would now reign. So the theory goes. Act II, scene ii, of *Cymbeline* may be said to exemplify the new mode. Iachimo emerges from the chest in Imogen's bedchamber, lit by a single flickering taper; he makes notes of the surroundings — the window, the adornment of the bed, the painted arras — and, more especially, of the sleeping girl with the mole on her left breast; then he removes her bracelet and tiptoes back into the chest, closing the lid over his head. It is easier to imagine such a scene in the enclosed, candle-lit Blackfriars than in the open-air vastness of the Globe.

Although the notion is intriguing, the actual stage provenance of *Cymbeline*, *The Winter's Tale*, and *The Tempest* is not clear; *Henry VIII*, we know, had its *première* at the Globe. For the King's men did not quit their Bankside theatre after 1609. The Blackfriars served as their winter house; come spring, they were playing at the Globe again. There, in 1611, Simon Forman saw *Macbeth* on 20 April, and *The Winter's Tale* on 15 May. He also caught a performance of *Cymbeline* but neglected to specify either date or theatre, although one guesses it was the Globe. In his *Bocke of Plaies* the astrologer has left for posterity his unique eyewitness accounts of these productions.[3] Autolycus's roguish antics pointed a useful moral: 'beware of trustinge feined beggars or fawninge fellouse.' The bedchamber scene in *Cymbeline* made an impression of a different sort. 'Remember . . .', Forman writes, 'in the depest of the night she being aslepe. he opened the cheste & cam forth of yt. And vewed her in her bed and the markes of her body. & toke a wai her braslet. . . .'

Whether they acted in small or large purpose-built theatres like the Blackfriars and Globe, or on temporary stages at Court or while on provincial tour, the King's men adapted the plays in their repertoire to changing conditions of performance. Such was the fabled flexibility of Elizabethan dramaturgy. The significance of the Blackfriars move lies more in its social and economic dimension, from which (needless to say) the aesthetic is not entirely separable. Sensing which way the wind was blowing, the company opted for the Court, not the city. Of course they could not have predicted that the fissures already present in society would eventually so widen as to plunge the nation into a civil war which would put an end to all but surreptitious theatrical activity. They did not need to make such predictions; the move made sense as a business gamble, and paid off handsomely. The King's men knew how to please the new, more narrowly based, audience. Tragedy now gives way to tragi-comedy as the dominant genre.

The Blackfriars lease of 9 August 1608 created a syndicate of seven sharers: Richard and Cuthbert Burbage, Thomas Evans, Shakespeare, Heminges, Condell, and Sly. Each member made his contribution of £5.14s.4d. towards the annual rent of £40. Later that year Sly died, so Shakespeare's share (and assessment) rose to one-sixth. The Blackfriars house proved much more profitable than the Globe. Twenty years after Shakespeare's death a share in the former was

---

1   The public and private playhouses, their audiences and repertoires, are analysed by Alfred Harbage in his influential *Shakespeare and the Rival Traditions* (New York, 1952).

2   G. E. Bentley, *Shakespeare and his Theatre* (Lincoln, Neb., 1964), p. 88. For a recent searching critique of Bentley, see J. A. Lavin, 'Shakespeare and the Second Blackfriars', *Elizabethan Theatre III*, ed. David Galloway (Toronto, 1973), pp. 66–81.

3   Forman also saw a performance of *Richard II* at the Globe on 30 April 1611, but his description does not accord with Shakespeare's play, and suggests that the King's men had another piece on the same reign.

Of Cimbaline king of England

Remember also the storri of Cymbalin king
of England in Lucius tyme. howe Lucius
Cam from Octauus Cesar for Tribut and
being denied. after sent Lucius wth a greate
Armi of Souldiars who landed at milford
hauen. and affter wer vanquisshed by Cimbalin and Lucius taken prisoner and all
by means of 3 outlawes of the wch 2 of them
were the sonns of Cimbalin stolen from
him when they were but 2 yers old by an
old man whom Cymbalin banished. and
he kept them as his own sonns 20 yers wt
him in A Caue. And howe on of them slewe
Cloten that was the quens sonne goinge
To milford hauen to sick the loue of Innogen
the kinge daughter whom he had banished also
for louinge his daughter. and howe the stalion
that cam from her loue conveied him selfe
into a Cheste. and said yt was a chest of plate
sent from her loue & others to be presented to the
kinge. And in the depest of the night she being
aslepe. he opened the cheste & cam forth
of yt. And vewed her in her bed and the
markes of her body. & toke a wai her bracelet
& affter Accused her of adultery to her loue &c
And in the end howe he came to her Deciphered into
England &c was taken prisoner and after
Reconciled to Innogen &c. who had turned her
self into mans apparell & fled to mete
her loue at milford hauen & chanchsed to
fall on the Caue in the wodde wher her 2
brothers were & howe by eating a sleping
Dram they thought she had bin deed & laid
her in the wodde & the body of Cloten by her
In her loues apparell that he left behind him
& howe she was found by Lucius &c.

176 SIMON FORMAN AT *CYMBELINE*, c. 1611. *Bodleian Library, MS. Ashmole 208, f. 206. Transcript: EKC, ii. 338–9. Forman's memoranda were first published by J. Payne Collier,* New Particulars regarding the Works of Shakespeare *(1836), pp. 6–26. The Collier connection has prompted some to impugn their authenticity (see, for example, Sidney Race, 'Simon Forman's "Bocke of Plaies" Examined',* Notes and Queries, *cciii (1958), 9–14); but conservative authorities generally accept the notes as genuine.*

A neuer writer, to an euer reader. Newes.

Ternall reader, you haue heere a new play, neuer stal'd with the Stage, neuer clapper-clawd with the palmes of the vulger, and yet passing full of the palme comicall; for it is a birth of your braine, that neuer vnder-tooke any thing commicall, vainely: And were but the vaine names of commedies changde for the titles of Commodities, or of Playes for Pleas; you should see all those grand censors, that now stile them such vanities, flock to them for the maine grace of their grauities: especially this authors Commedies, that are so fram'd to the life, that they serue for the most common Commentaries, of all the actions of our liues. shewing such a dexteritie, and power of witte, that the most displeased with Playes, are pleasd with his Commedies. And all such dull and heauy-witted worldlings, as were neuer capable of the witte of a Commedie, comming by report of them to his representations, haue found that witte there, that they neuer found in them-selues, and haue parted better wittied then they came: feeling an edge of witte set vpon them, more then euer they dreamd they had braine to grinde it on. So much and such sauored salt of witte is in his Commedies, that they seeme (for their height of pleasure) to be borne in that sea that brought forth Venus. Amongst all there is none more witty then this: And had I time I would comment vpon it, though I know it needs not, (for so

¶2   much

THE EPISTLE.

much as will make you thinke your testerne well bestowd) but for so much worth, as euen poore I know to be stuft in it. It deserues such a labour, as well as the best Commedy in Terence or Plautus. And beleeue this, that when hee is gone, and his Commedies out of sale, you will scramble for them, and set vp a new English Inquisition. Take this for a warning, and at the perrill of your pleasures losse, and Iudgements, refuse not, nor like this the lesse, for not being sullied, with the smoaky breath of the multitude; but thinke fortune for the scape it hath made amongst you. Since by the grand possessors wills I beleeue you should haue prayd for them rather then beene prayd. And so I leaue all such to bee prayd for (for the states of their wits healths) that will not praise it.

Vale.

177   PREFATORY EPISTLE TO *TROILUS AND CRESSIDA*, 1609, sig. ¶2. *Copy in the British Library; shelfmark: C. 34. k. 61. Greg 279. STC 22332.*

almost twice as remunerative as one in the latter, an interest of one-eighth in the Blackfriars returning £90 a year as opposed to £25 from a one-sixteenth interest in the Globe.[1]

In 1609 *Troilus and Cressida* was published under unusual circumstances. The play had been entered on the Stationers' Register for 'Master Robertes' six years earlier, with a note to forestall publication until 'he hath gotten sufficient aucthority for yt'. The King's men protected their playbooks. But on 28 January 1609 another two printers — Richard Bonian and Henry Walley — entered *Troilus and Cressida* on the Register, and issued it the same year, with a title-page advertising the play as 'Written by William Shakespeare' and 'acted by the Kings Majesties servants at the Globe'. A second issue later the same year removed the reference to performance from the title-page, and added an unsigned preface.

The play could have been 'new' only to readers. The 'grand possessors wills' thus insouciantly flouted must have been those of Shakespeare's company. Had the publishers got hold of a transcript in private hands? And what of the reference to a comedy 'never stal'd with the Stage' or 'sullied, with the smoaky breath of the multitude' — in direct contradiction of the statement on the first title-page? Are we to infer that *Troilus and Cressida* had never seen performance, or that it was acted privately? More likely the latter. One of the Inns of Court would suit this ratiocinative drama. There are some interesting biographical implications. 'A special audience of this

1   EKC, ii. 62–71.

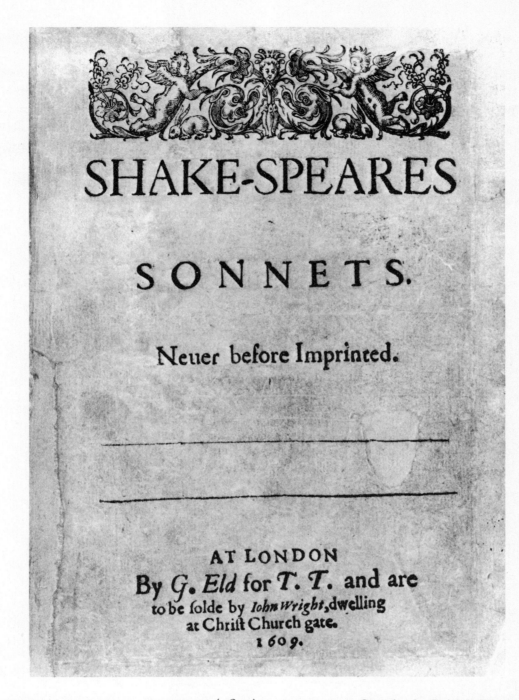

178 WILLIAM SHAKESPEARE, *SONNETS* (1609), TITLE-PAGE. *Copy in the British Library; shelfmark: C.21.c.44.* STC *22353ª*.

sort would allow one to discount any idea that the play reflects some deep-rooted cynicism in its author's attitude at this time; the satiric strain would be in part at least explained by the quality of persons in the audience and the time and place of the performance.'[1] However intriguing, this is, of course, mere speculation.

Vexing as they are, the problems surrounding the first publication of *Troilus and Cressida* pale into insignificance alongside those visited upon Shakespearian scholarship by Thomas Thorpe in the same year with his quarto edition of the *Sonnets*. Some, if not all, of these poems had circulated in manuscript since at least 1598, when Meres refers to Shakespeare's 'sugred Sonnets among his private friends'. Versions of two (138 and 144) had appeared in 1599 in *The Passionate Pilgrim*, a collection of short, mostly amorous, poems printed by William Jaggard with a catchpenny title-page ascription to W. Shakespeare — despite the fact that most of the items, including the

1 Peter Alexander, *Shakespeare* (1964), p. 247.

P*

well-known song, 'Crabbed age and youth', belonged to other hands. Ten years later Thorpe brought out his edition of the *Sonnets*.

All the signs point to unauthorized publication; unauthorized, that is, by the writer, not by Stationers' Hall. The numerous misprints indicate that the poet who took such pains with *Venus and Adonis* and *The Rape of Lucrece* had no part in supervising the printing of his most important body of non-dramatic verse. Few close students believe that the 154 poems of the cycle follow the sequence that their creator intended, although nobody has succeeded in rearranging them persuasively.

But the most mystifying problems of this edition are those posed by the dedication, supplied not in the usual downright fashion by the author, but by the publisher.

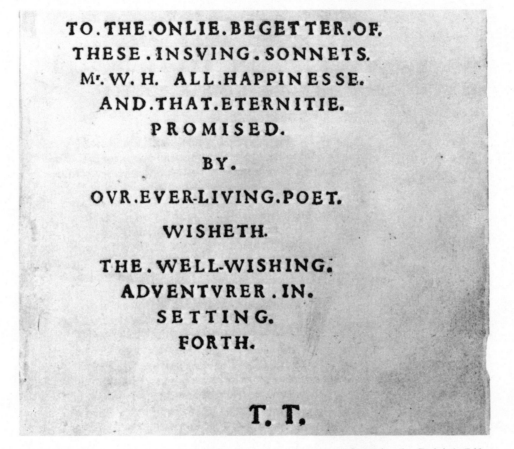

TO.THE.ONLIE.BEGETTER.OF.
THESE.INSVING.SONNETS.
Mr. W. H. ALL.HAPPINESSE.
AND.THAT.ETERNITIE.
PROMISED.

BY.

OVR.EVER-LIVING.POET.

WISHETH.

THE.WELL-WISHING.
ADVENTVRER.IN.
SETTING.
FORTH.

T. T.

179 WILLIAM SHAKESPEARE, *SONNETS* (1609), DEDICATION. *Copy in the British Library; shelfmark: C.21.c.44.* STC *22353ª*.

More than a century ago Richard Grant White wrote, 'Mr Thomas Thorpe appears in his dedication as the Sphinx of literature; and thus far has not met his Œdipus.'[1] He has still not met his Oedipus, although there has been no appreciable falling off in the number of well-wishing adventurers attempting to solve the riddle — or riddles — of the *Sonnets*.

Interest centres on the dedicatee. If Mr. W. H. is the 'onlie begetter' in the sense of inspirer of the *Sonnets*, then in identifying him we identify the Fair Youth who — cajoled, adored, chided — is, the speaker excepted, the principal personage of the drama. Is he Henry Wriothesley, third Earl of Southampton, with his initials reversed to deter the uninitiated? Not very likely. No strained ingenuity, however, is required to attach the initials to William Herbert, third Earl of Pembroke. Rich and handsome, liberal as a patron ('a most magnificent and brave peer, and loved learned men', Aubrey said of him), he was susceptible to feminine allurement, although stand-offish about matrimony. Moreover, this nobleman has a Shakespearian connection as one of the two brothers to whom Heminges and Condell dedicated their fellow's plays: those 'trifles' which their Lordships valued as something, and 'prosequuted both them, and their

1 Shakespeare, *Works*, ed. Richard Grant White (Boston, 1865), i. 152; cited by Hyder Edward Rollins in the New Variorum *Sonnets* (Philadelphia and London, 1944), ii. 166.

Authour living, with so much favour'. Herbert has attracted distinguished advocates, including Dover Wilson and Sir Edmund Chambers. In recent years, however, his star has declined. Born in 1580, he makes a precocious friend and lover, unless one assigns a later date to the cycle than most readers think likely. And it is doubtful that the obsequious Thorpe would insolently address a noble lord by the unhonorific 'Mr.'.

The other candidates are mostly non-starters. As early as the eighteenth century W. Hughes was put forward by Tyrwhitt (the great editor of Chaucer), and found favour with Malone. They detected a clue in Sonnet 20: 'A man in hue all *hues* in his controlling', and created the non-existent Hughes. Oscar Wilde resuscitated Hughes for his sublimated homo-erotic fantasy *The Portrait of Mr. W. H.* Should one prefer a more recent entry in the Thorpe sweepstakes, one may mull over the qualifications of William Hatcliffe, Prince of Purpoole — the Lord of Misrule — at the Gray's Inn Christmas revels of 1587–8. Dr. Hotson believes that this obscure Lancashireman, chronically in debt, journeyed to London in 1609 to peddle the *Sonnets* to Thorpe.[1] But Hatcliffe's claims have failed to generate much enthusiasm. Dr. Hotson's theory is perhaps less endearing than that of a German, D. Barnstorff, who proposed that Mr. W. H. is Master William Himself. The Variorum editor of the *Sonnets* is correct in saying that this is in fact not the most idiotic guess ever made.

Another school of interpretation, going back to James Boswell, the biographer's son, holds that *begetter* means *procurer*, and that the dedicatee has merited his ambiguous glory not as the inspirer of the *Sonnets* but as the unpoetical middle-man who furnished Thorpe with his copy-text. Again we have a choice of candidates. Sidney Lee is drawn to the stationer William Hall, who has the right initials, and, indeed, whose name stares at us from the dedication directly we remove the point after the *H* of 'M^r. W. H. ALL'. Another nominee is Shakespeare's brother-in-law William Hathaway. Most plausible of all, however, is Sir William Harvey, who in 1598 became the third husband of the Countess of Southampton. When she died in 1607, Sir William (this hypothesis holds) assented to the publication of a poetical testament which his wife regarded as too intimate to share with the public during her lifetime. The 'ETERNITIE. PROMISED BY. OUR. EVER-LIVING. POET' would be the dedicatee's progeny, for in 1608 Harvey took another wife, the young Cordelia Annesley. Precedent exists for addressing a knight as Mr.; Lady Southampton herself did so in her letters. But there is less precedent for *procurer* as an alternative definition for *begetter*. The reading is strained; the problem persists.

Indeed the entire dedication, not really punctuated at all but festooned with arbitrary points, is so syntactically ambiguous as to defeat any possibility of consensus among interpreters. Some would divide the lines into two sentences; others see 'Mr. W. H.', not Thorpe, as the subject of *wisheth*. All the riddles of the *Sonnets* — date, dedication, sequence, identity of the *dramatis personae* — elude solution, while at the same time teasing speculation. This writer takes satisfaction in having no theories of his own to offer.

In 1612 William Jaggard brought out a new edition of *The Passionate Pilgrim*, augmented by two long poems from Thomas Heywood's *Troia Britannica*. As Jaggard did not consult Heywood, or even give him credit on the title-page, the latter naturally felt offended, and vented his spleen, with more indignation than clarity, in an epistle to the printer following *An Apology for Actors*, also published in 1612. The passage holds interest for its Shakespearian allusion.

Here likewise, I muſt neceſſarily inſert a manifeſt iniury done me in that worke, by taking the two Epiſtles of *Paris* to *Helen*, and *Helen* to *Paris*, and printing them in a leſſe volume, vnder the name of another, which may put the world in opinion I might ſteale them from him; and hee to doe himſelfe right, hath ſince publiſhed them in his owne name : but as I muſt acknowledge my lines not worthy his patronage, vnder whom he hath publiſht them, ſo the Author I know much offended with M. *Iaggard* (that altogether vnknowne to him) preſumed to make ſo bold with his name.

180 THOMAS HEYWOOD'S EPISTLE TO NICHOLAS OKES, 1612. *From* An Apology for Actors, *sig. G4$^{r\cdot v}$. Copy in the Bodleian Library; shelfmark: 4°.H.34.Th. STC 13309.*

1 Hotson, *Mr. W. H.* (1964).

Apparently Shakespeare complained too, but privately and to the printer, for Jaggard cancelled the title-page and substituted a new one omitting Shakespeare's name. It survives in a single copy in the Bodleian Library. Thus the two sonnets, Heywood's poems, and the other bits and pieces now comprised an anonymous rather than falsely ascribed volume. Whether Heywood felt mollified is not known, but may be doubted.

The leading playwright of the age's leading company did not disdain to try his hand at trifling assignments no sooner completed than forgotten. For a fee Shakespeare devised the *impresa* to be borne by Francis Manners, sixth Earl of Rutland, as one of the contenders in the tourney at Court marking the King's Accession day, 24 March 1613. These *imprese* were insignia, allegorical or mythological, with appropriate mottoes, the whole painted on paper shields. The devices displayed at this tilt baffled at least one of the spectators, Sir Henry Wotton, who complained that 'some were so dark, that their meaning is not yet understood, unless perchance that were their meaning, not to be understood'.[1] Wotton thought that the Herbert brothers carried the best *imprese* that day. No matter; on 31 March, at Rutland's seat, Belvoir Castle, his steward Thomas Screvin recorded the payment of 44s. 'to m^r Shakspeare in gold about my Lordes Impreso', and another 44s. 'To Richard Burbadge for paynting & making yt'.

181   THE *IMPRESA* FOR THE EARL OF RUTLAND, 31 MARCH 1613. *Rutland MSS. iv. 494 (Accounts of the Steward of the Earl of Rutland) in Belvoir Castle. Transcript: TB, 74; EKC, ii. 153; BRL, ii. 449. The entry was first noticed in Belvoir Castle by Henry Maxwell-Lyte and W.H. Stevenson, and announced by Sidney Lee on 27 December 1905 in* The Times *('A Discovery about Shakespeare', p. 9.)*

Burbage was a talented amateur painter whose familiar self-portrait today hangs in the gallery at Dulwich College. The linking of his name with Shakespeare's effectively eliminates any doubt that it was the poet rather than some other Shakespeare — John Shakespeare, the royal bit-maker, for example — who created the Earl's *impresa*.

In the same month, March 1613, Shakespeare made his last investment. This time the house he bought was in London, not Stratford, and he seems not to have lived in it. Situated in the

Opposite:

182   THE BLACKFRIARS GATE-HOUSE CONVEYANCE, 10 MARCH 1613. *MS. in the Guildhall Library. Transcript: TB, 70–2 (extracts); EKC, ii. 154–7. The indenture was found in 1796 by Albany Wallis among the title-deeds of the Fetherstonhaugh family. Malone, who had known of the existence of the conveyance since 1783, when he referred to it in a manuscript note to his copy of Langbaine's* Account, *announced the discovery in his* Inquiry into the Authenticity of Certain Miscellaneous Papers and Legal Instruments *(1796), p. 119, and furnished a transcript in the Appendix (pp. 462–9). The Corporation bought the document in 1843. Its counterpart, the purchaser's copy lacking Shakespeare's signature, was acquired by H-P in 1872. He printed* A Facsimile of the Deed of Bargain and Sale of Shakespeare's Blackfriars Estate . . . *(Brighton, 1884). After his death the counterpart passed into the collection of Henry Clay Folger, and is now in the Folger Shakespeare Library (shelfmark: MS. Z.c.22 (45); formerly MS. 499.1). BRL provides a transcript (ii. 440–3). The conveyance is here reduced by about one third.*

1   Logan Pearsall Smith, *The Life and Letters of Sir Henry Wotton* (Oxford, 1907), ii. 17; quoted by EKC, ii. 153.

desirable Blackfriars district, the property was once, like the theatre, part of the vast Dominican priory complex. After the Dissolution the residence had been in the tenure of James Gardyner, Esq., and, after him, of John Fortescue, Gent.; in 1604 it was leased to William Ireland, a haberdasher, for twenty-five years. The owner was 'Henry Walker Citizein and Minstrell of London'. The 'dwelling house or Tenement', part of which was built over 'a great gate', was right up against the King's Wardrobe on the east, and abutted a street leading down to Puddle Wharf, where the Thames narrowed into a creek. On the west side the parcel included a plot of ground that the widow Anne Bacon had lately boarded up on two sides; an old brick wall enclosed the third side. The purchaser was entitled to free entry through the gate and yard, and also to 'all and singuler Cellours, sollers [i.e. upper rooms or lofts], romes, lightes, easiamentes, profittes, Commodities, and hereditamentes whatsoever to the said dwelling house or Tenement belonging, or in any wise apperteyning'. These details the conveyance sets forth. There are two copies, one for Shakespeare and the other for Walker. The transfer took place on the 10th. For the Blackfriars gate-house Shakespeare paid £140, of which £80 was in cash. He now had a house within a couple of hundred yards of the Blackfriars theatre; and at Puddle Wharf, just a few steps down the road, wherries were moored that could whisk him to Bankside. But this proximity would hardly matter much if, as seems likely, the playwright was now living in retirement at New Place; in the conveyance he describes himself as a Stratford man. In purchasing the gate-house he was merely following the example of his friend Richard Burbage, who had bought several parcels in the district. It was, apparently, an investment pure and simple.

In some ways perhaps not so simple. According to the title-deed, Shakespeare had three co-purchasers: William Johnson, John Jackson, and John Hemming. Hemming (or Heminges) was almost certainly the dramatist's old associate from the King's men.[1] Johnson presided as landlord of the Mermaid. The name Jackson is common enough, although he may be (as Dr. Hotson believes) the shipping magnate of Hull who enjoyed the company of 'noble wits' at the Mermaid, and was married to the sister-in-law of Elias James, a brewer at the foot of Puddle Dock Hill.[2] Despite the involvement of these parties in the transaction, Shakespeare was evidently the sole buyer. He put up the purchase-money; the others merely acted as trustees in his interest. The day after the sealing of the deed, Shakespeare mortgaged the gate-house back to Walker for the remaining £60. That sum fell due on 29 September next. If the buyer failed to pay it, the agreement stipulated that the seller would regain possession of his property 'from the feast of Thannunciacion of the blessed Virgin Marye next comming' for the term of one hundred years at the rent of 'a pepper Corne, at the feast of Easter yearlie'.

These elaborate arrangements, calling for trustees and a mortgage, place the Blackfriars purchase in a different category from Shakespeare's other investments. The mortgage, at any rate, is easily explained as a temporary expedient allowing the buyer some time to raise the balance of the purchase price. But why the trusteeship? The practical effect would be to deprive Shakespeare's widow of her dower right to a third share for life in this part of the estate; for in a joint tenancy, Chancery would not recognize Anne's privilege unless her husband had survived the other trustees.[3] Some biographers see dark overtones of marital discord; Sidney Lee remarks, 'Such procedure is pretty conclusive proof that he had the intention of excluding her [his wife] from the enjoyment of his possessions after his death.'[4] But, at the very least, this is to confuse the part with the whole: Shakespeare did not exclude Anne from the enjoyment of his other possessions. In his will (as we shall see) other considerations than the widow's right to dower moved him. In fact we do not know why he enlisted Heminges, Johnson, and Jackson as trustees.

A few subsequent developments respecting the gate-house require notice. Shakespeare let it to a John Robinson. In the spring of 1615, 'Ann Bacon beinge latelie dead', Shakespeare joined

1   Some biographers have without sufficient cause doubted the identification; e.g., H-P, *Outlines*, ii. 239.

2   Hotson, *Shakespeare's Sonnets Dated*, pp. 111–40, 207–17. An epitaph on Elias James, ascribed to 'W^m: Shakespeare', appears in Bodl. Rawlinson Poet. MS. 160, f. 41, and is dated 'about 1650' in the *Catalogue*; EKC gives the text (i. 551).

3   This legal opinion was given by Charles Elton, Q.C., to Sidney Lee (*A Life of William Shakespeare* (4th ed. of revised version, 1925), p. 488n).

4   Ibid., pp. 488–9.

several other property owners in the Blackfriars in petitioning the Court of Chancery to give the widow's son and executor, Mathias Bacon, authority to surrender the 'letters patentes and other deedes' pertaining to the said 'messuages, tenementes and premisses'. This was merely friendly litigation. Two years after the poet's death, Shakespeare's trustees conveyed the gate-house to John Greene of Clement's Inn and Mathew Morrys of Stratford, 'in performance of the confidence and trust in them reposed by William Shakespeare deceased, late of Stretford aforesaid, gent., and . . . according to the true intent and meaning of the last will and testament of the said William Shakespeare'.[1] This was on 10 February 1618.

About the same time as the Blackfriars transaction, Shakespeare's company was called upon to participate in the elaborate festivities at Whitehall celebrating the nuptials, in February 1613, of James's only surviving daughter, the Princess Elizabeth, and Prince Frederick, the Elector Palatine of the Rhine. She would reign for a few days as the Queen of Bohemia, and come to be known as the Winter Queen. But in the winter of 1613 those sad days lay ahead, unguessed at, and England toasted the marriage with plays, pageants, processions, masques, and fireworks. The King's men regaled the royal newly-weds with no fewer than fourteen plays, among them *Much Ado About Nothing*, *Othello*, *The Winter's Tale*, and *The Tempest*. For their contribution the troupe received the munificent reward of £153.6s.8d. In comparison, the Lady Elizabeth's men, the princess's own actors, played only three times.

Some historians believe that Shakespeare wrote the festive history of *Henry VIII* to celebrate the wedding of Elizabeth and Frederick. Such a performance is not mentioned in the Chamber Account, but conceivably it was the unnamed stage-play for which hundreds queued up on 16 February, only to have the performance cancelled in favour of the 'greater pleasure' of a masque. Many critics, although not all, think that Shakespeare wrote *Henry VIII* in collaboration with a rising young playwright, John Fletcher. The son of the Bishop of London, bred in the capital and educated at Cambridge, Fletcher would succeed Shakespeare as the ordinary poet of the King's men. Whether or not these two collaborated on *Henry VIII* we cannot say for sure, although most likely they did. That it was acted at Whitehall after the wedding is only a pleasant, perhaps idle, supposition. But a play on the reign of Henry VIII was performed at the summer playhouse of the King's company on St. Peter's day, 29 June 1613.

On that never-to-be-forgotten occasion the thatch caught fire, a sudden wind fanned the flames, and in a little while the great Globe itself was consumed. Three days later Sir Henry Wotton, not present himself, excitedly reported the event to his nephew, Sir Edmund Bacon.

The King's players had a new play, called *All is true*, representing some principal pieces of the reign of Henry VIII, which was set forth with many extraordinary circumstances of pomp and majesty, even to the matting of the stage; the Knights of the Order with their Georges and garters, the Guards with their embroidered coats, and the like: sufficient in truth within a while to make greatness very familiar, if not ridiculous. Now, King Henry making a masque at the Cardinal Wolsey's house, and certain chambers [i.e. pieces of ordnance] being shot off at his entry, some of the paper, or other stuff, wherewith one of them was stopped, did light on the thatch, where being thought at first but an idle smoke, and their eyes more attentive to the show, it kindled inwardly, and ran round like a train, consuming within less than an hour the whole house to the very grounds.

This was the fatal period of that virtuous fabric, wherein yet nothing did perish but wood and straw,

Opposite:

183 THE BLACKFRIARS GATE-HOUSE MORTGAGE, 11 MARCH 1613. *British Library, MS. Egerton 1787. Transcript: H-P, Outlines, ii. 34–6; EKC, ii. 157–9; BRL, ii. 445–7. Albany Wallis discovered the document in 1768 among the Fetherstonhaugh title-deeds. The Revd. Utrick Fetherstonhaugh presented it to Garrick, who died in 1779. Through the good offices of Horace Walpole, the mortgage deed was communicated to Malone, who printed it in the 1790 Shakspeare (vol. i, pt. 1, pp. 192–6). Subsequently misplaced, it resurfaced and was purchased in 1858 by the British Museum, where, somewhat faded, it is on permanent display in a case in the Manuscript Saloon. The document is here reduced by about one eighth.*

---

1 H-P, *Outlines*, ii. 36–7. Professor Brian Vickers has drawn my attention to a note on Shakespeare by George Coleman referring to the 'house formerly situated in Black-Friars, and but lately taken down on account of the new bridge, which belonged to that Poet' (*Prose on Several Occasions* (1787), ii. 165n).

184 WENCESLAUS HOLLAR, STUDY FOR THE 1647 'LONG VIEW' OF LONDON (detail). *Drawing (pen-and-ink over pencil) in the collection of Mr. and Mrs. Paul Mellon; item 4 in catalogue,* English Drawings and Watercolours 1550–1850 in the Mellon Collection *(1972). The drawing was obtained at Sotheby's on 10 June 1931 by Iolo A. Williams, and described and reproduced in 'Hollar: A Discovery of Iolo A. Williams',* The Connoisseur, *xcii (1933), 309–13. Theatre historians, however, neglected the item until I. A. Shapiro drew attention to its significance in* Shakespeare Survey 2 *(Cambridge, 1949), pp. 21–3.*

Some time during his residence in London, 1636–44, Hollar made this study of the 'West part o[f] Southwarke toward Westminster' for the foreground of his 'Long View' (item 78), although in the panorama the standpoint has shifted somewhat. Hollar sketched the scene in pencil, which was then mostly gone over, probably but not certainly by the artist, in ink. In the printed view the names of the Globe and Bear Garden are interchanged. Both study and etching depict the Globe Theatre as rebuilt after the fire of 1613; see C. Walter Hodges, Shakespeare's Second Globe: The Missing Monument *(1973), pp. 11–43.*

and a few forsaken cloaks; only one man had his breeches set on fire, that would perhaps have broiled him, if he had not by the benefit of a provident wit put it out with bottle ale.[1]

Such an event is calculated to inspire a pitiful ballad:

> No shower his raine did there downe force
> In all that Sunn-shine weather,
> To save that great renowned howse;
> Nor thou, O ale-howse, neither.
> Had itt begunne belowe, sans doubte,
> Their wives for feare had pissed itt out.
> Oh sorrow, pittifull sorrow, and yett all this is true.[2]

Puritans expectedly saw the hand of God in 'the sudden fearful burning'. But within a year a new Globe, with tiled roof, rose on the same site. On 30 June 1614 John Chamberlain called on a friend, but was told that she had 'gone to the new Globe, to a play'. As to whether the hand of God had anything to do with the miraculous restoration, the Puritans are silent. Rumour held that King James himself, with many of his noblemen, defrayed the cost of the rebuilding. In fact, however, the expense fell upon the housekeepers, required by the terms of their lease to maintain and repair the theatre. Each sharer was assessed £50 or £60 towards the charges. John Witter, already behindhand with the rent, could not put together his contribution, and bowed out from the syndicate.[3] We do not know what Shakespeare did. Perhaps, while pruning the vines in his Great Garden of New Place, he decided that this was a good time to sell his seventh share of the moiety in the company which he had served, to the best of his abilities, for almost two decades.

1   Smith, *Wotton*, ii. 32–3.
2   E. K. Chambers, *The Elizabethan Stage* (Oxford, 1923), ii. 421.
3   Not a player, but the wastrel who gained control of his share in the Globe by marrying the widow of Augustine Phillips.

15

Stratford Again

> Graves at my command
> Have wak'd their sleepers, op'd, and let 'em forth,
> By my so potent art. But this rough magic
> I here abjure; and when I have requir'd
> Some heavenly music — which even now I do —
> To work mine end upon their senses that
> This airy charm is for, I'll break my staff,
> Bury it certain fathoms in the earth,
> And deeper than did ever plummet sound
> I'll drown my book.

Ever since 1835, when Thomas Campbell, himself a minor poet, first made the suggestion, readers have identified the master of the revels in *The Tempest* with the master-reveller of the King's men, and interpreted Prospero's valediction, with its invocation of the supernatural potencies of art, as Shakespeare's own eloquent farewell to the stage.[1] In one respect at least, Prospero's words better suit the playwright than his puppet who speaks them. The magus of *The Tempest* has waked no sleepers from the grave, as has the author of *Richard III*, *Hamlet*, and *Macbeth*. It may, however, be objected that the soliloquy has its source in the *Metamorphoses*, which Shakespeare here consulted in both Ovid's Latin and Golding's translation. Nor does a speech of such evident dramatic propriety enforce us to read into it autobiographical reverberations. Prospero's revels have indeed ended; he must relinquish his magic, discase himself, and repossess his dukedom in Milan. Anyway *The Tempest*, performed in the Banqueting House at Whitehall on Hallowmas Night, 1611, was not Shakespeare's last play. *Henry VIII* followed, and the evidence points to his having had a hand, with Fletcher, in *The Two Noble Kinsmen*, around 1613. At most, then, in *The Tempest* he is saying *au revoir* rather than adieu. Certainly Shakespeare did not entirely give up visiting London during his last years. As we have seen, he was there in May 1612, when he gave evidence in the Court of Requests in the Belott–Mountjoy suit; again the following March, when he bought and mortgaged the Blackfriars gate-house; and presumably also in May 1615, when he joined in amicable litigation over the same property. But few plays issued from Shakespeare's pen after 1610; none, so far as is known, after 1613. When all factors have been duly weighed, there seems little reason to doubt the final non-literary phase that Rowe first summed up.

> The latter Part of his Life was spent, as all Men of good Senſe will wiſh theirs may be, in Eaſe, Retirement, and the Converſation of his Friends. He had the good Fortune to gather an Eſtate equal to his Occaſion, and, in that, to his Wiſh; and is ſaid to have ſpent ſome Years before his Death at his native *Stratford*.

185 NICHOLAS ROWE, *SOME ACCOUNT OF THE LIFE, &C. OF MR. WILLIAM SHAKESPEAR*, IN SHAKESPEARE, *WORKS*, ED. ROWE (1709), i, p. xxxv.

1 William Shakespeare, *Dramatic Works*, ed. Thomas Campbell (1838), p. lxiv. For a discussion of Campbell on Shakespeare, see *SL*, 312–15.

In 1611 the town rounded up subscriptions 'towardes the Charge of prosecutynge the Bill in parliament for the better Repayre of the highe waies and amendinge divers defectes in the Statutes alredy made'. In this period most road building and repair were financed by local philanthropists — Sir Hugh Clopton most notably exemplifies the breed — but Stratford now wanted the national government to assume some of the burden. Perhaps the matter had been mooted when the justices of the peace surveyed the highway in Bridgetown that year, and sat down together to a light refreshment of wine, sugar, pippins, and beer.[1] In the event, seventy-one citizens lent name and purse to the cause, the chief alderman, steward of the borough, and other aldermen heading the list prepared on 11 September. The steward, 'm^r Thomas Greene esquire', is the only subscriber for whom a sum is mentioned; he gave 2s.6d. Near the top of the list appears, added on the right, the name of 'm^r William shackspere' (about a third have their names prefixed by the honorific 'm^r'); perhaps he was in London when the sponsors first canvassed support. Bills for the repair of highways were before the Commons more than once in this period without progressing beyond the committee stage.[2] This one was no exception.

186 SHAKESPEARE ON THE CONTRIBUTION LIST FOR THE HIGHWAYS BILL, 11 SEPTEMBER 1611. *Shakespeare Birthplace Trust Records Office, Misc. Doc. I, 4. Transcript (extracts): EKC, ii. 152–3; BRL, ii. 416. H-P is the first to mention this document, in a note to the* Life, *p. 230.*

That autumn a neighbour in Henley Street, Robert Johnson, died. The inventory post-mortem, drawn up on 5 October by schoolmaster Aspinall, includes 'A lease of a barne that he holdeth of Mr Shaxper, xx^{li}'. Johnson, a vintner, was landlord of the White Lion Inn. Probably John

1 The suggestion is made by ME, 133.
2 Chambers notes that highway bills died in committee in 1610 and 1614; EKC, ii. 153.

Shakespeare built the barn, which stood at the back of the Birthplace property, in the waste known as the Gild Pits, through which the King's highway to London passed. The back gates of the Swan Inn adjoined the barn.[1] It was still being rented by a Johnson (Michael) in 1670, when Shakespeare's granddaughter made her will. In the late eighteenth century Jordan mentions 'the large barns, built with bricks, still standing in the Gild-pits, by the side of the Birmingham road'.[2]

Shakespeare's brother Gilbert was buried on 3 February 1612. The Stratford register lists the burial of 'Gilbertus Shakspeare adolescens', and, a year and a day later, that of Shakespeare's only remaining brother, Richard. Of the eight sons and daughters of John Shakespeare, now only the poet and his sister Joan survived.

In 1614 an unnamed preacher was entertained at New Place, the corporation paying 20d. 'for one quart of sack and one quart of clarrett winne' for his refreshment. He had come to deliver one of the three official foundation sermons with which the bailiff and council were edified in the chapel each year: the Oken on election day in September, the Hamlet Smith at Easter, and the Perrott at Whitsuntide. (In 1614 a fourth was established through the beneficence of Thomas Combe.) Probably it was the Easter or Whitsuntide sermon that he preached, for the payment is recorded in the Chamberlain's Account between entries dated 21 March and 30 June 1614. Visiting clergy sometimes stopped at inns, but they found entertainment in private houses too, and New Place — just a stone's throw from the Guild Chapel — was a likely place for the stranger to spend the night. On such occasions the corporation often footed the bill for gifts of wine, usually sack, but now and then an undesignated white wine. Sometimes they accompanied the wine with sugar.

187 A PREACHER ENTERTAINED AT NEW PLACE, 1614. *Shakespeare Birthplace Trust Records Office, Corp. Rec., Chamberlain's Accounts 1585–1619, p. 266. Transcript: EKC, ii. 152; ME, 135. H-P noted the entry in his* Life, *p. 270.*

That summer, on 9 July, a 'suddaine and terrible Fire' swept through the thatched houses of Stratford for the third time in living memory. Its force, the justices avouched, 'was so great (the wind sitting full uppon the Towne) that it dispersed into so many places therof whereby the whole Towne was in very great daunger to have been utterly consumed'.[3] Fifty-four dwellings burnt to the ground that Saturday, as well as barns and stables stored with grain and hay. A collection was taken up for the victims. Fortunately the Shakespeare properties escaped.

In the autumn a new crisis agitated Stratford's men of property. Enclosure was in the air again. Arthur Mainwaring (or Mannering), steward to Lord Chancellor Ellesmere, was promoting a scheme to enclose the common fields of Welcombe, and he had as his ally William Combe, a powerful new land-holder in the neighbourhood. At the age of twenty-eight Combe had just come into his bachelor uncle's estate. A previous attempt at enclosure had failed, although the prime mover was no less a personage than Sir Edward Greville, the late lord of the manor; but Mainwaring and Combe went confidently ahead. This issue touched people's pockets, and was thus calculated to arouse fierce passions. Shakespeare's tithe-interests were affected. His name stands at the head of the list of 'Auncient ffreeholders in the ffieldes of Oldstratford and Welcombe' which the Town Clerk, Thomas Greene, drew up on 5 September in response to the proposed scheme. Enclosure meant combining the yardlands — these were bundles of acre or half-acre strips in an open field — into larger units bounded by fences or hedges. Inevitably some boundaries would undergo alteration. The Welcombe fields were then meadowland boasting both hay for

1 Richard Savage describes the position of the barn in *The Athenæum*, 29 August 1908, p. 250.
2 *Original Collections on Shakespeare & Stratford-on-Avon, by John Jordan, the Stratford Poet . . .*, ed. H-P (1864), p. 50.
3 ME, 135–6.

mowing and grass for pasture. If these fields were enclosed, the remaining arable would be converted into sheep pasture, which as a rule yielded less income per square acre than grain and hay. Enclosure also reduced employment and forced up the price of grain. Hence the concern of the property-holders. On the other hand, enclosure also encouraged more productive agriculture, 'since the communal tillage of open fields was not conducted on scientific lines, and obviously no one would spend capital on improving his scattered and unenclosed plots for the benefit of his neighbours'.[1] Combe clearly felt that there was profit in enclosure. Shakespeare, wooed by both factions, seems to have kept cool.

188   THE WELCOMBE ENCLOSURE: GREENE'S MEMORANDUM, 5 SEPTEMBER 1614. *Shakespeare Birthplace Trust Records Office, Misc. Doc. I, 94. Transcript (extract): TB, 77; EKC, ii. 141; BRL, ii. 457. The episode was first discussed by R. B. Wheler, who included extracts from Greene's diary (see item 190) in* A Guide to Stratford-upon-Avon *(Stratford-upon-Avon, 1814), pp. 22–5. H-P first printed Greene's memorandum of 5 September in the* Life, *p. 267.*

Greene did not. As Town Clerk he looked after the minutes of corporation meetings in the Guild Hall, and also participated in council deliberations. He was Shakespeare's kinsman by blood or marriage — he speaks of himself as a cousin, and although Elizabethans used the term loosely, perhaps he was. The two seemed to get on. In 1609, when going about the purchase of a dwelling, he was the Shakespeares' house-guest, and in no hurry to move into the house George Badger sold him, 'the rather because [he wrote] I perceyved I mighte stay another yere at newe place'.[2] The mere suggestion of enclosure, however, made Greene exceedingly nervous, for he had lately invested £300 in a moiety of tithe-interests. Shakespeare owned the other moiety. Hence the Town Clerk's several references to Shakespeare in his memoranda.

At a meeting on 23 September Greene voiced his anxieties in the council, which voted unanimously to oppose enclosure. Two months later they agreed — with Alderman Cawdrey the lone dissenter — to use all lawful means to prevent Mainwaring's designs on the Welcombe meadowland. Meanwhile Shakespeare prudently entered into a covenant with Mainwaring's cousin, William Replingham of Great Harborough, who was the attorney acting as Mainwaring's agent. By these articles, drawn up on 28 October, Replingham undertook to compensate William Shackespeare or his heirs or assigns 'for all such losse detriment & hinderance' with respect to the annual value of his tithes, 'by reason of anie Inclosure or decaye of Tyllage there ment and intended by the said William Replingham'. At the recommendation of Thomas Lucas, one of the witnesses, Shakespeare and Replingham included Greene's name in the agreement.

He did not rest any easier as a result. In November he was looking for Combe in London, but not finding him, called on Shakespeare, who had come up from Stratford. Greene's memorandum of the 17th shows that Shakespeare tried to calm him:

at my Cosen Shakspeare commyng yesterday to towne I went to see him howe he did he told me that they assurd him they ment to inclose noe further then to gospell bushe & so upp straight (leavyng out part of the dyngles to the ffield) to the gate in Clopton hedge & take in Salisburyes peece: and that they meane in Aprill to servey the Land & then to gyve satisfaccion & not before.

1   EKC, ii. 146.
2   Shakespeare Birthplace Trust, Corporation Records, Misc. Doc. XII, 103; H-P, *Outlines*, ii. 378. Greene dated his memorandum 9 September.

189 THE WELCOMBE ENCLOSURE: THE SHAKESPEARE–REPLINGHAM AGREEMENT, 28 OCTOBER
1614. *Shakespeare Birthplace Trust Records Office, MS. ER 27/3. Transcript: TB, 75–6; EKC, ii. 141–2;
BRL, ii. 452. The document, a contemporary transcript endorsed 'Coppy of the articles with m[r] Shakspeare',
formed part of the Wheler Papers, and was presented to the Birthplace Museum (now the Birthplace Trust
Records Office) by Miss Anne Wheler. H-P printed it in his* Life, *p. 268.*

Greene adds that both Shakespeare and his son-in-law, Dr. John Hall, assured him they thought
nothing at all would be done. The survey took place, however, not in April but much sooner, in
December, and when the Town Clerk heard of it on the 10th, he was off to the Bear Inn and New
Place in search of Replingham. Greene missed him at both places.

However, he had the corporation behind him. They made a gingerly approach to Combe,
sending a deputation of six 'to present their loves & to desire he would be pleased to forbeare to
inclose & to desire his love as they wilbe redy to deserve yt'. Combe thanked them for their love,

190 THE WELCOMBE ENCLOSURE: GREENE'S MEMORANDUM, 17 NOVEMBER 1614. *Shakespeare Birthplace Trust Records Office, Corp. Rec., Misc. Doc. XIII, 26a. Transcript (extract): TB, 77; EKC, ii. 142–3; BRL, ii. 458–9. Greene's diary occupies four leaves (Corp. Rec., Misc. Doc. XIII, 26a, 27–9). Relevant extracts were first printed by R. B. Wheler,* A Guide to Stratford-upon-Avon *(Stratford-upon-Avon, 1814), pp. 24–5. Wheler describes Greene's hand as almost illegible. C. M. Ingleby published the whole diary in facsimile, with a transcript by E. J. L. Scott, in* Shakespeare and the Enclosure of Common Fields at Welcombe *(Birmingham, 1885), the usefulness of which is somewhat impaired by the transposing, in facsimile and transcript, of pp. 6 and 7.*

but budged not an inch — he saw gain from enclosure; Mainwaring had already gone too far to turn back; come thaw and he would begin digging his ditch and planting hedges. On 23 December the corporation dispatched letters, subscribed by 'almost all' the members, to Mainwaring and Shakespeare. 'I alsoe wrytte of myself', Greene adds, 'to my Cosen Shakspear the Coppyes of all our oathes made then, alsoe a not [i.e. note] of the Inconvenyences wold grow by the Inclosure'. That day the council sought to enlist other local land-holders in the cause: Andrew Archer of Tanworth, who held Bishopton manor and common, and Sir Francis Smith, who owned land at Welcombe.[1] The correspondence with Shakespeare has disappeared, but the corporation's letter to Mainwaring survives. They entreated him to remember the fires which had devastated Stratford, and warned that enclosure, by tending to the ruin of the borough, would bring on his head the curses of over 700 almsfolk living there.

All to no avail. The frost broke in December, and Combe's men began digging their trench, surrounded by hedge-mounds. Before long it extended over 'at least fifty perches': 275 yards. The council counter-attacked. On Greene's advice, William Walford and William Chandler bought a lease at Welcombe on 6 January 1615, thus becoming tenants with rights of common. Three days later, having sent their spades ahead, they began surreptitiously filling in Combe's ditch. When word of the activity reached him, he was predictably enraged. Before a crowd of onlookers, Walford and Chandler were thrown to the ground by Combe's men, while their master 'sat laughing on his horsback & sayd they wer good football playres'. He also abused the corporation as 'puritan knaves and underlings in their colour [i.e. the legal pretext by which they had insinuated themselves as commoners]'. Still, righteous indignation did not prevent Combe from offering Greene £10 to buy himself a gelding, in return for propounding a peace with the council. But Greene was not to be bribed. The next day women and children from Stratford and Bishopton finished the job of filling in the ditch.

On 28 March at Warwick Assizes, upon the petition of the bailiff and burgesses of Stratford, the court issued an order restraining Combe and any other from making an enclosure — which was against the laws of the realm—unless they could show good cause at open Assizes. Mainwaring and Replingham now acknowledged defeat, but Combe, beside himself, persisted. He threatened and railed; he beat the poor tenants, imprisoned them, and impounded their pigs and sheep. By buying up land and houses, he depopulated the entire village of Welcombe. In September, Greene made his most perplexing entry in his diary: 'W Shakespeares tellyng J Greene that I was not able to beare the encloseinge of Welcombe'. J. Greene was the diarist's brother John. But why should Shakespeare have communicated to John Greene a fact of which he could not have been unaware? And why did John trouble himself to pass it along to his brother? Finally, why should Thomas have regarded the intelligence as sufficiently interesting to record? Possibly 'I' was a slip for 'he'. Or possibly Greene meant to write 'barre', not 'beare'. He began by writing 'to he . . .';

1 ME, 137.

Q

maybe he intended to say 'to help', then changed his mind because of a possible ambiguity — 'to help' could mean either 'to aid' or 'to remedy'.[1] For that matter, 'beare' can be taken two ways also, as 'endure' or 'justify'. Any attempt to interpret the passage is guesswork, and no more.

After the staying order the case dragged on for another year. Then, at the Lent Assizes of 1616, the Chief Justice of the King's Bench, Sir Edward Coke, advised Combe to 'sett his heart at rest; he should neyther enclose nor laye downe any earrable nor plow any ancient greensward'. By April the force of the verdict had sunk in on Combe; he was 'out of hope ever to enclose'.[2] But if he abandoned all hope, he did so only temporarily. In June he was offering his 'verie lovinge freinds and Kinde Neyghbours' a new set of proposals, much more conciliatory; but the corporation refused to bite. They simply asked Combe to leave them in peace. He did not. Shakespeare, who seems never to have felt very keenly one way or the other about the controversy, now did not care at all. He was dead.

During his last years the retired playwright had his family with him in Stratford. So far as is known, his wife never strayed from the town, but for her the record is a blank between the baptism of her children and the drawing up of the poet's will, except for shepherd Whittington's concern about 40s. in Anne Shaxspere's hand. Her daughters' lives are more amply documented.

According to her epitaph, Shakespeare's eldest child was 'Witty above her sexe' and 'Wise to salvation' — 'Something of Shakespeare was in that', the memorialist, whoever he was, adds. Whether witty and wise or not, Susanna could sign her name, which is more than her sister demonstrates a capacity to do. She first appears in the records, after her christening entry in the Stratford register, in the spring of 1606, just before her twenty-third birthday. On 6 May she was cited in the act book kept by the ecclesiastical court that held 'peculiar jurisdiction' in the parish. Presided over by the vicar on his throne in Holy Trinity, with a notary present to record its acts, the court met approximately once a month. On this occasion twenty-two defendants, reported by the churchwarden and sidesmen, were charged with having failed to receive the Sacrament the preceding Easter, which that year fell on 20 April. The transgression may seem trifling, and ordinarily it was; but only six months previously a small band of fanatical Catholics had sought by violence to overthrow the government, and Parliament, having narrowly escaped being blown up in the Gunpowder Plot, was in no mood for toleration. It passed a number of vengeful statutes, among them an act aimed at 'persons popishly affected' who sometimes attended church 'to escape the laws in that behalf provided', but who evaded the Anglican Communion. Church papists, they were called, and the new law respecting non-receiving punished them with heavy fines, rising from £20 in the first year to £60 in the third and thereafter. In such an atmosphere parishioners missing Communion laid themselves open to grave suspicions of Catholicism. A third at least of the Easter Twenty-two were in fact known Catholics, or had recusant connections. There was Margaret Reynolds, for example, or Sybil Cawdrey. Margaret's husband paid his monthly fine for non-attendance; they had once sheltered a fugitive Jesuit priest. Sybil had a son in that order, and her family had been accused of harbouring seminary priests. The list also included Shakespeare's old friends the Sadlers, who required time (Hamnet petitioned) to clear their consciences. Susanna failed to show up in the vicar's court despite a personal summons by the apparitor. (The Sadlers were guilty of a similar negligence.) The word *dismissa*, added later to the entry for her in the act book, indicates that when Susanna did appear before the court her case was dismissed. Presumably she had meanwhile received the Eucharist, as we know ten of her co-defendants had.[3] A year later, on 5 June, 'John Hall gentleman & Susanna Shaxspere' were

1   The point is made by ME, 138.
2   C. M. Ingleby, *Shakespeare and the Enclosure of Common Fields at Welcombe* . . . (Birmingham, 1885), gives complete texts of Combe's letter and the corporation's reply (pp. 16–18). Greene records Combe's April despair in his diary (Ingleby, p. 12).
3   This plausible interpretation is offered by E. R. C. Brinkworth, *Shakespeare and the Bawdy Court of Stratford* (1972), p. 46. Brinkworth's book, which is helpfully informative on the proceedings of the parish ecclesiastical court, follows up the important article by Hugh A. Hanley, 'Shakespeare's Family in Stratford Records', *TLS*, 21 May 1964, p. 441. The same act book (p. 141) records that on 1 July 1608 Shakespeare's brother Richard was summoned before the church court for an unspecified offence, and fined 12d., to be given 'to the use of the poore of Stratford' (Brinkworth, pp. 110, 141). Eccles, reviewing Brinkworth, thinks the fault may have been Sabbath-breaking (*Modern Language Review*, lix (1974), 373).

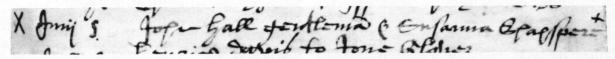

191 SUSANNA SHAKESPEARE CITED FOR FAILURE TO RECEIVE COMMUNION, 6 MAY 1606. *Act book (shelfmark: U269 Q22), pp. 37, 39; Sackville MSS. in Kent County Archives Office, Maidstone. Transcript: H. A. Hanley, 'Shakespeare's Family in Stratford Records', TLS, 21 May 1964, p. 441. The entry, in an act book formerly among family papers of the Sackvilles at Knole, was first published and analysed by Hanley, an Assistant Archivist in the Kent office, in the article cited. Margaret, wife of Thomas Raynoldes, heads the list of those presented 'for not receaving at Easter last'; Susanna's name appears in the sixteenth citation.*

192 JOHN HALL AND SUSANNA SHAKESPEARE MARRIED, 5 JUNE 1607. *Stratford parish register, marriages, f. 11. Shakespeare Birthplace Trust Records Office; shelfmark: DR 243/1.*

wed in Holy Trinity. The groom, in his early thirties, was impeccably Protestant.

The son of a well-to-do Bedfordshire physician, Hall was bred in the little hamlet of Carlton. At Cambridge, thirty miles away, he proceeded B.A. at Queens' College in 1594, and three years later took his M.A. there. Around 1600 he settled in Stratford, where he soon had a thriving medical practice. If Hall ever took a medical degree, no record of it has been found — the Royal College of Physicians never licensed him, nor did he obtain a Bishop's licence to practice. But in those days the profession was very loosely regulated. No matter; Hall was a dedicated physician with a large following. 'I kno by experyence: that hee is most excelent In that arte', Lady Tyrell informed Lady Temple when the latter's husband — the same Sir Thomas Temple so desirous of vine-sets from Shakespeare's garden — had suffered a mischance. A Linacre Lecturer at Cambridge, Dr. John Bird, speaks of Hall's 'great Fame for his skill, far and near', and of the 'Persons Noble, Rich and Learned' who benefited from his ministrations. Hall looked after humbler folk too — children, servants, barbers — and Catholics as well as Protestants. He did not scruple to ride forty miles on horseback to Ludlow Castle when the Earl of Northampton was down with a pleurisy contracted while following his hounds on a cold wet day. Twice the Stratford corporation elected Hall a burgess, and twice he refused because of the demands of his practice. When elected a third time he accepted, only to incur fines for missing sessions because he was out looking after his patients. One of these, Sidney Davenport, complained to the doctor that the magistrates ought not 'to lay this burthen upon you whose profession is to be most abroad'.[1] So too Hall declined a knighthood offered him in 1626 by the new monarch, King Charles I, preferring to pay a £10 fine.

Dr. Hall treated the whole gamut of human ills from measles to melancholy, and including black evacuations, cancer, bloodshot eyes, and the French pox. His medical diary records the case histories. Thus he cured the Countess of Northampton's chambermaid, laid low when her

1   ME, 115.

arse-gut fell out, and John Emes of Alcester, aged fifteen, unfortunately prone to 'pissing in bed'. The prescription for the latter included 'the windepipe of a Cocke, dryed and made into powder'. When his own wife lay 'miserably tormented with the collick', Hall gave her an enema — a pint of sack, made hot — which 'presently brought forth a great deale of wind, and freed her from all pain'. Hall's best remembered patient was the Warwickshire poet Michael Drayton, whom he describes as *poeta laureatus*. Drayton often called on the Rainsfords at Clifford Chambers, only two miles from Stratford; it was probably there that Hall treated him with an emetic infusion mixed with a spoonful of syrup of violets. Some of the physician's remedies, with their cocks' guts, spider webs, and excreta, may strike moderns as more alarming than the conditions they were designed to alleviate, but this doctor let less blood than others, and was in advance of his day in his treatment of scurvy, to which Elizabethans were prone by virtue of a diet rich in salted meat and fish but deficient in seasonal fruits and vegetables. This malady Hall fought with his Scorbutick Beer. He compounded water cress, brooklime, and scurvy grass with various herbs and roots, then boiled the mixture in beer flavoured with sugar, cinnamon, or juniper berries. The beer worked; it was rich in ascorbic acid.[1]

The motto 'Health is from the Lord' fittingly precedes the English edition of Dr. Hall's Latin case-book, in which time and again he gives thanks to God for a successful cure. Nowhere is his piety more fervent than in his account of his own miraculous recovery from a debilitating fever: 'thou hast saved me . . .', he addresses his maker, 'restoring me as it were from the very jaws of death to former health, for which I praise thy Name, O most mercifull God, and Father of our Lord Jesus Christ, praying thee to give me a most thankful heart for this great favour, for which I have cause to admire thee'.[2] Hall showed his gratitude more tangibly by giving Holy Trinity a carved pulpit, and serving as a churchwarden. His sympathies were Puritan. He zealously re-prehended parishioners who came to church late, slept there, swore, wore hats, or put their hands in ladies' plackets. Hall allied himself with vicar Thomas Wilson from Evesham (the doctor had in 1612 bought 'a close by Evesham way'), who had antagonized the corporation with his Puri-tanical views. The two men together sued the council in Chancery, Hall declaring that he had sold the town a lease of tithes for £100 'at the least' under their value, in order to maintain the salary of the schoolmaster and the vicar, who had six young children to worry about.[3]

The Lord blessed the Halls with only one child, a daughter Elizabeth, baptized 21 February 1608. She makes a solitary appearance in her father's case-book. He describes treating her for a 'Convul-sion of the mouth' in January and April 1624, and, a month later, for 'an Erratick Fever' — 'some-times she was hot, by and by sweating, again cold, all in the space of half an hour, and thus she was vexed oft in a day'. Hall purged Elizabeth, and anointed her spine. She responded to her father's care. 'Thus was she delivered from Death, and deadly diseases, and was well for many yeares.'[4]

The inscription on John Hall's gravestone describes Susanna as his most faithful wife (*fidissima conjux*), but that was not how John Lane, Jr., spoke of her in 1613. On 15 July Susanna sued Lane for slander in the consistory court at Worcester Cathedral, because 'about 5. weekes past the defendant reported that the plaintiff had the runinge of the raynes & had bin naught with Rafe Smith at John Palmer'. (To have 'the running of the reins' was to suffer from gonorrhoea ('reins' = kidneys or loins); but gonorrhoea did not then necessarily denote venereal infection, although in this context that appears to be what is meant.[5]) Lane, then twenty-three, came of good stock — Alveston gentry — but got into scrapes. He was sued for riot, and libelling the vicar and aldermen; the churchwardens charged him with drunkenness. Perhaps he was both drunk and pugnacious when he defamed Mrs. Hall. Ralph Smith, aged thirty-five, was a vintner's son, and by trade a

1   Hall's work as a physician is analysed by Harriet Joseph, *Shakespeare's Son-in-Law: John Hall, Man and Physician* (Hamden, Conn., 1964); see also ME, 114–5.
2   John Hall, *Select Observations on English Bodies* . . . (1657), pp. 227–8.
3   Edgar I. Fripp, *Shakespeare: Man and Artist* (1938), ii. 885–91.
4   Hall, *Select Observations*, pp. 47–51.
5   In the 'Alphabetical Table of Diseases' prefacing Hall's *Select Observations*, the first entry under 'G' is, '*Gonor-rhea, see runing of the Reines*'. The *Oxford English Dictionary* glosses the phrase under 'Running', II. 8; see also the corre-spondence in the *TLS* from A. L. Rowse (28 April 1974, p. 447), Ernest Mehew (3 May 1974, p. 477), Audrey Eccles (17 May 1974, p. 527), and myself (24 May 1974, p. 559).

hatter and haberdasher; he was Hamnet Sadler's nephew. Lane's sister Margaret was the wife of John Greene, the Town Clerk's brother, and his first cousin would marry Elizabeth Hall. His uncle, Richard Lane, in July 1613 appointed Thomas Greene and John Hall trustees of the property he settled on his son and daughter.[1] Stratford was a closely knit society, in which scandal — quick to circulate — had to be as quickly quashed. In the consistory court, Robert Whatcott, later to witness the poet's will, appeared on behalf of the plaintiff. Lane did not appear at all, and in less than a fortnight found himself excommunicated. The case was closed.

193   SUSANNA HALL SUES JOHN LANE, JR., 15 JULY 1613. *British Library, MS. Harley 4064 (Ecclesiastical Causes in Gloucester and Worcester, 1609–1613), f. 189. Transcript: EKC, ii. 12–13 (extract); BRL, ii. 450. H-P printed a facsimile in the sixth edition, 1886, of the* Outlines *(i. 242).*

Local tradition holds that the Halls lived in a handsome half-timbered house in Old Town, close to Holy Trinity, and even closer to New Place. The spacious dwelling had an ample garden in which Dr. Hall could cultivate the herbs and simples he used in his cures. Today the house is called Hall's Croft, but I have been able to find no reference to it by that name earlier than the listing of 'Hall Croft' in *Spenell's Family Almanack, Directory of South Warwickshire, and Annual Advertiser, for 1885.* It was earlier called Cambridge House, and served as a private school for girls. When Shakespeare died, the Halls moved into New Place. There they stayed for the rest of their lives.

194   HALL'S CROFT. *Shakespeare Birthplace Trust Records Office, PD. 29.5. The engraving appears as part of the letter-head of Cambridge House in the late nineteenth century.*

1   ME, 113.

Q*

The parish register records the burial of 'Johannes Hall medicus peritissimus' (most expert physician) on 26 November 1635. His remains lie in the chancel of Holy Trinity. On his gravestone, the second to the right of Shakespeare's, his arms, 'Three talbots' heads erased', impale those of his father-in-law. The inscription reads:

HEERE LYETH Yᴱ BODY OF JOHN HALL
GENT: HEE MARR: SUSANNA, Yᴱ DAUGH
& coheire
TER, OF WILL: SHAKESPEARE, GENT. HEE
DECEASED NOVEᴿ 25. Aᵒ 1635, AGED 60.

The Latin epitaph which follows eulogizes his healing skill ('Hallius hic situs est medica celeberrimus arte') and loyal wife.

Hall's medical fame prompted James Cooke of Warwick, Lord Brooke's surgeon, to call on the faithful widow when he was in Stratford during the Civil War. Cooke describes the visit.

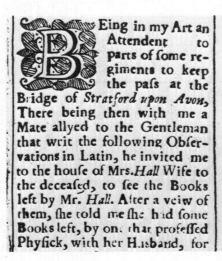

195   JOHN HALL, *SELECT OBSERVATIONS ON ENGLISH BODIES*, TRANS. JAMES COOKE (1657), sig. A3ʳ⁻ᵛ. *From Cooke's epistle 'To the Friendly Reader'.*

Odd that Susanna failed to recognize her own husband's hand. Could she read and write, or did she have learning sufficient only to enable her to sign her name? In any event, when Cooke found some spare hours he translated 200 of Hall's case-histories, from among 'no lesse than a thousand', and published them in 1657 as *Select Observations on English Bodies*. Although the surgeon refers to two books, only one of Dr. Hall's medical diaries is known to exist. Now in the British Library, it is Egerton MS. 2065.

Judith Shakespeare fared less well matrimonially than her sister, although her husband came from an unexceptionable family. He was Thomas Quiney, son of the Richard who was Shakespeare's loving countryman. When Richard died in 1602 he left a wife, Bess, and nine young children. Of these the best hope was the eldest son, Richard Jr., who would prosper as a grocer at the Red Lion in Bucklesbury, London, and with his partner, also from Stratford, buy two plantations in Virginia. But Judith married not Richard — he took a Sadler for his wife — but his brother Thomas, baptized 26 February 1589. He achieved no comparable triumphs in trade. Thomas became a vintner in Stratford; we hear of him selling wine to the corporation in 1608. Three years later he leased, for use as a tavern, the little house called 'Atwood's' near the top of the High Street, next door to his mother. On 10 February 1616 'Tho Queeny' was wed 'tow [i.e. to] Judith Shakspere', the assistant vicar Richard Watts probably officiating — he signed the marriage register this month. (Watts later married Quiney's sister Mary.) The groom was twenty-seven, the bride a mature thirty-one. One suspects she did not by then have a choice of suitors, if she ever did.

The marriage got off to an inauspicious start. Because the ceremony took place during the Lenten prohibited season that in 1616 began on 28 January (Septuagesima Sunday) and ended on 7 April (the Sunday after Easter), the couple should have secured a special licence from the

196 THOMAS QUINEY AND JUDITH SHAKESPEARE MARRIED, 10 FEBRUARY 1616. *Stratford parish register, marriages, f. 13ᵛ. Shakespeare Birthplace Trust Records Office; shelfmark: DR 243/1.*

Bishop of Worcester. They did not do so, although presumably they published banns in the parish church. Without a licence the minister was at fault in conducting the service. The upshot was that Thomas and Judith were cited to the consistory court in Worcester Cathedral. They failed to show up, were summoned again, and stayed away a second time. On 12 March or thereabouts, the court excommunicated Thomas. Possibly Judith suffered the same fate, although the record leaves that uncertain.[1]

197 THOMAS QUINEY EXCOMMUNICATED, 1616. *Worcestershire Record Office, MS. 802/BA 2760, Visitation Act Book 1613–17, f. 27ᵛ. Transcript: EKC, ii. 8; BRL, ii. 522. Joseph William Gray published a transcript of the minute in* Shakespeare's Marriage and Departure from Stratford *(1905), p. 248. EKC emends Gray, and is in turn corrected by ME, who reads the last word not as 'uxor' but as 'exco', for 'excommunicatio' or 'excommunicatus' (139).*

The offence was not serious. Others married in Lent — three weddings took place in Holy Trinity that February — and the Quineys may have just had the bad luck to fall victim to an apparitor hungry for a fee. Walter Nixon, who summoned them, does not have an especially savoury history: he had later to face accusations in Star Chamber of taking bribes and 'subtlely' forging the name of the registrar of the episcopal court on an injunction.[2] The excommunication anyway lasted only a short while, for before the year was out the Quineys were at the font to have their first-born christened in Stratford church.

Excommunication was the least of Thomas Quiney's worries that winter. Before marrying, he had got Margaret Wheeler with child, and by February she was dangerously pregnant.[3] Scandal turned to tragedy when, a month after the Quiney wedding, the unfortunate woman died in childbirth, and her infant with her. The parish register records both burials on 15 March.

1   ME, 139.
2   Public Record Office, Star Chamber Proceedings, James I, 26/10, *m.* 2; cited by Fripp, *Shakespeare* (1938), ii. 824, and by ME, 140. Fripp and ME are, in general, the most useful authorities on the Quineys, as well as on the Halls.
3   For the Wheeler episode and its aftermath, as for Susanna's non-receiving, my sources are Hanley ('Shakespeare's Family in Stratford Records') and Brinkworth (*Shakespeare and the Bawdy Court of Stratford*).

198 MARGARET WHEELER AND CHILD BURIED, 15 MARCH 1616. *Stratford parish register, burials, f. 46. Shakespeare Birthplace Trust Records Office, DR 243/1. The significance of the entry was first noticed by H. A. Hanley, 'Shakespeare's Family in Stratford Records', TLS, 21 May 1964, p. 441.*

Sexual delinquencies — what the homily denounced as 'whoredom and uncleanness' — fell within the purview of the ecclesiastical court held by the vicar of Stratford: the very court before which Susanna had been haled for not receiving the Sacrament in Easter 1606. Many of the cases heard by such courts of peculiar jurisdiction had to do with fornication and the like, so they became popularly, if somewhat disrespectfully, known as 'bawdy courts'. To the bawdy court of Stratford the apparitor Richard Greene (he seems to have doubled as the parish clerk) summoned the newly-wed Thomas Quiney.

The act book records the hearing and sentence on Tuesday, 26 March. In open court Thomas confessed to having had carnal copulation with the said Wheeler (*fassus est se carnelem copulacionem habuisse cum dicta Wheeler*), and submitted himself to correction. The judge, vicar John Rogers, sentenced the offender to perform open penance in a white sheet, according to custom, in the church on three successive Sundays before the whole congregation. But the penalty was remitted. In effect Thomas got off for 5s. This sum he gave for the use of the poor of the parish, and the vicar ordered him to acknowledge his crime, in ordinary attire, before the minister of Bishopton (*ad agnoscendum crimen in habitu suo prop[r]io coram ministro de Bishopton*). Falling as it did within Stratford parish, Bishopton had no church of its own, only a chapel; so Quiney was spared public humiliation.

199 THOMAS QUINEY TRIED FOR FORNICATION, 26 MARCH 1616. *Act book (shelfmark: U269 Q22); Sackville MSS. in Kent County Archives Office, Maidstone. Transcript: H. A. Hanley, 'Shakespeare's Family in Stratford Records', TLS, 21 May 1964, p. 441 (text and translation). The entry, in an act book formerly among family papers of the Sackvilles at Knole, was first published and analysed by Hanley in the article cited.*

His subsequent history had more downs than ups. In July 1616 Thomas exchanged houses with his brother-in-law William Chandler, and moved into the more spacious and imposing structure called The Cage at the corner of the High Street and Bridge Street. There, in the upper half, Quiney set up his vintner's shop, and also dealt in tobacco. He held several municipal offices: in 1617 he was named burgess and then constable, and from 1621 to 1623 he served as chamberlain, his pinnacle of municipal recognition. Quiney signed his account for 1623 with flourishes, and pretentiously ornamented it with a couplet in French from a romance by Saint-Gelais. Unimpressed, the council voted the account 'imperfect' in his absence, but later passed it. Quiney, no scholar, made a hash of the quotation.[1] (His wife was even less of a scholar, if we may judge from the fact that when in 1611 she witnessed a deed of Elizabeth Quiney and her son Adrian, she twice signed by mark.) The corporation never thought highly enough of Quiney to make him an alderman. He sued about a shipment of wine from Bristol, was fined trifling sums for swearing and suffering townsmen to tipple in his house, and was once in danger of prosecution for dispensing unwholesome and adulterated wine. Around 1630 he tried to sell the lease of The Cage, but his kinsmen stopped him, assigning the lease in trust to a triumvirate consisting of Dr. Hall, Hall's son-in-law Thomas Nash, and Richard Watts, now Quiney's brother-in-law and the vicar of Harbury. This move protected the interests of Judith and the children. Obviously Thomas was not to be trusted. In November 1652 The Cage lease was made over to Richard Quiney, the London grocer. When the latter died three years later, he bequeathed his brother an allowance of £12 a year and £5 for his burial. Thomas does not seem to have ever left Stratford (he was selling wine to the corporation as late as 1650), although the parish register fails to record his burial. Possibly he pre-deceased his wife, although he may have died in 1662–3, when the burial records are incomplete.[2]

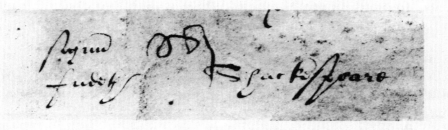

200 JUDITH SHAKESPEARE'S MARK, 4 DECEMBER 1611. *Shakespeare Birthplace Trust Records Office, MS. ER 27/11. The transaction witnessed was a deed of sale by Elizabeth and Adrian Quiney to William Mountford, wheelwright, of a messuage for £131.*

As parents the Quineys had bad luck. Their first child, whose name Shakespeare Quiney united the two families, died in infancy on 8 May 1618. There were two more sons: Richard, christened 9 February 1618, and Thomas, christened 23 January 1620. They died within a few months of one another in 1639, aged respectively twenty-one and nineteen. The Quineys had no more children.

Shakespeare lived to see neither these baptisms nor burials. He died on 23 April 1616. The Stratford register records the burial two days later of 'will Shakspere gent'. His brother-in-law, the hatter William Hart, who had been living in the Birthplace, was buried just eight days earlier, on 17 April.

If, as seems likely, Dr. Hall attended his father-in-law during his last illness, he may have kept notes about the progress and treatment of the ailment, although his interest as a medical diarist lies in patients who recovered rather than succumbed. The earliest dated history in the extant case-book belongs to 1617. Conceivably a second notebook exists somewhere — Cooke refers to two Hall books — and may one day surface. Meanwhile, our only information about the circumstances of the poet's death derives from the diary of John Ward. This is the Stratford vicar and physician who reminded himself 'to peruse Shakespears plays, and bee versd in them' so as not to 'bee ignorant in that matter'. Ward notes that 'Shakespear Drayton and Ben Jhonson had a merry meeting and it seems drank too hard for Shakespear died of a feavour there contracted.'

1   See Fripp, *Master Richard Quyny* (Oxford, 1924), pp. 206–7; also his *Shakespeare*, ii. 833.
2   ME, 140–1.

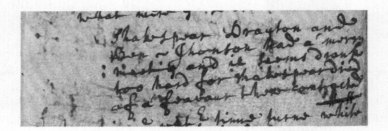

201 JOHN WARD'S MEMORANDUM OF SHAKESPEARE'S DEATH, 1661–3. *Folger Shakespeare Library, MS. V.a.292 (formerly MS. 2073.5), f. 150. Transcript: EKC, ii. 250; BRL, ii. 526. For the discovery and first publication of Shakespeare entries in Ward's diary, see item 116, above.*

Ward's report, half a century after the event, must be consigned to the mythos; he claims no more than to echo hearsay — 'it seems' is his qualifying phrase. Whether an evening's carouse could bring on a fatal fever is not for the medical layman to say, but Ward's story is in other respects not implausible. Shakespeare might well have gathered with his fellow Warwickshireman Drayton and his old theatrical comrade Jonson (no teetotaller) for a drinking party, and Judith's wedding provided a suitable pretext for such conviviality. Ward was, moreover, still in touch with a living tradition, for Judith, now advanced in years, dwelt nearby in Stratford (he refers to her as 'Mrs. Queeny').

During the winter of 1616 Shakespeare summoned his lawyer Francis Collins, who a decade earlier had drawn up the indentures for the Stratford tithes transaction, to execute his last will and testament. Apparently this event took place in January, for when Collins was called upon to revise the document some weeks later, he (or his clerk) inadvertently wrote January instead of March, copying the word from the earlier draft. Revisions were necessitated by the marriage of Judith, with its aftermath of the Margaret Wheeler affair. The lawyer came on 25 March.

Pages 243–5:

202 SHAKESPEARE'S LAST WILL AND TESTAMENT, 25 MARCH 1616. *Public Record Office, Principal Probate Registry, Selected Wills, Prob. 1/4. Transcript: TB, 82–6; EKC, ii. 170–4; BRL, ii. 478–80. The existence of this document was known, if not generally, for some time before it reached print. In October 1737, while visiting Stratford, George Vertue noted that a copy of the will was in the possession of Shakespeare Hart, the then owner of the Birthplace, and a descendant of the poet's sister; the original, Vertue remarks, 'may be Seen in Doctors Commons' (British Library, MS. Portland Loan 29/246, p. 19; see items 136 and 206, and Frank Simpson, 'New Place: The Only Representation of Shakespeare's House, from an Unpublished Manuscript', Shakespeare Survey 5 (Cambridge, 1952), p. 57). The copy mentioned by Vertue is very likely the one independently discovered by the Revd. Joseph Greene in Stratford a decade later. His transcript, with a covering letter (dated 17 September 1747) to the Hon. James West, is in the British Library (MS. Lansdowne 721, ff. 2–6). The copy found by Greene, which belongs to the first half of the seventeenth century and which was probably made after Dr. Hall's death in 1635, is now in the Shakespeare Birthplace Trust Records Office; shelfmark: DR 59/1 (see Levi Fox, 'An Early Copy of Shakespeare's Will', Shakespeare Survey 4 (Cambridge, 1951), pp. 69–77). EKC, ii. 169, and others have supposed that the original will was first printed in* Biographia Britannica *in 1763 (vol. vi, pt. 1, 3636–7), but it appeared earlier, as 'Extracted from the Registry of the Archbishop of Canterbury', in the posthumous third edition of Lewis Theobald's Works of Shakespeare (1752), i. 1–8.*

A few students — e.g. John Pym Yeatman, 'Is William Shakspere's Will Holographic?' (1901) — have argued that the document is in Shakespeare's hand. EKC, ii. 174, believes that a clerk in the employment of Francis Collins 'probably' drew up the will; BRL, ii. 473, has 'no doubt' that 'it was written by Collins' clerk or scrivener'. But there is doubt; ME, 141, identifies the hand as that of Collins. N. E. Evans, however, believes that 'in all probability' Collins did not draw up the will himself, 'for specimens of Collins's hand in other documents differ considerably from the writing in the will' (Shakespeare in the Public Records, p. 34). Collins or his clerk also set down John Combe's will in 1613.

Shakespeare's will was preserved in the Prerogative Office at Doctors' Commons (razed in 1861), and afterwards in Somerset House, before being removed in 1962 to the Public Record Office, where it is mounted and on permanent display in wall case XI of the Record Office Museum. A narrow strip of parchment formerly joined together at the top the three sheets of foreign-made paper on which the will is written. Although the document has suffered from folding and wear, it has been mended and is in reasonable condition. It is here reduced by about a quarter. On the first sheet what remains of Shakespeare's signature is in the decayed lower left-hand corner.

Tm Willm Shackspeare

In the name of god Amen I Willm Shackspeare of Stratford vpon Avon in the countie
of warr gent in pfect health & memorie god be praysed doe make & Ordayne this
my last will & testam̄t in manner & forme followeinge That ys to saye firste I Comend
my Soule into the handes of god my Creator hoping & assuredlie beleeveing through
thonelie meritte of Jesus Christe my Saviour to be made ptaker of lyfe everlastinge
And my bodye to the Earthe whereof yt ys made Item I Gyve & bequeath
vnto my sonne in Lawe and daughter Judyth One hundred & fiftie poundes of lawfull
Englishe money to be paied vnto her in manner & forme following That ys to
saye One hundred poundes in discharge of her marriage porcion wthin one
yeare after my deceas wth consideracion after the Rate of twoe shillinges in the
pound for soe long tyme as the same shalbe vnpaied vnto her after my deceas & the
Fyftie poundes Residewe thereof vpon her Surrendring of or gyveing of such
sufficient securitie as the overseers of this my will shall like of to Surrender or
graunte all her estate & Right that shall discend or come vnto her after my deceas or
that shee nowe hath of in or to one Copiehold tenemente wth thappurtennces lyeing
& being in Stratford vpon Avon aforesaied in the saied countie of warr being pcell
or holden of the mannor of Rowington vnto my daughter Susanna hall & her heires
for ever Item I gyve & bequeath vnto my saied daughter Judyth One hundred &
fiftie poundes more if shee or Anie issue of her bodie be Lyvinge att thend of three
yeares next ensueing the daie of the date of this my will during wch tyme my executours
to paie her consideracion from my deceas according to the Rate aforesaied And if she
dye wthin the saied terme wthout issue of her bodye then my will ys & I doe gyve & bequeath
One hundred poundes thereof to my Neece Elizabeth hall & the fiftie
poundes to be sett forth by my executours during the lief of my Sister
Johane harte & the vse & proffitt thereof Cominge shalbe paied to my saied
Sister Jone & after her deceas the saied lli shall Remaine Amongst the
children of my saied Sister Equallie to be devided Amongst them But if my
saied daughter Judith be lyving att thend of the saied three yeares or
anie issue of her bodye then my will ys and soe I devise & bequeath the
saied One hundred & fiftie poundes to be sett out by my executours & overseers
for the best benefitt of her and her issue and the stock not to be paied vnto her soe long as she
shalbe marryed & covert Baron but my will ys that she shall have the consideracion
yearelie paied vnto her during her lief & after her deceas the saied stock and
consideracion to bee paied to her children if she have Anie & if not to her
executours or assignes she lyving the saied terme after my deceas Provided that if
such husbond as she shall att thend of the saied three yeares be marryed vnto or att Anie
after doe sufficientlie Assure vnto her & thissue of her bodie Landes Answereable to
the porcion by this my will gyven vnto her & to be adiudged soe by my executours
& overseers then my will ys that the saied clli shalbe paied to such husbond as
shall make such assurance to his owne vse Item I gyve & bequeath vnto my
saied Sister Jone xxli & all my wearing Apparrell to be paied & delivered wthin one yeare
after my deceas And I doe will & devise vnto her the house wth thappurtenncs in Stratford wherein
she dwelleth for her naturall lief vnder the yearelie Rent of xijd Item I gyve & bequeath

unto her three sound [illegible] [illegible] Hart & Michaell Hart

three poundes a peece to be payed within one yeare after my decease
to be sett out for her within one yeare after my decease by my executors
with thadvise & direccions of my overseers for the best effitt of her
marriage & then the same with thincrease thereof to be payed unto
her Item I gyve & bequeath unto her All my Plate that I
have att the date hereof my will Item I gyve & bequeath unto
the poore of Stratford aforesaied tenn poundes to Mr Thomas
Combe my Sword to Thomas Russell Esquier fyve poundes &
to Fraunces Collins of the Borough of Warr in the countie of War-
gent thirteene poundes six shillinge eight pence to be paied within one yeare after my decease Item I gyve & bequeath to [illegible]
[illegible] xxvij viijd to buy him A Ringe to my godson William
Walker xxs in gold to Anthony Nashe gent xxvjs viijd & to my
[illegible] John Nashe xxvjs viijd Item I gyve & bequeath [illegible]
my Daughter Susanna Hall All that Capitall messuage or tenement wth thapp'tenances called the newe place wherein I nowe dwell
& two messuages or tenementes wth thapp'tenances scituat lyeing & being
in Henley streete within the boroughe of Stratford aforesaied And all
my barnes stable orchardes gardens landes tentes & hereditamentes whatsoever
scituat lyeing & being or to be had [illegible] receyved perceyved or taken
within the townes Hamlettes villages ffieldes & groundes of Stratford
upon Avon Oldstratford Bushopton & Welcombe or in anie of them
in the saied countie of Warr And alsoe All that messuage or
tenement wth thapp'tenances wherein one John Robinson dwelleth scituat
lyeing & being in the Blackfriars in London neere the Wardrobe & all
other my landes tentes & hereditamentes whatsoever To have & to hold All
& singuler the saied premisses wth their Appertenances unto the saied Susanna
Hall for & during the terme of her naturall lief & after her
decease to the first sonne of her bodie lawfullie yssueing & to the
heires males of the bodie of the saied first sonne lawfullie
yssueing & for defalt of such issue to the second sonne of her
bodie lawfullie yssueing & to the heires males of the bodie of the
saied second sonne lawfullie yssueinge & for defalt of such
heires to the third sonne of the bodie of the saied Susanna
lawfullie yssueing & of the heires males of the bodie of the saied third
sonne lawfullie yssueing And for defalt of such issue the same soe
to be & Remaine to the ffourth sonne ffifth sixte & seaventh
sonnes of her bodie lawfullie issueing one after Another & to the

Males of the bodie of the saied ffourth fyfth sixte & seaventh sonnes
lawfullie yssueing one after an other as yt ys before Lymitted to be & Remaine
to the first second & third Sonns of her bodie & to theire heires Males
And for defalt of suche issue the saied premisses to be & Remaine to my
sayed Neece Hall & the heires males of her bodie Lawfullie
yssueing for defalt of suche issue to my daughter Judith &
the heires males of her bodie lawfullie issueinge And for
defalt of suche issue to the right heires of me the saied William
Shackspeare for ever Item I gyve & bequeath to my saied daughter
Judith my broad silver gilt bole All the Rest of my goodes Chattels
Leases plate Jewels & Houshold stuffe whatsoever after my dettes and
Legasies paied & my funerall expences discharged I gyve devise
& bequeath to my Sonne in Lawe John Hall gent & my daughter
Susanna his wief whom I ordaine & make executours of this my
Last will & testament And I doe intreat & Appoint the saied Thomas
Russell Esquier & ffrauncis Collins gent to be overseers hereof And
doe Revoke All former wills & publishe this to be my last
will & testament In witnes whereof I have herevnto put my
hand the Daie & Yeare first above written.

Witnes to the publishing
hereof Fra: Collyns
Julyus Shawe
John Robinson
Hamnet Sadler
Robert Whattcott

By me William Shakspeare

Probatum coram magistro Willelmo Byrde
Legum doctore Commiss &c xxijᵈᵒ die
mensis Junij Anno Dni 1616 Juramento
Johannis Hall vnius ex &c Cui &c
de bene &c Jurat Reservata potestate
&c Susanne Hall alt ex &c cum
venerit &c petitur &c

A new first page was required, and numerous substitutions and additions in the second and third pages, although it is impossible to say how many changes were made in March and how many, *currente calamo*, in January. Collins never got round to having a fair copy of the will made, probably because of haste occasioned by the seriousness of the testator's condition, though this attorney had a way of allowing much-corrected draft wills to stand. Shakespeare validated each sheet at the bottom with his signature, prefixing the last with the emphatic 'By me'. He describes himself as 'in perfect health & memorie', a conventional phrase and not always to be taken at face value, although perhaps apt enough in January; the law anyway would be concerned with his memory rather than his health. In March a feeble hand held the pen. The invalid mustered all his strength for the firm strokes of 'By me William' in the third signature, then collapsed into the wavering scrawl of the surname. His two other signatures display (according to palaeographical analysis) 'weakness and malformation'. Shakespeare was dying that March, although he would linger for another month.

His will has given rise to even more discussion and debate than the marriage licence bond. Yet the first to pronounce on it, the Stratford antiquary Joseph Greene, who turned up a transcript of the testament in 1747, was positively depressed by his discovery. 'The Legacies and Bequests therein', he informed a friend, 'are undoubtedly as he intended; but the manner of introducing them, appears to me so dull and irregular, so absolutely void of yᵉ least particle of that Spirit which Animated Our great Poet; that it must lessen his Character as a Writer, to imagine yᵉ least Sentence of it his production.'[1] A twentieth-century student, B. Roland Lewis, who has lovingly annotated every provision, understandably takes a different view: 'Rowe said (1709) that the spirit of the man is to be found in his works. Rather the essential spirit of William Shakespeare is to be found in his will, its preparation constituting virtually the last act of his active life only a few weeks before he died.'[2] The truth lies somewhere between these extremes. Shakespeare's will is not a poetic testament but 'a characteristic will of a man of property in the reign of James I'.[3] In such a document it is futile to seek metaphor or dark conceit, or even intimate revelation. But the will does yield a glimpse of Shakespeare's purpose in building an estate from the proceeds of his play-writing, and it enshrines the names of those he cherished most in Stratford and in London.

The will begins with a pious declaration:

In the name of god Amen I William Shackspeare . . . in perfect health & memorie god be praysed doe make & Ordayne this my last will & testament in manner & forme followeing. That ys to saye ffirst I Comend my Soule into the handes of god my Creator hoping & assuredlie beleeving through thonelie merittes of Jesus Christe my Saviour to be made partaker of lyfe everlastinge, And my bodye to the Earth whereof yt ys made.

To find here a confession of personal faith is to consider the matter too curiously. The preamble is formulaic, following almost word for word a model included by William West of the Inner Temple in his *Simboleography, which may be termed the Art, or Description, of Instruments and Presidents* [i.e. *Precedents*]. West's second 'forme of a Will' commences, 'In the name of God Amen. . . . sicke of bodie but of good and perfect memory (God be praised) . . . First I commend my soule into the hands of God my maker, hoping assuredly through the onely merites of Jesus Christ my Saviour, to be made partaker of life everlasting. And I commend my bodie to the earth whereof it is made.'[4] Shakespeare did not have to supply Collins with these phrases; he set them down automatically.

Of his several heirs, Shakespeare considers first the case of Judith — because of her, the page required recopying. 'Item I Gyve & bequeath unto my sonne in L[aw]'; so the lawyer took down the dying man's words, but Shakespeare caught himself — Collins (or his clerk) crossed out 'sonne in L' and wrote instead 'daughter Judyth'. She is to have £150, with strings attached. One hundred pounds go to her for a marriage portion, but for the remaining £50 she must

1 British Library, MS. Lansdowne 721, f. 2. The existence of the will was known earlier; see caption 202.
2 BRL, ii. 471.
3 G. E. Bentley, *Shakespeare: A Biographical Handbook* (New Haven, 1961), p. 61.
4 William West, *The First Part of Simboleography* . . . (1615 ed.), Sect. 643.

renounce any claim to 'one Copiehold tenemente . . . being parcell or holden of the mannor of Rowington'; this was the Chapel Lane cottage. Shakespeare further bequeaths Judith 'One Hundred & ffyftie Poundes more if shee or Anie issue of her bodie be Lyvinge att thend of three Yeares next ensueing the daie of the date of this my will . . . .' Should she, however, die barren during this interval, his granddaughter Elizabeth Hall (in the will called his niece) will have £100, the other £50 going to his sister Joan and her children. If Judith, or any issue, is living after three years, then the executors will see to it that she enjoys the annual interest earned by the £150, although not the principal, so long as she stays married. Her husband can claim the sum only on condition that he 'doe sufficientlie Assure unto her & thissue of her bodie landes Awnswereable to the porcion by this my will gyven unto her' — in other words, that he settle on his wife lands worth the £150. Later in the will, on sheet three, Shakespeare gives Judith his 'broad silver gilt bole'. Chambers in 1930 guessed that Shakespeare's careful provisions respecting his younger daughter argued no great confidence in Thomas Quiney, and the suspicions have been borne out by the discoveries in the act book for the Stratford ecclesiastical court. It is perhaps not too fanciful to speculate, with Hugh Hanley and E. R. C. Brinkworth, that Quiney's trial and disgrace not only motivated the alterations in the will but also constituted a shock that hastened Shakespeare's end.[1]

Lesser bequests follow. Shakespeare leaves £30 and his wearing apparel to Joan Hart, who is permitted to stay on with her family in the western house in Henley Street for a nominal yearly rent of 12d. Her three sons — he names William and Michael, but then memory fails and a blank space is left for his third nephew Thomas — are bequeathed £5 each. Elizabeth Hall gets all the plate, except for Judith's broad silver-gilt bowl. Shakespeare, it seems, also considered providing Elizabeth with a marriage portion; but she was only eight — who knows? Susanna might bear more children — and so he changed his mind, ordering the incompletely stated clause to be struck out. The poet remembered the poor of Stratford with a donation of £10, generous enough for a man of his means; the town's richest man, John Combe, had three years earlier left £20 for the same purpose — a munificence thought worthy of mention on his monument in Stratford Church. Shakespeare gives his sword to Thomas, the nephew of the same Combe. The testator leaves £5 to Thomas Russell, the Alderminster squire connected by marriage to the author of *Willobie his Avisa*, and £13.6s.8d. to Francis Collins. Money to buy memorial rings, each to cost 26s.8d., he sets aside for old Stratford friends and neighbours: Hamnet Sadler, William Reynolds (the recusant landowner), and the Nash brothers, Anthony and John (they had witnessed Shakespeare's purchase of the Old Stratford freehold in 1602). Sadler's name replaces that of 'm^r Richard Tyler thelder', the butcher's son of Sheep Street whom the dying man may have known from his schooldays; Tyler had just come under criticism for his handling of collections for victims of the great fire — perhaps that is why his name was deleted from the will.[2] Shakespeare does not forget his eight-year-old godson, William Walker, whom he leaves 20s. in gold. Of all those he had known in London during his years with the Chamberlain's company and then the King's men, the playwright singles out three for affectionate remembrance: '& to my ffellowes John Hemynges Richard Burbage & Henry Cundell xxvi^s viii^d A peece to buy them Ringes'. Shakespeare neglects to mention Southampton, to whom, as an aspiring young poet, he had offered *Venus and Adonis* and *The Rape of Lucrece*; or the Earls of Pembroke and Montgomery; or, for that matter, any peer of the realm.

His wife he failed to mention too, at least at first; but then he did not have to provide for her. As the Victorian popularizer Charles Knight pointed out over a century ago, English common law entitled Anne to a life interest of one third in her husband's estate, as well as to residence in the family house. That was her dower right. Besides, the Halls, responsible folk, would look after her in New Place. But in an afterthought — the entry is an interlineation — Shakespeare refers to Anne: 'Item I gyve unto my wief my second best bed with the furniture', that is, with the hangings, valance, bed linen, etc. This provision has stimulated endless, mostly unprofitable, controversy. In the eighteenth century Malone saw the bequest as an expression of contempt:

---

1 Brinkworth, *Shakespeare and the Bawdy Court*, pp. 80–3.
2 ME, 136.

'His wife had not wholly escaped his memory; he had forgot her, — he had recollected her, — but so recollected her, as more strongly to mark how little he esteemed her; he had already (as is vulgarly expressed) cut her off, not indeed with a shilling, but with an old bed.'[1] Many, until this day, have echoed Malone's judgement. Another school, however, conscious of dower right, holds that the Shakespeares must have reserved their best bed for overnight guests at New Place and that the less valuable bed was the one rich in tender matrimonial associations. Investigators have turned over countless Elizabethan and Jacobean wills in search of analogous bequests, and their efforts have not gone entirely unrewarded. Thus William Palmer of Leamington in 1573 left his wife Elizabeth 'all hir wearing apparell' and his 'second best fetherbed for hir selfe furnished, And one other meaner fetherbed furnished for hir mayde'; he also doubled the income she would receive from the original marriage settlement, 'in Consideracion that she is a gentlewoman and drawing towardes yeres, And that' — the testator affirms — 'I wolde have hir to live as one that were and had bien my wief'.[2] This is apposite, and who would gainsay the conjugal tenderness informing the bequest? The problem, as regards the provision in Shakespeare's will, is that the scant attention paid to the spouse is unusual, and what is said is unaccompanied by any expression of testamentary emotion, as in the Palmer will; but Shakespeare includes no endearing references to other members of his family either, and perhaps his lawyer did not encourage, or permit, such embellishments. Hence our choice between cynicism and sentiment. The latter is surely the more attractive option, but this is a matter that can be no more than inferentially resolved.

As befitted an heirloom, the best bed would swell the value of 'All the Rest of my goodes Chattels Leases plate Jewels & household stuffe whatsoever after my dettes and Legasies paied & my funerall expences discharged'. The 'Leases' might include Shakespeare's shares, if he still held them, in the Globe and Blackfriars. All this he wills to his son-in-law John Hall and his daughter Susanna. She receives more — much more — besides: New Place, 'wherein I nowe dwell',

& twoe messuages or tenementes with thappurtenaunces scituat . . . in Henley streete within the borough of Stratford aforesaied And all my barnes stables Orchardes gardens landes tenementes & hereditamentes whatsoever scituat . . . within the townes Hamlettes villages ffieldes & groundes of Stratford upon Avon Oldstratford Bushopton & welcombe or in anie of them in the saied countie of warr And alsoe All that Messuage or tenemente with thappurtenaunces wherein one John Robinson dwelleth scituat . . . in the blackfriers in London nere the Wardrobe & all other my landes tenementes and hereditamentes whatsoever.

These properties, the bulk of the estate, are hers to have and to hold for the rest of her natural life. After her death the premises and appurtenances are to descend to the Halls' first son, and to that son's lawful male heirs, and (in default of such issue) to the second son's male heirs, and so on to the second, third, fourth, fifth, sixth, and seventh sons, and their lawful heirs. 'And for defalt of such issue the saied premisses to be & Remaine to my sayed Neece Hall & the heires Males of her bodie Lawfullie yssueing And for defalt of such issue to my daughter Judith & the heires Males of her bodie lawfullie yssueinge . . . .' In this way Shakespeare sought to hold together the material possessions purchased by his art. He could not have foreseen that nature would defeat his plans.

That the will lists no books or literary manuscripts has raised some eyebrows. This is not, however, as odd as might appear. Shakespeare's play-scripts were not his to dispose of — they belonged to the King's men. Books might have been separately itemized in the inventory postmortem, but this has not come down. In any event, they would form part of the 'goodes' inherited by the Halls, and perhaps thus found a place on the doctor's shelves alongside his medical treatises. If so, a special interest attaches to the 'study of Bookes' to which Hall refers in his nuncupative will of 1635, and which he bequeathed to his son-in-law, 'to dispose of them as you see good'. Two years later Susanna and her son-in-law charged in Chancery that Baldwin Brooks (afterwards to become the bailiff of Stratford) had suborned an undersheriff and some bailiffs — 'men of meane estate' — to break open the doors and study of New Place, and rashly seize 'Divers

---

1 *Supplement to the Edition of Shakspeare's Plays Published in 1778 by Samuel Johnson and George Steevens*, ed. Edmond Malone (1780), i. 657.
2 ME brings the will to notice and cites the salient bequest (164–5n).

bookes' and 'other goods of greate value'.[1] He had been frustrated in his efforts to collect a judgement against the Hall estate. During the Civil War, Queen Henrietta Maria, marching in triumph to Kineton with her forces, joined up with Prince Rupert and his troops in Stratford. There, in July 1643, the Queen kept her court at Stratford for three days. It was presumably on this occasion that Susanna Hall presented a member of the Queen's entourage, Colonel Richard Grace (he was chamberlain to the Duke of York) with a copy of Henri Estienne's *Mervaylous Discourse upon the lyfe of Katherine de Medicis* — if one may accept the title-page inscription in a seventeenth-century hand (not Susanna's): 'Liber R: Gracei ex dono amicae D. Susanne Hall'. Possibly the book originally formed part of her father's library. Reports about Shakespeare's manuscripts first began to circulate in the next century. In 1729 John Roberts, who describes himself as 'a Stroling Player', lamented that '*Two* large *Chests* full of this GREAT MAN's *loose Papers* and *Manuscripts*, in the Hands of an ignorant *Baker* of WARWICK, (who married one of the Descendants from *Shakespear*) were carelesly scatter'd and thrown about, as Garret Lumber and Litter, to the particular Knowledge of the late *Sir William Bishop*, till they were all consum'd in the general Fire and Destruction of that Town'. Sir William Bishop (1626–1700) did live in the Shakespeare country, and a conflagration inflicted much damage on Warwick in 1694; but no descendant of Shakespeare or of the Harts is known to have then dwelt there.[2] Malone reports that in 1742 Sir Hugh Clopton, born two years after the death of the poet's granddaughter Elizabeth, told the actor Macklin of 'an old tradition that she had carried away with her from

203 SUSANNA HALL AND THE *MERVAYLOUS DISCOURSE*, 1643(?). *Shakespeare Birthplace Trust Library; shelfmark: SR 93.2. STC 10550. This item, from the collection of Sir Thomas Phillipps, was no. 2511 in the Sotheby catalogue for the sale held on 26 and 27 November 1973.*

1 For the text of 'The Joynte and severall Answeres of Susan Hall widowe & Thomas Nashe gent', see Frank Marcham, *William Shakespeare and his Daughter Susannah* (1931), pp. 66–71.
2 *An Answer to Mr. Pope's Preface to Shakespear . . . By a Stroling Player* (1729), p. 45; EKC, ii. 272.

R

Stratford many of her grandfather's papers'.[1]

Shakespeare appointed Thomas Russell and Francis Collins overseers of his will. Five witnesses signed the document: Collins, July (or Julyns) Shaw, John Robinson, Hamnet Sadler, and Robert Whatcott. The last-named had testified for Susanna when she sued for defamation in 1613. Robinson was a labourer. Whatcott and Robinson may have been servants of Shakespeare or the Halls. The Halls were the executors. A note under Shakespeare's signature on the third sheet attests that the will was proved by John Hall on 22 June 1616.

204 WILLIAM SHAKESPEARE BURIED, 25 APRIL 1616. *Stratford parish register, burials, f. 46.* *Shakespeare Birthplace Trust Records Office; shelfmark: DR 243/1.*

Shakespeare was laid to rest in the chancel of Holy Trinity Church near the north wall. According to a report late in the century, they 'laid him full Seventeen foot deep, deep enough to Secure him'; but this seems unlikely so close to where the Avon flows.[2] On the slab covering the poet's grave — 'a plaine free stone', Mr. Dowdall described it in 1693 — appear these words:

> GOOD FREND FOR JESUS SAKE FORBEARE,
> TO DIGG THE DUST ENCLOASED HEARE.
> BLESTE BE Y^{E} MAN Y^{T} SPARES THES STONES,
> AND CURST BE HE Y^{T} MOVES MY BONES.[3]

Several correspondents in the late seventeenth century affirm that Shakespeare himself devised this epitaph, and ordered it to be cut on his tombstone.[4] The malediction, expressing a conventional sentiment in commonplace phrases, solemnly forewarns not the casual passerby — he would hardly come with spade in hand — but the sexton, who, because of the limited burial space available in the church, sometimes had to dig up graves and remove the bones to the adjoining charnel-house. William Hall, the rector of Acton in Middlesex, had something to say about the charnel-house and the curse when he wrote to 'Dear Neddy' (the noted Anglo-Saxon

1 William Shakespeare, *Plays and Poems*, ed. Malone (1790), vol. i, pt. 1, p. 136.

2 The report is by William Hall; see item 205, p. 251. Chambers makes the point about the improbability of a seventeen-foot grave (EKC, ii. 181).

3 BLESTE: a disputed reading, BLESE being a possible alternative.

4 Mr. Dowdall (item 218, p. 262) and Hall both have Shakespeare composing the epitaph, as does the author of an anonymous manuscript note 'written towards the end of the seventeenth century' in a copy of the Third Folio. H-P prints the note in his *Outlines* (ii. 357), and EKC reprints it (ii. 261).

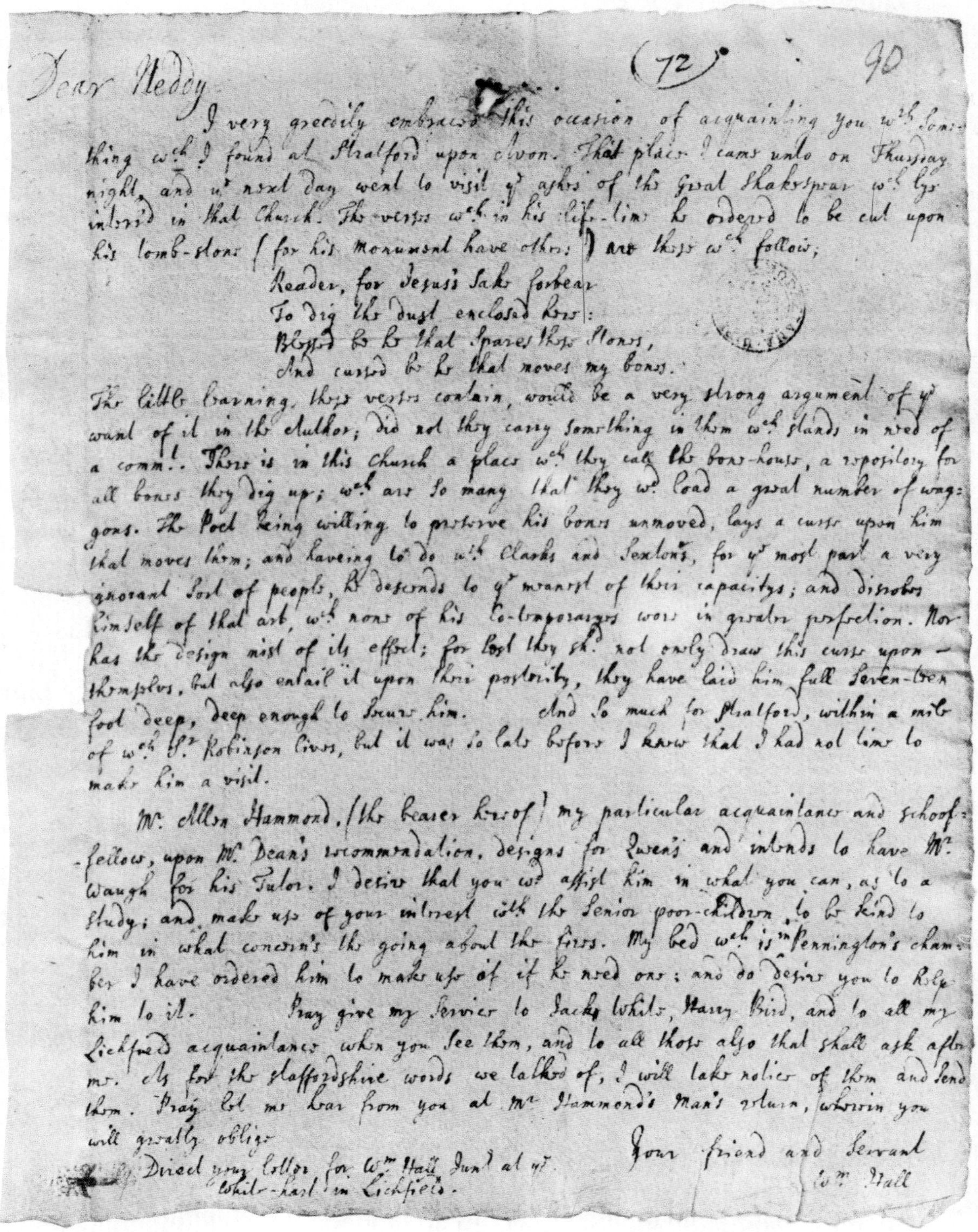

Dear Neddy.

... [handwritten letter, the legible epitaph verse reads:]

Reader, for Jesus sake forbear
To dig the dust enclosed here:
Blessed be he that spares these stones,
And cursed be he that moves my bones.

Your friend and Servant
Wm Hall

205   WILLIAM HALL'S LETTER, 1694. *Bodleian Library, MS. Rawlinson D. 377, f. 90. Transcript (extract): EKC, ii. 260–1; BRL, ii. 530. H-P discovered the letter and printed it in full in Shakespeare's Grave. Notes of Traditions . . . (1884).*

scholar Edward Thwaites) in 1694:

There is in this Church a place which they call the bone-house, a repository for all bones they dig up; which are So many that they would load a great number of waggons. The Poet being willing to preserve his bones unmoved, lays a curse upon him that moves them; and haveing to do with Clarks and Sextons, for ye most part a very ignorant Sort of people, he descends to ye meanest of their capacitys; and disrobes himself of that art, which none of his Co-temporaryes wore in greater perfection.

Whether or not actually written by Shakespeare, the malediction has effectively accomplished its purpose, for no sexton, clerk, or crank has moved the bones enclosed there. By the mid-eighteenth century, however, the gravestone itself (according to Halliwell-Phillipps) had sunk below floor level, and was so decayed that the overseers of the church replaced it.

There are those who suspect that Shakespeare's remains lie in the church rather than in the

no. 1.

*on shakespers
grave stone near the
rails of the commū
table.*

*Good frend for Iesus sake forbeare
to digg the dust enclosed tEare
blest be the man that spares these stones
and Curst behe yt moves my bones.*

*he left 2 daughters
Susanna daughter of
Shakespeare, married to John Hall
Gent*

*another Daughter married to
mr. Nash. of ....*

*no. 2. his wifes
grave stone.*

*anne ..... wife of
shakespeare dyd.
aug. 6. 1623.*

206   GEORGE VERTUE'S SKETCH OF THE SHAKESPEARE MONUMENT, 1737. *British Library, MS. Portland Loan 29/246, p. 17. Vertue made the sketch when he accompanied the Earl of Oxford on a tour in October 1737; see Frank Simpson, 'New Place: The Only Representation of Shakespeare's House, from an Unpublished Manuscript', Shakespeare Survey 5 (Cambridge, 1952), pp. 55–7. For Vertue's sketches of New Place, made during the same visit, see item 136, above.*

churchyard not because he was the celebrated poet of the London stage but because his purchase of an interest in Stratford tithes qualified him as a lay rector. However this may be, before the end of the century folk were finding their way to Holy Trinity 'to visit yᵉ ashes of the Great Shakespear which lye interr'd in that Church'. They also paused, as innumerable pilgrims have since done, before the effigy installed, about five feet above the grave, in the north wall of the chancel. As early as 1634 Lieutenant Hammond, passing through Stratford, found the 'neat Monument' worthy of note.[1] From a manuscript note in a 1653 almanac, we learn that it was made 'by one Gerard Johnson'.[2]

The name is an anglicized version, not unusual, of Gheerart Janssen, whose father (also Gheerart) had emigrated from Amsterdam to London around 1567 and set up shop as a stonemason in Southwark, not far from the Globe theatre. His four sons helped in the business, which prospered: the Janssens erected tombs in Bottesford church in Leicestershire for four Earls of Rutland, including the sixth, Francis Manners, who commissioned an *impresa* of Shakespeare and Burbage. When the elder Janssen died in 1611, his family kept the business going. Possibly Shakespeare and his fellows knew the shop. Certainly the poet's family were acquainted with the tomb, with recumbent effigy in a gown, fashioned by Gheerart the younger for John Combe. In his will Combe had allocated £60 for this memorial in Stratford Church.

For the Shakespeare monument, which is in Jacobean Renaissance style, Janssen worked mainly in white marble, with black for the two Corinthian columns, and black touchstone for the inlaid panels. The columns support a cornice on which sit two small cherubic figures, both male: the right one, holding a spade, represents Labour; the left, with a skull and inverted torch, signifies Rest. They flank the familiar Shakespeare arms, helm, and crest, carved in bas-relief on a square stone block. The design forms a pyramid at the apex of which sits another skull, chapless and hollow-eyed.

1   EKC, ii. 242–3; British Library, MS. Lansdowne 213, f. 332ᵛ; see also above, p. 185.
2   The note was set down by Dugdale; see *The Life, Diary, and Correspondence of Sir William Dugdale*, ed. William Hamper (1827), p. 99.

207   THE SHAKESPEARE MONUMENT, HOLY TRINITY CHURCH, STRATFORD-UPON-AVON.

R*

THE JOHN STOW MONUMENT, ST. ANDREW UNDERSHAFT CHURCH, LONDON. *The monument, installed in 1605, is discussed (in relation to the Shakespeare monument) by M. H. Spielmann, 'Shakespeare's Portraiture', in* Studies in the First Folio written for the Shakespeare Association *(1924), pp. 4–5.*

One suspects that the reverence inspired by the bust — actually a half-length figure carved from soft bluish Cotswold limestone — owes less to the execution than to the subject and setting. Wearing a sleeveless gown over a doublet, Shakespeare stands with a quill pen in his right hand, a sheet of paper under his left, both hands resting on a cushion. He looks prosperous, with unwrinkled brow, high bald dome, and thick, short neck. The side-locks are bobbed, the moustaches and beard neatly trimmed; the eyes (set too close together) stare vacantly ahead. One reminds oneself that it is unreasonable to expect lively touches of nature in a commissioned piece of funerary sculpture which tended as a class towards formalized rigidity; this effigy bears a generic resemblance to that of John Stow in St. Andrew Undershaft church in London.

Dover Wilson sees 'a self-satisfied pork-butcher' peering out from under the niched arch of the monument. Maybe so; but not all middle-aged successful writers look delicately consumptive. For better or for worse, the Janssen bust is an authentic portrayal, all the rest, save one, being derivative, spurious, or in varying degrees doubtful. The monument in Holy Trinity was presumably commissioned and paid for by one or more of the surviving adult members of Shakespeare's immediate family: the widow, the two daughters, the two sons-in-law, and his sister. Most probably Dr. Hall looked after the arrangements. Whoever took the responsibility, the family, whether entirely satisfied or not, must have found the likeness acceptable. It is even possible that Janssen, working as he did on Bankside, benefited from the suggestions of Shakespeare's former colleagues in the King's men. And however burgher-like the subject may appear, he stands before us as the poet, not the man of property, for his mouth is open to declaim his just-composed verses.

So too the tablet under the cushion celebrates the writer:

> JUDICIO PYLIUM, GENIO SOCRATEM, ARTE MARONEM:
> TERRA TEGIT, POPULUS MÆRET, OLYMPUS HABET.
>
> STAY PASSENGER, WHY GOEST THOU BY SO FAST?
> READ IF THOU CANST, WHOM ENVIOUS DEATH HATH PLAST,
> WITH IN THIS MONUMENT SHAKSPEARE: WITH WHOME,
> QUICK NATURE DIDE: WHOSE NAME DOTH DECK Ŷ TOMBE,
> FAR MORE THEN COST: SIEH ALL, Ŷ HE HATH WRITT,
> LEAVES LIVING ART, BUT PAGE, TO SERVE HIS WITT.
>
> OBIIT AÑO DOⁱ 1616
> ÆTATIS · 53 DIE 23 APᴿ.

The stone-cutter mistakenly carved 'SIEH' instead of 'SITH', but such slips of the chisel are common enough in monumental inscriptions of all ages. A more serious blunder is made by the unknown eulogist when he suggests that Death has placed the poet within the monument. About all he has to offer in the way of information is that Shakespeare died in his fifty-third year.

Around mid-century, Sir William Dugdale, born in Warwickshire on a day when (by happy omen) bees swarmed in his father's garden, visited Stratford to gather materials for his enormous *Antiquities of Warwickshire Illustrated: from Records, Leiger-Books, Manuscripts, Charters, Evidences,*

209 THE SHAKESPEARE MONUMENT IN DUGDALE'S *ANTIQUITIES OF WARWICKSHIRE* (1656), p. 520.

Tombes, and Armes: Beautified with Maps, Prospects and Portraictures, published in a splendid folio in 1656. Although Dugdale's compilation is invaluable, the engraving made by Hollar or his assisttant Gaywood from the author's sketch of Shakespeare's monument is perplexing rather than helpful, for we reconcile it with difficulty with the familiar artefact in the chancel. In the illustration in the *Antiquities* leopards' heads adorn the capitals, while on the outermost points of the cornice Rest and Labour perch precariously, the latter having exchanged his torch for an hourglass. The poet has parted with quill and paper; instead, elbows akimbo, he clutches the cushion—does it represent wealth? His cheeks have shrivelled, his moustaches droop disconsolately below the tight lips. The complacent pork-butcher has metamorphosed into a melancholy tailor.[1]

We are reminded that the monument too has had a history. Over the years it deteriorated, until by 1748 the statue, several fingers amputated, required repair and beautifying. Later in the century Malone, in a singular aberration, persuaded the vicar of Stratford to whitewash the bust, and for his pains was rewarded with an epigram inserted in the Stratford *Visitors' Book*:

> Stranger, to whom this monument is shewn,
> Invoke the Poet's curse upon Malone;
> Whose meddling zeal his barbarous taste betrays,
> And daubs his tombstone, as he mars his plays![2]

1   It is Chambers who thinks of a melancholy tailor (EKC, ii. 185).
2   R. B. Wheler, *The Gentleman's Magazine*, lxxxv (1815), 390.

In 1861 a limner applied fresh colours to the bust; a healthy glow suffused Shakespeare's cheeks, his locks became auburn and his doublet scarlet.[1] That these were Janssen's colours must remain uncertain, but no amount of restoration can have transformed the monument of Dugdale's engraving into the effigy in Stratford church.[2] The best and simplest explanation is that the illustration, like others in the *Antiquities*, misrepresents the object, in keeping with the liberty of seventeenth-century engraving. The main interest of Dugdale, who was later to become Garter King-of-Arms, lay in pedigrees, inscriptions, and the like. In the engraving the armorial bearings are accurately delineated. The monument in Holy Trinity, with its uninspiring bust, is authentic enough.

210 LEONARD DIGGES ON SHAKESPEARE, *c. 1613. Balliol College Library; shelfmark: 700 a. 14. Transcript: Paul Morgan, ' "Our Will Shakespeare" and Lope de Vega: An Unrecorded Contemporary Document', Shakespeare Survey 16 (Cambridge, 1963), p. 118. In this inscription on the fly-leaf of the third edition of Lope de Vega's* Rimas *(Madrid, 1613), Digges speaks of 'this Booke of Sonets, which with Spaniards here is accounted of their lope de Vega as in Englande wee sholde of our Will Shakespeare'. The Will Baker to whom the inscription is addressed may have been a University College, Oxford, contemporary of Digges. The 'M*[r] *Mab' referred to by Digges was a fellow of Magdalen College and a Hispanist. Paul Morgan discovered the inscription, and analysed it in the essay cited.*

It had been installed by 1623. In that year Leonard Digges, an Oxford scholar and translator and a Shakespeare enthusiast — he was the stepson of the Thomas Russell mentioned by Shakespeare in his will — alludes to Janssen's handiwork in his poem 'To the Memorie of the deceased Author Maister W. Shakespeare':

> *Shake-speare*, at length thy pious fellowes give
> The world thy Workes: thy Workes, by which, out-live
> Thy Tombe, thy name must: when that stone is rent,
> And Time dissolves thy *Stratford* Moniment,
> Here we alive shall view thee still.

1 The colours are thus described by M. H. Spielmann, 'Shakespeare's Portraiture', in *Studies in the First Folio written for the Shakespeare Association* (1924), p. 14; cited by EKC, ii. 184. Shakespeare's complexion has since darkened to a deep tan, and the eyes are almost black. On the monument Spielmann and Chambers are my principal authorities. The latter expertly sums up scholarship (ii. 182–5).
2 It has lately again suffered desecration. On the night of 2 October 1973 intruders removed the bust from the monument by chipping out part of the plinth. The police believe they 'were seeking valuable manuscripts written by the Bard' (Birmingham *Evening Mail*, 3 October 1973). These were regrettably unforthcoming. The bust, which I examined shortly after the incident, sustained only very slight damage, and has since been put back into its place.

The 'fellowes' here applauded — in a context that brings to mind a familiar *topos* of the *Sonnets* — are Heminges and Condell, and their piety of course lies in the gathering together and publication of the plays of the First Folio. That book has indeed, as Digges foretold, made Shakespeare 'looke/ Fresh to all Ages'.

211 THE FIRST FOLIO ENTERED ON THE STATIONERS' REGISTER, 8 NOVEMBER 1623. *Stationers' Hall, Register D, f. 69. Transcript: Arber, iv. 107; EKC, i. 138; Greg, i. 33.*

Mr. William Shakespeares Comedies, Histories, & Tragedies appeared at the end of 1623. The Stationers' Register entry, dated 8 November, lists sixteen plays 'not formerly entred to other men'. These include some of Shakespeare's best-loved works — *The Tempest, Twelfth Night, Julius Caesar,* and *Macbeth* — and represent all phases of his career; they are printed for the first time in the Folio. Not mentioned in the entry are *The Taming of the Shrew* and *King John,* which also find a place in the volume. Although new, they perhaps did not require registration because they passed as reprints of *The Taming of A Shrew* and the anonymous *Troublesome Raigne of John, King of England,* the latter, printed in 1591, being related, probably as source, to Shakespeare's play. Heminges and Condell excluded *Pericles* and *The Two Noble Kinsmen.* A consortium of Stationers sponsored the large and expensive book, but Edward Blount and Isaac Jaggard jointly held the copyright. It might appear odd that Jaggard should figure in the undertaking at all, let alone so prominently, for his father William had not only offended with *The Passionate Pilgrim* but had a few years later teamed up with Thomas Pavier to bring out a dubious series of Shakespeare quartos. Jaggard and Pavier were not too fussy about the texts they selected, which included the apocryphal *Yorkshire Tragedy,* and they were ordered to desist when the King's men complained to the Lord Chamberlain. Jaggard got round the restraint by ante-dating editions, from his shop, of *The Merchant of Venice*, *A Midsummer-Night's Dream*, and others; thus he put the year 1608 on the title-page of the 1619 *King Lear*. Evidently Heminges and Condell, leading members of the King's company, bore no lasting grudge against Jaggard for his piratical ways. The latter died before 4 November 1623, while the Folio was being printed, and his son took over management of the shop. A copy of the volume was bound by the Bodleian Library on 17 February 1624, this being the earliest reference to the published First Folio.

The title-page features a portrait of the author signed by the engraver, Martin Droeshout the younger, under the lower left-hand corner. Droeshout belonged to the third generation of a Flemish family of engravers translated to London; his grandfather John Droeshout, a painter and joiner, had come over from Brussels in 1566. Martin was only fifteen when Shakespeare died, and twenty-two when the Folio appeared; hardly very experienced in his craft. How he obtained the commission we do not know — perhaps his fee was as modest as his gifts. As the printing of the book proceeded, Droeshout's copper-plate was twice altered. In the exceedingly rare first, or 'proof', state, the ruff lacks shading under the ear. This is supplied in the second state; in the third, which is most common, a single out-of-place hair is to be detected on the right edge of the silhouette. For succeeding seventeenth-century folios, the printers used the same plate, which gradually coarsened. By 1685, when the Fourth (and last) Folio was published, a stubble covered the chin, and the complexion looked swarthy, with oily highlights.

The portrait has not gone entirely without admirers. 'What a powerful impression it gives', enthuses Dr. Rowse: 'that searching look of the eyes understanding everything, what a forehead, what a brain!'[1] But the engraver has not depicted the brain, only the forehead, described by another observer as that 'horrible hydrocephalus development'. Droeshout's deficiencies are, alas, only too gross. The huge head on a plate of a ruff surmounts a disproportionately small tunic. One eye is lower and larger than the other, the hair does not balance at the sides, light comes from several directions. It is unlikely that Droeshout ever sketched Shakespeare from the life. Probably he worked from a line drawing supplied to him. Still the Folio editors, who knew Shakespeare well, did not reject the likeness, and Jonson was able to bring himself to supply a few perfunctory lines of commendation, printed on the adjoining flyleaf. No doubt only an over-subtle reader will detect a latent irony in Jonson's conclusion — 'Reader, looke/Not on his Picture, but his Booke' — but the advice is sound enough.

Other preliminary leaves dedicate the Folio to William Herbert, third Earl of Pembroke (the Lord Chamberlain), and his younger brother Philip, first Earl of Montgomery, and offer commendations of the playwright in verse and prose. In an epistle 'To the great Variety of Readers', the editors praise the happy facility of their friend and fellow: 'His mind and hand went together: And what he thought, he uttered with that easinesse, that wee have scarse received from him a blot in his papers.' They also claim that 'as where (before) you were abus'd with diverse stolne, and surreptitious copies, maimed, and deformed by the frauds and stealthes of injurious impostors, that expos'd them: even those, are now offer'd to your view cur'd, and perfect of their limbes; and all the rest, absolute in their numbers, as he conceived them'. The implications of this statement, which has inspired volumes of gloss, lie outside the biographer's province.[2] There follows Jonson's eulogy of the sweet swan of Avon, the best-known such poem in the language. It too has received much commentary, and ever since 1693, when Dryden characterized it as 'An Insolent, Sparing, and Invidious Panegyrick', some readers have discerned sinister undercurrents of aspersion flowing beneath the surface level of compliment. It has also been pointed out that the praise, or much of it, has a lapidary conventionality. That no doubt is true, but to

Opposite:

212 THE FIRST FOLIO, 1623, TITLE-PAGE. *Copy in the British Library; shelfmark: C.39.k.15.* STC *22273.*

1   A. L. Rowse, *The English Spirit: Essays in History and Literature* (1966), p. 6.
2   For a masterly brief account of the First Folio, see Charlton Hinman's introduction to the Norton Facsimile, *The First Folio of Shakespeare* (New York, 1968). Authoritative studies on a large scale are W. W. Greg, *The Shakespeare First Folio* (Oxford, 1955), and Hinman, *The Printing and Proof-reading of the First Folio of Shakespeare* (Oxford, 1963), 2 vols.

Mr. WILLIAM
SHAKESPEARES

COMEDIES,
HISTORIES, &
TRAGEDIES.

Published according to the True Originall Copies.

Martin Droeshout sculpsit London.

LONDON

Printed by Isaac Iaggard, and Ed. Blount. 1623.

213 THE DROESHOUT ENGRAVING IN THE FOURTH FOLIO, 1685. *The engraving is here slightly reduced.*

the present writer, at least, Jonson's tribute seems sympathetic enough.[1] There follow the thirty-six plays.

Although the widow lived to see Shakespeare's monument placed in Stratford church, she died a few months before the publication of the Folio. The brass on her gravestone, which is to the left of her husband's in the chancel, informs us that she 'DEPARTED THIS LIFE THE 6TH DAY OF AUGUST: 1623 · BEING OF THE AGE OF · 67 · YEARES'. The Latin epitaph underneath fittingly memorializes the mother who gave life and milk. From the parish register we learn that she was buried on 8 August. Susanna died on 11 July 1649 at the age of sixty-six, and was interred five days later, to the right of her husband in the chancel. Dugdale records the epitaph, later erased and still later reinstated.

214 ANNE SHAKESPEARE BURIED, 8 AUGUST 1623. *Stratford parish register, burials, f. 51ᵛ. Shakespeare Birthplace Trust Records Office; shelfmark: DR 243/1.*

1 For a different view, see T. J. B. Spencer, 'Ben Jonson on his beloved, The Author Mr. William Shakespeare', *Elizabethan Theatre IV*, ed. G. R. Hibbard (Toronto, 1974), pp. 22–40.

215 SUSANNA HALL BURIED, 16 JULY 1649. *Stratford parish register, burials, f. 70ᵛ. Shakespeare Birthplace Trust Records Office; shelfmark: DR 243/1.*

Here lyeth the body of Suſanna wife of John Hall
gent. the daughter of William Shakeſpere gent.
She deceaſed the 2. day of July Anno 1649.
aged 66.

Witty above her ſexe, but that's not all,
Wiſe to ſalvation was good Miſtris Hall,
Something of Shakeſpere was in that, but this
Wholy of him with whom ſhe's now in bliſſe,
   Then P ſſenger ha'ſt ne're a teare,
   To weep with her that wept with all;
   That wept, yet ſet her ſelfe to chere
   Them up with comforts cordiall.
   Her love ſhall live, her mercy ſpread,
   When thou ha'ſt ner'e a teare to ſhed.

216 SUSANNA SHAKESPEARE'S EPITAPH IN DUGDALE'S *ANTIQUITIES OF WARWICKSHIRE* (1656), p. 518.

217 JUDITH QUINEY BURIED, 9 FEBRUARY 1662. *Stratford parish register, burials, f. 46. Shakespeare Birthplace Trust Records Office; shelfmark: DR 243/2.*

Judith lived on into the Restoration. On 9 February 1662, a few days after her seventy-seventh birthday, 'Judith uxor Thomas Quiney Gent' was buried, presumably in the churchyard. She had survived her twin brother Hamnet by sixty-six years. In this family the women outlasted their menfolk. Dowdall in 1693 reports a tradition that Shakespeare's 'wife and Daughters Did Earnestly Desire to be Layd in the same Grave with him', but 'for feare of the Curse' nobody dared 'Touch his Grave Stone'.

The Halls' only child Elizabeth in 1626 married Thomas Nash. He was the son of the Anthony Nash remembered with a ring by the poet in his will. Nash had studied law at Lincoln's Inn, but never seems to have practised, being comfortably off — he inherited, in addition to land, the inn called the Bear in Bridge Street. The couple lived for a time in the dwelling now called Nash House, adjoining New Place. Thomas died in 1647, at the age of fifty-three, and was buried in the chancel, to the right of Shakespeare, with the combined arms of Nash, Hall, and Shakespeare carved on his gravestone. Some fourteen months later, on 5 June 1649, Elizabeth took a second husband, John Bernard of Abington Manor in Northamptonshire. A widowed country squire, then forty, he had eight children by his first wife. When her mother died, Elizabeth inherited the joint Shakespeare and Hall estates, including the Birthplace and New Place, but the couple finished their days at Abington Manor. On 25 November 1661 King Charles II rewarded Bernard with a baronetcy, for he had done the state some service during the Civil War. Lady Bernard died childless in 1670, at the age of sixty-two, and was presumably interred with other Bernards in the village church, although no monument or gravestone survives for her. Judith Quiney's sons were dead too. 'He was the best of his family', Dowdall said of Shakespeare after visiting Stratford church in 1693, 'but the male line is Extinguished.' In fact the whole direct line — male and female — was now extinct.

The Henley Street houses passed to the Harts, who remained in possession until 1806. New Place eventually returned to the Cloptons who had originally built it. In 1702 Sir Hugh Clopton

218 MR. DOWDALL'S LETTER, 10 APRIL 1693. *Folger Shakespeare Library, MS. V.a.74. Transcript (extracts): H-P, Outlines, ii. 7; EKC, ii. 259; BRL, ii. 527–8. The letter, addressed to 'M*r* Southwell' and endorsed 'From M*r* Dowdall', was among the family papers of Lord de Clifford before coming into the possession of H-P. Eventually it passed, with other H-P papers, to the Folger. At the instigation of J. Payne Collier, the antiquarian bookseller Thomas Rodd first printed the letter in 1838 as* Traditionary Anecdotes of Shakespeare. *The parish clerk who showed Dowdall round was presumably the William Castle baptized in the church on 17 July 1614 (EKC, ii. 259).*

made extensive alterations along neo-classic lines. A later owner, the vicar Francis Gastrell of Frodsham, demolished New Place in 1759. Only the well and a few foundation stones remain. The vines and Shakespeare's mulberry are no longer there, but another ancient mulberry, grown from a scion of the one he reputedly planted, adorns the lawn in the Great Garden.

Acknowledgements of Facsimiles

Balliol College Library (by permission of the Master and Fellows): item 210.

Belvoir Castle (by permission of the Duke of Rutland): 181.

Birmingham Public Libraries, The Shakespeare Library: 150.

Bodleian Library (by permission of the Curators): 4, 7, 9, 50, 51, 53, 55, 56, 57, 58, 67, 68, 69, 70, 71, 72, 75, 77, 87, 92, 95, 96, 100, 101, 103, 107, 108, 111, 112, 113, 126, 133, 137, 147, 148, 162, 163, 166, 168, 170, 171, 176, 180, 185, 195, 205, 209, 213, 216.

British Library (by permission of the British Library Board): rear endpaper; 1, 2, 54, 73, 74, 80, 84, 85, 86, 97, 99, 102, 104, 106, 109, 110, 114, 115, 117, 118, 124, 127, 136 (by permission of the Duke of Portland), 145, 146, 149, 164, 167, 177, 178, 179, 183, 193, 206 (by permission of the Duke of Portland), 212.

Cambridge University Library (by permission of the Syndics): 76, 79.

Colgate University Library, Hamilton, New York: 64.

College of Arms (by permission of the Chapter): 128, 129, 130.

Fitzwilliam Museum, Cambridge (by permission of the Syndics): 91.

Folger Shakespeare Library (by permission of the Trustees): 8, 12, 52, 90, 93, 116, 131, 132, 138, 201, 218.

Greater London Record Office (by permission of the Corporation of Wardens of the Parish of St. Saviour, Southwark): 30, 31.

Guildhall Library: 29, 78, 172, 182.

Kent County Archives Office, Maidstone (by permission of Lord Sackville): 191, 199.

Longleat (by permission of the Marquess of Bath): 88.

Mellon Collection, Washington (by permission of Mr. and Mrs. Paul Mellon): 184.

National Monuments Record: 207.

Plume Library, Maldon, Essex: 33, 169.

Public Record Office (by permission of the Controller of Her Majesty's Stationery Office): 11, 48, 60, 81, 98, 105, 119, 120, 121, 122, 123, 135, 151, 154, 156, 157, 158, 159, 160, 165, 173, 174, 175, 202.

Royal Shakespeare Theatre, Stratford-upon-Avon, Picture Gallery (by permission of the Governors): frontispiece.

St. Andrew Undershaft Church, London (by permission of the Archdeacon): 208.

Shakespeare Birthplace Trust Records Office, Stratford-upon-Avon (by permission of the Trustees and Guardians of Shakespeare's Birthplace): front endpaper (Hall's Croft); 5, 6, 10, 14, 15, 16, 17, 18, 19, 20, 21, 22, 23, 24, 25, 26, 27, 28, 32, 34, 35, 36, 37, 38, 39, 40, 41, 42, 43, 44, 45, 46, 47, 49, 63, 65, 66, 125, 134 (New Place Museum), 139, 140, 141, 142, 143, 144, 152, 153, 155, 186, 187, 188, 189, 190, 192, 194, 196, 198, 200, 203 (Shakespeare Centre Library; photograph courtesy of Sotheby and Co.), 204, 214, 215, 217.

Stationers' Hall (by permission of the Worshipful Company of Stationers and Newspaper Makers): 89, 94, 161, 211.

Utrecht University Library: 82, 83.

Worcestershire Record Office (by permission of the County Archivist): 59, 61, 62, 197.

York Public Library: 3, 13.

INDEX

Note: *in this index titles have been modernized on the assumption that nobody can reasonably be expected to remember the old spelling. Also discretion has been exercised with respect to the spelling of Elizabethan surnames. Italicized citations refer to the page numbers of captions; roman type is retained for references to the facsimiles themselves.*

s*

POSTSCRIPT

This postscript, written while the book is printing, allows me to add a few more bits of information. At the Folger Shakespeare Library I have been able to identify the anonymous 'Old Warwickshire Boy' who wrote the doggerel ballad quoted on p. 8; he is one A. C. Hands. To 'All hail!' in *Richard II* (see p. 48) I would add the parallel usage in *3 Henry VI*, where Gloucester remarks aside after kissing his nephew: 'To say the truth, so Judas kiss'd his master / And cried "All hail!" when as he meant all harm.' The passage is not overlooked by Noble. In the Longleat Manuscript the date 'Anno m° q° g q^{to}' (cited in caption 88, p. 123) may be expanded as 'Anno millesimo quingentesimo quarto (or quinto)'; hence 1594 or 1595. In *Shakespeare and his Players* (1972), pp. 150–4, Martin Holmes informatively discusses the armour shown in the Peacham drawing, but he is more positive than the evidence warrants when he asserts that the sketch 'illustrates a production by Henslowe's company'. In an important essay, 'The Authenticity of Simon Forman's *Bocke of Plaies*', in *The Review of English Studies*, xxiii (1947), 193–200, J. Dover Wilson and R. W. Hunt argue persuasively for the genuineness of this Forman manuscript (see caption 176, p. 215).

I have also here the opportunity to make some corrections that reached the printers too late for incorporation in the text. Joan Hart survived her brother by thirty, not forty, years (Preface, p. ix), the Stratford register recording her burial on 4 November 1646. The information is correctly given on p. 25. On p. 38, for 'went on to repeat' read 'in the same certificate repeated'. In footnote 2, p. 38, for 'among the nine' read 'in the commissioners' list': the name 'Julian Coorte' appears not among the first nine, but with those 'presented for Recusantes' in the next grouping. On p. 56, for 'Castilo' read 'Castalio'. The reference is to Sebastian Castalio, whose *Dialogi Sacri*, prescribed at several schools, was apparently first printed in English in 1560; I have been able to include this correction in the Index. On p. 66, for 'seven altogether' read 'seven of them still living when he made his will'. In caption 118, p. 158, for '*catchword*' read '*speech prefix*'. On p. 178, for '*messuagio cum duobus*' read '*mesuagio duobus*'. It is George Colman, not Coleman, in the footnote on p. 224. On p. 240, for '*carnelem*' read '*carnalem*'. In the heading for the rear endpaper caption, for '1615 (?)' read '1616 (?)'. The customary date for Visscher's panorama, 1616, is probably correct, but Shapiro's discussion in his *Shakespeare Survey* essay, p. 27, should not be ignored.

The Shakespeare Third Folio with the purported sketch of Anne Hathaway is preserved in Colgate University Library. Credit is properly given in caption 64 (p. 74) and the Acknowledgements, but not in my Preface, which refers to Hamilton College (p. xi). Colgate University is situated in Hamilton, New York. There is also a Hamilton College in the same state. I have found this unwitting slip sobering. In addition to the usual disabilities of the scholarly vocation – limitations of memory, knowledge, or skill – one must reckon with the caprices of the unconscious. To the staff that received me so warmly at Colgate I can only offer the cold comfort that I have paid for my transgression with more than one night of sleepless remorse.

Evanston
November 1974

S.S.

Rear endpaper:

CLAES JAN VISSCHER, VIEW OF LONDON, 1615(?) (detail). *British Library Map Collection; shelf-mark: C.5.a.6. Visscher's view, the most familiar panorama of the capital before the Great Fire, shows the full expanse of the south bank, from the manor of Paris Garden (with the Swan Theatre) on the east, to beyond St. Olave's Church on the west. It is probably based on a drawing made around 1600, and thus antedates Hollar (see item 78). At Broken Wharf, Bulmer's Water Tower, built in 1594, is shown; but Salisbury House is absent, although construction was well enough advanced by 1602 for Queen Elizabeth to receive entertainment there. Tudor rather than Stuart arms appear on the Water Tower and the banner of the royal barge. The view depicts the Globe Theatre, which opened its doors in 1599, but the engraver has possibly confused this playhouse with the Rose, a Bankside fixture from 1587: the two theatres stood near one another, but only one is shown. There are many inaccuracies (as well as distortions of scale) in the panorama, which is derivative from previous maps and views, especially John Norden's 1600* Civitas Londini. *Norden shows a polygonal Globe, but the theatre is cylindrical in the inset map in the same panorama. The view reproduced is signed 'C. J. Visscher Delineavit'. An engraver and printer of Amsterdam, Visscher was only thirteen in 1600; his father had the same initials, but is described as a goldsmith or shipwright, not an engraver. Neither is known ever to have set foot in London. On the whole it is difficult to resist the conclusion of Darlington and Howgego: 'The view is pleasing to the eye, but its topographical value is small.'*

For more detailed information, see I. A. Shapiro, 'The Bankside Theatres: Early Engravings', Shakespeare Survey 1 (Cambridge, *1948*), *pp. 25–37; Irene Scouloudi,* Panoramic Views of London, 1600–66 (*1953*), *pp. 24–9; and Ida Darlington and James Howgego,* Printed Maps of London circa 1553–1850 (*1964*), *p. 9. Shapiro's essay is a masterly survey of the evidence as it pertains to the Southwark playhouses.*

Hamsted

Hamsted

St Brides

Whytefryers Stayrs

Baynards Stayrs

Blackfryars Stayrs

Baynards Castle

Pauls Wharfe

The Swan

Iohn Webb Delineavit